Sodomy in Reformation Germany and Switzerland, 1400–1600

The Chicago Series on Sexuality, History, and Society // Edited by John C. Fout

Sodomy
in Reformation Germany and Switzerland, 1400–1600

HELMUT PUFF

The University of Chicago Press
Chicago and London

Helmut Puff is associate professor of German and history at the
University of Michigan, Ann Arbor.

The University of Chicago Press, Chicago 60637
The University of Chicago Press, Ltd., London
© 2003 by The University of Chicago
All rights reserved. Published 2003
Printed in the United States of America

12 11 10 09 08 07 06 05 04 03   1 2 3 4 5

ISBN: 0–226-68505–5 (cloth)
ISBN: 0–226-68506–3 (paper)

Library of Congress Cataloging-in-Publication Data

Puff, Helmut.
    Sodomy in Reformation Germany and Switzerland, 1400–1600 /
Helmut Puff.
        p. cm. — (The Chicago series on sexuality, history, and society)
    Includes bibliographical references and index.
    ISBN 0-226-68505-5 (cloth : alk. paper) — ISBN 0-226-68506-3
(pbk. : alk. paper)
        1. Homosexuality—Germany—History.   2. Homosexuality—
Switzerland—History.   3. Sodomy—Germany—History.
4. Sodomy—Switzerland—History.   5. Homosexuality—Religious
aspects.   6. Reformation—Germany.   7. Reformation—Switzerland.
I. Title.   II. Series.
HQ76.3.G4 P84 2003
306.76'6'0943—dc21

                                                        2002013487

♾The paper used in this publication meets the minimum requirements
of the American National Standard for Information
Sciences—Permanence of Paper for Printed Library Materials,
ANSI Z39.48–1992.

Contents

Acknowledgments

This book would have remained unwritten if not for the happy confluence of several events. In 1984, as an exchange student at the University of Michigan, I enrolled in a graduate course taught by Martha Vicinus. Not only did I get a taste of the treasures of Victorian England, but also it was in this seminar that I first immersed myself in a text that radically changed my intellectual outlook, volume 1 of Michel Foucault's *History of Sexuality*. At German and Swiss universities in the 1980s, knowing Foucault was a secret pleasure one hardly ever shared in the public of seminars. I do not recall whether my friend and colleague Wolfram Schneider-Lastin knew of my Foucauldian leanings. At any rate, when asked in 1989 to decipher a document on the early history of homosexuality in Basel, he invited me to come along. Out of this experience grew a long, productive, and challenging cooperation that lasts to this day. However, this cooperation would have remained fruitless if my advisor, Rüdiger Schnell, had not trusted in my ability to work on the history of sexuality while writing a dissertation on a completely unrelated topic. For his support and for what I have learned from him, I have deep respect.

This book has been in the making for a long time. Over the course of more than a decade, I have accumulated more debts than I can acknowledge here. I have had the opportunity to do research in a number of archives, libraries, and research institutions. It is my pleasure to thank the Staatsarchiv Basel-Stadt, Staatsarchiv Luzern, Staatsarchiv Schaffhausen, Staatsarchiv Solothurn (especially Freddi Silvan), Staatsarchiv Zürich, Stadtarchiv Sankt Gallen, the Universitätsbibliothek Basel, and the Zentralbibliothek Zürich and their staff. In Germany, I am grateful to the Stadtarchiv Augsburg, Stadtarchiv Freiburg im Breisgau, Erzbischöfliches Archiv Freiburg im Breisgau, Stadtarchiv Konstanz, Stadtarchiv München, Stadtarchiv Speyer, and the Staatsbibliothek Berlin. I have also done work at the Österreichische Nationalbibliothek and the Haus-, Hof- und Staatsarchiv, both in Vienna, as well as at the Library of the Archdiocese in Kalocsa, Hungary.

This extensive research would have been impossible if not for the generous hospitality and financial support of many. In particular, I want to express my gratitude to Ewald Merkelbach for having offered me a Swiss home after I had moved to the United States. I wrote an early draft at the University of Michigan's Institute for the Humanities, where I held a faculty fellowship during the academic year 1997–98. A research fellowship and two extended stays at the Herzog August Bibliothek in Wolfenbüttel, Germany— a library with almost inexhaustible resources and an awe-inspiring staff— have enabled me to write the section pertaining to the Reformation. Special thanks go to Lorraine Daston for having invited me as a fellow to the Max Planck Institute for the History of Science in Berlin during the academic year 1999–2000, where I finished a first version of this book in a profoundly stimulating atmosphere. In addition, financial support and fellowships have come from a variety of sources: the Junior Faculty Development Award, the Rackham Summer Research Grant, and the project on gender-based censorship, directed by Domna Stanton, at the University of Michigan's Institute for Research on Women and Gender.

This book is in part an outcome of my straddling two academic cultures. An interdisciplinary group of medievalists and early modernists at the University of Basel, Switzerland—Susanna Burghartz, Valentin Groebner, and Martin Kirnbauer among them—greatly stimulated my progress during the early stages of my work. Yet this book would be slimmer without Claudius Sieber-Lehmann, who has accompanied its development and the growth of our (now transcontinental) friendship with a great sense of *savoir*, including *savoir vivre* and *savoir rire*. I thank Franz Eder, Klaus van Eickels, Ulrike Gleixner, Rainer Henrich, Bernd-Ulrich Hergemöller, Sven Limbeck, Matthias Meyer, Heinz Plancke, James Schultz, Dominik Sieber, and Elizabeth Wood for having greatly enriched my thinking. In Ann Arbor, I found an academic milieu congenial to my interdisciplinary outlook and intellectual pursuits. My colleagues at Michigan—Fred Amrine, Kathryn Babayan, Laura Downs, Geoff Eley, David Halperin, Julia Hell, Anne Herrmann, Valerie Kivelson, Yopie Prins, Elizabeth Sears, Patricia Simons, Carroll Smith-Rosenberg, Scott Spector, Karla Taylor, Valerie Traub, and Martha Vicinus—have offered their critical input on various occasions. As a friend, colleague, and historian, Kathleen Canning has supported me every step of the way in writing this book. I also benefited from discussions with participants in the University of Michigan's Colloquium on the

History of Law in Western Society. Christopher Wild from the University of North Carolina has been a model of collegiality and friendship. Lyn Coffin, Erik Huneke, Matthew Johnson, and Peg Lourie did formidable work in thinning out the thicket of my prose. Last but not least, I thank John Fout and Doug Mitchell for their unwavering support of this project.

✠✠✠

Small portions of the material presented here were previously published in the following articles: "Localizing Sodomy: The 'Priest and Sodomite' in Pre-Reformation Germany and Switzerland," *Journal of the History of Sexuality* 8 (1997): 165–95; "Männergeschichten/Frauengeschichten: Über den Nutzen einer Geschichte der Homosexualitäten," in *Geschlechtergeschichte und Allgemeine Geschichte: Herausforderungen und Perspektiven: Mit Beiträgen von Karin Hausen, Lynn Hunt, Thomas Kühne, Gianna Pomata und Helmut Puff*, ed. Hans Medick and Anne Charlotte Trepp (Göttingen: Wallstein, 1998), 125–69; "Female Sodomy: The Trial of Katherina Hetzeldorfer (1477)," *Journal of Medieval and Early Modern Studies* 30 (2000): 41–61; and "Sodomie in den Schriften Martin Luthers und in der Reformationspolemik," in *Das Geheimnis am Beginn der Moderne*, Zeitsprünge: Forschungen zur Frühen Neuzeit, vol. 6, no. 1–4, ed. Gisela Engel, Brita Rang, Klaus Reichert, and Heide Wunder (Frankfurt am Main: Vittorio Klostermann, 2002), 328–42.

Introduction

In the preface to his 1824 book *History of the Latin and Teutonic Nations from 1494 to 1514*,[1] Leopold von Ranke (1795–1886) provided history, an academic discipline in the making, with an often-invoked programmatic statement. According to the young scholar, the historian's craft is "to show how it actually was."[2] The *History* earned its author, a schoolteacher, a position at Berlin University in the year following the book's publication. Another passage from the same book, introduced as a "moral reflection" (*Moralische Betrachtung*), is virtually forgotten in comparison to Ranke's oft-cited historicist manifesto. There, the historian muses on why Italy, the same nation that disseminated much-needed "learning" (*Belehrung*) and "industrial impulses" (*Antrieb*) across Europe, was unable to pull herself out of the web of foreign powers on her soil. Ranke diagnoses a twofold "disease" at the core of Italy's loss of *Lebenskraft* (force of life): first, widespread "sexual violation of boys" (*Knabenschändung*), and, second, as "pederasty's rival" (*Nebenbuhler der Päderastie*), syphilis, "the French evil" (*das französische Übel*).[3]

When the nation, the military, and the sexualized male body were at stake, the project of a new historiography based on a critical assessment of sources came up against its limitations.[4] Confronted with sodomy in history, Ranke does not merely reconstruct "how it actually was." He refashions himself as an arbiter of morals, despite an avowal to the contrary.[5] History as the real thing gives way to history as the teacher of ethical lessons to moderns—an age-old concept of history, prevalent in Enlightenment historiography but much criticized in Ranke's scholarship as well as that of other historians after 1800.[6] The carefully erected methodological divide between the historian and the historian's object of study collapses in this passage. This rift in the Rankean method is all the more evident since, in passing, the author notes that some contemporaries viewed sodomy in a more positive light.[7] To be sure, moralizing does not befit the historian as

1

champion of a distant past in its own right. Yet moralization à la Ranke at least licenses one to express what supposedly evokes universal disgust (though, as I have noted, Ranke's own account allows for doubts about universality in this regard).

When Jacob Burckhardt (1818–97), arguably the most famous among Ranke's many well-known students, wrote his foundational 1860 study *Die Kultur der Renaissance in Italien,* he did not directly address the topic of sodomy.[8] Yet what Burckhardt meant by the sexual mores he veiled so conspicuously in his text is not hard to guess.[9] So closely do Burckhardt's passages on "Morality and Religion" (*Sitte und Religion*) correspond and respond to Ranke's "moral reflection"—despite the author's focus on matrimony and adultery—that sodomy remains legible "under erasure." Though often unacknowledged, sodomy has never been absent from the academic pursuit of history. Yet precisely these passages' familiar moralizations have kept historians from engaging Ranke's or Burckhardt's rhetorics critically or historicizing their claim to universal truth about sexuality and the body.

This book is devoted to reassessing the period which history's "founding fathers," Ranke and Burckhardt among them, first turned into a venerable area of historical research: the early modern era, especially the German Reformation. I set out to show that sodomy—the topic generations of historians have marginalized as beyond history proper, censored as inappropriate for the historically minded public, or condemned as monstrous—was inextricably woven into the cultural matrix of the German-speaking lands during the fifteenth and sixteenth centuries. Like few other concepts, sodomy touched mightily upon honor, both personal and communal—a nexus which turned this sexual sin into a social one and transformed suspicions of sodomy into perceived and strategically deployed threats to the body politic. Chronologically, my research stretches from the earliest known executions of sodomites in cities of the fourteenth century to the seventeenth century, when urban governments increasingly imposed silence on sodomy trials for fear of inciting precisely the sexual acts the trials sought to proscribe. Geographically, my investigation into court records focuses on the German-speaking part of what is now Switzerland, with occasional forays into highly urbanized southern Germany, a region closely connected with cities such as Zurich and Lucerne. Urban measures against sodomites coincided with the development of devotional literature in the vernacular after 1370. It will become evident that, around 1500, images of Sodom gained wide acceptance—images which the Reformers used in their polemical jousts at Rome, the papacy, and the Catholic Church. Pamphlets, those mouthpieces of social, religious, and political concerns, thus helped to inaugurate a new era in sexual politics—an era marked by the verbose embrace of matrimony and the equally verbose condemnation of sodomy.

Of all the sexual sins, sodomy merits our attention in particular; mentions thereof instigated rhetorical pirouettes and mechanisms of control administered by Church representatives as well as secular authorities. The Reformers' early polemics, for instance, broke with a rhetorical decorum that had previously reigned over representations of sodomy in many publications. Yet this moment was short-lived. After the middle of the sixteenth century, a more restrained sexual discourse emerged in all milieus, including confessional polemics. A discourse of manifold sins delving into layers of misbehavior such as sodomy was supplanted by an increasingly vague discourse on sex that propagated a singular dividing line between legitimate sexual behavior in marriage and illegitimate or "impure" sexual activities outside of marriage.

With its focus on words and narrations, rhetoric and textual patterns, the story that I want to tell is not a Rankean history of "how it actually was." This study is about the linguistic moves vis-à-vis sodomy. But it is not language in its abstraction that interests me. Rather, I research the ways in which historical actors, magistrates, officials, translators, redactors, experts, or defendants used language.

This book could therefore not have been written without the inspiration of the French philosopher-historian Michel Foucault, whose *History of Sexuality* launched an enormous project, historicizing what historicists like Ranke had placed outside of history, namely, sex and the body.[10] Foucault the "archivist" and "cartographer"[11] remapped a terrain occupied by the largely ahistorical, risqué histories called *La vie galante* in French (which eighteenth-century writers pioneered) or by "Histories of Life and Customs" (*Sittengeschichte*) in nineteenth-century Germany when sexology emerged as an interdisciplinary field of research on the margins of academe. In Foucault's vision, the history of sexuality took form conceptually not as a history of actual bodies or desires. Rather, the history of sex was cast as one of power relations mediated through words. Foucault thus rejected a classic notion which relegated sex to some private, personally liberating realm beyond the political. He argued that in modern times, discourses on sexuality constituted a regulatory mechanism through which power over the self was and continues to be established.

With regard to the discourse on homosexuality, Foucault set up the field of inquiry by suggesting a fundamental transition from the premodern "sodomite" to the modern "homosexual."[12] According to the *History of Sexuality*, the notion of temporary sinful aberration *in sexualibus*, characterized as sodomy, was superseded by the nineteenth-century concept of a class of persons, homosexuals, identified by sexual desire for the same sex—a shift emblematic of the historic progression from external forces of control, such as the state or the church, to internal technologies of the self.

Foucault's remarks on the emergence of the homosexual in *La volonté de savoir* were, above all, suggestively sparse. Put differently, they were ideally suited as a compass for efforts to explore the largely obscure terrain of a history of (homo-)sexualities. This appropriation of Foucault among historians is not without its ironies, however. The French philosopher-historian had offered a rather dark vision of modernity, approaching the ramifications of power in modern societies through a particular lens, the history of Western knowledge on sex. In subsequent research, this Nietzsche-inspired genealogy of the modern was often reframed as a project of a different order, a social history of sexual behavior.[13] Paradoxically, the fusion and friction between a Foucauldian archeology of discursive shifts and more traditionally minded history-writing proved tremendously productive. Within two decades, a flourishing literature on the history of (predominantly male) homosexuality came into being—a body of work covering diverse periods as well as various geographic regions. While critiques of Foucault's fragile factual framework abound in these studies, many authors nonetheless remain indebted to the basic problematic formulated by Foucault: the emergence of modern sexuality—its phenomenology, chronology, and "geography."

In light of Foucault's attention to the threshold of a modern sexuality, it is hardly surprising, for instance, that researchers of early modern Europe felt particularly attracted to the study of sex—history's terra incognita. In the course of their explorations, these researchers redrew Foucault's map significantly, taking its cartographer to task for periodization, the lack of agency in his work, as well as the nature of the suggested transformation. In a series of publications whose capstone is yet to appear, Randolph Trumbach has argued repeatedly for a shift from sodomy to homosexuality and, subsequently, heterosexuality during the early eighteenth century. The nascent psychiatry of the mid-nineteenth century rendered a phenomenon in writing, he contends, whose origins can in fact be traced to sociosexual practices—practices that emerged in Western Europe, particularly London, after 1700. In Trumbach's account, an older model of male libertinage in which either women or men were erotically desirable (provided the older male expressed his superior position by penetrating his partner, usually of a younger age) was superseded by the appearance of a group of men, derogatorily referred to as "mollies" or "sodomites," who desired fellow men exclusively and identified accordingly.[14] With regard to the eighteenth-century Dutch Republic, Theo van der Meer has linked the new figure of the homosexual to, among others, novel notions of selfhood: a modern sense of an individualized self that was less communally defined than physically bounded, thereby enabling a different form of desire.[15] Dirk Jaap Noordam as well as van der Meer point to a wave of persecutions in the Dutch Republic from 1730 to 1733 as a defining moment in the appearance of "a kind of homosexual": For the first time, the authorities' efforts to bring sodomites to trial coincided with the populace's cooperation—a confluence of forces motivated by a severe economic crisis and a novel willingness to defend matrimony against "sodomites"—resulting in the execution of several hundred men.[16] In all these accounts, the forces driving the gradual transformation of sexual experience and representation remain somewhat vague. Yet with a web of interrelated factors—legal, medical, and other discourses, various group mentalities, and individual actors—these studies offer a significant departure from Foucault's monolithic focus on the homosexual's genesis through scientific discourse.

The new ilk of historians also set out to embed their studies in frameworks other than the history of sexuality per se. As early as 1974, E. William Monter claimed that the history of witchcraft and the history of sodomy overlapped—a thesis still in need of verification.[17] Notably, Trumbach asserts that the emergence of a Third Sex revolutionized the whole gamut of sexual and social relations in Enlightenment England: the new form of exclusively male desire transformed notions of masculinity, since men now sought to distinguish themselves from "unmanly" sodomites. As a consequence, the "mollies" helped to crystallize "heterosexuality," with its concomitant rise in male adultery and female prostitution. By comparison, Michael Rocke's celebrated study of sodomy in fifteenth-century Florence—that is, before the "birth of the queen"—draws a large-scale portrait of sex between men as not only common at various stages of their lives but also as deeply enmeshed in forms of male sociability. Drawing on a uniquely rich set of sources, Rocke demonstrates with statistical accuracy that homoeroticism, far from being situated in the cultural or sexual margins, was integral to the social fabric of Renaissance Florence and Florentine masculinity in particular.[18]

Soon it became clear that the history of women who had effusive friendships and sexual liaisons with women—a topic Foucault had neglected entirely—followed a trajectory different from that of intimate male friends and lovers. Socially, the modern lesbian "appeared" after the male homosexual in the latter half of the eighteenth century—at least according to van der Meer, Trumbach, and a number of other critics.[19]

Unlike with men, however, evidence for the lesbian's literary presence predates her traceable social construct. In various English genres and writings, Valerie Traub excavates a veritable renaissance of lesbianism since the late sixteenth century.[20] In a study devoted to English rereadings of the Greek poetess Sappho, Harriette Andreadis shows that early modern Sapphists embraced and disseminated concepts of "lesbian-like" love as early as the late seventeenth century, the very time when there is increasing evidence for male-loving males in the labyrinthine European metropolis.[21]

Overall, the occasional cohabitation of research on male and female homosexuality under the roof of a history of sexuality has been an uneasy one. Many historians have therefore preferred to divide these narratives. Yet if they make us wary of gross generalizations, the discrepancies between the social and the literary or between the histories of gays and lesbians serve us well. The very concept of historical genesis is in need of explanation—a search for origins that, as Foucault once elaborated in a Nietzschean vein, "is an attempt to capture the exact essence of things."[22] We need to investigate the links between textual imaginations and social enactments, fragmented as these observations will be for the early modern period—studies that avoid the binary implicit in this formulation and potentially take their cue from Judith Butler's insights on the materiality of discourse.[23] At any rate, the occasional appearance of "homosexual-like men and women" before 1700—as documented by medievalists—may not constitute a reconfiguration of sexual culture akin to the one after 1700. Yet the picture of radical change as it has emerged from the history of sexuality is also overdrawn.

These investigations into the histories of men, women, their sexual acts, and erotic identities have severe shortcomings. For one, certain regions of Europe are much better researched than others. For the early modern period (roughly 1400–1800), England, Italy, and the Netherlands are particularly well represented while few studies exist for central, eastern, and some parts of southern Europe. Similarly, this historiography suffers from underlying assumptions of uniformity—a picture of fundamental shift in which the Western European metropolis often serves as the laboratory for changes of global relevance. It is the teleological orientation of many of the extant studies which seems to me Foucault's most problematic legacy, the single vanishing point of a somewhat elusive modern sexuality. The linearity of many historical accounts with their unequivocal transformations has—unduly, I believe—circumscribed the landscape of a history of sexuality. In contrast to the homogenizing force that writers, lawyers, psychiatrists, doctors, and historians have attributed to the term in the past, homosexuality harbors manifold, often contradictory, experiences. We need to allow for contradictions and work toward clusters of variously experienced sexual lives. In other words, the time has come to recognize this multiplicity in both premodern *and* modern sexualities.

The grand narrative of Michel Foucault's history of sexuality therefore needs to be revisited once more. I intend to replace Foucault's thesis of a linear evolution from sodomy to homosexuality with a more localized reading of past sexualities—an analysis that allows for a vast array of meanings, contestations, and diverse appropriations by historical actors. Homosexuals (in the sense of those who exclusively desire their own sex) are not absent from ancient texts, nor is the notion of the sexually fallen sodomite unknown in modernity. Importantly, notions of the sexual depend on the textual milieus in which they receive articulation. From a literary standpoint, Foucault's thesis relies on a problematic leap from one class of texts to another, that is, from religious to medical discourse.[24] In other words, the "fateful distinction"[25] between the "sodomite" and the "homosexual" changes significantly if we "compare like with like" and stay within one group of texts sharing the same features.[26]

Following Foucault's foundational charter, the study of homosexuality in history has in fact been riddled with questions of terminology and the application of contemporary critical concepts to past sexualities. In the process of investigating the history of sodomy's representations, a new and, as I will argue, problematic consensus has arisen among critics in the field of early modern sexuality, mostly among literary scholars: sodomy's instability as a term. It was Jonathan Goldberg who, in his groundbreaking *Sodometries*, contended that, in the Renaissance, the term sodomy "remains incapable of exact definition."[27] Thus, Goldberg expanded Foucault's aside about "sodomy—that utterly confused category"[28]—to indicate that Renaissance discourse on sexuality failed to close the book on sodomy, "that medieval catch-all."[29] Thanks to scholars like Jonathan Goldberg, Jacques Chiffoleau, Mark Jordan, and Allen Frantzen, we have begun to grasp that "sodomy" covers a terrain of meanings beyond a specific set of sexual acts. In medieval and early modern texts, sodomy appears linked to sins such as usury, treason, lèse-majesté, blasphemy, and concepts such as purity or ethnicity, to name but a few in a long list. We have learned to recognize that sodomy is not only about sex. The sexual is the idiom which channels and resonates with a multitude of themes. As a concept, it is often used to control the boundaries between the pure and the impure, rights and wrongs, the indigenous and the foreign.

Designed to throw into high relief the operative force of sexual categories, the idea of sodomy's instability, brilliantly deployed in critical readings, is in danger of becoming queer history's new credo, so widespread is its reach in contemporary criticism. "In the Middle Ages, sodomy encompassed diverse acts with a single common denominator: *all* thwarted conception," states Allen Frantzen categorically.[30] Others have concluded that sodomy is unlocatable, "a figure of cultural incoherence."[31] How can we write about what cannot be located? How is sodomy different from other categories in one of the most fundamental problems of all, the liaison between signifier and signified? Starting from the assumption of sodomy's polysemy, Frantzen registered surprise when he found that, in certain passages, sodomy holds a more narrow meaning (in Peter Damian's *Liber Gomorrhianus* or in *Cleanness,* for example).[32] As G. S. Rousseau indicated some time ago, there is a difference between sodomy's complicated taxonomy and its semantics.[33] What sodomy means in certain contexts is all too often knowable. In Catholic casuistry, theologians accorded the "unspeakable sins against nature" a firm place within Church dogma in commentaries on the Decalogue or the seven deadly sins (where religious commentators treated all sexual transgressions).[34] Seventeenth-century court records from Switzerland distinguished between *sodomia* (homosexual acts) and *bestialitas* (sex with animals),[35] though medieval theologians had grouped both nonprocreative acts under "the sins against nature" or *sodomia.* This is not to say that we always know what a certain author means by sodomy, that the category sodomy equals a modern category, or that all authors mean the same thing by it, even though there are indications that usage of the term became standardized during the early modern period. While in many contexts we *do* know what sodomy refers to, the term's genealogy as a history of ideas proper is contorted. Yet it may turn out to be a history that is not all that interesting to write.[36] After all, the cultural historian's task lies in investigating a term's situated meanings.

That we should not "assume that *sodomia* or *luxuria* or other such terms have a constant meaning across texts,"[37] may serve well as a heuristic device; it may serve us less well as an axiom. I propose that in future studies we critically examine the shift from one *un*-word to another, from the unspeakability of sodomy in medieval discourse to its undefinability in modern criticism. I do not intend here to attempt to unravel the Gordian knot whose name is sodomy, nor do I want to explain away the intricate problem of sodomy's meanings. Rather, I would like to ask, What kind of work does the claim that we cannot define sodomy accomplish? Why do we privilege terms as a key to researching sex and its representations in history?

Sodomy's instability has come to serve as another circumscription, namely, as a magic word which constantly yields new meanings. Not accidentally, this unstable term par excellence is frequently linked to terms such as ubiquity and proliferation in modern criticism. Rhetorically, these descriptions have something in common. They share a totalizing, all-encompassing quality, contradicting the claim to the particular which is so characteristic of queer studies' vision.[38] Introduced in historical writings to mark the medieval vis-à-vis the modern, "sodomy" has become a terminological convention, replete with modern associations and sharing many connotations with "queer."[39] Such associations enable critics to traffic freely between past sexualities and modern legal discourse, psychoanalytic theory, or contemporary sexual politics.

Both historical practice in the Rankean tradition and queer studies are locked in an embrace precisely because queer studies is one of the most radical departures of the historicist project: Where queer studies advocate the critic who is present in his or her writings, historicism tended to make its own constructedness invisible. But the relation of queer studies and the writing of history has primarily been cast as a question of what historians can learn by reading between the lines.[40] The answer was, and remains, much. But is there anything that queer studies might be able to take from current historical practices?

To describe sodomy as without essence has its price. As long as we insist on the term's unspecificity, we will find it hard to approach the historically specific, the changes and developments of rhetorical regimes, the patterns and formulations through time.[41] In his brilliant *The Invention of Sodomy in Christian Theology*, Mark Jordan has questioned whether it is possible to write a social history of sodomy (as a category? as sexual behavior?) and judged that such a history is "not desirable."[42] Like Jordan, I am skeptical whether there is something like "medieval homosexuality." Yet I desire to transfer a term such as sodomy, despite its contradictions, from the moment of its invention as an "artifact"[43] in the Christian theology of the Middle Ages into the messiness of history. Sodomy's appropriations and manifold usages, the practices that attached themselves to this term, be they textual in the narrow sense of the word (in the form of transmission of knowledge via manuscripts, prints, and manuals) or nontextual (as judicial sentences), will serve as my focus.

Thus, I am writing a particular form of social history that focuses on language. Sodomy may have had a highly speculative referent when it first appeared, but it acquired a deadly force in the term's long afterlife (which continues to this day). Concepts of sodomy are not merely phantasmata. They circulate widely at times and are embedded in social interactions. What we lack, therefore, is an analysis of particular tropes that bridge the social and the literary. As David Sabean suggested some time ago, "metaphors can be understood to provide a grammar of social relations."[44] Thus, this book is mostly not about the life of sodomites. It is about the social life of concepts, in a particular historical context, namely, that of early modern Germany and Switzerland. This move allows me to leave behind an aesthetics of production alone and move toward an intertwined aesthetics of production, dissemination, and reception. It is the historicity of rhetorical and sexual regimes that interests me as a result. In the course of investigating the cultural matrix of sodomy, I will therefore examine both historical documents and literary texts. In proceeding thus, I am indebted to pioneering scholars in the field like John Boswell and Alan Bray.[45] But in contrast to these authors, I will treat the different milieus separately in order to consider like with like.

In the context of current academic debates, such a critical intervention is most timely. The impact of poststructuralism on the humanities—the so-called linguistic turn, also known as the "deconstructive,"[46] the "literary,"[47] or the "rhetorical turn"[48]—has focused our attention on language as a mediator between things (*res*) and words (*verba*), between historical events and their reconstruction in the writing of history, a challenge that has been with us since Ranke based the historian's task on the realization that the past differed from the present. As a result of this much-celebrated, much-debated, and much-resisted rapprochement between literary studies and the writing of history, language and textuality have become key concepts in historical research.[49] Recently, however, many historians have again turned away from a Derridean focus on textuality only. Gabrielle Spiegel, Roger Chartier, and others have insisted on the irreducibility of the material world to discourse.[50] In literary criticism, Robert Weimann has called attention to "the 'instrumentality' of early modern representations, their engagements with the 'modalities' of living and communicating."[51] What is at stake in these debates is the category of difference, not Derrida's *différance* but the mundane difference between the (literary) text and the (social) context, the difference between the practice of writing and the written word, the textual body and the physical body, but also the differentiation of genres within the realm of discourse.

Unlike literary scholars, historians have found it less difficult to locate sodomy. Judith Bennett has in fact pointed to a disciplinary divide in the study of gay and lesbian history. She criticizes the dominance of literary criticism over social history.[52] In his recent "How to Do the History of Male Homosexuality," for instance, David Halperin rewrites Foucault's grand narrative, the birth of the homosexual in the nineteenth century. In a splendidly framed genealogical tableau, he calls attention to the premodern legacies which continue to haunt the category of the male homosexual in modern times. Yet the critic subsumes sexual practices under discourse without exploring the ruptures that run through and between the categories that he so comfortably aligns with one another.[53] One of these ruptures exists between cultural notions, on the one hand, in which, at least in many parts of Europe, it mattered who was "on top"—that is, older, socially superior, penetrating—and a Christian theology, on the other hand, in which both penetrator and penetrated were categorized as sinners, threatened with the same or a similar punishment. Yet, noticeably, the medieval (and, concomitantly, the religious) is absent from Halperin's genealogy. Whether the concept is effeminacy, active sodomy, friendship, or inversion, the materials to sustain these genealogical threads derive almost exclusively from antiquity and the Renaissance—drawing on the latter's familiar bond with secular modernity, the target of Halperin's intervention—but bypassing the medieval altogether. Has the uneven terrain circumscribed by "medieval sodomy" nothing to contribute to this narrative other than a confusing term that is still with us, sodomy? If anything, the medieval has left us with a challenge that is worth noting—unlike homosexuality or the homosexual, the term sodomy or sodomite rarely invited identification or self-definition.

This book thus investigates the multifarious relationships between acts and words with regard to a particular facet of early modern society and culture. The acts represented are sexual, the words encoding these acts often exceed the descriptive in order to effect the censorious or the punitive. Naming sodomy, therefore, was itself a powerful act, and a disruptive one at that, in practically all milieus where the various terms referencing same-sex behavior appeared.

This study is divided into two major, chronologically overlapping parts. The first traces the pattern as well as the rhetorics of persecution: their inspiration, logic, and transformation. The second part considers words acting injuriously, such as in slander.[54] The defamatory served as a mode of enunciation in which what was declared "unspeakable" in certain contexts became spoken frequently.

A road map for the chapters that follow: For much of the Middle Ages, sodomites seem to have gone without punishment. This situation changed drastically in the later medieval period, when episodic executions testify to the authorities' increasing grip on the sexual lives of their subjects. Chapter 1 explores the early documents of sodomy persecution from the German empire, outlining the political-legal matrix of (mostly urban) trials. When-ever fifteenth-century sodomy investigations were enmeshed in conceptual confusions, legal disputes, or political conflicts, the records thereof are par-ticularly rich. The fate of women, clerics, or members of the elite—treated in the second chapter—was often contested. These efforts to purge cities of sexual offenders coincided with the attempts by theologians to instruct lay believers on how to live according to God's will. Chapter 3 introduces the German-language discourse of sodomy in edifying literature from the pre-Reformation era. During the Protestant and Catholic Reforms of the sixteenth century—the time period covered in chapter 4—many authori-ties increasingly acted to contain knowledge about the so-called ineffable sin of sodomy, a caution first formulated in late medieval pastoral theology. Paradoxically, the rulers' attempts at enforcing silences came up against a sexual culture in communities such as Zurich and Lucerne in which men had sex with one another often without "labeling" their activities. As becomes evident in the defamation cases featured in chapter 5, this may have been so because allusions to such acts generated divisions and revealed conflicts along ethnic, political, and religious lines. Sixteenth-century Reformers, in their attempt to challenge religious authorities, then adopted the denigra-tory imagery that had proliferated with the spread of sodomy executions and defamations in the late medieval empire. Chapter 6 and chapter 7 fo-cus on published insults. Both chapters serve to contextualize the polem-ical discourse authored and authorized by Martin Luther. While chapter 6 introduces the slanderous tropes shared by humanists and Reformers, the following chapter analyzes a particular genre, the pamphlet, system-atically and chronologically. A concluding chapter positions my research in relation to the extant historiography on the German Reformation and to studies on matrimony in particular. Understanding sodomy in the context of the Reformation helps us to reassess the various transformations of the sixteenth-century Reforms. In the following pages, I invite the reader to traverse the divides of disciplines, topics, and genres, that is, to listen to the various resonances and echoes which configure the sexual imaginary in early modern Germany and Switzerland.

✢✢✢

A note on my own usage of terms: When medieval and early modern writers used "sodomy," they most commonly referred to male-male sexual activities. Importantly, in early modern German, "sodomy" is only one of many words to circumscribe—among other practices—same-sex sexual acts. Nouns such as "heresy," "pederasty," "sexual violation of boys," "Italian weddings," descriptions such as *puseron* or verbs such as "to commit heresy," "to florence," to name but a few, constitute a linguistic field structured by theological determinants but enriched by polemical *colores rhetorici*. All of these terms conjure up specific connotations; many of them refer to meanings beyond homoeroticism. Yet in different ways they center on same-sex sexual acts. In this study, I have made great efforts to work toward an inclusive textual analysis of the historical documents and literary texts which invoke the sins of Sodom. Rather than finding the "appropriate" term, the "right" definition, or bemoaning the lack thereof, we need to examine the clusters of words and their surrounding narratives. Using "sodomy" as shorthand in my own writing is thus a compromise—a compromise both with regard to privileging this term over a host of other expressions as well as with regard to my primary focus, male-male sodomy. This is a book about homoeroticism in discourse and practice, not a book about a term and its manifold meanings. Aware of the definitional intricacies, I will regularly point out a term's polysemy or indeterminacy of meaning in certain contexts. Moreover, I provide the reader with the German (or Latin) equivalent either in the text or in the notes.

In light of the goal of this study, I have chosen to stay as close as possible to the verbal manifestations of sodomy as evidenced in early modern German texts. In some cases, I therefore created English-language neologisms in order to render the linguistic repertory of my sources. If a document features the verb *florenzen*, I translate the word as "to florence" (note that the equivalent may vary according to context) rather than rendering it with a neutral verb such as "to sodomize" with its different connotations. In this particular example, I intend to enable my reader to partake of an imaginary in which Florence held a firm place as a haven for sodomites.

This proximity to the sources is especially significant when it comes to the vernacular term most frequently used with regard to same-sex eroticism, *ketzerie* or "heresy" (also used as a verb, *ketzern*, mostly for anal intercourse, or in phrases such as "to commit heresy" for a same-sex sexual act or a sexual act between a human and an animal). In fifteenth- and sixteenth-century sources, "sexual" and "religious" heresy often appear semantically distinct. Yet their entanglement never dissociated them completely. Starting with the drive against religious dissenters after the turn of the first millennium, inquisitors and religious writers portrayed unorthodox groups of Christian believers as sexual and sodomitical rogues, people whose contempt for God's creation was in evidence in their supposed sexual behavior. This strategy of vilification was so successful that "heresy" in German came to designate sodomy in addition to religious unorthodoxy (note that bugger in English or *bougre* in French follows a similar trajectory which originated in a religious "sect," the Bogomiles, just as the German word *ketzer* derives from *cathari*), a fact often overlooked by historians of heretical movements. Therefore, I have chosen to translate *ketzerie* as "heresy," a term that denotes sodomy and bestiality as well as religious dissent in south German and Swiss-German texts.[55]

Though this book is primarily about men and discourse on men, I have chosen to include same-sex eroticism among women wherever I found references to it. By doing so, I do not mean to imply that sodomy held the same significance when applied to men or to women. Rather, I have used similarities and differences to highlight the specifics of each. I found consolation in Eve Kosofsky Sedgwick's proviso that "There can't be an a priori decision about how far it will make sense to conceptualize lesbian and gay male identities together. Or separately."[56] In fact, Christian writers created a concept of same-sex sexual relations in which women and men resembled each other more closely than in ancient texts:[57] unlike in antiquity, Christian theology's understanding of male superiority did not license penetration per se, whether women or boys were the objects.

Part One

ACTS AND WORDS

1

The Politics of Sodomy (1277–1532)

In 1277 the German King Rudolf I of Habsburg (1218–91) sentenced a certain *dominus de Haspisperch* to be burned at the stake. According to a contemporary Dominican chronicle from Basel, the noble (*dominus*) had committed the "sodomitical vice."[1] This may well be the earliest document of an execution for the *vicium sodomiticum* in the German empire. The chronicle's sparse record leaves many questions unanswered—most pressingly, which sexual transgression the *dominus* had to die for.[2] What the chronicle documents, however, is significant enough to attract attention: When sitting in judgment, a newly elected king punished a sexual act that, whatever had occurred, met with the most severe reprobation among the age's leading theologians. A contemporary Dominican chronicler from a monastery with close ties to the king recorded this sentence, meted out by a secular ruler, through language that deployed the age's scholastic theology.

In the later Middle Ages, same-sex sexual behavior came under the purview of secular jurisdiction. On a case-by-case basis, judicial authorities in late medieval Europe developed an unambiguous and lethal tactic against the *vicium sodomiticum*, understood here as male-male sodomy. Kings, princes, prelates, and city councilors—all of them acting as judges—saw the criminal prosecution of same-sex relations, predominantly among men, as an age-old prerogative. Yet such prosecution became a regular feature of criminal proceedings only in the later Middle Ages, at a time when the authorities widened their understanding of what was deemed criminal and increased their efforts to punish offenders.

Around the time of Haspisperch's execution, concerns about same-sex sexual behavior intensified. When Thomas Aquinas (1224/25–75) worked previous references to *sodomia* into a more systematic treatment in his *Summa theologiae*, the "vice against nature" comprised a number of sexual acts all said to resist Nature's call for procreation (e.g., masturbation, bestiality), while

17

vitium sodomiticum—the term used in the chronicle entry—was reserved for same-sex acts.[3] Increasingly, theological writings were not the only ones featuring references to same-sex behavior. German poetry and legal texts followed suit. By the mid-thirteenth century, literary innovators composed didactic verses in the vernacular, condemning the "damned heresy" (*verwâzen ketzerîe*) when men turn to men instead of women for *minne* (love).[4] The most widely disseminated vernacular law code in south Germany, the *Schwabenspiegel* (c. 1275/76), compiled in an Augsburg monastery, calls those people traitors "who defame somebody by their speech" (*die mit ir rede einen verpalmundent*). Whether detractors vilify a person as "a sodomite" (*ein sodomite*), as having "committed sex with animals" (*er habe vihe geunreinet*) or as a "heretic" (*kezzer*), they ought to be broken on the wheel.[5] An Augsburg law code of 1276—a text inspired by the *Schwabenspiegel*—introduces distinctions among different kinds of "heresy." The city's lawmakers prescribed that a religious heretic (*ein chetzer umbe ungelauben*) ought to be transferred to the clergy (and, if found guilty, executed by the *vogt*), while a heretic of a secular kind should be taken to the urban court. In both cases, the crimes were considered to be acts against Christianity, and both "heresies" resulted in the same punishment, burning at the stake.[6] A Bavarian law code of 1328 elucidates the nature of "secular" heresy as mentioned in Augsburg in 1276. Ruprecht of Freising lists two kinds of sexual transgressors under the heading "heretic," a *maendlaer* and his sexual partner—both ought to be burned—as well as those who pollute themselves with animals (*vichunrainer*).[7] Practitioners of the law thus differentiated what heresiologists had successfully linked for generations—sexual deviance and religious unorthodoxy.[8]

The figure of the heretic never shed its manifold religious associations even when a more narrowly defined sexual heresy was prosecuted by secular institutions. Heresy—whose German version, *ketzerie*, derives etymologically from the sect of the Cathars—continued to evoke an uneven terrain, positioned between Latin and the vernacular, religious dogma and civic codes of behavior. Heresy thus concerned individuals as well as communities. It conjured up powerful notions of sexual as well as religious purity. And its most common punishment, burning at the stake, held Biblical associations that connected the fate of Sodom with that of imperial cities.

✝✝✝

This chapter seeks to uncover when and how sodomy came to be prosecuted as a crime in the German empire. Why did judges act so severely in cases of sodomy? What do the written records and the wording of the documents betray about the origins of civic concerns over same-sex sexual behavior? It is my claim that the increasing attention given to sodomy can be understood only in terms of the infusion of secular politics with religious ideas, though many cities pursued their own agenda in persecuting sexual "heretics." I will trace judicial responses to same-sex sexual behavior until 1532, when the *Constitutio Criminalis Carolina*, the first imperial law code, mandated burning at the stake for "heretical" sexual acts between men and between women. As the chapter unfolds, I will present fragments of past lives and past sexualities that, for the most part, historiography on Germany and Switzerland has tended to ignore.

State Formation and Sexual Discipline in the Late Middle Ages

The state that in the fifteenth century became known as the Holy Roman Empire of the German Nation encompassed lands much vaster than what is now Germany. It stretched from the Low Countries to Tyrolia and Italy, from Lorraine to Bohemia. The claim to preeminence expressed in its ceremonious title contrasted with a political reality much less glorious. Cohesion between regions different in language, economic output, and level of urbanization was low. These lands were nominally subject to one ruler, the emperor. Yet few imperial agencies existed apart from the feudal obligations, leagues, and corporations which made up the essence of this kaleidoscopic political entity in the midst of Europe.

The Swiss Confederacy, though formally a member of the polity, ceased to participate in imperial affairs in the fifteenth century. When Emperor Maximilian I (1459–1519) tried to enforce the Confederacy's allegiance militarily in 1499, the confederates were victorious over an imperial army and remained *de facto* independent. *De iure* independence followed only with the peace of Westphalia in 1648.

With its loose political structure, the Holy Roman Empire of the German Nation often does not get good press. Yet the fifteenth century went down in the annals as a period of great reforms for the imperial body politic. In order to alleviate conflicts, various estates rallied under the banner of peace. Constitutional change even provided the empire with something of a metastructure. The diets, irregular meetings of the imperial estates under the guidance of the emperor, developed into a political body whose composition was more stable than ever before. Institutions like the Imperial Chamber Court (*Reichskammergericht*), first instituted in 1495 as a high court (and after 1498 complemented by the *Reichhofsrat*), or the military districts

(*Reichskreise*), agreements like the Eternal Public Peace (*Ewiger Reichslandfriede* of 1495), as well as preparations for a general law code (which, ultimately, would include an article on sodomy and bestiality) seemed to herald even grander reforms to come. The reforms never came to full fruition, despite overblown rhetoric for the empire among humanists. Centrifugal political forces undermined an ever-fragile consensus, while confessional strife after the onset of the various Reformations would make agreements ever more difficult to achieve. [9]

Scholars rightly insist that the German lands remained rural in character throughout the medieval and early modern periods. Indeed, in urbanization the empire lagged behind Italy, the most urbanized society in Europe at the time. Yet the German cities which harbored diets were thriving centers of political and economic power, even though the same communities were politically underrepresented at these gatherings. [10] Places such as Nuremberg, Augsburg, Ulm, and Strasbourg accumulated unprecedented levels of wealth in the fifteenth century. The rise of urban trading centers also had an impact on the character of politics in this period. Medieval and early modern cities inaugurated the transformation of the communal body politic into a statelike entity characterized by both freedom and discipline. The freedom of German towns was proverbial, though freedom signified something different from individual rights. Above all, the status of a free city meant its right to rule the urban territory without interference from powers other than the king. Traditionally, decision-making resided in a city's assembly of free burghers ruled by councilors who also acted as judges. Though the tradition of cities as assemblies bound by the oath of individuals (*Schwurgemeinschaft*) never died, a city council's exercise of power and its juridical grip on its subjects greatly intensified during the period under consideration.

In an age of increasing social stratification, many forces set out to limit strife and foster a sense of commonality. As Heiko A. Oberman states, there was "a new awareness of all men being equal under the just will of God, which is seen as equally binding, embracing, and obligatory for the entire society, city and country, peasants and city folk, ecclesiastical and civil authorities." [11] According to this understanding, all citizens were jointly bound to maintain order, a concept closely tied to the divine will, Nature's rules (in the medieval sense of nature as God's creation), and political order. At least in intent, urban politics was universalized and, by individual measures, extended to all inhabitants, including the clergy, for instance. Increasingly, efforts were made to forge a more coherent body politic. Whereas the territorial expansion of cities met the resistance of neighboring powers, inward expansion knew few bounds. Criminal offenses were the appropriate place to test the juridical, moral, and political strength gained by the centers of urban power in their striving for independence from the princes and bishops.

Since the High Middle Ages, city charters had invested communities with privileges, including the right to punish criminal offenders. In many communities, however, criminal prosecution of sodomy and other delicts required the presence of a feudal lord or his representative well into the fifteenth century. Yet urban communities strove to increase autonomy in legal affairs, at the same time as new urban elites superseded the old rule of nobles in many cities. In an attempt to rid themselves of the rights of overlords or bishops, urban regimes extended their authority in criminal matters. Increasingly, they sat in judgment even on capital offenders (which had been reserved to the lords in earlier times).

Why did secular courts and urban communities start to persecute sodomites in the late Middle Ages? To answer this question, we have to leave behind urban politics and turn to the history of religious dogma, two spheres that corresponded in medieval times. It has long been acknowledged that the eleventh and twelfth centuries marked a watershed in Latin Christendom's attitudes toward same-sex eroticism. In his groundbreaking *Christianity, Social Tolerance, and Homosexuality*, John Boswell detected a lack of interest in homosexual behavior before the scholastic age. According to Boswell, neither "Christian society nor Christian theology as a whole evinced or supported any particular hostility to homosexuality."[12] Though sodomy was not condoned as a sexual practice, same-sex eroticism seems to have been of relatively little concern to theologians in the early Middle Ages.[13] Critics have shown that Boswell underestimated the handbooks of penance, manuals of tariffs for sins in which same-sex acts were regularly mentioned. Yet, even in light of these handbooks (whose relevance for interactions between priests and believers is a matter of dispute), one can still uphold the assessment of the Church's relative lack of interest in homosexual behavior, at least if one does not misinterpret lack of interest as signifying tolerance.[14]

In approximately the year 1050, one of the foremost proponents of Church reform as well as a brilliant rhetorician, Peter Damian (c. 1005–70), attempted to purge ecclesiastical institutions, especially monasteries, of sexual and other "impurities." His *Liber Gomorrhianus*, a treatise in the form of a letter addressed to Pope Leo IX (1049–54), was part of a campaign to enforce Rome's superiority over the ranks of the Church.[15] Unlike his attack on simonists, Damian's doctrinally inspired tirades against masturbators and sodomites found few followers among his contemporaries in the eleventh century. This lack of resonance notwithstanding, the *Liber Gomor-rhianus* set the tone for condemnations of sodomy among later generations of theologians. From the twelfth century onward, scholasticism and its rational theology created a new intellectual climate and a body of knowledge that reigned supreme in the following centuries. Scholastics introduced a dogma which castigated sodomitical transgressors severely. Theologians such as Peter Cantor (d. 1197), Albert the Great (1200–1280), and Thomas Aquinas singled out this sexual sin as one of the worst violations of the divine order and, except for bestiality, the worst among all sexual sins.[16]

The emergence of Catholic doctrine on sodomy and "the formation" of Western Christendom's "persecuting society" stimulated novel forms of sanctions across Europe, a "machinery of persecution" in the words of Robert Ian Moore.[17] In the course of the twelfth century, ecclesiastical councils as well as secular rulers enacted laws that, for the first time in medieval Europe, stipulated severe penalties for sodomy.[18] Though there is little evidence that these precepts were implemented, the fact that they were formulated is significant in and of itself. Legal norms and precedents created stimuli to penalize same-sex offenders. In the long run, trials and executions became occasions to legitimize rule by purging communities of sexual offenders. But if we start to hear about sodomy trials in the German empire in the thirteenth century, this is also because of the extended use of writing in civic administrations. In archives, acts of rulership such as the prosecution of criminals were documented.[19] Novel methods of record keeping alone do not explain why persecution became evident during the High Middle Ages. Both the prosecution of criminals and the emergence of civic bureaucracies testify to an expansive vision of rule. Towns in the well-populated and highly urbanized region between Germany's central mountains and the Alps (what is now south Germany and the German-speaking part of Switzerland) pioneered the development of models of civic administration as well as the penalizing of same-sex sexual behavior among men.

In the fourteenth and fifteenth centuries, city governments north of the Alps began occasionally to enforce severe disciplinary measures that regulated the fringes of sexual behavior—including same-sex behavior, predominantly among men. Yet when cities followed theological condemnations in actively punishing sodomites, the measures, though never systematic, became more stringent. For Boswell, medieval cities were places that attracted sexual adventurers, men who, like "gay people" in the modern West, left their homes to seek new lives in urban centers. This is much too romantic a view. Cities were places of close surveillance as much as places of sexual opportunities. Notions of *disciplina*, originally developed in monasticism, were tried out on the urban populace.[20] Cities were also social entities deeply affected by the upsurge of religious life in the late Middle Ages. Thus, I turn next to some of the first records of trials on same-sex sexual behavior, with an eye on the mindset that guided law enforcement in these cases.

The Beginnings of Urban Persecution

One of the earliest sodomy trials in the German lands occurred in Munich. In 1378 a civic court, chaired by the representative of the duke of Bavaria (*vicedominus*), sentenced Heinrich (Hainreich) Schreiber to death. Without the use of torture (as the document states), he had confessed to masturbation and mutual masturbation with a student and "three or four" (*mit dreyen oder mit viern*) other men.[21] The short entry's language is descriptive, using narrative, not legal terminology, to circumscribe the transgressions. By grouping masturbation and mutual masturbation together and arranging them progressively, the officials showed themselves somewhat familiar with the scholastic taxonomy of sexual sins in which both transgressions were viewed as *sodomia*, or sins against nature. For the purpose of legal proof, the record stresses ejaculation as the act's outward sign.

A few years later in 1381, the chronicler Burkard Zink (d. c. 1474) mentions that in Augsburg five "heretics" (*ketzer*)—a "peasant" (*ain baurn*), two monks, and two Beghards—were burned for "having committed heresy [i.e., sodomy] with one another" (*verprant man fünf ketzer umb ketzerei, die sie mit ainander gethan hetten*).[22] "Heresy," "heretic," or "to commit heresy" were the expressions most frequently deployed in the urban records of same-sex sexual contacts.

In 1399 a sparse entry in Basel's book of punishments records that Friedrich the cook was burned at the stake for a sex act with a man named Schregelin. His partner, who claimed to have been asleep while Friedrich "committed heresy" with him (*ketzerie mit jm tribe*), was only banished from the city, despite the fact that he had ejaculated.[23] In 1400 the council of Strasbourg had Johannes Rorer, the owner of a bathhouse, executed for "heresy" (*ketzerie*). The authorities also issued a search warrant for his fugitive sex partner, a carpenter named Heinzmann Hiltebrant. Councilors sent a messenger as far south as Lucerne to make sure the culprit would be arrested. While the search warrant featured only the term "heresy" to characterize the offense, the messenger also carried a note (*zedellin*) with him that explained the sexual doings between the two men in greater detail for a more restricted audience, probably the councils of neighboring cities. According to this note, Rorer and Hiltebrant had masturbated each other, first in a latrine and then also in various other locations.[24]

Premodern criminal records rarely reveal the circumstances under which same-sex sexual acts came to be prosecuted by the authorities. From scattered evidence, we can assume that it was a person's attested reputation for engaging in acts of sodomy which most frequently led to legal action. The Strasbourg council seized Johannes Rorer because he was reputed to be a "heretic" or sodomite (*ketzer*): they "interrogated him about the events in such a way as one rightly interrogates people with such a reputation."[25] In many proceedings, the whispers, rumors, and gossip surrounding people who appear as offenders in court were all too evident. Once these voices reached the level of a so-called shouting (*clamor* or *geschrey*),[26] in other words, a public outcry, the authorities took action *ex officio* against a breach of the communal order and initiated legal investigations. In court, proceedings for crimes such as blasphemy and heresy against God or the secular ruler took the form of an *inquisitio* during which the judges investigated these breaches.[27]

Many large or middle-sized civic communities north of the Alps experienced their first sodomy prosecutions during the course of the fifteenth century. A court in Constance ruled that two clerics would burn for the "heresy" (*kätzry*) they had committed with each other in 1418.[28] In Zurich, Hermann von Hohenlandenberg, a contentious noble and a burgher of the city (since 1406) accused of pillaging travelers outside the city gates (1419), was sentenced to death in 1431 for having had sex with many male adolescents.[29] Regensburg recorded its first trial for "heresy with several men and boys" (*keczerey mit manigem man und knaben*) in 1456.[30] In 1471 the same city witnessed the execution of four men who had engaged in sex with one another, three artisans and a merchant.[31] The city of Constance prosecuted a friar and a burgher for a "disorderly life" and "unchristian" acts they committed with one another (*jrs vnordenlichen lebens wegen so sy vncristenlich mit ain andern getriben*) in 1464.[32] In Fribourg, the pastry cook (*patissier*) Jehan Ruaulx lost his life at the stake in 1493 for numerous sexual acts he had committed and attempted to commit with boys (*garson*), men, and a cleric. Apparently, he caught the authorities' attention when he returned from France visibly dismembered. Interrogated by the city's council, he confessed to having lost his penis and one of his ears as punishment for having attempted to commit "sodomitical indecency" in Sisteron. He was made to confess to a string of transgressions in Fribourg and Lausanne.[33] Sometimes, even very small communities witnessed the persecution of sodomites. In 1464 the sexton of a pilgrimage church (Einsiedeln) and a boy he had "florenced" (*geflorentz*) were burned at the stake.[34]

In the sixteenth century many small urban communities followed the lead of larger communities in persecuting sodomites. The city of Solothurn witnessed the first execution for "the works and heresy of sodomy" in 1525,[35] while Schaffhausen documented its first sodomy case in 1530 when Hans Fritschi, a laborer in a monastery, was sentenced to death for "heresy," that is, "unchristian, malicious, shameful acts, evil, and misdeed" (*kätzry, vncristenlich, böß, schantlich handlung, vbel, vnd mißthun*).[36] No cases are reported from St. Gallen before 1533, when Conrat Mülibach died at the stake for having engaged in "indecent" (*vntzimlich*[]) sexual activity, that is, mutual masturbation with young men in and around the city over the course of fourteen years.[37]

In German and Swiss cities, the number of sodomy cases is small compared to other offenses, such as theft or murder.[38] In Basel, only eight legal proceedings in cases of sodomy or attempted sodomy were reported between 1399 and 1449.[39] During the fifteenth century, the council of Zurich issued a total of 388 death sentences. Theft (251) and murder (41) were the most common offenses leading to capital punishment. By comparison, only five persons had to die for same-sex sexual acts.[40] These figures are roughly comparable to the number of sodomites convicted in the Low Countries. According to Marc Boone, in Ghent—one of the largest cities in Europe (approx. 64,000 inhabitants)—eight individuals were found guilty of sodomy during the fifteenth century (three of them women). In the same period, authorities in Brussels executed the surprisingly high number of twenty-six sodomites. In Burgundian Bruges, by medieval standards a huge city of roughly 46,000 people, 15 percent of all condemnations between 1385 and 1515 concerned sodomy. Condemnations peaked between 1490 and 1515, when, among a total of twenty-one cases, sixteen people were executed. Only thefts had a higher incidence (46.3 percent), while homicide more rarely came to trial (8.8 percent).[41]

North of the Alps, the level of persecution remained substantially lower than in Florence or Venice, where thorough and extensive sodomy investigations took place. In Florence and Venice, most of the proceedings led to the imposition of fines rather than ending at the stake, as they frequently did north of the Alps. In the empire, sodomy was not a matter of continuous concern as it was in these Italian communities in the fifteenth century. Yet when such cases came to be known, executions of sodomites were frequent.[42]

The persecution of sodomites reflects the northern cities' increasing grip on moral and legal issues within their territories. The creation of a political center and the construction of the sexual margins were thus intimately intertwined. But why exactly did councilors act so strictly in cases of sodomy? Guido Ruggiero has convincingly argued that urban communities were indeed deeply concerned about sodomy. Councilors feared that if sodomitical acts were not punished, their cities would suffer the Biblical fate of Sodom and Gomorrah—cities that God had destroyed supposedly for the same-sex sexual acts of their inhabitants. Though this fear might have been particularly strong in Venice, Ruggiero's object of study, because of its vulnerable location on the sea, this notion was evident in other cities as well.[43] In the Regensburg trial of 1471, the council sentenced four culprits to death for having committed "the sin of unchastity which is called the mute sin against human nature." This formula was repeated almost word for word in all four verdicts. It was supplemented by a reference to God's wrath which had struck five cities (including Sodom and Gomorrah) as retaliation for "such sins."[44] When humans acted against their own nature—to be imagined as the nature of the species and not their individual nature, to further interpret the formula—offenders deserved the harshest of treatments for their so-called unnatural acts. Penal authority in capital offenses like sodomy derived directly from God who, according to Genesis 19, had destroyed the city of Sodom in retaliation for the transgressions of its inhabitants. Whatever breach of the divine order to which the Old Testament story originally referred, medieval tradition saw the offense as sexual. After Emperor Justinian's (527–65) law code (528/542) first linked same-sex sexual acts among men to the destruction of Sodom as well as to other disasters, epidemics, or earthquakes, Sodom's offense was frequently interpreted as male homoeroticism.[45] Genesis 19 thus amounted to a divine mandate, a law binding all Christians. If the representatives and guardians of God's order on earth acted against offenders, a divine response similar to the destruction of Sodom (and the other four cities) would hopefully be avoided and, unlike Sodom, their own city might be saved from its ruin or the death of innocent inhabitants. The Biblical reference thus provided legitimation for the city's judges.[46]

Linguistically, the Regensburg entry fuses expressions with distinct genealogies into one compelling cluster: "unchastity" as an umbrella term for illegitimate sexual acts (described in more detail in the proceedings), "the mute sin," an equivalent for male-male sodomy, masturbation, and—rarely—bestiality, sodomy as the sin of the inhabitants of Sodom, and "the sin against nature."[47] In their entanglement, these phrases might have been compiled to convey unequivocally the delict in question, sexual acts involving several men. Since all locutions refer to a number of acts, officials might have felt the need for terminological clarification. In this and other trials, profuse narrations of the events served the same purpose. Be that as it may, the complex formula from Regensburg shows an unusual degree of learning for a fifteenth-century court—a time when trained experts only rarely handled judicial affairs in imperial cities.

In general, city councils increasingly assumed responsibility for protecting the city's moral integrity: sodomy was only one of the greatest violations, more heinous than transgressions such as drunkenness, gambling, adultery, and the like.[48] City authorities tried to ensure that urban society lived according to divine law. According to a Basel source, councilors were "bound . . . to punish all their subjects' misdeeds as well as malicious and boisterous words and actions which are against the Christian order and the Ten Commandments of God Almighty."[49] Sexual roles and activities were thought to be part of God's order as enshrined in the Ten Commandments. Lay concepts of an honorable body politic and the theological condemnation of sodomy reinforced each other. In the urban milieu, therefore, the theological thrust against sodomy acquired a new intensity. The magistrates felt compelled to intervene. Otherwise, a community's honor would be damaged and God's wrath would strike all of society, regardless of individual guilt or innocence.

The Legal Framework

As a rule, cities within the German empire had no sodomy laws on the books.[50] While many Italian communities issued severe legal edicts against same-sex sexual acts after the mid-thirteenth century, and especially during the fourteenth century,[51] few German communities had such prohibitions.[52] This lack of formal legislation notwithstanding, commentators took the existence of legal prohibitions against sodomy and bestiality for granted. "Imperial law punishes this shameful sin severely and contends that storms and plagues originate from it," writes Ulrich of Pottenstein in his catechetical *summa* (c. 1400), obviously alluding to Justinian's *novellae*.[53] References to sodomy legislation rested on the assumption that the Roman Empire had never ceased to exist,[54] though the relevant articles of Roman law were quoted in court documents only in the sixteenth century.[55] It was by the standard of customary law that sodomy was judged a delict deserving of a death sentence. Divine law permitted urban rulers to apply their powers of life and death to same-sex offenders. Referencing customary and Roman law, Ulrich Tenngler (1447–1511) called for punishment at the stake in cases of same-sex sexual acts (as well as cases of bestiality). The relevant article in this state-of-the-art manual in German for practitioners of the law, first printed in 1509 and frequently reedited, refers to common legal practice, while the margin references Justinian's law code.[56]

The absence of urban sodomy legislation notwithstanding, the surviving trial records testify to a legal mentality that guided civic judges in assessing the gravity of an offense. First, ejaculation had to have occurred. If no emission of semen had been established, judges often refrained from issuing a capital punishment. In 1427 the council of Basel banished the fisherman Peter Keller from the city "for [his] bad reputation for having attempted to commit heresy [sodomy], if one would have let him."[57] The authorities specified the exact distance from the city an offender had to remain—a distance that reflected the gravity of the transgression. While Keller swore an oath to stay twenty miles from the city, a repeat offender with a reputation for having attempted "heresy," possibly the same person, was banished "behind the Alps" (*ennent dem Lampertisch gebirge*) in 1441.[58] Milder than capital punishment, banishment was nevertheless a severe sentence, likely to disrupt a person's life, especially if expulsion was, as in the case of sodomy, eternal (banishment in the case of perjury lasted one year, homicide meant five years, and the expulsion for magic, like sodomy, was lifelong). In the year of Keller's punishment, 1427, a guildsman took up his cause and successfully intervened with the council so that Keller's banishment was reduced to two miles from the city (which might have enabled him to settle close to the city and do business more easily).[59] The council of Basel also commuted the banishment of Friedrich Schregelin from "behind the Alps" to banishment outside the city.[60] While the man who had shared his bed, Friedrich the cook, ended at the stake, Schregelin was only banished, despite his having experienced orgasm. According to the records, Schregelin acted as if asleep, thereby diminishing his responsibility in the eyes of the judges.[61]

Second, the frequency of sexual intercourse affected penal severity. Though some same-sex offenders were executed even if they had had sex only once, milder punishments were also an option in these cases. If sexual encounters had taken place over time, capital punishment was the rule. This is why interrogators usually noted the number of sex acts and, sometimes, a liaison's duration.

As a rule, investigators also extorted information from defendants as to how they had achieved sexual satisfaction. As far as one can tell from these widely differing records, judges treated mutual masturbation, the sexual practice that men adopted most frequently, as severely as intercrural (i.e., between the legs) intercourse (while oral sex is rarely reported). Yet many regarded anal intercourse as more deserving of punishment than other sex acts among men. In a 1493 protocol from Fribourg, the scribe termed anal sex "la propre sodomitique, c'est assavoir par derriere" (the true sodomy, that is to say, from behind).[62] Suspects sometimes advanced similar views. They presented anal sex as a severe transgression, while mutual masturbation or intercrural intercourse were conceived of as less egregious. Penetration, with its manifold associations of power and domination, physical integrity and gender inequality, emerges as a central tenet in the offenders' male sexual ideology. Yet the question of who penetrated whom seems to have rarely interested legal investigators. It had practically no effect on the punishments meted out, unless a passive partner was underage.

Age was the third important factor in mitigating the severity of a sentence.[63] As long as offenders could be seen as victims and had not actively solicited sex, they often escaped punishment.[64] In other words, the judges took a case's specific circumstances into consideration. Since intergenerational sexual activity was common, this means that many persons involved in sodomy trials faced no punishment or a punishment short of a death sentence.

Court documents claim burning at the stake as the punishment usually meted out for this offense. Upon the accused's request or because of the youth of an offender, burning at the stake was sometimes mitigated to decapitation, an execution less damaging to a person's honor (and also less painful). In Regensburg in 1471, the stakes had already been prepared for the execution of four culprits when the authorities granted their last-minute requests to be decapitated.[65]

With the introduction of the Constitutio Criminalis Carolina in 1532, criminal prosecution of sodomy for the first time gained an unmistakably clear legal basis in the German empire. In article 116 of the Constitutio Criminalis Carolina, women and men found guilty of same-sex sexual acts were to be sentenced to death: "If anyone commits impurity with a beast, or man with a man, or a woman with a woman, they have forfeited their lives and shall, after the common custom, be sentenced to death by burning."[66] Yet the effects of the Constitutio Criminalis Carolina were less immediate than this formulation suggests.

The process that led to the enactment of the Constitutio Criminalis Carolina, first discussed at the diet of Freiburg in 1498 and finally achieved in 1532, spanned more than three decades. Therefore, the code originated long before the Reformation and was finally enacted by Emperor Charles V in a religiously fractured empire. In fact, the *Constitutio Criminalis Carolina*, article 116 was copied word for word from another criminal law code, the *Constitutio Criminalis Bambergensis* of 1507, which regulated crimes in the diocese of Bamberg. Whereas other statutes taken from this 1507 model were revised and a special committee debated legal issues at the diets of the 1520s, the complicated search for consensus did not affect the sodomy statute in any way.

The statute evidences a continuation of late medieval practice more than a radical departure from earlier measures. Like the codification and systematization of law itself, the inclusion of sodomy statutes followed the lead of Italian city-states, which in turn relied on models from antiquity. Unlike antisodomy laws of late antiquity, article 141 of Bamberg's 1507 *Constitutio Criminalis*, on which the 1532 *Constitutio Criminalis Carolina* article was based, calls for the stake as punishment and also includes women offenders.[67] The sodomy article thus epitomizes the fusion of several legal traditions—Roman, Germanic, and customary law—as is characteristic for the code as a whole.[68]

Moreover, since the *Constitutio Criminalis Carolina* was subsidiary to customary and local law, it took many principalities and territories more than a century to implement the code. Whereas Basel, the site of a university, is said to have utilized this code soon after it was promulgated,[69] few documents from as late as the seventeenth century prove its use in Lucerne.[70] Even in Basel, court documents frequently refrain from mentioning the relevant paragraphs.[71]

✠✠✠

Divine standards of behavior are hard to achieve in any community. In medieval societies, the tremendous task of ensuring a code of behavior thought to be God's and the small forces set up to penalize transgressors of this same order made for a striking contrast. As a result, prosecution remained episodic, unlike the systematic persecution that emerged in some Italian communities. Instead, the response to same-sex sexual behavior was tied to highly localized episodes, reflecting personal enmities, clashes between institutions, and conflicts over how to enforce what was considered to be divine law. This did not change even when a new criminal law, the 1532 *Constitutio Criminalis Carolina*, might have provided a novel stimulus for trials of same-sex sexual acts. The following chapter will introduce sodomy trials from a local perspective.

2

Cases, Conflicts, Contexts

Despite an increasing attention devoted to same-sex sexual behavior, criminal prosecution of same-sex acts was haphazard during the late Middle Ages. It is especially noteworthy that church institutions remained largely inactive on a judicial level. At the same time, their secular counterparts regularly took offenders to court. But urban prosecutions variously affected different sectors of society—women, clerics, foreigners, the elite. In these fifteenth-century cases and the conflicts they created, extensive records reveal the significance of local conditions in shaping official responses to same-sex offenses.

Women Offenders

The episodic nature of trials for "heresy" becomes particularly apparent when we look at women who were accused of same-sex sexual behavior. The late medieval period witnessed the first criminal prosecutions of women for sexual relations with women. Strikingly, northern European powers were more active than Mediterranean societies in penalizing female homoeroticism.[1] In Rottweil in 1444 two women—one religious woman, the recluse Katharina Güldin, and one unnamed laywoman—were incriminated. Only a short and hardly legible transcript of a letter from the vicar general to the deacon of Rottweil survives.[2] Apparently, the city officials complained that the two women had practiced the "vice against nature which is called sodomy."[3] Notably, it was the city which became active in the matter and approached the representatives of the Church—a pattern I will address further below. Because of the women's different legal status— one of them belonging to a clerical, the other to an urban jurisdiction— several authorities became involved. The vicar general ordered the local deacon to conduct an investigation of the religious woman and to afterward transfer the case to the bishop's court in Constance. What happened to either the laywoman or her religious partner remains unknown.

The earliest known trial in which the judges issued a death sentence for female same-sex relations targeted Katherina Hetzeldorfer. For her crime (which bears no name in the protocol of the proceedings), she was drowned in the Rhine River near the imperial city of Speyer in 1477.[4] Some two years before the proceedings, Hetzeldorfer had left her native Nuremberg (where a "middle-class" family by the same name is well-documented).[5] She migrated to Speyer in the company of a woman whom she had "abducted" (empfuert) from a noble in Wertheim, as one witness stated, and, upon her arrival in Speyer, presented her companion as her "sister" (swester).[6] Whereas Hetzeldorfer's appropriation of a masculine identity seems to have gone unnoticed until the case came to court, rumors and whispers in the city raised suspicions about the couple's true relationship. According to one witness, Hetzeldorfer "had deflowered her [sister] and had been making love to her for two years."[7] She described herself as her companion's "husband" to a confidante who later appeared as a witness in court.[8] Moreover, Hetzeldorfer adopted the masculine code of a rogue, a sexually aggressive character and a potent lover. S/he actively sought out two women as sexual partners, called on one of them, Else Muter, at home (when her husband was out), and offered the substantial amount of eight florins to make her bend to her "manly will."[9] Hetzeldorfer's account is transmitted with minute attention to details of sexual role-play, including this description of how she made a dildo: "she made an instrument with a red piece of leather, at the front filled with cotton, and a wooden stick stuck into it, and made a hole through the wooden stick, put a string through, and tied it round."[10] Much to the judges' bewilderment,[11] this tool had enabled her to pass as a man in the eyes of her female sexual partners until the case came to court, or so they claimed in their testimony.

Viewed from the vantage point of legal thinking or theology, female homoeroticism inhabits the same category as male homoeroticism: in Rottweil's ecclesiastical records, the two women's crime was described as "sodomitical vice"; in the civic investigation of Agatha Dietschi (1547), the word heresy (ketzerey), the German equivalent for male-male sodomy and bestiality, came up during the interrogation.[12] These similar descriptions notwithstanding, magistrates responded differently to same-sex eroticism between women than to same-sex behavior between men. Whereas with men investigators often focused on sexual acts exclusively, they subjected women to more thorough investigations of their lives. In the records, these women appear to be torn between multiple social and religious identities as women and "men," "husbands" and lovers; in some cases, they were religious dissenters or "wayfaring" women. [13] In the case of Hetzeldorfer, the judges focused on the question of how Hetzeldorfer was able to pass as a male so successfully. Compared to men suspected of sodomy, women suspects created confusion for the judges. Their gender and their manipulation of expected female behavior apparently made the application of sentences to identifiable sexual acts difficult. It is, therefore, anything but accidental that the few trial records of "lesbian-like" [14] offenders are more extensive than comparable cases among men, whose condemnation is sometimes transmitted with little ado.

In addition, though coded with the same legal term as in other cases, the *crimen contra naturam* among women came to court much less often than the same crime among men. In court, women passing as men met quite different fates. Drowning, Hetzeldorfer's punishment, was considered an extremely degrading death sentence, meted out mostly to women and children transgressors and rarely imposed on men. [15] To the inhabitants of Speyer, Hetzeldorfer's execution reinscribed the "right" gender on her body and thus publicly legitimized urban rulers in their attempt to ensure a supposedly natural order of creation. In the case of "gay-like" males, the authorities responded in ways that can be rendered with some precision, as I described in the previous chapter on the legal framework of persecution. In the case of "lesbian-like" women, prosecution occurred so rarely that judicial responses may have varied more than in the case of male sodomites.

In the cases of both Agatha Dietschi and the unnamed "woman in men's clothes" (*ein frow in manszkleydung*) (the latter reported by the chronicler Fridolin Ryff [d. 1554] in 1537), [16] the accused had worked as farmhands and had married. However, the latter was drowned in the Rhine near Grenzach (not far from Basel), and the former, apprehended in nearby Freiburg im Breisgau in 1547, was pilloried in an iron collar and banished from the city. [17] In both cases, the women's "wives" claimed ignorance about their "husbands'" true sex, at least at the time of the wedding. (Dietschi's "wife" found out that her "husband" was a woman in the second year of their marriage.) [18] While in the case of the woman executed in Grenzach the chronicler declares that no sex between the spouses had taken place (theft and a dissipated lifestyle were at issue), in the case of Dietschi several hints suggest that the spouses had engaged in sex. Nevertheless, Dietschi received a relatively mild punishment compared to the death sentence meted out in Grenzach.

How was it possible that Dietschi got away with banishment, when in a nearby locale and only ten years earlier a woman had been sentenced to death for a similar transgression? Under the name of Hans Kaiser, also known as Schnitter Hensli (reaper-Hans), Dietschi had worked as a farm-laborer in the Danube valley since 1538. There, she married Anna Reuli with the community's approval. According to observers, they constituted a model marriage for eight years, until Reuli got involved with a man named Marx Gross. Obviously willing to separate, Anna then revealed her husband's sex to her brother-in-law, who in turn triggered the legal investigation by approaching the authorities. After initial wavering, Anna denied any sexual involvement with Agatha (alias Hans Kaiser) during their marriage. Marx Gross, who presumably wanted to save Anna from punishment, seconded her version of the events by stating that Anna Reuli's virginity was intact when they first had intercourse. Another villager, however, had found the two spouses in a barn, clearly engaged in erotic play. Moreover, when Anna had discovered that she was married to a cross-dressing woman in the second year of their marriage, she had continued to live with Agatha, supposedly for fear of saddening her aging mother or being ostracized by the community. During the investigation, it also came out that Agatha had been married a number of times, in the role of a husband *and* of a wife. Originally, Agatha was married to a man in her native village (Wehingen). She arrived in the principality of Fürstenberg in the Danube valley (Niedingen) in the company of a wife and a grown-up child. When she later returned to Anna's village without them, she claimed the two had died and thereafter started to court Anna Reuli.

As with Hetzeldorfer, a phallic tool, called either an *jnnstrument* or a *rüstung* (armor), featured in this case. Not only was Agatha found to possess such an instrument when she was arrested in Freiburg, but she also confessed to having improvised one "behind a willow tree" in the first days of her marriage and having used it with Anna three or four times. [19] The seriousness of such a revelation is indicated by the fact that Anna, the plaintiff, was also arrested. Possibly, only the perception that penetration had not been achieved saved them from a more severe sentence. If Anna Reuli was punished at all, her sentence does not appear in surviving records.

It is widely assumed in recent criticism that the use of penislike instruments marked the dividing line between the *tribade* who was executed for her reversal of the ordained gender hierarchy and the *femme* who, as the weaker partner, might have been subject to punishment, but was rarely if ever found guilty of a capital offense. [20] To be sure, this commonplace holds true for the trial of Katherina Hetzeldorfer, who was executed for having appropriated a phallic identity. Yet in cases like Dietschi's, uncertainties remain not only as to what happened between the women "in bed," but also what moved the judges to release the suspects. The application of *vicium sodomiticum*, a legal term primarily identified with males, raised confusions that could not be easily resolved when suspicions of female homoeroticism reached the male sphere of urban jurisdiction. Penetration offered a point of comparison to which the judges frequently resorted. Yet comparability did not go far with a sexual offender whose aberrant behavior was trumped by her gender deviance in the eyes of the judges. In order to act like a sodomite, a man did not have to be different from other men. But how could a woman act sodomitically, if the images this term invoked had to do with anal sexuality and penetration?

It is important, however, to remind ourselves that indeterminacy of sex surfaced not only with women. While women passing as men became an object of great curiosity in the sixteenth century, men whose biological sex troubled notions of sexual dimorphism entered the records mostly as enigmatic beings. As with the women discussed above, sexually indeterminate males caused confusion among the authorities in early modern Europe.[21]

Male-Male Sodomy and the Clergy

The confusion that occasional accusations of clergymen created was of a different kind than that created by women taken to court for same-sex sexual behavior. From the perspective of secular authorities, cases against clergymen provided an occasion to challenge the fundamental jurisdictional divide that separated the ecclesiastical from the secular realm. Because of the different authorities involved in disputes over delinquent clerics, the records exceeded those in other cases. More than in cases where only one jurisdiction was involved, the documents therefore reflect the highly localized contexts in which these cases arose. Before presenting the cases of clerical offenders whose prosecution became a matter of conflict, I next discuss the responses, or the lack thereof, within the Church.

A statute first issued at the Third Lateran Council (1179) decreed that clerics who had sinned *contra naturam* were to be either expelled from their orders or forced to do penance in a monastery.[22] Yet this decree does not seem to have been enforced on a regular basis. There is little evidence that ecclesiastical authorities or monastic orders purged their own ranks of same-sex offenders in court. Overall, ecclesiastical courts were much less active than civic courts in prosecuting sodomites.[23] Among the monasteries under the rule of Cluny, for instance, thirteenth- and fourteenth-century regulations governing monastic life do not betray a particular interest in the brethren's same-sex acts. In the same period and order, prosecutions with regard to the "vice against nature" were extremely rare.[24]

The clergy had a unique forum to deal with sodomitical transgressions, be the offenders laypeople or clerics, the *forum internum* of confession. These interactions left no records in the archive. A survey among confessors in Cologne (1484) shows that priests were not unanimous in how best to deal with the "mute sin" of sodomy.[25] While hard-liners wanted to castigate and punish this sin more openly, a majority was not willing to embark on a course fraught with danger, preferring to keep the issue silent. By keeping the actual occurrence of sodomy as secret as possible, representatives of the Church expanded their options beyond the discipline-and-punish approach of urban councils.

Unlike their secular counterparts, Church institutions were also more prone to act leniently in court. When in 1457 it became known that a Knight of the Teutonic Order had had sex with a priest in Weissensee near the city of Erfurt—an area ruled by the archbishop of Mainz—the bishop's court interrogated both men. In a first hearing, the Teutonic Knight confessed to having engaged in sexual intercourse with a person he perceived as a woman. Despite this finding, neither of the two was arrested. When summoned to court a second time, not surprisingly, the priest failed to appear and the case was dropped.[26] In 1504 the ecclesiastical court in the same city sentenced a priest known to have committed the *peccatum Sodomiticum* with seven boys and two women (anal intercourse?) to perpetual banishment from Thuringia, a relatively mild punishment compared to the sentence of urban courts in comparable cases.[27] If proceedings were instigated and a sodomy case entered the *forum externum*, ecclesiastical courts showed more leniency than secular ones. In some cases, the accused even tried to take advantage of ecclesiastical leniency in the prosecution of sodomites when they attempted to avoid being tried in secular courts.[28] When the Franciscan Hans Surer confessed before a civic commission in 1499 to having slept with a young boy, the monk's father successfully requested that his son be transferred to the Dominicans in Bern to await a prison sentence according to canon law rather than leaving the sentence to the council of Fribourg.[29]

There is some evidence that the interest of ecclesiastical courts in sodomy prosecutions increased on the eve of the Reformation. These courts served both laypersons and clerics, primarily with regard to sexual sins. Despite some overlap, they complemented rather than competed with civic jurisdiction. (Civic marriage courts were only instituted after the Reformation.) The judges issued fines and no corporal punishments, since the Church had no authority to execute defendants. Though sexual offenses—adultery and fornication—made up 90 percent of the cases brought before the Basel ecclesiastical court between 1463/64 and 1469/70, same-sex violations were never tried during this period. In the sixteenth century, a new category surfaced in the same records—*propter puerum*, "because of the boy (child)." If we take this to mean a same-sex liaison (which is complicated by the fact that this category is once applied to a woman), as Thomas Albert suggests, the court fined 3 percent of lay offenders in this category, as opposed to 10 percent for adultery, and 61 percent for fornication (1513–15). Among clerical offenders, *propter puerum* ranked second after concubinage (25 percent) with 9 percent (1509–22).[30] Around 1500, there was also an increase in sodomy trials in the realm of civic jurisdiction. The evidence from ecclesiastical courts, therefore, resonates well with an increasing number of urban sodomy trials on the eve of the Reformation.

The Church itself was a complex institution where varying interests came together. Regular and secular clergy, prelates and lower-rank clerics, members of the orders and priests often found themselves at odds over how to respond to breaches of sexual decorum, as the following case shows. When in 1416 it became known that Heinrich of Rheinfelden, a respected and educated Basel theologian, was suspected of sexual overtures to lay workers in the city's Dominican monastery, the city council initiated an investigation.[31] Six witnesses were interrogated by city officials. As a cleric, Heinrich was subject to ecclesiastical jurisdiction and could not be forced to respond to questions by the city commission. But the laborers gave the council detailed depositions of Heinrich's eros-laden interactions with his inferiors. The Dominican had showered them with gifts, invited them to his room, visited a baker at his workplace, indulged in bawdy talk about the others' sexual exploits with women, asked a worker to expose his genitals, exposed his own genitals, touched another's penis, and asked others to touch his own. In light of their inferior social position, the workers responded cautiously yet firmly in order to protect their sense of honor, or so they stated in the hearing. One of the main witnesses, Heinrich Böpplin, it is recorded, talked loudly while Heinrich of Rheinfelden whispered during their meetings; the laborer threatened to go public. The Dominican Heinrich sought one-to-one encounters with these men and begged them to remain silent. According to the council, the statements confirmed initial suspicions about the "roaming" sin of "sodomitical depravity" in Basel (*infamia seu crimine sodomitice pravitatis volante in dicta civitate Basiliensi*).[32] But no sexual intercourse seems to have taken place—if we believe the witnesses (who could have been prosecuted had they admitted to the act). Once the council got wind of the rumors, it took action, collected information on the suspect, and approached the bishop's court in the matter.

Conflicts arose in the local monastery about how to avoid scandal over Heinrich's doings. By intending to punish the culprit "in secret" (*in einer gheim*), the Dominican monks wanted to save "their monastery's honor" (*ires closters ere*) even before the city convened its commission.[33] Some fellow brethren conspired against Heinrich, and a series of very contentious discussions took place within the Dominican monastery. An emergency hearing of the regional Dominican chapter was held in Basel to discuss the matter. There, supporters of Heinrich and those who sought to cover up the whole affair won their case. The investigators played Heinrich off against his "detractors," suggesting that the testimony of an "honorable and pious man" (*biderbe man*) like Heinrich trumped their account.[34]

In this and other cases, the local clergy was more willing to collaborate with the council than the order's superiors were. The high-ranked Dominicans whom Heinrich was able to win over guarded the order's interests against infringements of any kind. It was feared, probably rightly, that a scandal would undermine the monastery's position in the city. The most desirable course of action must have been to put a lid on the affair of Magister Heinrich, especially in light of recent tensions over religious politics in Basel. At the beginning of the century (1401–11), Heinrich of Rheinfelden and the Dominican monastery had been embroiled in a highly publicized dispute over the legitimacy of Beguine congregations in Basel. The Franciscans (who had defended the Beguines and lost their cause) could easily have exploited accusations of sodomy against a prominent Dominican in town—all the more, since the Franciscans had been supported by the city magistracy.[35]

In Heinrich's case, no serious action ensued. Probably, Heinrich left the city—he does not show up in the documents for a couple of years—to let the dust settle on the affair. His prestige was not permanently damaged. He returned to Basel. In 1431 he preached at the Council of Basel for the Dominican order.[36]

Conflicts also arose in 1475 over the fate of another clergyman, Johannes Stocker, chaplain at the cathedral of Basel. Stocker was made to sign his confession in August of the same year as *presbiter et sodomita*, "priest and sodomite." In harshly condemning legal rhetoric, an ecclesiastical commission sentenced him in accordance with Lateran III to perpetual exile in an unspecified Italian monastery for "having perpetrated in the current year, at the most nefarious instigation of humankind's foe and oblivious to his spiritual salvation and his honor, the abominable sodomitical vice several times with a youth named Johannes Müller from the town of Bruck in the diocese of Constance who then lived in Basel in his [Stocker's] house."[37] After the arrest in June, faced with execution, Johannes Stocker complied with the prosecution. He voluntarily (*incompulse*) confessed his deeds without the use of torture. To be more precise, he confessed only acts committed with Johannes Müller, a young student and choirboy who lodged with Stocker. From rumors in the city echoed in the proceedings, we know that Müller was likely not the first youth toward whom Stocker had felt a strong affection.[38] Conradus, a teacher at St. Leonhard's school, warned Müller, mentioning sexual relations that Stocker had previously had with two other youths.[39] Stocker's affection for Müller perhaps was different from his earlier experiences only in that it knew no bounds. If we are to believe Müller's statement, Stocker assured him that he "loved him [Müller] more than any other man. Never was he [Stocker] overcome by a stronger desire to make love to a boy than with him. And when he [Müller] was in the choir, [Stocker] never turned his eyes away from him and begged him to do his will and let him make love to him."[40] In a "spontaneous confession," written down immediately after his arrest, Stocker discloses that he had not "tried nor done such things with another youth or man."[41] Stocker confessed only to having "florenced" (*geflorentzet*) Müller fourteen times on the premises of the cathedral.[42] While Stocker claimed Müller's consent to their encounters, the boy reported resistance and, after Stocker had forced himself on his object of affection, pain.

Several persons and various institutions participated in the scandalous Basel affair to make Stocker an example. His fate was a matter of dispute within the bishop's quarters. As a tattletale and informer, Stocker was hated by many and supported by the mighty few.[43] After his initial confession in June 1475, he was sentenced at first to the loss of all his possessions and perpetual imprisonment on bread and water. This was not the final outcome of the case. At the beginning of the following month, Oswald, count of Thierstein and steward to Johann V von Venningen (d. 1478), bishop of Basel, came to the city of Basel. Having assumed that Stocker would "be sent away and disgrace [would] be avoided,"[44] Oswald was dismayed to realize that the bishop's representative in town already had arranged for a public trial the following day. The trial, Oswald claimed, would have led to Stocker's execution, according to the motto: give him a fair trial and hang him. Such a measure required the collaboration of secular and ecclesiastical authorities, because only secular authorities could carry out a death sentence. With difficulty, Oswald convinced the vicar general to postpone the trial until the following Monday, thus gaining time to get support from the bishop. Then, in a somewhat agitated letter, Oswald appealed to the bishop's own interests, noting that a public procedure could hardly be "useful" (*nützlich*) and imploring the bishop to keep his representative from executing his plans. As an alternative action, he suggested secretly trying Johannes in a place outside the city of Basel and exiling him afterward. The bishop proceeded exactly as Oswald had suggested. Stocker was sentenced to perpetual exile from the area north of the Alps. Thus, public knowledge of his doings was contained and further damage to the bishop's quarter avoided. Notably, members of the urban elite advocated a public trial, whereas Oswald, count of Thierstein, and the bishop favored a more secretive handling of Stocker's case.

According to canon lawyers, sodomy was "a *delictum mixti fori*, that is, a crime within the jurisdiction of either secular or religious courts."[45] The *Summa de casibus* (1317), the so-called *Summa Astesana*, by Astesanus d'Asti, one of the most widely used handbooks for confessors north and south of the Alps, recommended that ecclesiastical and secular authorities collaborate in cases of sodomy.[46] Yet, as a rule, the Church did not actively participate in sodomy trials in the Holy Roman Empire. The well-functioning collaboration of spiritual and secular authorities in the prosecution of male-male sodomy turns out to be a myth. To be sure, medieval theologians condemned same-sex acts in their teachings. Yet theoretical condemnations of homoeroticism emerged long before drastic measures were regularly taken. Within Church institutions, theological condemnation was seldom transferred rigidly into judicial action, especially when clergy were the offenders.

The coexistence of two jurisdictions made sodomy cases involving the urban clergy a matter of dispute between several competing institutions. In the city of Augsburg in 1409, four clerics—two chaplains, one priest, and a Dominican monk—and a craftsman, a tanner, were arrested on charges of having committed sodomy with each other—the "mute sin against nature" (*stumede sind wider die natur*) or "heresy" (*ketzerei*) as it appears in various chronicles. A conflict with the bishop ensued (whose contours remain somewhat vague) over how to treat the clerical offenders.[47] At any rate, the different forms of executions testify to the offenders' different legal status; the clerics died a brutal death, yet they died without bloodshed. Whereas the layman was burned at the stake, the clerics were locked in a cage, pulled up on the city tower for everybody to see, and starved to death. Though no documents are preserved, chroniclers well into the sixteenth century provide an account of this event.[48] Most urban governments stopped short of violating church rights, however, by choosing not to execute clerics.

Conflicts between the secular and the ecclesiastical swords over the treatment of sexual "heretics" had many political, legal, and moral reverberations. For the council, the seizure of power within the city walls inevitably led to clashes with the clergy, and sodomy was only one among many such conflicts over concubinage, property rights, and so on.[49] Urban rulers brought legally fixed boundaries into question by referring to sexual norms and by extending their claim to moral rule over sodomites among the clergy. Clerics suspected of sodomy became a test case for urban power in legal affairs. Indeed, one of the Swiss Confederacy's declared objectives was to contain the scope of clerical jurisdiction.[50] City councils usually respected the limits of their authority vis-à-vis ecclesiastical institutions, however. They preferred legal means to expand their power, it seems. Though they threatened their counterparts, they did not go beyond what was legally warranted in most cases.

Though the cities appear to have been the more dynamic agents in the exchange, the Church was flexible in meeting the challenge to its status. Once secular authorities translated theological-legal axioms into action, ecclesiastical institutions fought against an interference with clerical prerogatives. A Lucerne case testifies to the growing tensions between one city and the Church.[51] When a Benedictine monk was found guilty of "heresy" and detained by city officials in 1489, the two laymen involved were sentenced immediately and burned to death. All three men had apparently "rubbed their penises against one another until they ejaculated."[52] The city councilors respected clerical immunity by saving the monk from immediate execution. Yet by arresting the culprit, the council also showed its willingness to go further in this case. Both the bishop of Constance and the father superior applied to the council for jurisdiction over the monk's case. But Lucerne's councilors made clear that they wanted to retaliate for this crime on their soil. Following a recommendation by other members of the Swiss Confederacy, they threatened to obtain papal permission to punish this monk, or so they said in a letter to the bishop of Constance.[53] The council claimed that the Church had often been negligent in judicial matters, underscoring its argument by verbally mustering broad-based consent: "The common man," as the council's handbook says, "does not like to do this [that is, to hand the priest over], for one is always afraid, he might not be punished at all."[54] The entry expresses a concern that the failure to issue a sentence in this case would undermine the burghers' religiosity and disrupt both civic and religious discipline, which were posited as mutually supportive.[55] At the same time, the council of Lucerne stopped short of the ultimate violation of clerical privilege in criminal matters. When they extradited the accused to the bishop, they sent an accompanying letter in which they openly threatened not to cooperate with the Church any longer if the accused sodomite were not adequately punished. (What became of the monk is uncertain.) This case shows the city more active than church institutions in publicly penalizing sodomy. In general, the city councils acted more Catholic than the pope—always with an eye to their own advantage.

Conflicts over clerical immunity, especially in sexual matters, remained a feature of urban society into the Reformation era. Yet these conflicts would be misinterpreted if we took them for evidence of a continual enmity between towns and the Church. Conflicts arose only sporadically. To the contrary, clashes over sodomites within the clergy also testify to the degree to which urban leaders were open to religious ideas. Where ecclesiastical authorities were found lacking, their urban counterparts felt called upon to enforce divine law. Italian city statutes on sodomy demonstrate how religious concerns influenced secular legislation.[56] There are no such laws from the medieval period in the German empire. Nonetheless, the records of urban sodomy trials resonate with religiously inspired arguments and anxieties.

The vernacular term most frequently used to describe same-sex sexual behavior in civic court records, "heresy," testifies to the degree to which urban life was infused with religious clichés, notions, and ideas, including the Christian condemnation of sodomy. "Heresy," meaning religious unorthodoxy *and* sexual transgression, echoes long-standing church polemics against groups considered to be heretical. What is more, the judges in sodomy trials concatenated sexual crimes in ways comparable to a scholastic theology of sin: a Munich court listed solitary masturbation with mutual masturbation; in Lucerne, a convict was said to have engaged in sex with animals as well as with men. The application of "heresy" in urban courts thus reflects the usage of "utterly confused" scholastic categories such as *sodomia, vicium sodomiticum,* or *vicium contra naturam.* At the same time, these records also betray distinctly urban concerns about communal standards of behavior, individual as well as communal honor, and, ultimately, a community's purity.

In order to be effective, albeit to a limited degree, urban control of sexual behavior had to be regularly rehearsed. The council's willingness to bring the community in line with divine mandates demanded that such a standard be communicated to the urban populace. From time to time, an example would have to be set. Well-publicized, scandalous incidents were particularly effective in this regard. But as in the above conflicts between secular and ecclesiastical authorities, exposure of same-sex sexual acts frequently served particular interests.

Burgundian "Florentines"

Male-male sodomy often entered the urban scene spectacularly, as illustrated by the cruel fate of a group of eighteen Lombard soldiers executed as sodomites on Christmas Eve day in 1474. These mercenaries, in the service of the duchy of Burgundy, were captured in battle and subsequently transferred to Basel, a member of the anti-Burgundian league that in 1477 would prevail against one of Europe's most splendid powers.

With conspicuous unanimity, these soldiers confessed under torture to having been involved in acts of male-male sexuality.[57] Only two of the eighteen were able to resist the allegations. A third later recanted. Many of these Lombard men confessed to having been "florenced" by their superiors, and many of them had proceeded to "florence" their inferiors.[58] While reconfirming the notion that Lombards, especially Lombard mercenaries, were avid practitioners of sodomitical intercourse, they also shifted the responsibility for these acts to others and often moved the acts' occurrence to distant places during their adolescence in Italy. In other words, the mercenaries cited the distant location of the crime, youthfulness, and inferior social position as mitigating circumstances. Sometimes, the witnesses went beyond general indicators of frequency such as "once" or "often," and mentioned the number of their sexual encounters (1, 2, 3, 10, 20, 40, 50, 1,000). Anthony Parmisan confessed to having "florenced a thousand times before he took a wife."[59] The accused men claimed to have been abused by their teachers, raped by soldiers, or beaten to comply with their superiors' sexual desires. One mercenary even stated that he was "florenced" by unspecified "evil people," by which he probably meant criminals.[60] Another portrayed himself as having been forced into sodomitical acts by sheer need. Still another soldier had received financial remuneration for consenting to an act of sodomy. Often, sexual abuse led them to instigate the same sexual practice, or so they confessed.

Yet why did investigators so persistently link war crimes with male-male sex acts in a trial that targeted mercenaries of a foreign power? And why did the defense strategy adopted by the Lombards turn out to be futile in the end? The proceedings against the Lombard mercenaries must be understood against the backdrop of the anti-Burgundian war propaganda—a well-orchestrated campaign that preceded the war and was elaborated throughout its duration (1474–77). During the war years, commentators portrayed the Burgundian forces as immensely cruel and prone to sexual perversion. According to the chronicles, the Burgundian forces burned villages, killed their inhabitants, raped boys as well as women, and left great suffering behind them. Persistently, Basel and other members of the anti-Burgundian league had branded the Burgundians as heretics in the heart of Christendom.[61] According to Johann Knebel's (1414/16–81) Basel chronicle, the Alsatian landvogt serving Burgundy, Peter von Hagenbach, was a *tyrannus, traditor, sodomita, obpressor tam virginum quam mulierum*—"a tyrant, traitor, sodomite, oppressor of virgins and women."[62] At the same time, an envoy to the imperial court was told to expose the "murderous, villainous, unchristian and unnatural" way the Lombards had behaved during their raid on a region west of Basel.[63]

These stories reflect the conviction, as anti-Burgundian propaganda maintained, that the Burgundians represented an emanation of evil forces prone to the greatest sexual transgressions. Thus, when the Lombard mercenaries serving Burgundy were captured during the war and executed in Basel for everybody to see, Burgundian misdeeds could finally be punished and thereby made known to the broader populace. As mercenaries, these men evoked images of sexual licentiousness and unruly masculinity. As Italians in the service of the duke of Burgundy, they could be vilified as sodomites.[64]

Not all of the captives were in fact Lombards. As Claudius Sieber-Lehmann has shown, a few Burgundian and French soldiers were among them.[65] The trial's propagandistic intent is clearly revealed by the fact that the two Frenchmen were forced to confess to crimes other than sodomy. Sieber-Lehmann has rightly called the proceedings "a show trial," swiftly conducted and even more quickly brought to a deadly end.[66] The authorities exploited and reinforced notions that opposed Italian sexual depravity to "German" innocence in matters of sodomy. Through this anti-Burgundian propaganda campaign, the league members intended to mobilize their populaces for war with one of Europe's foremost powers. The Basel episode of 1474 demonstrates how different modes of communication intersected and thereby acquired a deadly force. To incite popular indignation against the Burgundians, many "media" propelled images of sodomitical sex to a large urban public. Yet the machinations of sexual suspicions could turn against the powerful themselves if the political context made such an outcome seem expedient.

In 1463 a contentious nobleman, Richard Puller von Hohenburg, was stripped of many of his Alsatian holdings.[67] Another noble, Wirich von Berstett, had apprehended one of Puller's servants, Ludwig Fischer, who attracted attention by conspicuously displaying clothes unbecoming a servant. Under torture, Ludwig confessed to having been courted by Richard—a fact which had enabled him to improve his economic lot by blackmailing his master. As a result of the proceedings that followed, Hohenburg lost his fiefs to the bishop of Strasbourg. Yet no formal trial seems to have ensued. Hohenburg was released from arrest soon thereafter.

This would not be the last time that rumors about Hohenburg's sexual doings circulated among the Alsatian nobility. Under scrutiny, Hohenburg aggressively undertook to conceal the traces of his activities. On his orders, a servant who had witnessed a sexual act was drowned. Hohenburg's enemies claimed to have found the written order for the killing when they confiscated one of his castles.[68]

Hohenburg's sexual proclivities did not cause his downfall, as the nineteenth-century historian Heinrich Witte contended.[69] A nobleman's sexual doings in and of themselves would hardly have sufficed to bring about his demise. It was the explosive mix of endless conflicts over possessions *and* his interest in same-sex eroticism that made Hohenburg a target for his numerous foes. Having overcome the first accusation more or less successfully, he was targeted a second time and arrested in 1474. As a noble, Hohenburg was not sentenced to death for sodomy. In 1476 he was released conditionally after signing a confession of his misdeeds and relinquishing his possessions. He never began his term of imprisonment in a monastery, as he had agreed, however, but fled and continued to fight for his possessions.

Hohenburg's complex life story demonstrates that accusations of sexual ill-repute sometimes targeted nobles. Yet the powerful and members of the nobility could manipulate court proceedings, even in cases involving such a severe charge as sodomy. Hohenburg used his social position to have depositions nullified. A brilliant tactician, he played local competitors off against other powers. By turning to the emperor and his court—the highest (though distant) secular authority of all—he circumvented the authority of other Alsatian nobles and obtained imperial support instead.

Several times in his life, Hohenburg was able to turn the tables on his persecutors. Although firm evidence existed to the contrary, he presented himself as innocence personified and convinced others that all the allegations against him were fabricated. To prove his honorable status, he came up with letters that testified to his good *fama* (when he was not able to procure such letters, he forged one).

After having been stripped of his lands a second time in 1476, Hohenburg wisely turned to the Swiss Confederacy—at that time said to be a haven for the criminally suspect. After long deliberations, the city of Bern rejected his plea for assistance in winning back his property in Strasbourg and Alsace. Subsequently, he approached Zurich where, surprisingly, he found support. By taking up his cause, city authorities embarked on a course fraught with hazard. In subsequent events, conflict arose not only, as expected, with Strasbourg (where Hohenburg was a citizen and had married) over a host of legal and financial issues, but also with other Swiss territories over the risk of a feud with Strasbourg, one of their close allies. At this juncture, Hohenburg and his servant Anton Metzler were suddenly discovered to be "heretics." The charge surfaced conveniently when it became politically expedient to sever connections with Hohenburg.

Under torture, Hohenburg confessed that he had had sex with Metzler and several other men (also that he had forged documents). At the stake, however, asked to repeat his confession, he refused to do so, claiming that his fortune was the true reason for his execution and thereby implying that Zurich authorities had unjustly tried him in order to seize his properties. He singled out one member of Zurich's elite as the particular villain who was responsible for his death, Hans Waldmann. Shortly before Hohenburg and his servant died in the flames, he asked Waldmann to do penance in the next life for having betrayed him.

Only a few years after this well-publicized event, Hans Waldmann was himself executed and, again, "heresy" was part of the accusations. Waldmann's delicate diplomacy during the Hohenburg case—when conflict with Strasbourg and the Swiss allies was successfully avoided—marked the beginning of a spectacular yet short-lived political career. One year after Hohenburg's execution, Waldmann became mayor of Zurich (1483). He distinguished himself as a statesman and acquired fame far beyond Switzerland—an unusual career considering the parochialism of Swiss politics. Whatever his merits or faults as a statesman, Waldmann's ascent and political moves attracted deep resentment within the city of Zurich—the discontented included members of the elite as well as the populace—and among the cantons of the Confederacy.[70]

Sodomy accusations emerge as one of the major links between Hohenburg and Waldmann. Even before his execution in 1489, Waldmann became an object of libel. He was accused of having been bribed by foreigners and particularly by the Milanese. This slur implied a linkage between illicit political and financial deals on the one hand and illicit sexual doings on the other. As somebody who had socialized with the executed sodomite Hohenburg, Waldmann also remained guilty by association. In 1485 a certain Hanns Krut was reported to have smeared Waldmann's reputation by labeling him a "traitor, perjurious villain, and pederast [*knebenschinder*]." Not a burgher of Zurich himself, Krut backed his authority with that of his "masters" in Bern and Strasbourg, and he cited these councilors as experts on the subject of Waldmann's villainy.[71]

Detractors like Hanns Krut created insults by clustering slanderous words. By conjuring up treason as well as sexual depravity, Krut called Waldmann's abilities as a political leader into question. Yet the cluster of accusations that he deployed is vague and stereotypical. Powerful notions of impurity had for a long time blurred the distinctions between betraying God (religious heresy), betraying God's creation (sexual heresy), and betraying one's financial obligations or political loyalties.[72] Once Waldmann's political fate began to turn in the context of a peasant rebellion, previous accusations—a concoction of rumors about illicit financial dealings, foreign connections, and sex among men—surfaced again and this time were taken seriously.[73]

In 1489 Waldmann met the fate that Hohenburg had met seven years earlier. But more inventive means of humiliation were employed. After his imprisonment, Waldmann was relocated to a dungeon where a "heretic" (*ketzer*) had been held before (and who was evicted to make room for Waldmann). He was forced to eat from this "heretic's" plate and received no privileged treatment as a former mayor of the city. Influential friends were barred from visiting him.[74] In other words, the city's leadership invented a strategy that not only figured Waldmann as a social, sexual, and religious outcast but also reinforced the accusation against him with potent rituals of exclusion. All the rumors converged to shape a narrative which breathed life into the accusations that had circulated before he was apprehended. When Waldmann was finally executed in Zurich, Hohenburg's last words at the stake must have resounded in the ears of the spectators.

The executions of Hohenburg and Waldmann were political spectacles in the Confederacy and beyond. The fates of Richard von Hohenburg and Hans Waldmann attracted exceptional attention among contemporaries: numerous chronicles covered their life stories in remarkable detail.[75] Chroniclers elaborated, for example, on the romance between Hohenburg and his servant Anton Metzler.[76] They crafted a "textbook version" of the incidents that led to the executions. But knowledge about the executions also filtered down to the streets of Swiss cities.[77] The polyphonous chorus of voices reveals political factions, lines of conflicts, and the Confederacy's antiaristocratic outlook. Thus, the executions of Hohenburg and Waldmann for a congeries of offenses, sodomy prominent among them, emerged as political events that spread images of sodomy to the populace.

The publicity given to Hohenburg and Waldmann had reverberations well beyond those intended by the rulers of Zurich. According to one speaker—clearly not a member of the elite—the two cases taken together testified to Zurich's greed: "my masters [the councilors] have accepted the eight thousand florins from Strasbourg unjustly [the sum Zurich received to avoid a feud with Strasbourg in the Hohenburg 'deal']. When they had received the sum, Sir Richard von Hohenburg was easily burned and not before, although he was a villain as well before as after."[78] The defamer did not dispute the fact that Hohenburg was "a villain" and was, therefore, justly burned at the stake. Rather, his comment points to his cynical awareness of the expediency of Hohenburg's downfall and the financial gain connected with it—an allegation to which Hohenburg himself alluded at the stake. The speaker regards Hohenburg and his masters as all practicing morally questionable behavior.

✠✠✠

In the second half of the fifteenth century, sodomy trials became a political weapon in the empire.[79] Accusations of sodomy were still relatively novel in urban politics in the north. Yet their novelty made the delict's spell on urban communities in this time period all the more potent. Only from time to time did sodomy surface in cities north of the Alps. Despite occasional scandalous episodes, judges showed no signs of a continuous alarm over same-sex eroticism in the fifteenth century. The trials differ widely in scope, execution, and outcome. Therefore, any one of them can hardly be regarded as typical. However local these events were, they suggest that an episodically high visibility of same-sex sexual acts was emerging as a corollary of late medieval politics. Many urban communities had to work through the topic of male homoeroticism at one significant point or another. By comparison, prosecutions for female homoeroticism were extremely rare.

Despite the episodic nature of sodomy trials, proceedings in secular courts offer glimpses into male-male and, to a more limited extent, female-female eroticism in imperial cities of the late Middle Ages. Prosecution of these sex acts enabled secular authorities to display on occasion their willingness to control sexual mores, thereby legitimizing a council's rule. The records of urban sodomy trials resonate with both communal and religious concerns. Yet the application of a Biblically inspired code of law was riddled with limitations and contradictions. Within a city's walls, councils faced clerical immunity. The councilors' approach was further troubled by a world suffused with gendered bodies and various forms of desire. Their focus on the sexual act, defined by a phallic sexuality, was hardly applicable to women's sexual acts with women, for instance. Notions of gender dimorphism and what a man's or a woman's body meant seemed to be inapplicable to certain individuals. Overall, the measures of state authorities were haphazard. Punishment depended largely on the specific circumstances of a case—whether defendants were accused for political reasons, whether women became the object of legal proceedings, or whether members of the clergy were involved—a trait of judicial life I capture with the term episodic. The casuistry of medieval court cases has thus introduced the intricacies of urban politics as well as a maze of conflicting motivations, actions, and desires.

Judicial activity against sodomites during the late Middle Ages coincided with the clergy's newly intensified efforts to disseminate the Word of God among laypersons. In the following chapter, I will delve into the instructional material addressed to the laity and analyze how religious teachers negotiated their role as experts in sexual dogma in the case of sodomy.

3

The Discourse of Experts

The sins of Sodom occupied a religiously and symbolically elevated terrain in the pastoral theology of the late Middle Ages. A rhetoric of extremes and superlatives *in pessimo* regularly came into play when religious writers treated *sodomia*.[1] Sometimes, because of the sin's severity, the sodomite even served as the epitome of the sinner.[2]

In the *Speculum exemplorum* (*Mirror of Exempla*)—a voluminous collection of more than twelve hundred stories used in sermons—the very last story features a sinner so enmeshed in his sinful life that he is unable to pull himself out and embrace God.[3] Sexual sins, sodomy in particular, represent the sinners' ultimate "insanity," in that they knowingly trade hell for redemption when giving in to the desires of the flesh. The *Speculum exemplorum*, largely an anthology of earlier works, was published as a printed resource for priests.[4] A detailed index guides its user to the relevant themes. Twelve entries refer to *sodomia* (whereas only eleven feature usury). In moral theology, *sodomia* usually covers transgressions such as masturbation, nonprocreative heterosexual intercourse, and bestiality as well as sexual contacts between men and between women. Significantly, where we leave the realm of religious dogma and enter the wealth of examples offered by the *Speculum exemplorum*, *sodomia* signifies same-sex sexuality among men (though, as an example, the story is applicable to an array of transgressions other than sodomy).

The story runs as follows:

In the diocese of Duisburg, a young man had confessed to sodomy on many occasions, but always experienced relapses after confession. Refusing to further absolve the sinner unless he were to revoke his deeds on a permanent basis, the father confessor eloquently tried to cajole the young man into conversion. The youth, however, gushing with tears, stated that he could not make any more false promises about his ability to resist physical temptation. Agitatedly, he described a vision in which he saw the flames of the inferno on one side of his body, whereas the other was pulled toward "some young man with whom" he would "perpetrate the crime" (*adolescentem aliquem cum quo crimen possim committere*). The imminent punishment of the two in eternity notwithstanding, he clung obstinately to his "malice" (*malum, scel[us]*) and left without absolution. The confessor (and the story's commentator) revels in the powers of the divine that, even in such a severe case, could have reconciled the sinner with a forgiving God.[5]

In this *exemplum*, sodomy figures as a test case for the conversion of a sinner enmeshed in what amounts to the ultimate sin. Neither the sodomite's vision nor the father confessor's enlightening words have power over sodomitical desire. Caught in the throes of lust, the sodomite cannot disentangle his soul from "demonic forces." Thus, the sodomite serves as a warning for the loss of control brought about by corporeal desires. Where the body rules the mind, human order is perverted. Yet nowhere does the body rule one's being more obstinately than in sex and, among the sexual sins, in sodomy.[6]

Confession, the story's theme, and sermon, the story's pragmatic function, are the loci where Christian dogma encounters the actual sinner. Intriguingly, in order to authenticate this story, the sinner and sodomite seems to speak for himself. Yet it is doubtful whether there is any position from which "the Sodomites do indeed speak for themselves."[7] Rather, the actual sodomite emerges as the ideal sinner. His own horrifying vision testifies to his inevitable punishment in eternity. Applying religious moralism to his own life, he serves as a mouthpiece of didacticism, warning others who lead similarly sinful lives.

In this chapter, I seek to investigate the (imagined) conversations between theological experts and the laity on same-sex eroticism. I focus on the functions assigned to the so-called unspeakable in the religious discourse of the waning Middle Ages. Historians of sexuality have often circumscribed the scarcity of materials on same-sex desire by resorting to this and similar expressions. This chapter works against prevailing scholarly practice that perpetuates medieval metaphors regarding the so-called unspeakable. With its various resonances in moral theology, the "unspeakable" is in fact ill-suited to express that which eludes our desire to know for sure. It is equally ill-suited for the purpose of writing a history of hidden sexualities. In fact, the "unspeakable" occupied a specific locus in the edifice of medieval moral theology. In religious writings, the suggestion of the unspeakable served, above all, as a powerful metaphor cast in words themselves and meant to have an impact on words yet unspoken. The omissions and obfuscations associated with the unspeakable were crafted. These silences originated, at least in part, in the nature of textual genres and their particular functions. Subsequently, these silences can be understood as resulting from textual or social conventions, interventions by individual actors, and the intricate structure of early modern communicative practices. The linguistic lacunae, the euphemisms, as well as the specific rhetorical strategies around same-sex desire will serve as my starting point for investigating how the sexual was communicated in history.

I am less interested here in the literary trajectory of notions of unspeakability in medieval and early modern Europe than in furthering a thesis that the discourse of unspeakability was a discourse of experts: the mandarins of medieval and early modern society—professors of theology, scholastics, jurists, teachers, Reformers—developed and appropriated this notion. The mediators of elite knowledge for the laity, clerics whose vocation and writings situated them at the interface of religious expertise and lay knowledge, made frequent use of the metaphor and its manifold variations.

The following remarks can be understood as a foray into the vast terrain of instructional materials for the laity, the modes of their dissemination, and the transmission of expert knowledge to a broad audience.[8] I will discuss how the unspeakable operated as a metaphor as well as a guideline to censorship and analyze instances in which expert theology encountered lay religiosity. I have selected three texts for this purpose, written at important stages in the history of religious lay instruction: the first from the early phase of edifying literature in the vernacular (Ulrich of Pottenstein's catechetical *summa*), the second and third from a time when printing transformed lay instruction (a printed manual for confession, *The Mirror for the Sinner,* and a sermon by Johann Geiler von Kaisersberg). I will also discuss the classroom as an instructional milieu where teachers were forced to confront eros-laden canonical texts deemed unfit for the ears of students.

A Trope of Communication

During the Middle Ages, theologians actively disseminated Christian dogma to the clergy and an increasingly diversified laity. In the lives of ordinary Christians, sites for religious instruction were scarce, however. Apart from auricular confession—obligatory for, yet certainly not practiced by, all believers once a year after 1215—the only institutionalized occasion for teaching the laity was the sermon. Experts of the faith had experimented with lay instruction throughout the Middle Ages. In the fourteenth century,

they embarked on the difficult path of adapting scholastic theology to linguistic vessels largely unexplored as a channel for theologically complex
subject matters, namely, European vernaculars.[9] Erudite clerics launched
edifying literature as a new vehicle for disseminating religious doctrine.
They created tools for the "popularization" of religious teachings, to use
Leonard Boyle's term.[10] By means of a "wave of popular treatises,"[11] doctors
of the soul (animarum medici) waged "a campaign to reach out effectively"
to believers.[12] This literature's proliferation in the century preceding the
Reformation depended greatly on a lay readership eager to commission,
buy, and consume vernacular publications on religious matters. The use of
more affordable paper as a writing surface (instead of parchment) helped
the dissemination of such innovative instructional tools. Literacy spread
beyond the clergy, and learning increasingly occurred outside of clerical
institutions, though we should not underestimate the degree to which nuns,
lay brethren, and priests were themselves the target of religious instruction
by pastoral theologians.

Religious teachers acknowledged that "unchastity," the whole arena of
erotic desires and sexual acts, was a treacherous ground for humans. In a
widely available handbook of canon law (c. 1400), Brother Berthold held
that "many sins derive from unchastity."[13] The Alsatian sermonizer Johann
Geiler von Kaisersberg (1443–1510) used the metaphor of the sword to
characterize the dangers emanating from the "seven capital sins," among
which "unchastity" stood out as "the last sword which nobody overlooks or
escapes."[14] According to Geiler, young children as well as priests, poor as
well as rich people were endangered by this deadly weapon in the devil's arsenal.[15] "Unchastity" was especially dangerous because it lay hidden under
the guise of virtues such as affability, love, or saintly behavior.[16]

As guardians of Christian tradition and teachers of ordinary believers,
mediators of religious dogma navigated a course of restraint regarding
Catholic doctrine on sex, and sodomy in particular. Sodomy, one of the
gravest sexual sins according to scholastic taxonomy, is a revealing litmus
test for conversations between religiously trained experts and the recipients
of their message. Appropriating the vast terrain of terms of the unspeakable, religious writers of the late Middle Ages unfolded communicative
scenarios whose plots were driven by the extremely delicate topic of conversation. In religious writings, the unspeakable thus functioned as a trope
of communication. In the context of religious instruction, unspeakability
is primarily identified with the range of sins covered by sodomia, and especially sexual activity between men (and between women).[17] Via tropes of
unspeakability, sodomy emerges as a vaguely knowable sin, though these

same tropes operate in ways that severely curtail descriptions of sexual practice.[18]

There are examples of passages where theologians chose not to articulate sexual practices such as sodomy. Mark Jordan has called our attention to a "dramatic displacement" in Thomas Aquinas's (1224/25–74) first *Scriptum* on the *Sentences*. There, St. Thomas divides the species of *luxuria* (lust): "since *luxuria* against nature is unnamable, it will be set aside."[19] According to the modern critic, the New Testament letter to the Ephesians 5:3 inspired this censorious move (". . . all impurity or covetousness must not even be named among you, as is fitting among saints"). By St. Thomas's time, the association of unspeakability with the sins against nature in general and sodomy in particular rested on more sources than simply this quote from the Bible. It was a Church Father, Jerome (c. 347–419/20), who, in his book on Hebrew names (*Liber interpretationis Hebraicorum nominum*), first explained the name *Sodoma* etymologically as "silent beast" (*pecus silens*).[20] Subsequently, French theologians of the High Middle Ages elaborated on this notion. At a time when the *sodomitae* of Genesis 19, the inhabitants of Sodom, were viewed as sodomites, William of Auvergne (d. 1249) presented "mute" (*mutum*) as an equivalent to sodomite (*sodomita*)—an explanation motivated by an assumed phonetic resemblance.[21] The same theologian expounded the Pauline term *passio ignominiae* literally as the "unspeakable disease," explaining *ignominia* as "not worthy of a name," *non dignum nomine*.[22] In the following centuries, many theologians perpetuated this spurious etymology.[23]

Like St. Thomas, some religious teachers used the rhetorical device of *praeteritio* to avoid discussing sodomy and other sexual sins. Yet "passing over" indicates that there are words, though they may not be appropriate in a particular context. The anonymous author of a fifteenth-century religious manual stated that he, like St. Thomas, did not want "to expound the sins against nature," though by his omission he noted their existence.[24] Geiler von Kaisersberg concludes that "it would be better [*nützer*, literally, more useful] to remain silent than to speak about" sexual practices, explained as masturbation and the sin for which one is burned at the stake, sodomy.[25] Many other writers, however, preferred to elaborate on this notion. Often, they embedded their appropriations of phrases of the unspeakable in imagined scenarios of ruptured conversations.

For some theologians, to name sodomy was a stigmatized act. According to Guilelmus Peraldus (William of Peyraud) (c. 1190–1255), "no man should speak about this sin."[26] In Berthold of Regensburg's (d. 1272) sermon on "leprosy of the soul," tremendous guilt and shame are associated with articulations of this sin.[27] Other writers added short explanations as to why people ought not to speak about the "mute sin." Martin of Amberg (second half of fourteenth century) states that "unchastity against nature," the "mute sin," is "so vile or revolting that, because of its vileness, people prefer not to speak of it."[28] Sodomy counts as a "mute sin" (*peccato muto*) or an "unspeakable vice" (*vitio indicibili*) because "naming this sin is very bad" or, in a different passage, very shameful.[29]

Not only naming *sodomia* was problematic. "One should not even think of this sin," states a fifteenth-century sermonizer.[30] The mere memory of it displeases God. This is why Lot's wife was turned into a pillar of salt gazing at the city of Sodom in fire.[31] Naming *sodomia* verbally was also likened to its referent, the sexual act. Both activities were said to pollute.[32]

Since communication is a two-way process, in which naming implies listening, mentions of the so-called unspeakable not only "pollute the mouth of the speaker" but also "the ears of the listeners."[33] According to Stricker, an erudite thirteenth-century German poet and didacticist, even the most shameless person cannot bear to hear about sodomy.[34] A fifteenth-century manual contends that mentioning *sodomia* "hurts the ears of good [people]."[35] Thus, all the senses become involved in enunciations of the unspeakable. Several theologians circulated the notion of listeners or readers being severely "angered" (*geergret*) by these sins' mention.[36]

Hearing of sodomy also moves listeners to action. Angels run away when overhearing mentions of "the sins against nature" (note the allusion to Genesis 19, with the story of the angels who visited Lot in Sodom and left before the city's destruction).[37] The author of the *Confessionale*, a fifteenth-century German manual of confession, seems to follow the angelic example when he refuses to delve into the matter in this context (*praeteritio*).[38] Martin of Amberg suggests that "angels flee as far as the voice reaches" when people mention "unchastity against nature" (*unchewsch wider die natur*) "in a sinful way," thus indicating that the contrite might be safe in their enunciations.[39] William of Peyraud describes a less violent reaction to "the novelty of such great and unheard of malice"—a listener's bewilderment and disbelief.[40] Echoing Genesis 18:21, Denis the Carthusian (1402/3–71) expresses the notion that God could hardly believe these sins' existence, "wondering whether such abominable misdeeds between humans can exist."[41]

Not only angels are presented as eavesdropping on conversations that mention the unspeakable; the forces of the devil sometimes participate in these scenarios as well. According to William of Peyraud, angels and demons agree about sodomy: demons are said to blush (though the sins of lust in general please them).[42] Another text echoes the idea that many evil spirits are afraid of sodomitical acts (not only of naming them).[43] The notion is widespread that even the devil is ashamed when confronted with this sin.[44] One fifteenth-century sermonizer explains that "some demons abhor this vice because of Nature's nobility."[45] Johann Geiler von Kaisersberg has the devil embark on an apotropaic rite intended to purge the air: in response to *sodomia*, he spits and utters a preverbal "yuck, yuck."[46]

Further proof for this sin's ultimate status is that the devils, "the masters of all sins" (*meister aller sünden*), "never dared to give it a name"; some devils do not "advise [this sin] publicly"; or, like their comrades Nimrod and Astarot, they "could not give this sin [one of the crying sins, *peccata clamantia, sodomia*] a name."[47] Since "neither men nor devils gave the sin a real name," "the damned sin" has many names, or "cognomina."[48] Berthold of Regensburg proceeded to call sodomy the "mute sin" or the "red sin" (*rôte sünde*). According to the thirteenth-century Franciscan sermonizer, the sin's lack of a real name thus led to a proliferation of circumlocutions. If we take "red" to refer to the color of blood, this singular term may stand for the many innocents who died in Sodom or in other disasters that struck humankind because of sexual deviance.[49]

Metaphors blend verbally what is incommensurate, designating a particular phrase for a meaning out of context. Metaphor is thus the trope of excess par excellence. Viewed in this light, "the unspeakable" emerges as an extremely intriguing expression, exceeding in fact the comparison that is always implicit in the metaphorical. In lieu of sexual description, notions of unspeakability call attention to language as a medium for articulating sexual activity. What is more, tropes of unspeakability switch registers when replacing the descriptive with the emotive. Noticeably, when the unspeakable was referred to, religious writers wrote with an emotionally heightened affect. As I have shown, their writings brought up the theme of horror and shame in a variety of ways, with shame serving as "a tool of discipline."[50] Rhetorically, the emotional range of horror and shame often came to stand in for the sin itself. This configuration replicates the story of Sodom: God's wrath was commensurate with the horror of the sins that caused the city's destruction. The Strasbourg sermonizer Johann Geiler von Kaisersberg elaborated on this notion when he linked the fate of the city of Sodom to a sin for which people die at the stake.[51]

Medieval metaphors like the unspeakable sin forge links between the textual and the extratextual. Frequently, they spill over into realistic scenarios. Not surprisingly, therefore, the unspeakable is also imagined to occur because of a speaker's inability to speak. In view of the enormity of their sin, sodomites may fail to confess.[52] Their refusal to speak up puts pressure on the father confessor. He is called upon to move the sinner to confession, for, if unrepentant, the sinner risks eternal punishment.[53] Sodomites are struck by muteness in the presence of God (*coram Domino*); during the Last Judgment, they remain silent about their sins.[54] Guilty of the unspeakable sin, the sinner sometimes confesses without making clear the sex of his or her sexual partner. Confessors ought to know, though, that this is not a practice that will save one's soul. In cases where a father confessor does not grasp the transgression in question, absolution is not valid.[55] The preacher Paul Wann (d. 1489) therefore exhorted the sinner to confess in such a way that the priest will know "sufficiently" the exact circumstances of a sexual encounter "against nature."[56]

Not surprisingly, a euphemistic way of speaking creates barriers of understanding. The discourse on the sins of Sodom is sometimes so vague as to cause miscommunication. This is what the great Franciscan preacher, Berthold of Regensburg, contends. This writer inserted a scene of failed understanding between himself and an imaginary listener into one of his sermons. Like other sermonizers, Berthold made use of fictitious interlocutors who interrupt his sermon (*fictio personae* or *prosopopœia*)—a sign of staged orality which in this case is the ultimate marker of the literary pretending to be oral (what was published as Berthold's German sermons was, in fact, a redaction by a circle of Franciscans from Augsburg). In response to Berthold's elusive remarks about the sin that dare not speak its name, a fictitious listener interjects: "Brother Berthold, how shall I guard myself from committing this sin?" Without delving into the matter, the sermonizer responds by saying: "God almighty help me that you do not understand"— a posture emphasizing the unequal distribution of knowledge and power in this soliloquy of a sermon masquerading as colloquy.[57]

Tropes of unspeakability constituted a common way of referring to sexual sins against nature. Invented to circumvent explicitness, this textual strategy became identified with what it euphemized. There is no way to assess whether this rhetoric was effective in teaching Christians vaguely about the sins of Sodom, as pastoral theologians intended. Yet appropriations of phrases of the so-called unspeakable sin outside religious literature proper indicate how commonly these circumlocutions were deployed, if not understood.[58] A humanist's humorous story from the late sixteenth century illustrates how firmly erudite readers identified locutions of the unspeakable with the sins against nature: "Urged to confess, a peasant boy alluded to something which he did not want to disclose. Whereas the priest translated the boy's words and his unwillingness to speak up as a most scandalous deed (*enorme facinus*), the boy himself had in fact only thought of a puerile trivium."[59] In this *facetia,* expert discourse confronted the ways of an ignorant youth, a communication that resulted in great misunderstanding and, even worse, ultimately in the boy's turning to the devil.[60] Yet the pun of the story played into an erudite audience's familiarity with the trope of the unspeakable—without subverting the reticence imposed on invocations of sexual acts.

✤✤✤

Metaphors of the "unspeakable" indicate a cultural and educational setting of great significance. They resonate with the communication between the confessor and the imagined penitent, the literate cleric and a more or less illiterate layman, the knowing priest and his student. In other words, the unspeakable is a metaphor of control. Two impulses are closely intertwined in these various scenarios of communication taken from religious didacticism: the impulse to disseminate knowledge about sexual sins to the laity—an audience seen to be greatly in need of religious guidance—and the impulse to control and limit conversations on this same topic.

With few exceptions, historians of sexuality have hardly begun to access the vast array of materials written to inform and instruct a diverse audience of laypeople on sexual behavior. As a rule, scholars have focused on canonical works, such as St. Thomas's *Summa theologiae* or other major works of scholasticism. Yet how did academic theology filter down to the level of lay beliefs? What precisely was the basis for lay belief? What did Christians in the fifteenth century hear about the sins that dare not speak their name(s)?

Teaching in a Vernacular Summa

Authors of religious manuals repressed, retrieved, and, to a limited extent, disseminated doctrinal knowledge on sodomy in a variety of ways in order to educate a lay audience. As the following example demonstrates, far from providing their readers with free access to Christian dogma, the disseminators of religious norms tailored their representations to specific audiences and vehicles of communication—a strategy also advocated by manuals on how to preach (*artes praedicandi*).

With twelve hundred folios, Ulrich of Pottenstein's (c. 1360–1416/17) early fifteenth-century catechism is arguably the most comprehensive catechetical text ever written in the vernacular.[61] Its author belonged to a circle of Austrian clerics who were among the first to make the vast body of theological manuals in Latin available to a German-reading audience— an undertaking with few precedents. Though other literary experiments

in teaching the religious essentials in writing are found in the period after 1370, the so-called Viennese School contributed significantly to popu-
larizing religious doctrine in the vernacular.[62] The University of Vienna,
founded in 1365 and reorganized at the end of the fourteenth century,
functioned as the circle's nucleus, and Heinrich of Langenstein (1325–97),
former professor at the Sorbonne and author of a pioneering manual of sins
in the German language (*Erchantnuzz der sund*), was its mentor. The circle's
devotional writings count among the most widely disseminated fifteenth-
century texts and shaped the late medieval German religious discourse for
the laity.[63] These writers' personal network encompassed a range of social
groups, among them the dukes of Austria, other prominent members of
the Austrian nobility, the faculty at Vienna's university, wealthy Viennese
burghers, and the local clergy. In this socioliterary milieu, Ulrich was able
to carry through a risqué project whose dimensions left behind everything
previous generations had produced in terms of baedekers for the soul in
German.

Ulrich looks at the topic of sodomy in the context of the Ten Commandments. The sixth (or, according to the tradition Ulrich adheres to,
seventh) commandment—"You shall not commit adultery" (Ex 20:14), often rendered as "You shall not commit unchastity"—as well as the ninth—
"You shall not covet your neighbor's wife"—were the appropriate loci for
furthering sexual ethics. Among the pillars of Christian piety, the Decalogue reigned supreme as a structurally and mnemonically useful format for
furthering Christian doctrine among the laity. Like other foundational texts
of medieval and early modern Christianity, the Decalogue became firmly
embedded in liturgy and religious life in the age of scholasticism.[64] Under
the rubric of the commandment "You shall not commit adultery," Ulrich
discusses the different categories of lust, among them the "vice that cannot
be named"—"in whatever form," as Ulrich euphemistically refers to it: "The
seventh transgression concerns the command to desire naturally and where
nature is naturally inclined to. These are the [sinners] who pollute themselves with the vice that cannot be named and of which one cannot speak
properly; the [sinners] who sin against nature and [by their sins] do offend
the works of nature in whatever form that occurs."[65] Though the gravity
of the offense is clearly expressed, the specifics remain obscure in this as
well as in the following paragraphs. Ulrich marshals an army of authorities
to demonstrate the sin's sinfulness, which is repeatedly said to exceed that
of all other sins. Its "muteness" testifies to its ultimate status. Paradoxically,
the unspeakability tropes were balanced by a competing concept, the concept of a "crying sin," that is, a sin that called for retribution.[66] Unlike with

other sins, this sin's disastrous consequences defined its essence—the punishments prescribed in divine, natural, canon, as well as imperial law, and God's various interventions said to be motivated by this form of behavior (the Great Flood, the destruction of five cities, Onan's death, etc.). For an audience of "simple laymen" (*slechten layen*), narrations of wrath and revenge, therefore, represent the utmost of sexual transgressions.[67]

At this interface of Latin and German language, theology and homily, clerical and lay culture, Ulrich, a translator and a redactor of a vast body of Latin texts, filters out any description of sexual activities, including the sex of potential participants. Only when Ulrich expounds St. Paul's letter to the Romans (1:26–27) does he admit that both men and women are endangered. Yet Ulrich adds a particular misogynistic twist that is not strongly suggested by St. Paul: he states not only that women preceded men in "polluting" themselves but also that they seduced men to follow them.[68]

According to the genealogical approach, sodomites can claim a pedigree. While Ulrich of Pottenstein suggested, based on St. Paul, that women had invented the derided erotic practice, in *The Defense of Women*, Henricus Cornelius Agrippa of Nettesheim (1486–1535), the German humanist, would retort to similar suspicions of Eve's perennial guilt by portraying men—the inhabitants of Sodom—as the initial culprits.[69] Whether women or men were thought to have invented same-sex eroticism, whether misogyny or profeminism surfaced in debates on the sin's origins, remarkably, religious manuals of the later Middle Ages addressed both men and women as (potential) sodomites. Though often enough women-transgressors were mentioned only in passing and, importantly, men served as examples more often than women, religious discourse had a systematic edge to it that, for better or for worse, was lacking in other arenas. To religious writers, clearly, women as well men were capable of committing the sins of Sodom.[70]

To pastoral theologians, educating an uneducated clergy or a fairly educated laity meant tightrope walking. The condemnation had to be clear enough without instilling reprehensible ideas in the minds of potential readers or listeners. In other words, in order to fight illicit forms of sexuality, clerics wanted to make sure that subjects under their moral guidance grasped the derided practices intellectually. To some extent, condemnation required verbalization.[71]

There is a particular problem associated with encoding prohibitions against the so-called unspeakable sin of sodomy, however. In the form of published writings, readings could not be controlled or potential misuse held at bay. Authors of religious manuals could not be sure who the recipients of their doctrine would be. Where should the lines be drawn between linguistic clarity and well-calculated obfuscation? Without a profile of individual readers or listeners, writers had to navigate a middle ground between what was deemed speakable and what was better left unspoken, that which could be voiced in intimate conversation, expressed in public, or rendered in writing and that which preferably was to be kept silent. Jean Gerson (1363–1429), therefore, prefaced his treatise on masturbation (and sodomy) with an apology to the reader, stating that "the obscenity of the subject matter and the words" are licensed by "the necessity to teach remedies."[72]

This core problem of religious instruction *in sexualibus* was exacerbated by the choice of language. Though centuries of colonization and missionary activity had contributed to the creation of a liturgical language in the German tongue, though "religious movements" (Herbert Grundmann) such as mysticism had experimented with German as a channel for the divine message, this same language was still a medium deemed unfit by many for the intricacies of Christian dogma. A catechetical manual in manuscript form from the fifteenth century stated explicitly that, while "I do not want to expound" the sins against nature, one could find a fuller treatment of this "great sin against nature" in Latin, "but in Latin it is written" (*awer in der latein stet es geschriben*).[73] The author not only called attention to his role as mediator of Christian teachings, he also presented German as a devotional language that stayed pure of certain defiling words. The rhetoricity of the unspeakable was well suited for the large audience authors of catechetical texts had in mind.

In fact, many religious texts in Latin were written in the same cautious style that characterized vernacular publications dealing with sexual sins. Once we acknowledge the impetus to reach the ordinary believer, the divide between Latin and German writings breaks down. The enormously prolific Denis the Carthusian, for instance, embraced a discourse of sins designed to uplift the literary recipient spiritually and motivate him to change his ways. In his *Summa of Vices and Virtues* (*Summa de vitiis et virtutibus*) and numerous other works, Denis, like many theologians, barely touched upon sodomy.[74]

In many ways, the production of catechetical texts replicated problems associated with the confessional.[75] The confessor as well as the catechist was called upon to assess transgressions of Christian doctrine. At the same time, religious educators voiced the concern that overly explicit prohibitions enticed addressees to enact what was prohibited. Explicit language describing the illegitimate was thought to produce undesired results.[76] Disseminators of Christian norms thus feared that explicit acts of verbal condemnation would instigate unwanted sexual acts—acts that would not have been committed without doctrinal teachings—rather than uprooting the decried practices.[77]

Prohibitions with regard to sexual behavior were therefore subject to severe rhetorical constraints. Though it can be argued that Ulrich addressed an exclusive group among the political and educational elite of Austria (whose members are known to have commissioned manuscripts) and thus safeguarded his catechism against illegitimate readings, it is clear from his own wording in the preface that he envisioned this vernacular *summa* as a venture to re-create the body of Christian thought for all of Christendom (including both clerics and lay believers).[78]

Ulrich's caution in negotiating his complex role as translator and educator is amply evidenced in his writings. In Ulrich's, as in other didactic texts, the expression "inexpressible sin" ("the vice that cannot be named") served as a stock metaphor to denote sodomy and other sins against nature. Paradoxically, an expression of inexpressibility invoked a particular set of sexual practices. The phrase permitted writers to evade an explicit description while supplying them with a metaphor whose wide usage safeguarded them from criticism by other theologians for sharing scholarly topics with the academically untrained. Yet tropes of unspeakability not only were commonly used to express the so-called sins against nature, they also guided theologians in their conversations with the laity. These metaphorical phrases, vacillating between the descriptive and the prescriptive, invited censorship. What was described as unspeakable thus also led some theologians such as Ulrich to omissions that rendered the message opaque.

Yet vernacular *summae*, like Ulrich's, which offered systematic treatments of a field by means of a manual, were less successful in disseminating religious messages to a vernacular readership than small, primerlike publications on topics of practical interest for believers. In his *Mirror of Conscience* (*Der Gewissensspiegel*, before 1382)—an early experiment in edifying a German readership, Martin of Amberg claimed that his small treatise was more useful to read and memorize than "larger and more profound books" (*grozzer und tüffer pucher*).[79] Because of their size, small treatises were conducive to large-scale distribution. By comparison, Ulrich's lengthy catechism found few readers.

A Printed Mirror of the Soul

No radical shift occurred when manuscripts for the laity were slowly replaced by printed matter such as the German *Mirror for the Sinner* (*Der spiegel des sunders*, c. 1476) after the invention of printing around 1450.[80] Many of the early religious publications relied on manuscript models and were not, like the *Mirror for the Sinner*, specifically composed for the medium. Printing greatly expanded the audience for devotional literature. The city of Augsburg, where the *Mirror for the Sinner* was printed, excelled in producing German-language publications. In the fifteenth century, its output of vernacular publications was higher than that of any other German or European center of printing, and most of these books were exported.[81]

The book's colophon explains succinctly how the *Mirror for the Sinner* could alter the general reader's life. Its anonymous author, or rather compiler, presented the book as a text "in which man may learn how he should betake himself to God and approach God by truly realizing one's sins" ("In wôlichen bûchlin der mensch lernen mag wie vnd durch wz gestalt er sich zû got soll viegen vnd nâhen. das ist durch ware erkantnus seiner sunden").[82] Addressed to the confessing sinner, this psychologically astute treatise furthers the insight of male and female readers into human culpability. Authors of manuals like the *Mirror for the Sinner* assimilated mostly Latin models to a new medium. The author of *The Mirror for the Sinner* sought inspiration in an array of manuals in both Latin and German that were geared toward a similarly broad readership.[83] Compiling his manual from various sources, the anonymous author also viewed himself in the tradition of the Viennese School, and Heinrich of Langenstein in particular—the literary-religious context that had brought forth Ulrich von Pottenstein's *summa*.[84] Though designed for a comparatively broad audience, the *Mirror for the Sinner* did not abstain from addressing the "sins against nature" in print. *Sodomia* held its firm place in the clearly structured edifice of sinful behavior within Christianity. It is listed both under the seventh of the capital sins, *luxuria* (lust), and, as in Ulrich's catechetical *summa*, under the commandment "Thou shalt not commit adultery."[85] These two passages differ significantly from one another, pointing to different rhetorical conventions in the treatment of the sins of Sodom.

First, I will turn to the short paragraph on "the sin against nature that is in Latin *peccatum contra naturam* or *sodomia*" (*dy sund wider die natur das ist zelatein peccatum contra naturam oder sodomia*) in the context of the manual's discussion of capital sins.[86] Structurally, this reference is prominent. Verbally, however, it is both short and extremely restrained. Whereas this text's hierarchy of sins puts lust in the prominent last position, and, among the subtypes of sensual sins, accords *sodomia* a highly prominent place (after fornication, whoredom, adultery, rape, sex with clerics, and incest),[87] the author does not match this structural prominence with descriptive fullness.[88] Instead, he refuses to go beyond a mere definition ("where the natural practice of intercourse is reversed"—*do die natürliche brauchung der vermischung verkert wird*) that does little to explore the topic, since it does not specify the kinds of reversions in question. Instead, after supplying us with two Latin equivalents (*peccatum contra naturam* and *sodomia*), the author-compiler refuses to delve into this sin further "whereof one cannot write purely nor give [further] distinctions" (*daruon lauter zeschreiben nit vnderscheyd zegeben ist etc.*) as would have been customary in an academic milieu.[89]

Tapping into a vast body of moral theology, the author, compiler, and translator virtually banned verbal representation of the matter at hand for a vernacular audience. The brevity of the paragraph on the sins of Sodom is highlighted by the fact that the whole section on lust concludes with a sin that is treated in great detail, excessively "lustful marital intercourse" (*libidinosus coitus coniugalis*) and other matrimony-related transgressions.[90] While up to this point the treatment of *luxuria* in the *Mirror for the Sinner* follows a scale of egregiousness in which *sodomia*, the most severe of the sins of unchastity, comes last, the desire to conclude with a sin pertaining to the union of husband and wife, the only place of legitimate sexual activity, gestures toward the broad audience which this manual envisions. Despite the length of the entry on marital sexuality, the author concludes the whole chapter by stating that one would have to write much more about the sin of unchastity (contrary to the topos of unwritability in the context of *sodomia*).[91]

In this first passage on *sodomia*, the tone is unemotional. By contrast, the second time Sodom makes an appearance (still short, though significantly longer) in the *Mirror for the Sinner*, the text's anonymous "I" voices disgust in verbose invocations of unspeakability.[92] In his treatment of the Decalogue, the author provides his reader with an explanation of *sodomia* by differentiating people who "commit the sin against nature with themselves, other humans, or animals."[93] If catechetical literature proffers definitions of the sins against nature at all, most manuals present us with *sodomia* as derived from scholastic theology, though portrayed in abbreviated terms.[94] With regard to *sodomia*, differentiations and subdivisions often replace full descriptions.[95]

Positioned prominently, *sodomia* opens the discussion of other unchaste acts. It is described in terms of its disastrous effects on humankind. From the outset of this section on *sodomia*, the author divides his readership into two groups, organized around opposite poles or types: the ignorant and the experienced. While the former are to be protected from defilement, practitioners of *sodomia* are extremely vilified. Linguistically, they are dehumanized ("inhuman sin"—*vnmenschliche*[] *sunde*[]) and made to resemble devils ("many devilish people"—*vil teufelhafftig menschen*), and their sinful acts are described with epithets such as "grave" (*schwere*), "unnatural" (*vnnatürlich*), "stinking" (*stinckende[] sunde[]*), or, repeatedly, "poisonous" (*vergift*). The priest's pressing urgency is noteworthy, since he believes that "many devilish people" adhere to the practices prohibited by this commandment—doings that incur an expression of regret ("unfortunately"—*leider*) by the author.[96] At one point, the author labels not only their sins "poisonous" but also the sinners themselves. Their transgressions have caused destruction and deluge throughout the history of humankind, exemplified by the Biblical Flood and the destruction of five "royal cities" (*kuniglich stet,* including Sodom and Gomorrah)[97] as well as inflation, wars, plagues, floods, and sudden deaths—effects of sodomitical behavior that, the writer seems to suggest, can be witnessed every day.[98]

Bipartitio of a fictitious audience is a common strategy in audience-oriented passages of medieval literature. Frequently, authors divided their imagined audiences into two opposite groups and then invited their readers and listeners to join the enlightened (like Gottfried of Strasbourg in the strophic prologue to *Tristan*): The envious are contrasted with the good-spirited among an imagined audience. Subsequently, rights and wrongs are mapped onto this division. When *sodomia* makes an entry, however, there is no passageway between the two groups. Thus, *bipartitio* is not about an author's plea for sympathy staged in order to allay potential criticism, but instead adherence to an unequivocal religious and ethical dogma that allows no wavering on the part of the imagined audience. Indeed, the division of the audience is apt to strengthen the position of the expert. The innocent have to be protected while those who have sinned can never return to the blissful state of ignorance. Partitioning the audience thus seeks to drive a wedge between the innocent and the sinner in order to prevent the sedition of the former. Yet these rhetorical moves also allude to the schism between supporters and foes of God during the Last Days of the world.[99]

The split audience implicates the teacher himself. Clearly, the text's pastoral teacher aligns himself with the innocent part of his audience. The German expression for "to elucidate," *klar vnd lauter machen,* jibes well with "purity," the attribute characterizing the sodomitically innocent, in contrast to "stinking" and "inhuman." With consideration for the innocent, the author cites an injunction against exploring unspeakable doings any further in order not to ruin the innocent. But who is to speak if the author, teacher of the laity, is not to?[100]

The audience for catechetical publications covers the whole spectrum of Christians. Teachers who educate the laity therefore also have to address those whose behavior must be corrected. In a moment of rupture, the anonymous author-compiler switches roles from a preacher-in-print to that of a father confessor. He implores readers guilty of one or several of the sins in question to confess. Powerfully, the text's anonymous "I" involves the sinner's "thou" in a conversation. The priest in print raises his voice to a rhetorical climax when addressing those "members of the devil" face-to-face: "Woe to you, man or woman, that you commit these poisonous things and talk to other humans about them or teach them how to commit these acts."[101] By contrast, the "innocent" (*vnschuldige[] menschen*) part of the *Spiegel des sunders's* audience is endowed with "pure ears and chaste hearts" (*reinen oren vnd keuschen hertzen*), whose very purity and chastity is endangered by exposure to information on *sodomia*. Moreover, the innocents may even be annoyed when these sins are expounded, the author muses.[102]

Within a few lines, we traverse different notions of unspeakability. We move from the priest's caution about articulating his expertise for fear of contaminating the listener, to his addressing sinners who are prone to remain stubbornly silent in view of the sin's enormity. The refusal to verbalize shifts from the writer as father confessor to his imagined audience, the sinners. Ironically, the instructor foresees manifold inhibitions on the part of the sinner in enunciating what he himself was hesitant to name. What terms is the sinner supposed to use in confession, we might ask? The author does little to provide his audience with a language for confession.

The textual politics of "Don't ask, don't tell" has often been credited with causing the proliferation of words about what is supposedly unspeakable. I would suggest distinguishing the "rhetorical effect" of the unspeakable, to refer to a phrase by Judith Butler,[103] from its overall discursive effect. Rhetorically, tropes of unspeakability spill over: wordy euphemisms were deployed for a heightened effect on the reader. Discursively, the unspeakable was far from everywhere. Rather, the metaphor occupied a certain place in the overall edifice of Church doctrine. Containing knowledge on how to speak "it" was an object of prime concern to the ecclesiastical and erudite elite, and tropes of unspeakability were designed precisely to serve this containment.

A Censorious Metaphor and Its Discontents

Many theologians designated specific milieus and settings where the sins of Sodom ought not to be mentioned. Addressing the clergy as disseminators of the divine word, William of Auvergne stated categorically, that "there is nobody who should dare to name it ["the sin of shame," that is, *sodomia*] when preaching."[104] This or similar prohibitions are not truly "taboo[s] forbidding public discussion of sodomy," as Elizabeth Keiser has described the trope.[105] *In praedicando* (when preaching) circumscribes a specific setting characterized by the presence of an audience of believers and a sermonizer endowed with ecclesiastical authority. William deemed a discussion of the unspeakable sin inappropriate in sermons—a concern reiterated by clerics of later generations.[106]

Despite cautionary notes against preaching on *sodomia*, many sermons transmitted in manuscript or in print contain material on the "mute sin," though references usually remain vague.[107] The Dominican promoter of Church reform Johannes Nider (c. 1380–1438) provided priests with guidelines for achieving rhetorical decorum: the sermonizer ought to make a sodomite's guilt unequivocally clear, yet should refrain from describing the specific acts subsumed under the rubric vices against nature, at least in a public sermon.[108] As I have shown, many texts lived up to this guideline for sermonizers. Frequently, we do not know for sure the specific sexual practices in a modern taxonomy to which references in religious literature refer.

Compared to the sermon, the confession allowed for more explicit enunciations. Theologians such as Nikolaus of Dinkelsbühl, Jean Gerson, Johann Geiler von Kaisersberg, and Martin Luther (before 1517) viewed the confessional as an appropriate site for putting words to so-called unspeakable actions. Thereby, they reserved the license to speak on *sodomia* for conversations shielded from exposure and guided by an expert of the soul.[109] In confession, confessors had to be moved to speak on the unspeakable. In a vernacular exposition of the Decalogue, for instance, the Nikolaus of Dinkelsbühl-redactor divided his imagined audience into those who are innocent of "unchastity against nature" (and therefore needed to be protected by silence) and those who have committed *sodomia*—a set of sins circumscribed as comprising all sexual acts against the order of nature (only masturbation was mentioned explicitly). The latter group he encouraged to speak to their confessors without inhibition: "If he has not experienced shame when he committed the sin, much less ought he be ashamed when he confesses."[110] In order to extract a confession from a sinner who committed masturbation (or sodomy), Jean Gerson called for "an adroit and circumspect father confessor," because otherwise the "infected" would not reveal his involvement.[111]

The difference between sermon and confession is a difference only of degree. Verbal caution was the primary guiding principle in both contexts: "One ought not to preach or to interrogate in confession about this sin, unless with acute caution," stated Denis the Carthusian.[112] In a collection of sermons in Latin, intended as models for sermonizers, Johannes Herolt (d. 1468) concluded by addressing his colleagues (when mapping sodomy he referred to masturbation, heterosexual intercourse involving an unfit vessel, same-sex sexuality, and bestiality): "in sermons one must speak of this worst sin very cautiously; also, the father confessor must act with caution regarding this sin in the confessional, so that nobody is scandalized nor given occasion to sin."[113] As early as the thirteenth century, Raimund of Pennaforte cautioned against taking the license to speak on the unspeakable in confession too far. Interrogations regarding the "mute sin" must be conducted with more circumspection than those regarding other topics in confession; sodomy is to be treated "with caution and fear," he argued.[114] The Franciscan preacher Berthold of Regensburg issued a strict "Don't Ask" policy, addressed especially to priests in confession, yet valid for all believers—as if banishing any mention thereof could make the practice disappear.[115]

Cautionary notes invoking the unspeakable were anything but original. Prohibitions against verbalizing sodomy and other sexual sins amounted to a *locus classicus*. The rhetorical reticence of pastoral theology contrasted with the mode of explicitness which characterized early medieval handbooks of penance—to refer to an astute observation by Allen Frantzen.[116] Notions of unspeakability were not merely metaphorical, however. Authors of catechisms understood their role as preachers in the medium of writing. When composing manuals in German, they put into practice cautionary notes for the preacher on sodomy. Religious writers transferred the metaphor into action in their adaptations and translations of Latin models for the audience of religious instruction in writings.[117]

When Johann Geiler von Kaisersberg addressed the laity in his translation of a catechetical work by Jean Gerson, he therefore used "common ways of speaking"—*modi generales loquendi*—a rhetorical mode which those familiar with the sins of Sodom would supposedly understand but those innocent of them would not grasp (note, once again, the split audience). According to this treatise, mentions outside of confession were not appropriate because of the horrendous "indecency" (*unfletikeit*) of sins against nature.[118] Some theologians resisted the experts' "consensus" not to speak (or write) on the "mute sin." Instead, they opted to castigate *expressis verbis* what in their view severely endangered human souls. By inverting a common stance among the Catholic experts of the faith, these writers forged a powerful position for themselves from which to vent their pastoral concerns and urge their audience, be it in writing or in speech, to reform before it was too late.

In the case of the famous Strasbourg preacher Johann Geiler von Kaisersberg, this frankness was all the more potent since, as I just noted, he espoused rhetorical discretion. When preaching in Strasbourg Cathedral in 1506, Geiler revisited a common rhetorical policy of restraint and claimed to turn it on its head. Referring to a *communis opinio*, he reiterated an argument familiar to the disseminators of religious knowledge: "They say one should not speak about [sodomy, because] one learns it [through speech]." Geiler refers to sodomy as the sin of the *bübenketzer*, those "heretics" who have sex with boys.[119] On this occasion, he rejected the expediency of pastoral caution. He held that those ignorant of the sin would in fact *not* "learn" sodomy by the words of his sermon.[120] Thus, Geiler distinguished between verbal representation of sex and the sexual actions that might ensue as a result of verbal explicitness—a distinction that many theologians had blurred. For the occasion, Geiler converted, so to speak, from a proponent of rhetorical restraint to a vociferous zealot in the fight to uproot sodomy. Thereby, he inverted the injunction to be opaque to an injunction to become vocal on the unspeakable sin par excellence.[121]

What made preachers like Geiler von Kaisersberg so effective was, among other things, that they wove observations on their listeners' everyday lives into the pastoral message. In his 1506 sermon, Geiler presented splinters of social existence when castigating same-sex eroticism—a path untrodden by most other sermonizers from the German-speaking lands. He distinguished those who "florence" "actively" from those who "let themselves be florenced" "passively" (*der sich laßt florentzen etc. / noch keiner der florentzt etc. / nim es [Actiue vnd passive]*)—a differentiation rarely exhibited in homiletics north of the Alps.[122] Also, in a sinner's life cycle, same-sex sexuality was primarily identified with youth.[123] He calls upon parents to guard their "young, pretty boys" (*iungen hübschen knaben*), suggesting remedies intended to protect young men from being seduced. According to Geiler, the youth of those first initiated into the practice of sodomy and masturbation presents several problems. At the time when boys are led to commit these acts, "they do not know what it is" (*sie werden geschent sie wissen nitt was es ist*). This is not the only way in which the metaphor of the unspeakable is read into a man's life. In later life, sinners might turn away from these sins but fail to confess their deeds. Worse, they might develop sodomitical sex into a lifelong habit, and if they remain in this sin until the age at which Christ died on the cross (thirty-three) they will never be able to reform. In order to break this vicious circle of youthful ignorance, alluring habits, unrepentance, and the sinner's ignorance or silence, an explicit sermon is the appropriate response.[124]

Geiler von Kaisersberg's sermon opens with a reference to a public event that rendered visible the invisible sin in the city of Strasbourg, the execution of two men immediately preceding the date of his sermon—a certain Jerome and a bottlemaker who had left their wives and had sex with one another. [125] Significantly, the sermon's occasion underscores the ineffectiveness of a policy of rhetorical restraint. On the occasion of this sermon, the moral theologian and preacher reflects on his success as the corrector of urban mores: "Thirty years ago, I wrote against this vice so well and concisely that one should have heeded it [his message]. A good friend and a scholar told me: 'Doctor, it is enough of this'" (meaning he should stop writing about it). [126] On several accounts, Geiler's rationale for outspokenness deserves our attention. Via this sermon, the sermonizer shared a debate among scholars with his audience. It was the experts, scholars like Geiler, who advocated verbal restraint with regard to same-sex sexual behavior. Via this anecdote, Geiler presents himself as a consistent advocate of outspokenness, silenced by a theologian's response to his publications for the laity. While his own catechetical writings expanded the horizon of religious instruction for the laity, they never openly challenged rhetorical decorum.

Teaching the Unspeakable Sin of the Romans

Sermon, confession, and catechetical instruction were not the only sites where scholarly experts had to balance disseminating knowledge of sexual matters against containing that same knowledge. The classroom functioned in a similar way as an interface between the cognoscenti and the ignorant— a site where suggestions of "indecent lusts" had to be confronted, especially in a period of renewed classical learning that brought to the fore "obscene" ancient writings for the purpose of instruction. Like a father confessor, a teacher disseminated ideas to an audience of presumably ignorant youths whom experts—pedagogues like Erasmus (1466/69–1536)—wanted to protect from exposure to indecencies.

In *Defenders of the Text*, Anthony Grafton has commented on a passage in Erasmus's *De ratione studii* (1511)—a treatise on the teaching of classical literature or, to quote Jean-Claude Margolin, a "plan d'études," a "programme scolaire," and a "méthode d'enseignement." [127] There, the skill it takes to navigate between the Scylla of corrupting the text and the Charybdis of corrupting students is discussed with regard to a sin that could not be easily verbalized. [128] Erasmus "takes as his example the worst line—from a Christian point of view—in the entire Virgilian corpus: *Formosum pastor Corydon ardebat Alexim* ('Corydon the shepherd was hot for pretty Alexis'), the beginning of the second Eclogue."[129] For the humanist, censorship of Virgil, an author central to the Christian tradition, is not an option. Rather, a strategy of transcending the supposedly offensive comes into play.[130] With regard to the topic, one man's erotic desire for another, Erasmus suggests a digression on good and bad friendships. Good friendship can only be predicated on similitude, unlike the *ardor* that Corydon, described as *rusticus*, experiences for Alexis, the *urbanus*.[131]

Thus, the offensive was transformed into a moral precept on friendship—a metamorphosis of literary words into ethical concepts that was greatly valued in the Renaissance classroom. "If the teacher gives this preface . . . I think that nothing shameful can occur to a listener who is not already corrupt."[132] The *corruptus*—note the allusion to St. Paul's letter to Titus 1:15 ("To the pure all things are pure, but to the corrupt and unbelieving nothing is pure")—will have no opportunity to corrupt other students, because he is forced to keep his "poison" to himself.[133] Did teachers heed Erasmus's advice? Did students ever smell a rat? I am more optimistic than Anthony Grafton that from time to time students might have subverted such an attempt to neutralize a literary passage. Be that as it may, what is of keen interest is, first, the fact that erotic desire between two men becomes *the* locus where the transmission of texts in the classroom is problematized. Second, Erasmus very consciously uses friendship to cover over the traces of what in other contexts might have been termed sodomy. By absorbing erotic desire between men into male-male friendship, Erasmus comes dangerously close to collapsing the figures of the male friend and the sodomite, often kept at great distance discursively.[134]

The most common pre-Erasmian textbook commentary on Virgil's *Eclogues* knew no such qualms. Without much ado, Hermann Torrentinus (Hermann von der Beeke, d. 1520) calmly set out to explicate the love between the two men, softening *ardebat*, which Grafton translates as "he was hot for," to a weaker "he loved very much" (*valde amabat*).[135] Yet the commentator contains the passage's explosive content allegorically, or, as one could also say, historically. He equates Corydon with Virgil and Alexis with Emperor Augustus. Had Torrentinus grasped the passage? Not accidentally, Torrentinus became the object of ridicule (as commentator of Virgil's *Aeneid*) in the famous humanist satire, the *Epistolae obscurorum virorum* (1515/17).[136]

Authors of textbooks in the vernacular voiced concerns similar to Erasmus's *De ratione studii* about the sexual depravities of the ancients. As a commentator on Ovid's *Metamorphoses* in German, Gerhard Lorichius (1485/90 to before 1553) legitimated the publication of Jörg Wickram's vernacu-

lar Ovid in a poetological excursus (*Zuschreibung*), because this literary endeavor at the interface of Latin and German erudition was so unusual—
German was considered "unnoble," "clumsy," and without the desirable *or-
natus*.[137] Like Erasmus, Lorichius compared the literature whose reading he
advocated to "heathen poison" (*Heydnischem gifft*), and, again, same-sex desire became something of a test case for humanist learning.[138]

Lorichius's prefatory caveats are not without reason. Medieval commentators defended Ovid against the reputation of having been a sodomite.[139]
Yet all texts are subject to potential abuse by readers, Lorichius argues (as
did Erasmus and many other theologians mentioned in this chapter), alluding to Titus 1:15 and the "corrupt" reader. In that sense, ancient literature
equals the Holy Scriptures—except that Roman authors trump all other,
even Biblical, writers in both eloquence and bawdiness. As antidote[140] to
the dangers of corrupt reading, Lorichius, like Erasmus, proposes to ad-
minister a *mélange* of didacticism. In class, doses of uplifting moral messages
from the Bible ought to alternate with excerpts from ancient literature. In
the printed book at hand, Lorichius offered a "didactic exposition" (*Eyn
Außlegung der Sitten*)—moralizing passages that interrupt the flow of Ovidian
tales—without which, he felt, the common man would surely be irritated
(*ein groß ergernüß dem gemeinen unverstendigem man*).[141]

In Lorichius's view of books, reading is like going to class. The common
reader is in danger of reading literally and therefore is badly in need of a mediator. According to his preface, it would be wrong to assume that ancient
poets represented the depravities of their own time faithfully. Rather, these
authors invented bawdiness in order to castigate debaucheries, even when
they drew their own portraits as bawds. What is more, licentiousness helps
in memorizing the sentences to be learned from the examples. Like ancient literature in its own time, printed books thus contribute to the grand
project of humankind's betterment, whose progress, Lorichius suggests, is
already evident in Mainz, the city where printing was first invented and the
German translation of Ovid saw the light of day in 1545. What does this
mean for sodomy?

As every reader of the *Metamorphoses* knows, to cast Ovid as a heathen
Christian poses something of a challenge to the interpreter. Having portrayed the sin against nature as an ultimate offense in his preface, the commentator faces an acute problem in books 10 and 11. Orpheus, inconsolable
about Eurydice's final loss, turns away from women and seeks erotic pleasure with boys, thereby introducing a heretofore unknown way to have
sex to Thracia.[142] The German translation by Jörg Wickram, Lorichius's
collaborator, however, deletes all allusions to same-sex sexual practice, not

only here, but also with regard to other relevant narrations. According to the German Ovid, Ganymede, for instance, is cast as the eagle who flies to Mount Olympus to become the gods' cupbearer, a version of the myth that strangely collapses the enamored Zeus, the eagle, and his object of love, Ganymede.[143] After Eurydice's death, the German Orpheus starts to scorn women but, unlike the Orpheus of Ovidian myths, does not satisfy his lust with boys. Rather, the German *Metamorphoses* explains Orpheus's farewell to women with a rather un-Ovidian curse by Pluto, the god of the underworld: "Since he has lost his wife, he shall avoid all women."[144] Taking Orpheus's repudiation to heart, Thracian women avenge themselves and brutally kill the singer—a version of the story from which Orpheus emerges as something of a hero of misogyny instead of dying as the inventor of sodomy in Thracia.

To be sure, Jörg Wickram, the sixteenth-century translator—by his own, overly modest words ignorant of Latin[145]—did not adapt Ovid's text from the original Latin but from a Middle High German model text by Albrecht of Halberstadt (c. 1200) whose translation Wickram modernized, primarily with regard to its linguistic form.[146] Unfortunately, only fragments of Albrecht's *Metamorphoses* and nothing of the relevant books ten or eleven survive. We are therefore unable to decide whom to credit with these literary acts of censorship by way of translation—Albrecht, a contemporary of Wolfram of Eschenbach and Gottfried of Strasbourg, or Wickram, a contemporary of Martin Luther (though, it seems likely that Wickram did not intervene substantially).[147]

Whatever the case, Wickram's collaborator, Lorichius, a *litteratus*, whose commentary ennobled their unconventional publishing venture, clearly modeled his commentary on Ovid's original (he may not even have known Wickram's German text at the time he was writing his commentary). As a result, he was forced to confront the text's offensiveness on a sexual plane. Ironically, therefore, the much discussed common man would get a glimpse of Orpheus's true transgression only through the moralizing comment whose very intent was to defuse Ovid's explosive representation of "indecencies." Traversing different sins "against nature" (*wider die natur*), Lorichius states that Orpheus's sin, the "mute sin" (*stümmende sünde*) is graver than incest (treated earlier) because "it is more against nature," substantiating his view with a number of authorities.[148] By dint of this Christian taxonomy, the representation of strange *amours* metamorphoses into a mirror for the Christian soul.

Yet Orpheus is a particularly challenging case. Like Ovid himself, Orpheus, "a priest and poet" (*Priester und Poeten*),[149] embodies the height of poetic expression—an unsurpassed ability to move others by songs makes Orpheus an exemplar of a poet in the good sense of the word—while he also incarnates the *poète maudit*, an "erring poet" (*ein irriger Poet*) who violated divine reason by committing "the horrible vice" (*grausam laster*) of sodomy. [150] It is precisely his compulsion to castigate the ever-growing sins in his own times that enables Lorichius to thwart the challenge of sodomy. In his exposition, the mute, sodomitical sin against nature is transformed into other sins, misogamy and refusal to procreate in heterosexual unions: "What could be more against nature than to want to have sex with women and not want to father children?" [151] Thus, Orpheus, the ur-father of Orpheunists (*Orpheunisten*), alias sodomites, [152] becomes an emblem for behavior "against nature" in general. The myth's homosexual plotline is hidden behind a veil of utterly confused moralizations.

✢✢✢

In early modern culture, the dissemination of knowledge to ever-changing communities of readers and listeners depended on manifold processes of mediation, translation, and adaptation. Mediators of expert knowledge such as theologians, sermonizers, religious instructors, teachers, commentators, and translators populated late medieval literary endeavors. Tropes of unspeakability resided in these nodes of communication. As a metaphor, the unspeakable thrived particularly in settings where an educated elite "spoke" to an audience supposedly little familiar with the erudition of experts. Designed for a nonacademic audience encompassing both clergy and laity, these expressions constituted a traditional locus in pastoral theology. Though forever ambiguous, invocations of the unspeakable could therefore be decoded as signifying sexual acts centered around same-sex eroticism. Readers appropriated, commented upon, adapted, and even resisted the implications of this metaphor. Associated with destruction and disaster, sodomy and the other sins against nature did not destroy language. Rather, control was at issue. According to the experts of Christian dogma, the so-called unspeakable connoted an imperative to censor, a "one should not speak about it," at least not in certain contexts, rather than a "one cannot speak about it." The metaphorical was thus linked to taking action. As I will show in the following chapters, both the censoriousness as well as the highly emotionalized rhetoric of shame and disgust affected various textual arenas, from pamphleteering to the state's archival records. Increasingly, secular elites saw themselves as called upon to manage knowledge of same-sex eroticism.

4

Acts without Words, Acts of Silencing:
The Sixteenth Century

In a letter written in 1539, Peter Kunz, minister in Bern, thanked Joachim von Watt (1483/84–1551), the great humanist and Reformer of St. Gallen, for his opinion on how to proceed in a case of male-male sodomy—documentation of which is lost.[1] Apparently, the letter's addressee had argued against harsh retribution, making a plea for taking the defendant's youth into account—as noted in chapter 1, a common legal practice before the Reformation.[2] After the Reform had been introduced in many German and Swiss cities in the 1520s and 1530s, Reformers debated issues that touched on ecclesiastical life and civic morality in Protestant communities. In a phase of consolidation, Reformers discussed with their colleagues the appropriate evangelical forms of action in affairs of religion as much as of the state. Kunz mentioned in his letter that he had contacted other ministers with regard to the same matter, Wolfgang Capito from Basel and Sebastian Meyer, one of Kunz's colleagues in Bern. Thus, the single surviving document, Kunz's epistle, reflects a nexus of interlocutors and opinions that goes far beyond the one letter we have.

Invoking standard epistolary convention, Kunz praises the friendship that the elder once demonstrated toward the younger in Zurich. Watt had received the "stranger with open arms" (*benigniter es amplexatus incognitum*), a candor that now also characterizes his humane response to the youth's sexual transgression.[3] An aside on how rare the sexual act in question was—*rari exempli eventu*—barely separates "two kinds of intimacy," to adopt a phrase by Alan Bray, the affective relationship of friendship between men and its sexual counterpart, sodomy.[4] In fact, the revulsion against "the monstrous atrocity of that unspeakable pederast" (*de nefandi illius* παιδεραστοῦ *prodigioso nimis facinore*) serves as a link between friends of bygone days.

The crime's wording merits our full critical attention. I am pointing to Kunz's shift from Latin, the elevated language of the letter, to Greek, the

even more elevated idiom that offered the letter writer an elegant circumlo-
cution for sodomite, *paiderastes*. This passage is one of the earliest examples
of circumscribing sodomy by means of codeswitching to Greek, a language
and culture that increasingly came to be associated with male-male eroticism in later centuries.[5] To be sure, switching from one language to another
has proven a common strategy to name subjects ranging from the slippery
to the monstrous. By such a device, the letter writer artfully displays resistance, veiling what was conventionally described as an ineffable monstrosity, the *nefandum,* and branding the act in question as foreign (a rhetorical
strategy that will become a major theme in the second part of this book).
Whatever source inspired Kunz to adopt such a wording in a legal context,
the term *paiderastes* represents more than a learned synonym for sodomite.
The recherché word evokes a humanist revival of ancient literature that
included the unspeakable sexual practice known by the German name of
"heresy."

A reading of a letter opened this chapter, and a letter will conclude it. The
body of the chapter deals with court proceedings in the sixteenth century. In chapter 2, I argued that the nature of sodomy trials in the early
modern German lands was episodic. The present chapter will delve into
sixteenth-century episodes of same-sex acts, first, to uncover the traces of
a sexual culture in which these acts occurred quite regularly and, second,
to investigate changing responses to these acts. Sexual acts that were embedded in everyday interactions of a nonsexual kind solicited severe and
censorious responses—responses in tune with a new self-understanding of
post-Reformation authorities, both Catholic and Protestant. An investigation of one Reformer, Werner Steiner, will illustrate the dialectic of disciplining and silencing that guided early modern authorities whenever they
confronted same-sex sexual behavior.

The records that inform this chapter were drafted in the preeminent
cities in the German-speaking part of Switzerland. For the sake of comparison, I have focused on a Catholic canton, Lucerne, and a Reformed canton,
Zurich (Protestant since 1525). Documents from Basel, Schaffhausen (both
had joined the Confederacy as recently as 1501), and St. Gallen, all of them
Protestant, and Catholic Solothurn, complement this picture. What makes
this material particularly precious in the context of historiographical efforts
to recover the social history of sexuality, and especially of sodomy, is that
most of the proceedings originated outside the cities. Both Lucerne and
Zurich ruled over rural territories. Considering that the bulk of published

archival records pertain to the persecution of sodomites in European cities, this material is an especially welcome addition to our reconstruction of past sexualities.

Trial records are texts unlike others. While religious literature often invoked burning at the stake to represent the sin in question (chapter 3), the wording of legal proceedings was linked to a proscribed course of action (often left unexplained in the records themselves). The words recorded in trials, often formulaic, are anything but transparent. Yet they are slippery in ways different from literary texts. Court narrations were guarded by oaths; confessions were extorted by the threat of torture—according to the authorities, a method of inquisition that ought to be used as little as possible. Moreover, depositions and verdicts render trial records multivocal—a polyphony streamlined by the recording practices of scribes. But these records nonetheless allow us to reconstruct the actions that preceded prosecution. Any such reconstruction needs to take into account the rhetorics of persecution, however. Therefore, I propose a twofold exploration of court documents. I will read them as pointing toward a male culture that included the erotic and as documenting a changing societal and judicial approach to sodomy.

Domestic Sodomy

What is remarkable about the sodomy cases that Protestant and Catholic law courts heard in sixteenth-century Switzerland is their everyday quality. The men who were investigated were, as a rule, ordinary people, simple folk, not members of the elite. And, what is more, the sexual activities that surfaced in the courtroom were embedded in everyday interactions—a striking contrast to the stark rhetoric used to describe these sexual practices in court proceedings or verdicts. Men met each other while drinking together. They reported engaging in suggestive erotic slurs. Farmhands slept in the same bed while harvesting or after a long night out. Inns and hostels fostered close physical encounters between males with few if any social obligations toward one another. Master-servant relationships also provided a haven for sexual activities among men. The everyday quality of these sexual encounters as brought to light in court proceedings is further evidenced by the fact that many of these proceedings did not start as sodomy trials but rather became such after having been initiated for offenses other than sodomy.

According to the trial records, everyday interactions and social networks led to sexual transgressions. Frequently, shared bedrooms or beds set the scene for eroticism. In the canton of Lucerne, a Catholic priest was accused of having pestered an adolescent while staying overnight at a farm.[6] In another case reported to Lucerne authorities, an innkeeper and his wife entered the bedchamber in order to pacify altercations between overnight guests. One man had moved toward another, supposedly with erotic intent.[7] Over a period of fourteen years, Conrad Mülibach of St. Gallen was accused of having sought and had sex with males, many of them working in his trade, weaving.[8] A farmer's wife discovered two guests *flagrante delicto* in an alcove in her farmhouse's living room; after having asked one of them "what he was doing," she berated them unmercifully.[9] Sexual doings between men were said to have been caused by the fact that one man's wife was in confinement.[10] In Augsburg, erotic contacts among a group of men had lasted for years and, in some cases, extended beyond the date of their weddings.[11] Lyndal Roper captures this everydayness as it appears in the documents by the term "domesticated homosexuality."[12] Yet in its implicit reference to the untamed sexual beast, "domesticated homosexuality" remains uncomfortably attached to demonizing sodomy. As the records show, same-sex eroticism was neither universal nor anything out of the ordinary, if by ordinary we mean sodomy's social nexus, not government or community responses to same-sex activities.

The quotidian world in which people experienced male-male sexual encounters functioned without categories such as "homosexuality" that could have structured the variety of acts, subjects, and responses which constituted homoeroticism in this period. Judging from the surviving court records, homoerotic seduction lacked a language of its own. When approaching other men, males appropriated a linguistic code used in heterosexual encounters. The slang expression *hinacht minnen*, for instance, qualifies *minnen* for "to have sex" with "from behind."[13] One man described another's unsolicited advances as wanting him "to act like with a woman."[14] Men who initiated erotic activities often couched their bodily moves toward male intimacy in words alluding to the other sex. "If only I had a beautiful girl," one farmhand was said to have told a fellow before suggesting that they get intimate.[15] More graphic statements could also be heard. One man exclaimed: "A great fat cunt for me," adding "I don't have one, so be one for me."[16] During a night in an inn, Franz Kessler pretended to be a woman by tucking away his genitals and thus put the moves on a fellow guest, or so he claimed in court.[17]

In erotically ambiguous situations, heterosexual sex could also serve as a cover-up for erotic encounters of the same-sex kind. When a city guard named Roman discovered Hans Pröpstli and a boy in a guardhouse in Solothurn, Pröpstli explained his intrusion by claiming he had been awaiting a tryst. In the course of the argument that followed, Pröpstli intimated the name of a woman to lend credence to his story. The boy present was supposed to have acted merely as a messenger.[18] Sex with women might have been an offense for a married man like Pröpstli, but it definitely counted as a lesser transgression and could therefore be cited as an excuse. When an innkeeper caught the same defendant in the company of a boy while both had their pants down, Pröpstli claimed that they had had sex with a woman who had just left.[19] The same Pröpstli, an artisan in the small urban community of Solothurn, asked one servant permission to spend the night with him in the latter's tiny alcove, arguing that he did not want to wake up his wife and children late at night. There, he brought up the topic of young women twice and his searching hands reiterated the erotic message nonverbally. The servant's response was suspended between an unwillingness to accommodate his employer and an obligation to respect his request. First, he asked Pröpstli to go to his wife, then, stressing social distance, stated that he had been working all day and needed to sleep.[20]

In one of the empire's largest cities, Augsburg, we also find a picture of sodomitical sex embedded in everyday activities. There is little evidence for distinct locations where men met. Nor is there evidence for coded language. What distinguishes the Augsburg records from the Swiss proceedings presented above is that the urban pursuit of sodomy brought together people from vastly different social backgrounds. In 1532 legal proceedings exposed a circle of men who not only had sex with each other but also exchanged sexual trade on a rather grand scale. Among them were not only a priest and a teacher—professions expected to lead model lives—but also a member of one of Augsburg's richest families, Sigismund Welser. With their keen interest in both sexual techniques and the locations of sexual intercourse, the authorities could hardly have been reassured when they learned that, besides a public bath and several inns, sexual encounters between members of the same sex had taken place in a presbytery and a schoolhouse.[21] Evidence across Europe shows that same-sex eroticism did not inhabit a sphere of its own. Rather, sodomy, as the legal category went, appears absorbed into larger social patterns, at least until it came to court.

In court, defendants often insisted that moves leading to their arrest be understood as actions undeserving of criminal prosecution. Many of the accused portrayed behavior that had led to charges of sodomy as nothing out of the ordinary. Hans Bröpstli, for instance, assured the court that all his life he had never been "tempted by evil will or lust to commit such things with a man."[22] But he added that he had lain physically close to many a man "when it was cold."[23] According to this suspect, physical proximity between men was a remedy against frost *and* a common pastime. Another suspect stated that if he had grabbed other men's private parts it was to assess the state of their health.[24] By embedding their actions in the everyday, suspects erected a strategic line of demarcation between their own doings and what legal scholars called *sodomia*. They depicted their doings as congruous with a code of behavior in the male communities to which they belonged, thus attempting to avoid the grip of the courts.

This male code was far from being universally accepted. What one suspect viewed as everyday, another described as transgressive. When authorities from Zurich investigated a violent incident between farmhands, the defendant remembered a friendly social gathering until he was hit, whereas a peer recounted in great detail that the defendant had groped his genitals several times. According to a witness, the defendant had guided the other man's hand to his exposed penis, asking him to expose himself also.[25]

Occasionally, individuals used their status "to persuade" dependents or people of lower rank to have sex. Not only were the socially inferior obliged to follow their superiors, but also the legal system favored the more respectable. Gifts of clothes or money were an integral part of early modern sexual culture. One boy-servant received generous remuneration from his master for sexual services. When the same adolescent threatened to leave, his employer asked him to procure another boy for similar duties. After his return with such a specimen, "a young, handsome, poor student" (*einen jungen hüpschen armen schüler*), the master, obviously pleased with the choice, handed him the substantial sum of twenty florins.[26] The Augsburg trials reveal that gifts of both money and clothes as well as excessive wine consumption—itself a target of urban regulation—played a major part in leading newcomers to grant sexual favors to other men.[27]

Fragments of a Communal Self

In court, male-male eroticism did not appear as a self-induced lust. Even in light of evidence that strongly suggested the contrary, many of the accused asserted innocence by revealing their inner purity to the investigators. Men said that the thought of sexual acts with members of their own sex had never crossed their minds. A fourteen-year-old suspect from Basel, Jacob Fischer, stated somewhat credibly that "he had had no idea what it was and also did not know what it meant."[28] Claiming ignorance, Fischer nevertheless confessed to having committed "indecent works" (*vnzimbliche werck*) twice with Georg Wüst when each pushed his penis into the other's back (it is unclear whether this meant penetration).

Court narratives allow "evil desire" to exist but often project it onto a realm beyond personal control. Defendants insinuated, for instance, that one had to learn sodomy. Even those who themselves had become gifted educators of other men in sodomitical sex often blamed the culprits who had first seduced them for their initial involvement.[29] When an apprentice was chided for having disgraced his master—"you haven't learned this from your master"—he responded by blaming a companion: "Of course he had learned [the sexual practice] from nobody else than Uli Somerauer" who had committed "such acts."[30] In a case of bestiality, the defendant cited the dirty talk among laborers as having induced him to have sex with cows.[31] One apprentice tried to convince a reticent fellow apprentice to consent to a sexual act by citing previous experience, according to which "it did not harm."[32]

Genealogies of seduction in court regularly led to regions where Romance languages were spoken. Jacob vom Schloss (1515), Hans Pröpstli (1525),[33] Balthasar Bär, Balthasar Fölck (1532), Werner Steiner (1542), and Jephat Scheurmann (1609) all claimed to have learned the practice of male-male sexuality from *welsche*, a derogatory term used primarily for Italians but also for other speakers of Romance languages. Bär quotes his sexual partner from Fribourg[34] as having lured him into a sexual encounter by saying that "this is the way the *welsch* have sexual intercourse."[35] Jephat Scheurmann confessed to having been "seduced" (*verfüert*) as a young man while "in foreign countries" (*an der frömbde*). He mentioned an apprentice from Fribourg as his preceptor. The precise wording is of interest here. Scheurmann stated that "he was brought into this vice" (*inn diß laster gebracht worden*) as if an alien force had intruded upon a core self. He attributed his failure to protect his innocence of sodomy to youthful ignorance: "he did not know that it was a sin" (*das er nidt gewisset, es sünd sÿe*).[36] After his initial experience, Scheurmann was seduced again in his hometown, Zofingen, and proceeded to seduce others. Others, like Hans Pröpstli from Solothurn, had acquired the habit while traveling in Italy (Rome and Milan are mentioned specifically).[37]

Sleep or drunkenness held a similar significance, signaling to the judges reduced responsibility on the part of the accused. Whatever happened in these states of mind should not be prosecuted or should be punished with a lesser sentence.[38] Suspects tried to convey a sense of a self that remained pure, severe criminal prosecution notwithstanding. Among other things, sleep signified that a person had no capacity to remember. Ambrosius Suter mused that he might have dreamt of his wife, "whom he often asked to move closer," while asking his male companion to do likewise. Suter even proffered a double explanation for his sodomy: he was deeply asleep and in a drunken stupor.[39] Andreas Pfister did not deny that he had grabbed another man's genitals but hastened to add that he had been "drunk" and acted "in jest."[40] Sometimes, the molested shared this notion. One of the young men who had been approached by Bröpstli amended his deposition to remark that "if he [Bröpstli] did it while asleep he [Thonj Balthasar] will forgive him."[41]

If no other explanation was plausible, the accused claimed to have been tempted by man's foe, the devil, one of the stock figures of moral theology and popular belief.[42] An apprentice who had asked a companion to "commit the bodily acts with him" said his intentions were induced by "the evil spirit."[43] Another stated that the devil had seduced "his person" (gmüt) to commit sodomy; otherwise he was "untouched" by that sin.[44]

Notions of magic also surfaced when defendants answered to the courts for sodomy. In Schaffhausen in 1530, Hans Fritschi confessed to having committed "unchristian and heretical acts" innumerable times, as the scribe put it, with a fellow laborer named Hans Räss.[45] For more than a year, the two men had had sexual intercourse. In court, Fritschi admitted only minimal involvement in the two men's affair, despite its considerable duration. What must have looked like a consensual relationship to the judges, Fritschi portrayed as having happened against his will. (Since Räss had not been apprehended, no competing account challenged Fritschi's version of the events.) According to the transcript of Fritschi's confession, Räss, the older of the two, had forced the younger to have sex by making him drunk and showering him with small gifts. With regard to a pair of new pants, Fritschi stated that he had worn them only twice, because Räss had these pants in his control. In other words, by dint of these clothes, his companion could force him to perform the evil act. The wording suggests that wearing the magic pants meant loss of control over one's own body. The judges showed little mercy: in light of the accused's youth they mitigated the punishment from death at the stake to decapitation.

The pragmatic context of statements in court—charges of criminal behavior—explains why individuals came up with apologetic notions of the self, a self susceptible to the influences of others and, ultimately, beleaguered by evil forces. Thus viewed, the self appears as fleeting, its expressions as momentary, dictated by external circumstances. Indeed, such explanations provided the accused with a defense and potentially a sense of integrity in the face of imminent punishment. In the context of court proceedings, the self gone public was a regulated entity defined by a common set of rules. Though differentiated by social status, these rules encoded in the expressions of the self were commonly shared; otherwise they could not have served their pragmatic function. In court, the "self" was communal, not an individual persona. Defendants reinscribed individual behavior into the behavioral standard with which they were familiar.[46] By invoking these formulas, they intended to separate a momentary or repeated lapse with potentially serious consequences from a more permanent idea of personhood.[47] The opprobrium associated with terms like sodomy or heresy was such, however, that practically nobody claimed the label "heretic" or "sodomite" once in the dock. These words invoked such a severe transgression that their application other than for the purpose of defaming another person was extremely rare. On the individual level, male-male desire and sodomy were thus presented as belonging to the self's Other.

Infamous Fama

In encounters with erotic overtones, men often responded aggressively to other men's moves on them, or so they told the judges. Accused of the "heresy of sodomy" (*kätzery der Sodomy*), Hans Pröpstli of Solothurn confessed to having offered sex to an unspecified number of males "with whom he had lain at night," but "they refused."[48] Though Hans Bröpstli of Zurich wrapped his version of the events in notions of reciprocity, the three adolescents he had approached stated that they had labeled him an *arsbruter* (buttfucker) in response.[49] Men, touched in ways they considered indecent, started to argue or caused an uproar in order to attract the attention of others in the same room or house.[50]

Verbal vilification was one mode of response to unsolicited advances, while physical rejection was another. When Conrad Mülibach fondled the genitals of his host's son, the latter hurled him to the ground.[51] The line between aggressive words and aggressive actions was thin. One witness reported a sequence of aggravating responses to Pröpstli's nocturnal pesterings, for instance. When the latter thought him asleep and tried "to sting" him, he first turned on his back. When he tried again, the witness reportedly became agitated and forced Pröpstli to leave.[52] Naturally, court records are weighted toward accusations of aggression and sexual coercion. Judicial archives harbor information primarily concerning those incidents where conflicts escalated and came to court. Witnesses also felt the need to exaggerate their resistance to sexual advances in order to avoid punishment.

In court, men often explained aggression against a supposed sodomite by referring to the suspect's *fama* or social reputation.[53] People claimed to know their neighbors' sexual doings and exploited this information when need arose.[54] In his testimony, Jephat Scheurmann sketched the contours of a sodomitical society in his native Zofingen, a small town north of Lucerne. A civic dignitary himself, he claimed to have "seen" how, among others, Vincenz Kuhn, a local glazier, had had dealings with a number of boys.[55] Many a witness cited rumors or claimed they had "heard" that a certain suspect had molested another person of his sex.[56] The surveillance of sexual behavior extended even beyond a community's physical boundaries. When it became known that a Swiss mercenary in northern Italy had engaged in sex with a boy, an outcry (*geschrei*) arose in the platoon. The soldier was forced to leave. Codes of behavior were not suspended when Swiss men participated in warfare outside of Switzerland.[57] Rules might even have become more rigid in the face of a foreign "onslaught."

Fama was based, above all, on suspicious behavior. A man who physically approached another man during a night in an inn or on a farm might be tolerated a first time. Violent reactions became more likely when a man's allegedly erotic intentions had become evident through a repetition of similar moves. This vision linked the sodomite's traits not to the essence of an identifiable character, but to a sequence of actions that constitute subjectivity.[58] The likelihood of a conflict often depended on a suspect's social standing, with elite suspects commonly shielded from prosecution.

Nevertheless, responses to same-sex desire were often equivocal. When farmhands refused to lodge in the same bed with a fellow laborer, they voiced only vague explanations as to why they preferred different sleeping arrangements.[59] Hans Pröpstli moved physically close to a servant with whom he shared a bed. After a while, the servant got up and refused to stay with him. Asked by his companions why, he apparently stated, "it is not good to lie with him."[60] An adolescent threatened to leave his father's house, should Conrad Mülibach be allowed to stay there overnight again. According to the records, this young man provided no explanation for his strong antipathy. Despite numerous attempts to return, Mülibach was always turned away at the door, as the boy had desired.[61] In one case, an apprentice moved on to a different employer without indicating a reason for his departure. When a second hire felt physically molested by a fellow worker, the first's departure started to make sense.[62]

It is possible that commoners engaged in drastic language with regard to a suspected sodomite among themselves. With persons above their rank or in court, they guarded their choice of words and used circumlocutions instead. They coined formulas such as doing "it," "the things," or "such behavior."[63] When a fifteen-year-old spoke of a priest's pesterings, he complained incoherently that "the whole night, especially before midnight, the other would not leave him alone but always wanted to lie on him." Interrogated further, he pointed to a bed as evidence "where one found what we did not like," as the local records stated enigmatically.[64] An innkeeper confronted a neighbor about an "atrocious deed" (*wüste handlung*) without mentioning the deed's precise nature, so he stated explicitly during the interrogation. He forbade his wife to take bread from the suspect, however.[65] In the context of everyday conversations reported in court as well as in the depositions, there is little doubt that these responses and circumlocutions referred to sexual activity. In daily interactions, there was in fact no need to use terms with a legal or religious valence, such as heresy or sodomy. Rather, there was incentive to avoid legally relevant expressions, since using them could have severe consequences. Even if members of a small rural community did not use a term like sodomy, with its religious and legal implications, they nevertheless could have known the sexual actions to be punishable.

Sometimes victims were strongly encouraged to speak up. A servant woman in whom a farmhand confided about being sexually molested urged him "to say" to the authorities "what [had] happened" (*er sölles segen wiess gangen sÿg*). An investigation was initiated.[66] In the case of sodomy, vociferousness coexisted with deep-seated injunctions to remain silent. Frequently, sodomites asked their sexual partners to remain silent about their sexual doings.[67] When a master asked his apprentice workers about a complaint that one of them lay on top of others, they responded somewhat elusively. Their bed was big enough, they stated, yet added that the culprit "perpetrated other things which they were not supposed to talk about."[68] In fact, many a perpetrator seems to have had an acute sense of the danger or sinfulness of his doings. Melchior Brütschli went on a pilgrimage in order to confess anal intercourse with a male companion.[69] In another case, five boy apprentices fled their master's disciplining hand after one had complained to him about an apprentice who molested the others by lying on top of them.[70]

Tellingly, when witnesses related sexual encounters in court, they sometimes expressed diametrically opposite impulses, like wanting to stay still or to act aggressively. One suspect explained that although he had tolerated a suspect's physical intrusion, he nevertheless felt deep hatred for him. By stating his conflicting emotions in court, the accused tried to ensure that officials would not take his toleration for complicity.[71]

Sodomitical acts were often represented as threatening the social fabric. Apprentices expected their masters to act against perpetrators. When

Hoder Wasser replaced Hans Heinrich Vogler as a shoemaker's apprentice, he was dismayed to hear that his predecessor had put the moves on a fellow apprentice and blamed his master for it. When the shoemaker heard about the incident, he reacted strongly. He used corporal punishment on the apprentice who had been assaulted but kept silent, dismissed him, and forbade him to speak about the incident—a silence with which the apprentice refused to comply. It was the attempt to silence him that induced the apprentice to tell his father and raise an "outcry."[72]

Social familiarity kept people from embarking on actions fraught with conflict. The sexually suspect often lived unremarkably among neighbors before being made the object of a public outcry or being taken to court. In other words, members of a community were somewhat protected, despite a *fama* that included hints at their illegitimate sexual doings. At the same time, others, especially the young, were warned not to socialize with people said to engage in illegitimate sexuality.[73] At any rate, the barrier against reporting a neighbor was high. Immigrants and foreigners became the target of criminal prosecution more frequently than natives. This is not to say that for the locals, social life in the cantons of Switzerland was harmonious. Yet repercussions in case of conflict could be prohibitive. Restraint was especially strong in the case of crimes punishable by death, like sodomy. Inhibitions against denouncing a suspect were, of course, overcome in particularly severe conflicts.

It is hard to determine precisely why an elusive *fama* turned into legal proceedings or why suspects became defendants. Accusations became more vociferous, for example, when several men jointly raised charges.[74] A political context may explain why communal knowledge was shared with superiors who then initiated legal action. In the territory of Lucerne, accusations against Hans Portmann surfaced in the aftermath of a rebellion against the city's taxation.[75] In another region that belonged to Lucerne, a number of charges, sodomy among them, were brought against an incompetent priest.[76]

Surveillance on a local level fed into the state's policing efforts. Conflicts escalated once people voiced communally shared knowledge in public, especially in situations fraught with tension. If conflicts were not resolved, gossip, rumors, voices, and suspicions amounted to a *geschrei* or *clamor*, which legally forced the authorities to initiate a trial. "Outcry," a community's discursive response to what was perceived as transgressive, is a consistent feature of the reaction to sodomy on the local level.[77] Legal proceedings then provided a mechanism by which good reputation could be restored to communities.

The above episodes shed new light on the so-called repression hypothesis—the idea that state powers were the primary agents in persecuting sodomites. To be sure, legal action against perceived criminals relied on a functioning state apparatus, and prosecution certainly could not take place without the authorities' support. Yet cases from Zurich and Lucerne tell a story that differs significantly from the textbook account that seeks the origins of persecution in the state. The above episodes demonstrate how the populace's monitoring of sociosexual mores fed into the state's activities and how governments were sometimes forced to act according to communal concerns.

Rare Cases, Strong Responses

Although same-sex sexual activities often surfaced in a casual context, their casual appearance should not be confounded with lenient treatment. Once the authorities got wind of sexual doings among males, the full weight of their investigative apparatus was brought to bear against suspects. When information reached officials that two six-year-old boys had engaged in what was termed "unchristian acts" (vnchristenliche werch)—according to witnesses they had lain on top of each other with their pants down—the authorities conducted a thorough investigation.[78]

In the case of Paulus Leemann, a Catholic priest from the territory of Lucerne, accusations were fabricated in order to rid the parish of an unpopular cleric.[79] His behavior was offensive on many accounts, but it was not until 1577, when a fifteen-year-old complained of having been pestered by Leemann, that action was taken: a list of the priest's wrongdoings was hastily compiled by the villagers. The charge of sodomy proved useful not only in marking his character as utterly depraved but also in urging the council of Lucerne to action. Once the council took over, investigators focused on the charge of sodomy, letting the other charges virtually drop from sight. In order to establish the true course of events, the priest and the boy were each interrogated numerous times. The adolescent toned his previous statement down by stating that the priest had tried his luck only once. For his part, Leemann dismissed the boy's statement, explaining that he had put an arm around the boy in an effort to relieve the pain he had felt from a physical ailment. He stated that the adolescent could easily have called on others in a neighboring room if he had felt threatened by his actions. There was no talk of his being drunk, of course, as the boy had claimed.[80] Step by step, the evidence against Leemann evaporated during the course of the investigation.

These records demonstrate the great strides urban authorities had made in a long-standing conflict over clerical jurisdiction since the early fifteenth century. In 1423 the council had taken note in its manual that "heresy" had occurred between monks without taking any action at all (the exact wording makes it likely that we are in fact dealing with sodomy): clerics were subject to a different jurisdiction.[81] In a comparable case in 1489, the council risked a major conflict with the bishop of Constance yet refrained from infringing on the latter's judicial rights.[82] Now, in 1577, magistrates initiated an investigation against a priest and interrogated him.[83] Leemann's case in fact coincided with a Counter-Reformation campaign to enforce moral and sexual standards among the canton's clergy.[84] This time, civic authorities made sure that the case was given serious consideration by the ecclesiastical court in Constance. They also banished Leemann from the territory of Lucerne.

In the early modern court, interrogations into a variety of offenses included an investigation of a suspect's character and past misdeeds. As a result, charges of theft, for example, were sometimes trumped by charges of sodomy, though both amounted to capital crimes.[85] In the case of Thöni Rüttiman, a vagrant initially seized for larceny, investigators uncovered not only a whole string of thefts but also sexual offenses. The defendant confessed to having "florenced" a boy while a mercenary in Italy and to having committed bestiality with a donkey.[86] When Ambrosius Suter and Peter Sifrid were imprisoned on charges of embezzlement, one of the accused attempted to blacken the other's name by claiming that the latter had molested him sexually.[87] Once sodomy allegations were made, authorities usually pursued them with a vengeance. In the case of Suter versus Sifrid, the ambiguity of the accusation led to a different result. Suter pointed out that if such activities had taken place at all, which he could not remember (citing alcohol and sleep as an explanation for his uncertainty), Sifrid had mentioned them first in court and never before. Thereby, he successfully discredited the other party's sincerity in bringing up the charge.[88] The authorities dropped the charge altogether.[89]

Authorities in Swiss cities did not prosecute same-sex sexual behavior consistently. When it surfaced, however, it was taken very seriously. In a particularly telling case, Zurich authorities seized Wilhelm of Mühlhausen for having sold two shirts "in a suspicious manner" (*argwöniger wyß*). Suspicions that he had stolen the goods could not be corroborated during a first investigation. Subsequently, Wilhelm was put up in the local *Spittal* or "poorhouse," where he attracted attention by verbally abusing his fellow inmates as well as railing against the government. Wilhelm's cantankerous personality disposed him to a sequence of verbal disputes, many of which included drastic homoerotic overtones. What is more, Wilhelm suggestively lay on top of a young boy, declaring that he wanted to make love to this fellow inmate. The publicity of these acts made him the target of further disciplinary scrutiny, first in the *Spittal*, then in a second investigation by the authorities. Imprisoned again, Wilhelm was forced to confess to a great number of thefts and two instances of "unchristian and unnatural acts" (*vnchistenliche vnd vnnathürliche werck*) with members of his own sex in Säckingen and Einsiedeln, outside the territory of Zurich. For all his crimes—verbal transgressions, thefts, and sodomy—he was burned at the stake.[90] Restraints on severe punishment were obviously of less import in the case of vagrants or foreigners like Wilhelm.[91]

Despite the haphazardness of law enforcement in early modern states, the prosecution of sodomites in some cases reached beyond the boundaries of territories.[92] In court, officials interrogated defendants about their sexual partners and tried to bring these men to trial. Investigators questioned the accused about the locations where they had engaged in sexual activities. They not only listed these locations but also proceeded to notify neighboring territories about transgressions of the proscribed sexual order on their soil. They sent arrest warrants for suspects on the run to neighboring territories. Authorities provided legal assistance to one another and cooperated in tracking culprits.[93] Within the Confederacy, a long-standing tradition of legal cooperation took precedence over confessional differences even after the Reformation.

Authorities who notified other rulers about acts of sodomy apologized in order to rid this information of any presumption of political enmity. They presented their practice of shared moral rule beyond the borders of judicial authority as a sign of friendship among the ruling elites.[94] When officials in Schwyz notified their Swiss compatriots in Zurich about a certain Hans Blatter's confession, no *zedellin* (secret note) was used as had been done in Strasbourg in 1400.[95] Blatter had admitted to having "florenced" Ulrich Vogel (also Vogler) from Thalwil (near Zurich) twice, supposedly with the youth's consent. The authorities arrested Vogel and questioned him. The suspect stated that one of his father's guests, a doctor, was put up in his room. Though the chamber had two beds, the older man had forced himself on the youth and had sex with him twice intercrurally. On the occasion of a second interrogation, Vogel admitted that he had also lain on Blatter once, but put great emphasis on the fact that no anal intercourse had occurred. Instead, Vogel claimed to have resisted the other's desire to penetrate him.[96]

Of the eighteen investigations that involved the charge of sodomy in sixteenth-century Zurich, a city of about five thousand inhabitants, only ten started as sodomy investigations. In the remaining cases, sodomy became a topic only when the investigation was already under way. To be sure, the use of torture and the authorities' inquisitiveness helped to bring sodomy to the surface. Yet not all "convicted sodomites" were punished by death. In six of the proceedings, no formal sentence is transmitted. If anything, this lack of documentation can be interpreted as evidence that no severe punishment and probably no death penalty was meted out.[97] Defendants in cases where officials found no clear evidence of intercourse usually received relatively light punishments. The three young men who had responded with verbal abuse to Bröpstli's sexual advances were reprimanded by Zurich authorities for speaking rashly and exhorted to keep peace; Bröpstli was warned to desist from "groping" (*griffen vnd grappen*) men in the future.[98] In eight cases the accused were burned at the stake (five) or decapitated (three). One was banished from the territory of the Confederacy. Three other cases ended in an exhortation by the authorities. One ended in house arrest. In one case, five young suspects fled and thus escaped prosecution. In comparison to offenses such as theft, blasphemy, bestiality, fraud, and murder, sodomy rarely came to court. Of 572 executions during the sixteenth century (1501–1600), theft was the delict that most frequently led to the death penalty (338), followed by blasphemy (73), and bestiality (56).[99]

Twelve sodomy investigations are documented for the sixteenth century in Lucerne, and thirteen men appeared in court. One, a minor of fifteen years, was drowned for sodomy and petty theft;[100] one youth was decapitated, and three men died at the stake. In cases that involved other serious charges, such as bestiality and murder, the authorities sentenced offenders to be broken on the wheel (two). While investigations led to no sentence at all in two cases, the other investigations resulted in banishments. A boy of ten years from a small rural community, for example, was flogged and then, after being instructed by a priest, banished from the canton's territory forever.[101] In general, proceedings for bestiality outweigh those for sodomy. Between about 1530 and 1607, authorities in Lucerne acted on charges of bestiality in thirty-six cases, sentencing thirty-one men to death. Twenty proceedings thereof involved accusations of sex with animals only (while in the remainder of cases charges such as theft or murder were part and parcel of the trial).[102] Only the trial against Jörg Sigler featured charges of sex "with people and cattle" (*mit lüten vnd fech*).[103] According to a nineteenth-century source, Lucerne, a city of roughly four thousand people, witnessed death sentences in 181 cases between 1501 and 1600. Seventy-seven people were sentenced to death for theft, twenty-three for murder, twenty for bestiality, twelve for counterfeiting, seven for sodomy, five for rebelliousness, and two for fraud. [104] When it came to sodomy, Zurich and Lucerne provide a rather similar picture. No women were put on trial. Prosecution targeted mainly male adolescents and foreigners, men with little social capital. At least four of the seven men who were executed came from regions other than Lucerne. By comparison, members of the elite were relatively safe. [105]

For good reasons, the large-scale judicial records unearthed in Florence by Michael Rocke have no equivalent north of the Alps. As his work demonstrates so convincingly, the Officers of the Night, the civic commission set up in the fifteenth century to contain same-sex sexual activities in Florence, was able to bring such a great number of men to court because they lowered the punishment to fines and banishments in most cases. In cities north of the Alps, which regularly meted out the death penalty, barriers to acting against perceived sodomites remained high. Persecution of sodomy in Florence thus differs in various ways from the picture that I am drawing here.

In Swiss courts, for instance, little importance was given to sexual roles. The records show little concern over who was active and who was passive in sexual intercourse. Neither do the daily interactions portrayed in these proceedings convey popular conceptions that attach significance to the question of who penetrated whom. Whereas Rocke found a rigid distinction in sexual roles for Renaissance Florence, where elder men were expected to penetrate younger men and stigma was attached to role reversal, Swiss sources do not share the same preoccupation. [106] North of the Alps, the records are more in tune with Christian theology, which as a rule failed to distinguish the severity of the crime according to who penetrated and who was penetrated. Though there are hints that sexual actors themselves attached a particular opprobrium to anal sex, taking it to represent sodomy while holding other sexual practices to be significantly less severe, even these actors betray little concern over activity/passivity in sexual intercourse.

In both Zurich and Lucerne, sexual activity between men often cut across class, rank, and age. Many scholars have called attention to the fact that before 1700, as a rule, sodomitical relations were inscribed into social hierarchies: a mature man penetrated a person below his rank and age—an encounter that the younger male, just as in ancient Athens, was not to enjoy (though he might benefit socially). [107] Social superiority had to be aligned with what was figured as sexual domination. What has become a standard account runs the risk of reducing the complexities that shaped the early modern culture of sex. I want to argue for an early modern "sexual system," following Isabel Hull's suggestion, [108] that allows for multiple locations of same-sex eroticism—locations that were neither entirely separate from one another nor conflatable into one. Same-sex behavior unfolded in a variety of social settings: it was practiced among adolescents; it existed in the milieu of workers or laborers with negligible age or social distinctions; and it flourished in cross-class and intergenerational relationships of masters with their dependents. Though most of the erotic arrangements that were brought to light in courts lasted only for one or a couple of sexual encounters, a few liaisons lasted longer, indicating that there were people who habitually practiced sodomy. [109] Given the paucity of source material, I cannot gauge the dominance of one of these "settings." Yet the records are telling enough to underline the significance of any one of them. In fact, Rocke's account offers a similarly multilayered picture, replete with fragmentary evidence that cannot be subsumed easily under one model of sexual behavior in which hierarchies reigned supreme. This variety is remarkable in light of the unifying forces of a male culture that was, unlike in the empire, at work in Florence—a culture resonant with public discourses and artistic representations of sodomy. North of the Alps, same-sex encounters, though—needless to say—culturally mediated, escaped the disciplining forces of such a distinct sexual culture. In the words of Isabel Hull, sex "was not a thing-in-itself, nor did it have value or meaning except in its various contexts." [110] Yet sex received meaning in the wording of trial records.

The Shifting Rhetorics of Persecution

The idiom that shaped the protocols of early modern court proceedings was not exclusively inspired by legal models. Rather, legal experts used a medley of registers and styles. When verbalizing sodomy, the authorities drew, for example, on religious manuals such as those discussed in chapter 3. During the sixteenth century, religiously inflected terms such as "unnatural" started to appear in legal documents more frequently. [111] Also, concerns about the wording of the so-called unmentionable vice surfaced in court records. In early modern legal casuistry, for instance, commentators applied the pastoral caution developed by confessors and religious teachers to the sphere of legal proceedings. [112] As religious instructors had done, practitioners of the law avoided drastic language and used euphemistic ways of speaking in legal documents.

At the end of the sixteenth century, it became customary for scribes to dissociate themselves from what they reported, for instance. Distancing locutions such as *mit gunst zemelden* (to note with goodwill), *mit Reverentz zů melden* (to note with reverence), *mit Reverentz zeschrÿben* (to write with reverence), *leider* (unfortunately) or the Latin *reverenter* (reverentially) became part of the judicial archive's linguistic repertoire in introducing concepts deemed offensive to superiors.[113] With regard to sexual acts between men, formulas were invoked when it came to expressions such as "pressed his male member c.v. [*cum venia*, "with permission"] in his back body."[114] While verbal decorum was not entirely new in legal records in the sixteenth century, the standardized formulae of shame were.[115]

Clusters of stark and condemnatory phrases set the culprit apart from his or her community. A scribe from Willisau (Lucerne) indulged in phrases such as "of gross, previously unheard of . . . sodomitical action" and added "to note with reverence" in order to express his noninvolvement and to avoid offending the reader.[116] The sentence against the leader of the Augsburg clique, Bernhard Wagner (named Berlin in the court records), concludes with the warning: "May everybody know how to be on guard against . . . the detestable evil and vice against nature for themselves and with others," thereby blending different styles, that of religious didacticism with that of legal descriptiveness.[117] In the proceedings, city clerks avoided graphic language. At one point, the expression for anal intercourse was discreetly replaced by *N.* for *nominandum*, "to be named" (though the context makes clear what one must fill in). Rhetorical expressions of revulsion became a regular feature of court records.[118]

Local authorities were not always well prepared for sodomitical crimes to occur in their region. When Hans Herter, a father of three and owner of a small piece of land, was apprehended for having grabbed other men's genitalia and, in some cases, for having engaged in mutual masturbation over the course of twenty years, the vogt of Kyburg (north of Zurich) declared that he was at a loss as to how to act. He wrote to his superiors, asking "for directions" (*ordnung vnnd wägwyssung*) on how to punish the offender, claiming that he and the judges of Kyburg had never encountered such an offense. According to his letter, officials feared they would either "act too little or too much."[119] They may have wanted to dispose their superiors toward clemency by arguing that "though [the offender] was accused of having committed heresy with these persons and they lay on top of each other as if they wanted to have sex (*lybliche werch begen*), in fact he did not do it at all except through stimulation of their genitalia."[120] He complicated what might have been a plea for mercy by saying that Herter and his partners had acted "as if they had lain with women," a wording reminiscent of the Bible.[121]

Documents from sixteenth-century Zurich provide researchers with a unique opportunity to see the authorities at work crafting archival records of same-sex sexual behavior. Whenever a case came up, the competent vogt of Zurich's territory asked the council for assistance. Subsequently, the council nominated two investigators, usually from its own ranks. These councilors then conducted the investigation on location, interrogated witnesses as well as defendants individually, and carefully recorded the results of their investigation. In fact, the protocol was of the greatest importance, since the council pronounced its judgment on that basis.[122] Many cases are therefore transmitted in two versions: first, the protocol of the proceedings (including pieces of evidence and correspondence); second, in the case of severe penalties, an entry into the *Council's Book of Punishments* (*Rats- und Richtbuch*). In this second set of records, the findings of the proceedings were copied, summarized, and recast in legal terminology. When the death penalty was meted out, a section was added on how a culprit was to be executed. Entries on a case usually end with an oath of truce, intended to protect the city from revenge by the executed person's relatives.

Descriptions of the crimes vary significantly between the ledgers of the investigations and that of the sentences. As a rule, the *Council's Book of Punishments* inflated the legal concepts that had been used during interrogation. Whereas the protocols were relatively descriptive (though they did not shun the moralistic register altogether), the *Book of Punishments* indulged in formulaic wordiness. Jacob Müller, for instance, who had coerced an apprentice into sex, was executed for "such an unchristian, shameful, vicious atrocity, malice, knavery, and heresy . . . against divine, Christian, and human law as well as against nature, all honor."[123] These and similar phrases were common in cases of bestiality or sodomy. What local investigators had captured rather straightforwardly as "unchristian acts" (*uncristenliche werch*), the *Book of Punishments* retold using a plethora of terms for (homo)sexual behavior, "to commit harmful mischief" with another (*schadtlichen mûtwillen gethriben*), "to florence" (*geflorentzet habe*), or "to commit shameful, unnatural heresy" (*volbrachte schandtliche vnnatürliche kätzerÿ*).[124]

The records of Rudolf Bachmann's and Uli Frei's trial are a good case in point. Both men were decapitated in 1567 for having repeatedly engaged in anal sex. The protocol of the investigation is so descriptive that the register of moral condemnation is almost absent. According to the protocol, Frei and Bachmann shared a bed while Bachmann's wife was in confinement. An inebriated Bachmann and Frei felt each other's members. They became so aroused that Frei guided Bachmann's penis into his anus, a practice they repeated six times on different occasions. In contrast to such a factual description, the entry into the *Book of Punishments* recasts a straightforward narration in the terms of sixteenth-century professional legal discourse. The sexual act was rendered by "to florence," a word used in everyday conversations and in legal language as a technical term for anal intercourse. When consecutive acts were mentioned, the full verbal register of a bureaucratic rhetoric of horror unfolds. The document states that the two men committed "shameful, unchristian, unnatural acts."[125] The verdict repeats these formulas, stating that they were to be decapitated for "such shameful, unchristian, unnatural heresy, great evil, and crime."[126] In other words, the *Book of Punishments* greatly intensifies the rhetoric at work in the previous protocol.[127]

Occasionally, the protocols of the investigation themselves testify to a preference for guarded and veiled language. One scribe summed up the witnesses' statement, according to which the suspect had "fucked them in the ass" (to be sure, he had inserted the distancing formula "to mention with reverence"); a different hand replaced this phrase with "to attempt to commit his shameful malice."[128] If the *Book of Punishments* evaluated crimes according to locales and the number of times the crimes had been committed, the writers of the initial protocols for individual cases in sixteenth-century Zurich started to follow the same procedure.[129]

It is hard to generalize from evidence that depended greatly on the training of individual administrators. Yet it is clear that one process of recording informed the other and vice versa, testifying to the transformation of the legal system in this period.[130] In the territory of Zurich, a gradual process of standardization occurred. By 1600, the most commonly used phrase to describe sodomitical sex (as well as bestiality) was "unchristian acts."[131] Other documents described these acts a little less obscurely as "unnatural and unchristian." This novel wording has no exact equivalent in documents of the fifteenth century. Their dissemination is an effect of the new legal professionalism.

Under the aegis of this new rhetorical regime *in sexualibus*, expressions proliferated that preface a particular notion by the prefix *un-*.[132] Obviously, this class of words contains the concept which is being negated. The unnatural, for example, conjures up nature as the arbiter of human actions. Yet in the case of the word unnatural, the prefix *un-* also exceeds the semantic function of denoting the contrary. Unnatural is not simply nonnatural, the opposite of natural. By the sheer weight of the rhetorical tradition and frequent usage in moralizing contexts, *un*-words take on additional connotations, the other side of the norm. From the point of view of the speaker, they articulate a polemical stance. *Un*-enunciations condemn that which is expressed, declare it as dangerous, treacherous ground (like "un-American" in Senator Joseph McCarthy's House Committee on Un-American Activities). As a word in context, this expression of "symbolic extremities"[133] also contains an "ought," a call for action. Unnatural and un-Christian connote a wretched state that ought to call forth the most vocal condemnations. The terms are meant to activate their readers or listeners, though the precise nature of the implied action remains, of course, undefined.[134] On the one hand, expressions such as unnatural or un-Christian differ from the notion of unspeakability in the ways they operate semantically, because these phrases call attention to their own rhetorical production. On the other hand, these proliferating un-words map easily onto the more established notion of the un-speakable, the standard description for sins such as masturbation, anal intercourse between man and woman, bestiality, and, most prominently, same-sex sexuality.

In court records, officials constructed criminal personalities, prominently featuring sexual transgressions such as sodomy or bestiality. Mention thereof was frequently moved to the beginning or end of a list, where a criminal's personality was most in evidence.[135] Under torture, Marx Anthoni from Ferrara admitted to having stolen a knife, clothes, shoes, a woolen shirt, and one florin. His "unchristian acts" (*vncristenliche[] werch*) with an Italian twelve-year-old (*welltschen bůben*) exceeded the other crimes in severity by far, and that is probably why they headed the protocol.[136] Wilhelm of Mühlhausen was made to confess a great number of petty thefts (a total of twelve), but two acts of sodomy in two different houses for the poor topped the list.[137] This pattern of categorizing crimes reserved a highly visible position for same-sex sexual acts. Authorities in Zurich were not the only ones to classify sodomy in this way.[138]

The language of Protestant law courts and Catholic ones did not significantly differ. In Lucerne as in Zurich, authorities used an increasingly moralistic tone over the course of the sixteenth century. Documents switched from German, the language of regular legal practice in this time period, to Latin, so that terms taken from a professional discourse on legal matters (*more sodomitico, reverenter*) could be included.[139] In Zurich and Lucerne, similar formulas were used to paraphrase a crime that supposedly evaded formulation.[140] In both cities, the new language of law enforcement gave expression to a particular understanding of rulership. The political elites emphasized patriarchal hold over a state's subjects and gubernatorial control of moral behavior, a notion reinforced in communications with lower-level authorities. It also reflected an early modern notion of statehood that rested on a close association of the secular and religious realms.

The legal discourse analyzed here is not a matter of words alone. The terms of discipline and punishment were intimately intertwined with an intrusive course of action by early modern authorities to enforce sexual discipline within their populace. This picture is still a far cry from a well-functioning state machinery policing sexual behavior extensively. Statehood and the presence of government in local contexts relied primarily on individuals taking action. These actions were haphazard and often inefficient. In some cases, investigations were started long after the incriminating events. The scandals that surfaced disrupted lives long after the people involved had engaged in same-sex acts. Some had married. Others had died. Others had become respected members of their communities. The interventionist aspect of enforcing a strict code of moral probity had to be reconciled with another element of early modern rule, the effort to ensure social peace in the populace. Among other factors, membership in the elite cautioned authorities against taking severe measures, as will become evident in a case from Zurich, that of the Reformer Werner Steiner.

A Case of Many Tales

As a follower of the great Reformer Huldrych Zwingli (1487–1531) and a friend of Heinrich Bullinger (1504–75), Zwingli's successor, Werner Steiner (1492–1542) was a major figure in the early history of the Reformation in Switzerland.[141] He was involved in an attempt to establish the evangelical creed in Zug, a part of the Swiss Confederacy that borders on the territory of Zurich. Because of his association with the new belief, Steiner, a priest and wealthy burgher, had to find refuge in the newly reformed Zurich once religious reform had been rejected in Zug. In light of the events which surfaced in 1541, Steiner's whole life is seen to have been overshadowed by an earlier episode.

The proceedings against Steiner take us from the year 1541 to the year 1518, about the time when a monk named Martin Luther first became the object of talk in Saxony and beyond. While waiting for a Church benefice, Werner Steiner was working as steward to a priest in Schwyz, when Hans Kern, a farm laborer, passed through. During the night which followed, the two, though of widely different social origins, shared the same bed. As both men confessed separately in 1541, Steiner volunteered "to teach" his bedfellow the pleasures of mutual self-enjoyment on this occasion— pleasures which, as Steiner professed readily, equaled sexual intercourse with women.[142] With Steiner and Kern, little or no age differential came into play. Both were probably in their twenties.[143] It was the difference in their social status that shaped the encounter. The future priest, it emerged, had not only questioned the uneducated lower-class man about his amorous pursuits but had also, at least according to Kern, coaxed him to confess to Steiner.[144] By giving Kern small gifts of money and clothes, Steiner further urged Kern to consent to mutual masturbation.[145] The defendants agreed that Kern had refused the lesson in shared pleasures among men. Kern, who had come to Schwyz to secure the local priest's support for his marriage to a servant, fetched a woman known to be a prostitute. The two men presumably had sex with her, though the confessions gloss over this question. In 1541 what was at issue was whether Steiner's actions constituted sodomy or not.

Intriguingly, Steiner's chronologically organized confession recounts a gradual discovery of homosociality's erotic potential—a fascinating account of male-male desire from a period in which autobiographical texts reported such longings only rarely.[146] Steiner turned to introspection in order to explain why he, a revered and erudite member of the same elite that investigated his case, had satisfied his lust in such an unorthodox fashion. Before attempting to "teach" Kern, Steiner himself had been "taught" the practice, he stated. While traveling as a student in France, he was molested by a Frenchman who "tried to manipulate his male member" (*der hette jm an sinem mannen glid zirlen wellen*); yet Steiner shoved him away. Once in Paris, he frequently observed how Frenchmen caressed their genitalia and proceeded to follow their example. Presumably upon request, Steiner added that having sex with women did not stop him from pleasing himself in this way. Steiner's youthful initiation into a "French sexual practice" in fact triggered a lifelong interest in the erotic side of homosocial bonds. When the investigators had him recount his sexual biography, he admitted that once in a bath he was so overcome by desire for an attendant that he felt nauseated. Lust went right to the heart; this bodily sensation "repeated on him" and "made him feel like throwing up," all the more since he suppressed the impulse without seeking sexual release.[147]

Steiner's overpowering desire did not develop into an exclusive sexual persona, however. Like other Reformed priests, Steiner married and subsequently had several children with his wife. If one were to judge the success of his marriage by his family's prosperity or, more to the point, whether he was able to muster the support of his kin during the proceedings, his marriage was certainly a model alliance.[148] What distinguishes the above episodes from other same-sex encounters that I have presented in this chapter is the almost lifelong extortion that resulted from it.

Steiner did not narrate his desires voluntarily—his confession stood at the end of an extensive investigation. As in many comparable incidents, the 1541 investigation had begun over allegations other than sodomy. When Uli Kern, Hans Kern's brother, was arrested for having disrupted public peace, the authorities were loath to find that simple farmers like the Kerns had ready access to cash. They quickly discovered the source of their "income," Werner Steiner, who, over the course of many years (at least since 1527), had regularly paid large sums of hush money, barely disguised as loans or charity for a destitute family. The Kerns construed Steiner's encounters with Hans Kern as acts bordering on sodomy (they shrank away from the term with its severe associations) and exploited this information to blackmail him. By his willingness to pay, Steiner became complicit in their "reading" of the events. When the Kerns grew ever more demanding (1537–38), their benefactor brought in influential friends, Conrad Pellican (1478–1556)[149] as well as Heinrich Bullinger, to ward them off. Uli Kern authored a threatening letter that spoke of "lighting a flame under [Steiner's] behind" (*jm dem Steiner ein facklenn vnder den hindern anzünden*)—words Bullinger rightly interpreted "as if" Steiner were charged with "having committed heresy" (*luthete alls ob er kätzery begangenn*). Steiner assured Bullinger that he "had done nothing worthy of the stake" (*hette er nüdt gepflägenn, das füÿrs wert were*), encouraging his friend to inquire himself into the allegation. During a confrontation, Uli Kern toned down the charge referring to nocturnal pesterings rather than "heresy." Yet ultimately, though pressured by Zurich's most eminent theologians, the Kerns did not want to reconcile with Steiner—in one conversation, Uli Kern refused to shake Steiner's hand.[150]

Even in his final confession, however, Steiner denied categorically that his desires, let alone acts, bore any resemblance to the derided practice of anal intercourse. Clearly, homosocial bonds were erotically charged for Steiner in ways that linked masturbation and mutual masturbation. Yet male-male intimacy differed from the abhorred practice of anal sex or "florencing"—acts that, unlike his own, he presented as worthy of the stake.[151]

Far from reveling in a victorious crusade against sexual impurity, the elite became uneasy whenever sodomitical behavior became publicly known. Partially, a lack of established rules for dealing with sodomites made a response difficult. Would a Reformed city government have to handle cases of sodomy differently than in pre-Reformation times? The uneasiness among post-Reformation authorities with regard to sodomy was not attributable solely to the yet underdeveloped state of Protestant theology or the lack of legal precedents, however. Sometimes, the need to preserve the status of the ruling class also inspired caution.

In the case of Steiner, the leaders of the Reform found themselves in a dilemma. They had to decide between a personal obligation to a prominent supporter of Protestantism and a civic obligation to enforce what they understood as God's injunction. This situation was aggravated by the number of judicial authorities involved in the proceedings. Given the territorially fissured political state of the Swiss Confederacy, it is not surprising to find four cantons involved, one of which, Zurich, had adopted the Reform while the others safeguarded their Catholic beliefs with increasing fervor. Steiner's indictment gave them a welcome opportunity to point their fingers at a well-known member of one of the Reformed territories. Complying with Protestant Zurich's request for severe measures against one of the Kern brothers, the local magistrate of Catholic Schwyz sharply demanded that Zurich proceed against Werner Steiner with comparable severity. [152]

For the upper-class Steiner, the episode resulted in lifelong house arrest, a punishment mitigated upon his family's request. [153] Shortly thereafter, in 1543, he died.

Enforcing Silence on Sodomy

During the early modern period, a proliferation of words accompanied the disclosure of sodomy in law courts. At the same time, there were increasing pressures to veil one's language in the abstract as well as powerful incentives to remain silent. Raising the issue of sodomy meant airing dirty clothes in public, a battle of words in which losers and winners could not be easily made out and discretion was to be recommended. High-level experts intervened to make sure silence on sodomy prevailed. In Calvin's Geneva in 1568, the famous jurist Germain Colladon stated that it was unnecessary "to describe minutely the circumstances" of a case of same-sex intimacy between women except for saying that the punishment was "for the detestable crime of unnatural fornication." [154] Similarly, in a counsel on an investigation of witchcraft from 1647, two renowned experts from Basel, the jurist Johann Jakob Faesch (1570–1652) and Theodor Zwinger (1597–1654), leader of Basel's Church, argued vehemently not to pursue a theme that had troubled the case's previous investigators, the "sodomitical sin" (*Sodomitischen sündt*) between the supposed witch Elisabeth Hertner and her female cousin. [155] These authors concurred with all legal authorities not only in the most severe reproof of sodomy but also in opining that "as much as possible this vice be kept in secret and not be shared with the common people in order not to stimulate curiosity among young and old people and not to spread this shameful misdeed in the future, neither in the city nor in the territory [of Basel]."[156] They ordered that the unmarried woman be locked up in an asylum and instructed in religious matters. Catholic authorities acted no differently. When two boys, one sixteen and the other ten years of age, were interrogated in Lucerne in 1637 about having fondled their genitals *more sodomitico*, they were released after confession and corporal punishment. In addition, the authorities enjoined them to remain completely silent on the matter.[157]

Besides the micro- or macropolitics that motivated a censorious stance in individual cases, there was a general concern that words could not be controlled once they had been made public. Verbal caution was especially an issue in the case of executions. Before executions, the criminal's confession was commonly read aloud in public. Yet in the two recorded cases of same-sex eroticism in sixteenth-century St. Gallen, only heavily edited and abbreviated versions of the verdicts reached the public.[158] Like religious educators before the Reformation, post-Reformation authorities tended to argue for secretiveness in cases of sodomy.[159] In Lucerne in 1599 a boy of ten years was "publicly reputed to have acted in an unchristian way" (*er verlümbdet worden, daß er vnchristenlich sölle gehandlet haben*), but it remains impossible to judge which sexual act he had attempted but failed to commit, although the records clearly state that he had confessed. Yet what did he confess? This and other records evade our desire to categorize clearly.[160] The records bespeak a willingness to guard and veil what was defined by a centuries-old discourse as in need of guarding and veiling.

Postlude

In 1567 the magistrate of Basel received an inquiry concerning two youths by the small neighboring city of Delsberg (Delémont) in the Swiss Jura. Three years earlier, these adolescents had, "by the instigation of an evil man," engaged in "unchastity" with one another. While the third party, an adult man, was executed in Valengin[161] immediately after the three had been apprehended, the two adolescents were kept in prison.[162] Both the culprits' youth and the fact that, unlike the main culprit, they were natives, must have weighed against an execution. Now, three years later, the magistrates wanted to close the case.

The Delsberg officials decided to obtain expert legal advice in the matter. The question they asked through their envoys to the council of Basel was straightforward enough: Should the two boys be punished by being burned at the stake or should they be pilloried, flogged, and banished from the city's territory?[163] Not long after the visit, Basel councilmen responded in a letter that they had discussed the matter amongst themselves, but "could not remember that such a crime had been committed here"—a rather formulaic response, to be sure, and one which signaled noninvolvement.[164] Instead, they turned to expert advice themselves, the faculty of law at Basel's university. They added the professors' statement (*Ratschlag*) to their letter while declining to comment further.

In line with common legal opinion, the professors argued for clemency in the case of the Delsberg adolescents. Quoting the relevant statute of the *Constitutio Criminalis Carolina* on "unchastity against the order of nature," these experts rehearsed the enormity of the crime in rather conventional wording—a crime that cries to heaven for divine justice and a crime that had caused the destruction of cities and peoples. Yet even in the case of such a "horrendous" incident (*greüwel*), they said, mitigating circumstances had to be taken into consideration.[165] Intent emerged as a central category in the experts' *consilium*. Not only were the two adolescents merely fifteen— "youth being inclined to commit vice more out of simplicity and lack of reason than out of evil intent" (*Diewill die jugent vonn einfalt vnnd vnverstandt mher dan vß boßhait vnnd fürsatz zun lastern genaigt*)—but also, the youths had been prompted by a third party's "devilish command" (*teuffelische anweyßung vnnd anstifftung*). They had willingly collaborated with the authorities in the proceedings and were not known to have committed the same act since. Without having interrogated the culprits, the professors discerned from written evidence that the two boys had acted out of "ignorance" (*vnverstandt*) and were, therefore, likely to be susceptible to future "improvement" (*besserung*). Having rejected the death penalty, the professors stopped short of suggesting a specific retribution and left the assessment of a sentence to the Delsberg authorities.

This episode is worthy of closer scrutiny from the perspective of legal history as a history of communication. In the context of sixteenth-century jurisdiction, adjudicating a case and meting out punishments meant negotiating between well-established legal customs on the one hand and law codes on the other hand. In 1438 Enea Silvio Piccolomini, the later Pope Pius II, had drawn a picture of legal life in Basel as a community where "custom is more in use than codified law."[166] By 1567, the legal system had changed considerably. The case of the youths from Delsberg shows that the notion of codified law was now very much on the minds of the authorities. Magistrates of a small urban community like Delsberg turned to a befriended city like Basel in order to gain access to the latest legal expertise.

In Basel itself, specialists from the local institution of higher learning were approached as experts.[167] At the same time, the old customs had not disappeared altogether and continued to shape the ways in which magistrates enforced the law.[168]

This episode drives home forcefully how changing patterns of communication were of supreme importance in forging the legal discourse on sodomy. Legal experts cast their opinions in a rhetoric that claimed persuasive force via a hodgepodge of registers ranging from Biblical references to law codes. They engaged a general discourse of moral improvement and also adopted the tone of religious didacticism. They provided a standard language and, at the same time, instructed the recipients of their advice on how to act. Insisting on general rules of procedure, they also argued against a judiciary practice of mere retribution and in favor of circumstantial circumspection. Yet importantly, within this professional standard deemed fit for Protestant communities, they also argued for the authorities' silence on matters of sodomy. While the Delsberg authorities had sought advice only with regard to whether the sentence ought to be more or less severe, the experts strongly favored a more secretive approach. They proffered an argument widespread in religious didacticism before the Reformation, namely that public punishments would "implant the seed" to the many "who otherwise would have not thought of such an abominable sin," adding that it was better to "silence this vice completely than to make it known." They even ended on a terminological note, stating that this is why sodomy is called "the mute sin."[169]

In many territories, the Reformation resulted in an increase of power for the ruling elites. Only rarely did post-Reformation authorities become more active against same-sex sexual offenders, however.[170] Nonetheless, there was a noticeable shift in the politics of sodomy in German-speaking Europe. During the course of the sixteenth century, the legal discourse on sodomy was silenced in many ways and public exposure of sodomy became rare. State officials increasingly espoused a rhetoric of disgust and a politics of silence reminiscent of a medieval theology of sin. The courtroom became the site where this expansive vision of rule—a rule committed to the control of acts and words—met actors who frequently resisted applying these terms to themselves. At work in many delicts, this discrepancy was particularly stringent in the case of sodomy—a transgression whose verbalization excluded self-description. Yet punitiveness pertains not only to the official responses but also to that of local communities. Though erotic companionship among men was, as far as one can tell, not uncommon, their sexual acts, once unearthed, were held in harsh condemnation at the local level.

What sixteenth-century court records reveal among other things is the power accorded to certain words, especially words as severe as those referring to same-sex sexual acts. In the second part of this book, I will turn to words spoken and written in spite, that is, with the intent to insult or harm. Sodomy defamations were an extremely powerful way of vilifying a person, one that, as I will show, permeated many social and textual arenas.

Part Two

ACTING WORDS

5

Defamation as Practice

Defamation provided speakers and writers with a vast and diffuse forum for voicing the "unspeakable sin of sodomy." Court documents with their narrative explicitness were virtually inaccessible to the public, and didactic texts had to veil the forbidden in order to provide exemplars for the moral life. Whereas entertaining texts frequently avoided representations of sodomy, the defamatory mode of speech served ironically as an educational tool—a popular vehicle to circulate concepts associated with sodomy. Yet how can one approach defamatory speech within a conceptual framework like mine that focuses on different forms of representation? Can we assume a referential relation between categories of sexual acts and linguistic vehicles of derision? Is not the practice of defamation by its very nature irreconcilably far removed from the sexual practices derided in the verbal act? Does not defamation thrive on falsification and distortion, and escape any sort of "reality check"? For all these reasons, sexual defamation has not been a widely discussed topic among historians of sexuality. Although early modern historians have devoted increasing attention to verbal feuds in small communities, they have done so primarily from an anthropological perspective.[1] Their findings have rarely been analyzed from the point of view of learning what these verbal acts contribute to our understanding of the "sexual system," to engage a term coined by Isabel Hull. Historians of sexuality, though interested in discourse, have avoided these utterances as ephemeral and instead focused on more canonical texts such as religious, legal, and medical commentaries. Following Alan Bray's seminal work and Eve Kosofsky Sedgwick's theoretical lead, scholars such as Jonathan Goldberg, Winfried Schleiner, Cameron McFarlane, and Carolyn Dinshaw have recently started to explore the topic of sodomy vilifications.[2] From a variety of perspectives, they have demonstrated how the defamatory structures discourse on same-sex eroticism. "The evidence of same-sex desire is never far removed from the evidence of homophobia," observes Cameron McFarlane.[3] As I will show, this observation is especially pertinent to the times "before sexuality," that is, before the medico-scientific complex gained a central position for defining the sexual.

We cannot be certain what sixteenth-century people associated with terms like "bugger," "catamite," or "sodomite," any more than we can assess what modern-day speakers of English picture when they are exposed to the equivalents of these catch-all names. Whether slanderous remarks were intended to invoke the sexual per se or not, ideas of same-sex sexuality attached themselves to a variety of practices. By means of accusations, mentions of sodomy were introduced into a wide range of textual milieus, both written and oral. While name-calling targeting female-female sexuality was virtually nonexistent in early modern Germany and Switzerland, defamation created an arena where fantasies about male-male sexuality could roam under cover of denouncement. Condemning sodomy or defaming sodomites protected the detractor from association with the derided sexual practice (although, of course, the defamer risked negative responses by the community or court action). In other words, by means of slander, malice, calumny, and libel, the so-called unspeakable was spoken in many contexts and many people gained at least some degree of familiarity with same-sex symbolism.

Modes of accusation—the manifold appropriations of defamatory topoi in social and political contexts—are part and parcel of the stuff from which history is made. Yet investigating defamation means asking a reader to depart from established ways of thinking about the past. For the historian, it means to move from history as that which *truly happened* to what was *plausibly imagined to have happened*. Raphael Samuel has given this turn to semiotics in writing history a venerable pedigree—a pedigree encompassing some of the most innovative pieces of scholarship in nineteenth- and twentieth-century historiography. "Reading the signs," as he argues, "transfers attention from the study of 'objective' reality to the categories in and through which it was perceived, from collective consciousness to cognitive codes, from social being to the symbolic order."[4] Viewed thus, the question of whether sexual slurs were in fact true or not holds less interest than the cultural matrix which allowed defamatory topoi to gain credence among contemporaries.

This is not to say that one can never assess the truth-content of sexual slurs nor that one should not try to do so. Rather, it is to state that the charge of sodomy rarely relied on voyeurism. Whoever seeks to gauge the historical truth-content of sexual insinuations risks embracing polemical thinking where it is most slippery, on its own terms. Significantly, sexual defamation operated by sowing the seeds of belief precisely where what actually happened could hardly be validated. As a rule, sex acts are fleeting by nature, leaving few traces in the archive. Frequently, therefore, contemporaries were no better equipped than today's historians to assess what happened "in bed." The secrecy of sexual acts is precisely why sexual slurs are so useful a weapon. They make "known" that which eludes scrutiny. As Cynthia Herrup writes in her recent account of the spectacular case brought against the Second Earl of Castlehaven in seventeenth-century England: "Intuiting whether sodomitical acts inspired these accusations or were convenient, even disingenuous, afterthoughts to other suspicions is less important than recognizing the social utility of sodomy as an accusation."[5]

As I have already described in previous chapters, in early modern Europe, the terrain delineated by sodomy was an expedient vehicle of defamation for a host of reasons—religious beliefs, notions of purity, and codes of masculinity among them. Like charges of heresy, sodomy's sister concept, accusations of sodomy tended to set the individual apart from the body social (without which little sense of self could—and can—be gained). What is more, sodomy allegations often impaired whole communities. As I will argue in the chapter that follows, sodomy was a particularly disruptive and therefore potent suspicion undermining the fabric of hierarchically organized social relations. Such accusations could be effective, because sodomites were not viewed as a distinct category of human beings. Potentially, all Christians, especially Christian men, could act as sodomites and be typed as a *ketzer* or "sexual heretic."

I will delve into a variety of slanderous forms, ranging from face-to-face invectives to epistolary slanders—interactions that have left a written record because they led to court proceedings. The defamatory will emerge as a highly regulated form of speech, replete with clichés of vilification—a violent form of verbal interaction that induced the state to try to regulate the phenomenon. Yet not all groups were equally targeted in early modern society. In fifteenth- and sixteenth-century Switzerland, sodomy was a charge especially associated with foreigners, Italians most of all, and with the elites, that is, a charge often exchanged between members of the elite or leveled against the elite.[6]

Significantly, sodomy accusations began to circulate more widely at the very time when Church reformers launched, and subsequently elaborated, a theology of *sodomia*; when sexual accusations, sodomy among them, became a preferred weapon in the Church's fight against what orthodox theologians saw as heresies.

A Genealogy of Sodomy Defamation

Sodomy defamations follow a historical trajectory. During the medieval period, suspicions of sodomitical doings surfaced in clashes over Church reform among members of the ecclesiastical elite. "In the eleventh century, the western clergy, Europe's intellectual elite, reinvented itself," to borrow a formulation by Dyan Elliott—a reinvention unthinkable without the polemical as a vehicle for reconceptualizing the Church as well as theology.[7] In the polemical wars between proponents of clerical celibacy on the one hand and defenders of clerical concubinage on the other hand, the latter group sometimes labeled the former as sodomites, thereby collapsing celibacy and sodomy. At issue were what represented abuses to the former faction—clerical marriage, simony, a lax sexual morale—and well-founded traditions to the latter. As a result of the conflicts over Church reform, sins like sodomy and simony were grouped together—a cluster that would survive several centuries into the age of the Reformation as an association of financial with sexual misdoings.[8]

In fact, polemicists on both sides of the clashes over Church reform promulgated images of Sodom, sins they held in abhorrence. While Peter Damian, arguably the most brilliant among the proreform theologians, saw *sodomia* (defined as masturbation, mutual masturbation, intercrural, and anal intercourse) among clerics as an evil "cancer" in the holy edifice of the Church,[9] the antireformers and defenders of clerical marriage argued that sexual sins of all kinds, but those against nature most notably, were the obvious outcome of enforcing prohibitions against marriage among the clergy.[10]

Yet this same stigma was also applied outside of the clergy. Soon rulers were targeted as sodomites. During the schism between the empire and the papacy, propapal writers assailed King Henry IV (1054–1106) as an opponent of Church reform. In addition to the reproach of multiple adulteries (motivated by his wanting to divorce his first wife), Henry was said to have engaged in incest and *sodomia*. There is no indication as to whether the latter charge signifies "homosexual relations," as Bernd Schütte suggests. Wido of Ferrara hints at such a transgression when writing that Henry "took pleasure in the frequent company of boys and very old men" (*Gaudebat multum consortio puerorum et maxime venustorum*), but refrains from the charge when he states there is not enough evidence to say whether these meetings occurred "in vice" (*sed utrum id vicio fieret, ut aliqui confinxerunt, non satis compertum erat*).[11] In his biography of Pope Innocent IV, the Franciscan Nicollò da Calvi (d. 1273) denounced Emperor Frederick II (reigned 1220–50) as a heretic. Not content with excessive heterosexual intercourse, Frederick supposedly turned to practicing and "openly preached" (*aperte predicabat*) the "sodomitical vice." This reproach, presented as Frederick's ultimate violation of God's order, must have had resonance for an audience familiar with this ruler's interest in cultural exchange with Muslims, who, as I will show, were often typed as sodomites. [12] Political alliances also lent themselves to suspicions of sexually illicit friendships—as when the German King Louis of Bavaria (1314–47) and his rival, King Frederick, known as the Fair, formed a politically motivated union in 1325. [13]

The polemical sword forged in the eleventh century was then turned against the ecclesiastical elite itself. Famously, the French King Philip IV, the Fair (1285–1314), and his counselors successfully adopted this form of detraction. In the case against Pope Boniface VIII (1294–1303), a vague sexual insinuation (1297) materialized into shaky evidence (after 1303). [14] During the posthumous legal proceedings, the antipapal party mustered depositions from witnesses in Boniface's entourage as well as references to a general *fama* according to which Boniface had engaged in the crime of sodomy (*sodomitico crimine*), all aiming to demonize the pope as a heretic and sexual rogue (whose transgressions spanned many of the practices subsumed under *sodomia*, with the exception of bestiality). [15] A similar medley of accusations—heresy, simony, sodomy—proved effective when the French crown initiated proceedings against a whole order, the Knights Templar, after 1305. [16] This amalgam of accusations was so successful as to be copied in other European countries. [17] As James Brundage notes, "the charge of sodomy became a more or less routine ingredient of political and social invective just when secular penalties for homosexual practices were becoming markedly more savage." [18] "Routine" as a term captures well the topical clusters of associations in these episodes. It is less apt, however, to indicate the brutish force with which these accusations entered the political arena, so novel and so strong was this defamatory strategy. [19]

Whether members of the clergy or secular rulers became the objects of vilification, sodomy was a charge specifically associated with the elites. Moreover, sodomy accusations were often enmeshed in political conflicts. [20] In the secular realm, insulting strategies that originated in ecclesiastical conflicts might in fact have been reinforced by an indigenous tradition of vilifying men who (supposedly) had sex with men. But by the time vernacular law codes like the *Schwabenspiegel* (c. 1275) mandated severe punishments against slander and vernacular courtly literature of the thirteenth century featured slurs against "heretics," Christian terminology had superseded these Germanic forms of detraction beyond recognition. [21]

At any rate, by the fifteenth century, accusations of sodomy entered upon the stage of urban politics in the north. As I discussed in chapter 2, they were used against Burgundian mercenaries, nobles such as the Alsatian Richard Puller von Hohenburg, and Zurich's mayor Hans Waldmann. But they also resonate with communal concerns about honor and suspicious behavior, as analyzed in chapter 4.

Fama *and* Diffamatio

The notion of *fama*, an individual's reputation, and *diffamatio*, the attempt to strip someone of this reputation by means of verbal insults or injurious remarks, are interdependent. *Fama* was infinitely more meaningful in early modern European cultures than in today's societies in the West—and consequently *diffamatio* was more charged as a social practice. *Fama* was understood spatially as a person's social extension, that which determined his or her standing within a community. Like property, a good *fama* could be gained or lost. A vernacular handbook of law from circa 1400 stipulated not only that detraction was a mortal sin (if committed in the absence of the detracted), but also that it was worse than robbing a person of all his or her goods.[22] Theologians valued a good *fama* highly because it was said to keep people from committing sins. Its perceived loss could have serious consequences, all the more so since *fama* was deeply enmeshed in power relations and difference of class and gender. Threatening a person's reputation was, therefore, considered to be a heinous crime.

In Lucerne in the fourteenth century, if somebody was tried for having "injured" somebody's honor by the accusation "You fucked a cow"—the example given in the council's manual—the punishment amounted either to a fine of one pound or a one-month banishment of one mile from the city. In 1395 the city council mandated in the future to take such breaches of a citizen's honor more seriously.[23] Two and a half decades later, the council refined this measure by differentiating between detraction in secret (*hinterred*) and face-to-face verbal duels (*zureden*). Whereas the latter received the aforementioned punishment, the former was punished according to its gravity and the council's discretion.[24]

In 1414 Thöni Diener, an innkeeper in Lucerne, was anonymously rumored (*verlûmdet*) to have "buggered"—the record features the Italianizing verb *pûlscherûnet*—a man in Milan.[25] The magistrate of Lucerne ruled to clear Diener of the charge.[26] Although the councilmen heard no case, it is nevertheless evident that they were aware of the rumors. News damaging to Diener's *fama*, traveling by word of mouth, aroused the authorities' attention and entered the written record when his case was discussed during a council meeting.

Despite the council's intervention, Diener's ill-repute persisted for quite a while. Eight years later, in 1422, the council addressed his case for a second time. Diener appeared in person and swore that he had never committed an act of sodomy but that a thief had called him a "sodomite" (*pulscherun*) in Milan.[27] After first denying the slur verbally, he had proceeded to beat his accuser and "would have liked to stab him" (*wolt* [*den*] *erstochen han*). It was decided to put the case to rest and not to inquire further into the matter: "The Councilmen want rather to believe him [than not]; they will view him as a respectable man and he shall be in good standing." Diener's oath put closure on the matter.[28] The episode makes clear that slanderous words often led to violent actions. This was one of the reasons why city councils took such keen interest in speech utterances, acting as mediators in conflicts that threatened to disrupt the urban peace.[29]

The council had to convene yet another time to address a slanderous remark directed at Diener. A burgher was said to have called him a sodomite (*ketzer*) and added, "as one knew from Lombardy" (*es wurd wol kuntlich von Lamparten her vs*). In 1433, said burgher had to swear an oath before the council stating that he knew nothing of Diener other than that he was honorable. The council seems to have grown tired of having to deal with the same charge over the course of almost twenty years. Both men, the slanderer and the slandered, were fined ten florins.[30] News about words uttered on an Italian street thus triggered several investigations into a townsman's respectability north of the Alps. Fellow burghers took sexual slurs as indicators of actions and passed them on by word of mouth. Yet spoken words were also able to exonerate those whose honor was damaged. An oath did much to establish one's respectability.

In Brother Berthold's manual, the author distinguished between detraction in "words and letters"—in other words, between spoken and written slander.[31] An anonymous writer from the mid-fifteenth century who devoted a series of sermons to the topic of detraction listed a panoply of slanderous forms: whispers, street-talk, public gossiping, *libelli famosi* or "insulting letters" (*schendtbrief*), defamatory songs, and, lastly, nonverbal communication such as finger-pointing, conspicuous silence, and so forth: "Wherever people gather, as in courts and inns, they mostly talk to diminish one another's honor and good name."[32] The sin of detraction, in this writer's view, thus comprises not only face-to-face interactions but also written statements circulated in *schendtbrief* or *libelli famosi*. People, he says, "post [these letters] on Church doors, throw them in houses or on streets so that they will be found and read, and damage people."[33] The catalogue also lists songs "in which a person's good reputation is tainted" that "are carried to many areas and cities,"[34] drawing our attention specifically to the widespread wanderings of the minstrels of musical calumny.[35] Only one kind of detraction seems to escape this author's listing, *picturae famosae* or defaming images.[36]

Depending on the type of accusation and the status of the participants, *libelli famosi* offered a distinct advantage over an orally transmitted verbal exchange.[37] Distributed anonymously in public spaces, written accusations provided the safety of anonymity to the detractor as opposed to face-to-face encounters, which, in village or urban communities, rarely happened without witnesses. Anonymity was crucial if social superiors or the powerful were targeted. Viewed from the perspective of the defamed, anonymous defamations, in whatever form, must have inspired anger and fear since the personal attack could not be matched with an equally personal counter-attack.

At the end of the fifteenth century, the council of Cologne first undertook an investigation when it learned that the "unspeakable mute sin" (*unsprechliche[] stumme[] sunde[]*) was rampant in the city.[38] Immediately, a commission was appointed to collect information on this serious matter and asked to levy punishments on the culprits, surely an unusual measure for a German city. Yet the council's original intention to intervene with force was quickly replaced by an attempt to cover up the commission's key finding, namely that a late former councilman, Johann Greeffroide, had stood at the center of the accusations. Anonymous letters leveling sodomy charges against him had been distributed publicly.[39] A priest at one of the parish churches had called attention to this breach of the divine sexual order after one of Greeffroide's sexual partners had confessed to him on several occasions. During the investigation, he did not reveal the sinners' names but described the main wrongdoer as a "powerful" and "dead man" who "was married and had children": He "used to be a member of the Council and belonged to [the city's] rulers."[40] The priest's tirade was ultimately censored. Civic authorities were alarmed and hushed up the affair.

Defamatory practices belong neither solely to the oral sphere of social interaction nor to the sphere of literacy. Often, defamation involved both oral and written practices of communication: strife in the streets ended up in the courtroom and therefore entered the archives; everyday conflicts involved literate media such as letters, pamphlets, and the infamous *libelli famosi*; spoken charges were taken up and perpetuated by urban chronicles; highly literate sparrings among the elite were passed on by word of mouth.

Some who had suffered loss of their *fama* took their detractors to court. In 1490, in a rural area near Lucerne (Hiltisrieden), one parish priest brought an accusation against another "that he was a heretic and had committed heresy with his servant who was stabbed thereafter."[41] Conveniently, his alleged sexual partner could not be summoned to testify since he had died as a result of the stabbing. The defamed priest brought his case before the secular court in the city, apparently convinced that the judges would rule in his favor and punish the slandering colleague. The judges ruled that the defamed priest had to vacate his office and leave the territory. It may be that the Hiltisrieden priest's claim of having been slandered was ill-founded, or the judges may have assumed that the accusations of "sexual heresy" were in fact well-deserved. At any rate, as a cleric, the defamed was exempt from more serious punishment and thus suffered only banishment.

Whereas in the preceding case the defamed priest sought protection from a court against a detractor, in many if not most cases, ill-repute itself triggered a judicial investigation.[42] When sodomy charges against a canon from Hildesheim became known, for instance, ecclesiastical authorities undertook to investigate his *fama*. The cleric was suspected of having committed the "horrifying and detestable vice of sodomy" (*horrendo illo et detestabili vicio sodomie*). The context provides no further information as to the precise nature of his alleged misconduct, but we are well informed as to how the canon's superiors proceeded; the judges interrogated fellow canons—interrogations that were apparently conducted with great care. Subsequently, the *patres* of his order, having listened to witnesses' statements and consulted legal experts, offered a written assessment of the canon's *fama*. The allegations were found to be false. His personal integrity was vindicated in a letter that carefully outlines the legal procedures followed. This document was preserved as an example of correct judicial process to be followed in cases in which potential loss of *fama* required legal action.[43]

Defamation gives insight into a highly gendered arena of verbal exchange. Verbal assaults were based on notions of sexual difference. The assignation of injurious epithets varied from sex to sex, for instance. Evidence abounds that, across Europe and including the German lands, "whore" was the label most frequently attached to women in injurious exchanges, both between women and between men and women.[44] When men (or, more rarely, women) accused men of sodomy, the body became the battleground for determining reputation just as when female physical integrity was scrutinized in charges against women.[45] Whereas the idiom of verbal aggression drew on the sexual for both sexes, the injurious register as deployed by men and women does not correspond. Female integrity centered primarily on sexual behavior, whereas male reputation occupied a wider range of values. Unlike female "whoredom," male "sodomy" featured associations of male homosociality, reminiscent of powerful political, ecclesiastical, or professional all-male institutions or gatherings. Accusations of treason, bribes, and similar breaches were frequently associated with sodomy defamations, reflecting the superior social position of men in early modern society. Sodomy defamations, in short, carried multiple layers of significations that do not find a parallel in accusations of whoredom. With few exceptions, "sexual heresy" was an all-male insult, professed mostly by men and addressed mostly to men. By comparison, female sexual autonomy hardly entered the ideological formations of early modern Europe (unless women held significant power, as in sixteenth-century and eighteenth-century France).[46]

Recent studies suggest convincingly that, contrary to stereotypical notions of womanhood in medieval and early modern Europe, which marked the "sins of the tongue" as typically female, both men and women were active in the culture of defamation.[47] Yet men insulted mostly men, while women defamed mostly women. Only rarely are women reported to have invoked the severe sexual register associated with sodomy against men. A man from Entlebuch, a rural area within Lucerne's territory, brought a case before the council that had been instigated by a woman. He claimed to have been vilified as a "heretic" (kätzer). It is clear that we are dealing with a sexual slur, yet whether it is homosexual activity, bestiality, or both that became a vehicle of verbal attack remains obscure. The young woman who had supposedly so labeled him denied she had committed such a verbal breach of communal harmony. Rumors surfaced that she was "a witch and an evil woman" (einn hex vnd einn böß wîb). She was imprisoned and tortured to extract a confession. Though no evidence was found against her, she was banned from the Swiss Confederacy.[48]

Defamation in all its forms was an important vehicle for venting social or political dissatisfaction. In 1514 Jakob Nadler, a mercenary, was summoned to the tagsatzung, regular meetings held by the Swiss Confederacy. He was known to have criticized Swiss rulers for siding with Matthaeus Schiner (c. 1465–1522), bishop of Sitten (Valais), against France. According to an informer, he had stated that "the king of France has maintained me for twenty-seven years, and I prefer to serve him than the buttfuckers." And he added: "The bishop of Valais is a buttfucker and a liar." He also volunteered intimate knowledge of the bishop's and other clerics' sex life, especially the pope's: "He [the pope] kept a boy whom he florenced, and he inspired the boy to wish to become pope. And if he became pope, he would let his dick—with which he has ridden [i.e., had intercourse with] donkeys—hang through the throne." After invoking the stereotypical link between Lombardy, a part of Italy, and sodomy[49]—"the Lombards are buttfuckers and heretics [sodomites] and he does not want to serve them"—Nadler articulated a full-fledged political ideology. He expressed a credo that rested on the complete division of secular and ecclesiastical power: "and the pope should live without the king and [only] bless holy water."[50] This lengthy and detailed diatribe, full of spicy words, weds popular political ideology to sexual defamation. Two sexual depravities were alluded to, bestiality and sodomy, both portrayed as clerical sins. Nadler invoked Rome as the site of the Holy See and artfully reinforced the Italian localization of sodomy by using the verb "to florence" to describe male-male intercourse.

Jakob Nadler's verbose vituperations are situated in a very specific and highly politicized context. During the Franco-German Wars in northern Italy (1494–1527)—wars that relied heavily on the manpower and military expertise of Swiss mercenaries—accusations of sodomy became a convenient method of scapegoating, commonly applied to unpopular superiors, and used to justify resistance against military discipline or to characterize adversaries.[51] According to the Swiss chronicler Fridolin Baldi, the Pavia campaign of 1512 was directed against "heretics"—meaning "sodomites."[52] In the context of the Italian wars, at least from a northern perspective, to defame a man as a sodomite amounted to suggesting that he was a traitor, submitting sexually and politically to foreign forces. While Arnold Esch suggests that the simple folk took these associations literally,[53] Jakob Nadler's case is a welcome reminder that sodomy accusations used for political ends were not reserved for the elites.

Yet the gist of Nadler's accusations was also in tune with Swiss foreign policy. Due to long-standing political ties with France and large payments to Swiss leaders (*Pensionen*), the majority of cantons sided with the French king and opposed the imperial-Milanese alliance against France. Bern was one of the few cantons to support the anti-French alliance. Around 1496 a certain Lienhart of Grünenmatt criticized the Bernese for forming an alliance with "the buttfuckers [i.e., Italians] and Germans [*Schwaben*]." Beyond the cluster of treason, sexual deviance, and bribes alluded to here, the accusations referred mostly to questions of political alliance: notwithstanding a long-standing loyalty to the French king, Bern's political elite were rumored to be conspiring with the German emperor. Lienhart alludes to the city's alliance with Count Ludovico Sforza, named il Moro, of Milan (1452/80–1508) and the German Emperor Maximilian I (1493–1519), claiming that such an allegiance threatened Swiss unity (many people held that Swiss mercenaries should not fight each other). Lienhart's suspicions and reprimands are cast in graphic physical images replete with suggestions of obscene bodily contact: "they should kiss the Roman king [the king of the Holy Roman Empire]," alias "swine," "in the ass."[54] Individuals and communities were typed like their political allies and defamed accordingly. The allegiances of mercenaries thus became part of intra-Swiss conflict. When encountering Anton Brügler, a Bernese citizen, the knight Dietrich von Endlisperg from Fribourg said, "if he [is] Bernese, then he is also a Lombard and, with permission, a buttfucker." As a punishment, the knight was ordered never to set foot in Bernese territory again.[55]

Swiss court cases after 1500 testify to the popularity of notions defaming the Latin Other. In Zurich, a young man insulted a molester by saying that "he fit well into the *welschland,* [since] he was a buttfucker [*arsbruter*]."[56] (*Welschland* refers to countries where Romance languages are spoken; here, it is a derogatory reference to Italy.) One hospital inmate accused another, who was *welsch,* of wanting "to love him through the ass."[57] In the territory of Lucerne, during a brawl, a French-speaking man from Fribourg was maligned as perverted—"You *wallch,* you are a depraved person, a thief and a villain."[58] When the local authorities appeared on the scene, they added slander to insult by stating, "Having to do with that *walch* amounts to fucking a mare."[59] In close encounters with people from regions where a Romance language was spoken, suspicions of sexual misdoings surfaced frequently. In court trials, a slanderous concoction surfaced that connected theft, bestiality, and sodomy and preferentially targeted the foreign. After having been seized by the authorities in Zurich for theft, Jacob vom Schloss was found to have had a string of lucrative erotic liaisons with men his superior in age and social status: notaries, academics, and merchants, mostly in France. In the dock, he attributed his ruin to the *welsch.* Having confessed that the first man to have seduced him in Geneva was a notary at the court of Savoy, Jacob proceeded to warn "every honest man . . . that he does not send his children to the *welsch,* neither the French, the Savoyards nor others, since they try hard to cheat us Germans of our children [literally: "shit on our children"] and introduce such viciousness to us."[60] These instances show how, on the one hand, defamations were tailored to the specific circumstances of their utterance. On the other hand, their repetitive nature reminds us that verbal slurs were far from original. They drew on a well-established reservoir of injurious expressions.

Defamation is predicated on the power of recognition and the force of repetition. In this, it is much more structured than gossip.[61] The familiarly packaged can be processed with ease, or, viewed from the other end, the well-known tropes of defamation are easily tagged on to a variety of events or people. Under certain circumstances and independently of its truth content, defamation acquired an extraordinary power, as in the following episode from Solothurn.

Sodomiticus Redivivus

In 1515 the authorities of Zurich felt compelled to inform the council of Solothurn—a small city not far from Bern and a full member of the Confederacy since 1481—about a capital offense that had occurred on Zurich's soil.[62] Apprehended in Zurich for theft, the aforementioned Jacob vom Schloss from Lucerne had implicated Ulrich Conrad of Solothurn by his confession. Zurich officials may have been aware of the fact that their letter indicted a member of one of the city's most wealthy and powerful families. Ulrich Conrad (1477/78–1541) was a canon at the collegiate church of St. Ursus (where he would rise to the position of associate provost). His brother, Niklaus Conrad, served for many years (as in 1515) as *Schultheiss* (*scultetus*), the city's highest-ranking official. In fact, during the Italian wars, Niklaus Conrad represented a type of locally based power broker involved in the grand scheme of European politics.[63]

According to the executed sodomite, Ulrich Conrad had repeatedly invited him to dinner. The adolescent's educator, a chaplain at St. Ursus, warned the youth about taking his fellow canon up on the offer. He alluded to rumors—a *geschrey* or *clamor*—about sexual relations between Conrad and an organ player from Büren whom common *fama* regarded as sexually suspect, though unjustly so, as this canon said. Jakob, already familiar with the practice of same-sex sexuality at this point, may have taken these warnings as a hint. Invited another time, he had dinner with Conrad, stayed overnight, and Conrad "committed heresy on him" (*ketzertj jnn ouch*).[64]

Solothurn authorities did not take the matter lightly. Immediately after the letter from Zurich arrived, the council convened and decided to forward "this very severe matter" (*negocium quod nobis gravisimum visum est*)[65] to the bishop. Conrad went to Lausanne with two letters of support, one by the city's council and another by the chapter of St. Ursus, both written in such a way as to dispose the bishop in his favor. The chapter even called the scoundrel's confession "the most severe lies" (*gravissimorum mendatiorum*) against a member of an "honorable family, native to this town" (*honesta familia huiusce oppidi ortus*).[66] Soon thereafter, Conrad returned from the bishop's court with a letter nullifying the charge and certifying his personal integrity.

Certificates of honor emerge as an important legal device for formally restoring one's honor, available primarily to the clergy or the upper echelons of the social hierarchy.[67] We know little about how or whether these documents were used in daily interactions, but if Conrad had hoped the bishop's letter would clear his name and permanently silence the rumors about him, he had underestimated the pertinaciousness of *sotto voce* talk or the obstinacy of communal memory. Subsequently, over the course of almost a decade, suspicions hovered about Conrad—suspicions that surfaced from time to time in the form of slurs.

In 1524, nine years after obtaining the certificate, Conrad decided to corroborate its validity and initiated legal proceedings for libel before the council.[68] For members of the elite like Conrad, the courtroom offered an arena to clear one's name of a charge as damaging to one's honor as sodomy. According to the protocol, during an informal gathering, a chaplain at St. Ursus, Jost Zigerli, had intimated that Conrad and the aforementioned organ player had engaged in sex.[69] Taken to court, Zigerli named a superior, a canon called Bartholomäus von Spiegelberg (d. 1541),[70] as having initiated the detraction by vilifying Conrad as a "sodomite" (*kätzer*).[71] Subsequently, Conrad also took Spiegelberg to court for slander. It is both the publicness of these accusations—the fact that the verbal attacks had happened in the presence of others (*under ougen*) but without the slandered being present[72]—and the urban locations where the slurs occurred—the places of attack were recorded with great accuracy—that left Conrad apparently little choice other than to take his slanderers to court.[73]

The severity of the accusations in this case became evident when defendants were hesitant to talk about this "monstrosity" in the public of the courtroom. As a capital offense, sodomy was, as both defendants stated, *malefitzisch*, so every utterance with regard to these events touched on the lives of others.[74] Cautiously, the councilors worked toward urban peace. The proceedings were recorded with the greatest care. Every step and every maneuver were documented in great detail, so severe were the charges and so prominent the litigants.

In separate trials, the defendants proffered strikingly similar defense strategies. First, they questioned the authority of the court in this matter, suggesting the case be transferred from the council to ecclesiastical jurisdiction. Asked to comply with the proceedings, they were willing to collaborate with their secular "masters," the councilors. Compared with the vociferous resistance to secular juridical authority in cases involving clerics during the fifteenth century, the council's drive for legal authority met little resistance—not surprising given the close ties between the urban community and St. Ursus.[75] Second, the defendants downplayed their own participation. Both Spiegelberg and Zigerli contended that no enmity existed between their own and Conrad's family. The defendants also portrayed their part as mere participation in a chorus of libelous rumors. More to the point, one of them argued that Conrad should clear himself first of libels voiced in the chapter itself—a reproach to which Conrad responded that he had not been present, had not heard about the slanders, and therefore could not have taken the libelers to court.

Despite the almost material qualities with which theologians and others invested personal reputation, honor is obviously a muddy terrain. In this case, it was hard to find a culprit who could be held responsible for damage to Conrad's honor. Yet legal procedure and a prestigious family's strategy required that such a culprit be found. Otherwise, nobody could have formally cleared Conrad of the accusations. A solution worthy of Solomon was found. Zigerli confessed to having slandered Conrad only from hearsay; the plaintiff bore the financial burden in this case in order not to further delay a settlement. Spiegelberg stated that he could not remember his insults; should he have vilified Conrad, however, his verbal attack referred to nothing but the "affair" of 1515 which the bishop's letter had already nullified. Ironically, the insinuation that Conrad had had sex with an organ player from Büren dropped out of sight entirely. Thus, everybody saved face, and the personal honor of all parties remained intact.[76]

Ulrich Conrad's court case against his detractors does not match the demise of a Hohenburg or a Waldmann in historical-theatrical splendor (chapter 2). On a small scale, though, this incident illustrates what happened when a member of a local elite was implicated in the charge of sodomy. The trial against Conrad's supposed detractors reveals that a community was actively engaged with sexual misdoings in the form of rumors. Once invoked, whether rightly or wrongly, sodomy was a charge that stuck to the person thus defamed for a long time. By breaking codes of behavior and disrupting public peace, verbal offense posed a danger to both political order and social cohesion. The fact that the derision cast on superiors and peers was transmitted with painstaking accuracy demonstrates that the authorities took these verbal transgressions seriously. These acts of speech are transmitted to us because face-to-face slander invaded, satirized, transgressed, and, in some cases, provoked court proceedings—especially when the slander involved members of the elite, who were more likely to go to court.

Not surprisingly, therefore, early modern rulers seriously attempted to regulate disruptive verbal behavior. Their attempts attest not only to concerns about the health of the polity, but also to an increase in their disciplining power over burghers and subjects. Like Solothurn, many early modern communities adopted legislation to control slander. Councils passed laws that imposed severe punishments on slanderers or those who accused others of verbal injury unrightfully.[77] To prevent the proliferation of derogatory remarks, the city of Bern, for instance, passed laws that imposed severe punishment on the slanderer. Lawmakers distinguished between vilifying words (such as "heretic") spoken impulsively and those slanderous incidents that were premeditated.[78] Thus, the city claimed authority over verbal conflicts. "Heresy" was mentioned frequently, among other crimes, in these laws—laws that were reissued and reformulated several times over the course of the fifteenth century and adopted in cities under Bern's rule.[79] By the early seventeenth century, those guilty of severe verbal aggression were forced to make restitution for the insulted person's loss of honor and pay the city a heavy fine.[80] These regulations express a deep-seated concern over the potentially unsettling effects of verbal feuds within urban society.

Defamation was an important element in the early modern culture of information. In societies like early modern Germany and Switzerland, which relied in many ways on oral forms of communication, the spoken word had a different and a more significant status than in today's societies. In the cities, street-talk and rumor in its many forms fed into political systems that were largely nonparticipatory but nevertheless had to rely on responses of the urban population. Slander was part and parcel of the production and dissemination of information through oral networks of communication. Defamatory speech thus emerges as a prime means by which at least fragmentary knowledge about same-sex sexual relations spread in communities.

Accusations of sodomy occurred with relative frequency in Swiss politics before and after 1500. It involved both individuals and whole communities. Politically, the Confederacy rallied round a notion of *teutsch*—German—a battle cry that reflected its location on the borders of other cultures and linguistic communities.[81] As speakers of German, the Swiss partook of a mindset that differentiated the world south of the Alps from that north of the Alps by allegations of illicit versus licit sexual practice.[82] As I have shown in this chapter and will continue to discuss in the following chapters, sodomy-laden imagery provided an important link between different social groups. It revealed social hierarchies and political loyalties, notions of sexual difference, and concepts of sexual order. Yet defamation as a cultural practice also involved writing and publishing. Many an author explored the borderland of the obscene by engaging in the art of defamation. In fact, libel established an arena of cultural exchange between social strata marked by different layers of erudition. Words of slander circulated broadly in different textual settings.

There is no clear division between the social practice of defamation, which was the topic here, and its counterpart in the world of the written, published word—the subject of the next two chapters. They are two sides of the same imagistic coin. The tropes of sodomiphobia as detected in the social art of defamation—the Italian connection, the association between bribery and sodomy, the image of sodomitical sex as a pursuit of the elite, and so forth—remain evident when sodomy defamations come up in published texts, mostly in religious pamphlets or treatises, but also in poetry collections and encyclopedias. Obviously, polemical arguments permeated a variety of genres. Needless to say, the printing press greatly facilitated the broad dissemination of literary works, including those publications that exploited a thirst for slanderous conflict. Importantly, rhetorical tradition considered polemic a strategy apt to enliven a text emotionally, heighten its affect, and ultimately make it more persuasive.

6

The Art of Defamation: Humanists and Reformers

Images of Sodom were important, if not central, to the dissemination of Reform ideology across a wide spectrum of the population. The pervasiveness of this imagery in the context of the Reformation is nothing less than remarkable. This is all the more noteworthy because publications of an entertaining or instructional kind often failed to represent sodomy, before and after the Reformation.[1] In the didacticism that characterizes so many literary enterprises of the period, representations of sodomy could not be inverted into a lesson to be learned, unless the lesson was to shun or repudiate even the mention of it. A poetics of teaching by inversion often excluded sodomy, a transgression that set its perpetrators apart from Christian society, so much so that these sinners and their sin could not be made into a lesson. In Reformation polemics, however, these limits of representation in didactic literature were regularly set aside for the purpose of vilification.

In order to fathom the Sodom-related rhetorics of the Reformation, we need to consider the images current in a related movement, humanism, from which the Reform of the *imaginaire* drew its inspiration. In this chapter, I will therefore contextualize Martin Luther's writings in the published polemics that preceded the Reform. While the previous chapter mostly focused on defamation against individuals, literary forms of vilification or polemics shall be my topic in this one. Devices such as inversion, enumeration, codeswitching, and the construction of authority via "experience" count among the most common strategies to rhetorically display the so-called unspeakable.

Humanists Defaming, Humanists Defamed

Humanism as a scholarly endeavor stimulated exchange across political and linguistic boundaries. Growing numbers of Germans migrated south to complete their education. The German humanist Albrecht von Eyb (1420–75) spent sixteen years of his life in Italy, befriending such eminent scholars as Barzizza, Chrysolaras, Valla, and Filelfo, before he finally returned to Bavaria. Albrecht Dürer (1471–1528) gained access to artistic circles in Italy, where painters admired his mastery. Mercantile exchange also intensified in the period. Italian merchants traveled north of the Alps, while tradespeople from Augsburg, Nuremberg, or other south German cities were to be found in the great Italian trading centers. In an age of nascent German patriotism, the constant reinvention of Italy as a sodomitical south was part and parcel of these encounters.[2] Upon his return from Italy, Albrecht von Eyb owned a personal copy of Mercurino Ranzo's (d. c. 1469) comedy about a sodomitical cleric, De falso hypocrita,[3] and an image of Italian origin inspired Dürer to produce his 1494 drawing "Orpheus, the first sodomite" (Orfeuß der Erst puseran).[4]

The attitudes of many northern humanists vis-à-vis Renaissance Italy were conflicted, alternating between veneration of a philologically advanced society and suspicions of the Italian Other. Ulrich von Hutten (1488–1523), for instance, an imperial knight and a champion of a secular humanism, expressed his shame "in being German every time conversations with Italians touched upon the persecution of [Johannes] Reuchlin," the accomplished Hebraist whose scholarly endeavors had caused a clerical backlash, "and they asked him whether monks were really so powerful in Germany."[5] While an intellectual elite north of the Alps might have reached out to a pan-European movement of learned literati, as a romanticized view of the past wants us to believe, German humanists also voiced stereotypical slurs concerning Mediterranean sexual depravity.[6]

Literary forms of verbal assault can be illustrated by texts produced during a gathering of German writers in the city of Regensburg in 1493. There, an informal circle of intellectuals launched an attack against their Italian counterparts—an attack both erudite and rude, learned and crudely offensive. In carefully crafted poetic diatribes, the German poets, led by the first German poeta laureatus, Conrad Celtis (1459–1508), tried to establish their textual and sexual superiority by vociferously slandering Italian humanists as pederasts.[7] The poems of the Regensburg circle float defamatory topoi while, at the same time, taking them to extremes: "You Italian shit-shot licker of asses, . . . You jump boys: in your impious embraces / You go coddling bristling hairy hollows. / Cannot shame, poor man, keep you from pretending / To be sober: intoxicated jerkoff, / Flaccid cocksucked pathic and masturbator?"[8] Incensed by Italian attacks on German linguistic shortcomings, the circle resorted to the most graphic language in order to defend German masculine honor against the perceived Italian onslaught. Thus, German emulation of Italian ways in matters of perfect Latinity was accompanied by ferocious verbal hostility in matters of sexuality.

Images of Italy as the country of sodomy continued to flourish throughout the period that witnessed the spread of the Reform movement in Germany. In the year 1519, the German humanist Johannes Crotus Rubeanus (1480–c. 1545) sent a letter to Martin Luther (1483–1546) from Bologna— a letter filled with disgust about the "imprudish women and male hustlers" who supposedly constituted the following of the pope.[9] He implied that by selling so many "pallia, indulgences, bulls, pranks, [and] farces" the Holy Fathers financed their "whores and mignons" (*cynaedos*).[10] Rubeanus thus saw the Catholic Church's financial schemes as fostering aberrant sexual practices.[11]

Descriptions à la Celtis or Crotus Rubeanus were potent rhetorical weapons because they often blended premeditated perceptions with claims of authenticity. In an anecdote in Felix Hemmerli's (1388–1459) *De matrimonio* (*On Matrimony*, 1456), a German cleric condemned Italians as sodomites authoritatively, because he had spent time at the Roman curia—as had the author, Hemmerli—and "had experience" (*quoniam expertus*).[12] Some of the "Regensburg humanists" had spent time in Italy. Their poetry in arms betrays intimate acquaintance, for instance, with cultural constructs of sodomy south of the Alps, where penetration and notions of activity and passivity in sexual intercourse were far more central than north of the Alps. Mobility in university education therefore not only resulted in a number of German students attending Italian institutions of higher learning, but also raised awareness of difference in "national" character—perceptions that could then be cast in familiar tropes, like that of the Italian sodomite. In fact, according to Kurt Stadtwald, Germans living in Rome took an active role in both shaping and disseminating stereotypes of sexual depravities among Italians.[13] Like Ulrich von Hutten, they propagated notions of Rome that drew on clichés of Italian bawdiness.

Images of sexual unruliness were certainly not the only images humanists attributed to the Holy See, but they formed an important element in a larger set of perceptions, including extravagant waste of resources, pastoral neglect, and loss of touch with Christian doctrine. In the words of Kurt Stadtwald, "the humanists created the Rome that Luther loved to hate."[14] "The Roman misdeeds are incredible," Martin Luther is reported to have exclaimed during a so-called table talk, everyday conversations recorded by his students: "Nobody can believe the amount of [Roman] depravity unless he experiences it with his own eyes, ears and experience."[15] Only retrospectively, years after his travels to Rome, had Luther acquired such a clear vision of the state of Italian, especially Roman, morals. In this conversation, he concocted a panoply of vices: avarice, contempt for God, perjury, and sodomitical sins, as if such sinfulness was visible, audible, and self-evident on the streets of Rome.

As is evident in these passages, anti-Italian sentiment was mapped onto another ideological force, anticlericalism.[16] Anticlericalism has attracted much attention, especially in the historiography on the German Reformation. However, anticlericalism is a recurrent theme in late medieval social life. Popular tales, satire, and political and humanist literature all thoroughly exploited the topos of a sexually debauched clergy long before the onset of the various Reforms.[17] Anticlericalism as well as antimonasticism found a powerful expression in an almost reflexive antagonism to Rome and the Holy See among humanists. Under the hands of the Reformers, these notions turned into a weapon against the Catholic Church. These writers forged a close alliance between the figures of the depraved cleric and the sodomite as the ultimate transgressors of divine creation—figures that, contrary to a modernist bias, were conflated only rarely on the eve of the Reformation.

Toward a Geography of Perversion

In ever new variations, images, and word combinations, the link between the Italian south and sexual depravity was reconfirmed in Martin Luther's writings. Terms like *welsche practiken* or *welsche hochzeiten (nuptiae Italicae)*— "Latin" or "Italian weddings"—dislocated the practice of sodomy, more precisely, that of anal sex, to the Mediterranean world and, more to the polemical point, to Rome as the center of Catholic Christianity.[18] If the "Italian sin of sodomy" was compared with an indigenously German sin, it was the Germans' ever-growing alcoholism (*Sauffen-Laster*). Not only was alcohol consumption a far older habit than the supposedly novel sins imported from Italy—Luther quotes Tacitus as an authority on the subject—drinking threatened the divine order to a much lesser degree than did "Italian mores" (*Welsche sitten*).[19] "Every country has its vice," Luther explained in one of his sermons in 1538 and proceeded to type the Greeks as "whorers," while presenting the Italians as perpetrators of the sin that the apostle Paul expounds in Romans 1:24–25, sodomy.[20] By contrast, the Germans were introduced by their enmity toward the Italian sin of sodomy.[21]

Not all Italians were equally associated with sodomy. The practice was especially identified with inhabitants of the Tuscan city of Florence and, in the context of the Reformation, the Holy City of Rome. In a list of social groups occupying different parts of Europe, one fictitious letter among the satirical body of epistles published as *Epistolae obscurorum virorum* (1515/17) placed "heretics in Bohemia, drunkards in Saxony, courtiers in Rome, and sodomites in Florence."[22] Johann Fischart (1546–90), a poet of great virtuosity from Strasbourg, varied this list but seconded the *Epistolae's* view of the Florentines: "Junkers in Germany, bishops in Italy, nobles in Austria, little doctors and trainees in Speyer . . . sodomites in Florence."[23] Early New High German incorporated the word "to florence," the very term confirming the identification of this Italian city with same-sex sexual activity among men. When Luther disparaged Pope Clement VII (1523–34) as a "Florentine rascal" (*Florentzisch früchtlin*, literally "Florentine fruitlet"), he was alluding to Florentines as practitioners of male-male sexuality.[24] The fact that a particular site, whether Florence or Rome, was portrayed as a haven of sodomites inevitably evoked the fate of the Old Testament Sodom as the city that had given these sinners their name in the first place.

Yet the polemicists' "geography of perversion" does not reflect a geographical map.[25] Cartographers of defamed desire often created composites where Italy, the Muslim Turks, and all heathens were linked by their supposed defiance of Christian norms. In Luther's assemblage of heresies, attacks on the one group were frequently linked to the other. In the verbal guise of a textual travesty, for instance, the Jewish and the feminized, "papist" Other were blended in a polemical Pater Noster: *Aue rabi, du heylige Jungfraw S. Paula Bapst*—"Hail rabbi, you holy virgin Pope Saint Paula" (Pope Paul III).[26] Yet it would be insufficient simply to insist that sodomites be counted in this list. Because of their insidious invisibility, because of the supposed ease with which humans were seduced into committing sexual irregularities, sodomy was portrayed as particularly threatening.

German was not the only culture in which the practice of same-sex sexual activities among men was associated with foreignness. In medieval Russia, sodomy was viewed as an import from heathen places.[27] In France, vehement anti-Italianism predated the close political association of the two countries during the reign of Catherine of Medici.[28] In early modern England, Mediterranean societies, both Christian and Muslim, were continually typed as the places most prone to sodomitical intercourse, despite the fact that several well-publicized scandals involved Englishmen.[29] In the early modern Dutch Republic, if sodomy was talked about at all, it "was thought to be a Catholic, or more particularly, an Italian vice."[30]

According to some late sixteenth-century writers, the ultimate haven for sodomites was not to be found in Italy but in the Americas, securely removed from firsthand experience for most readers of German.[31] The Americas attracted adverse projections, including the noble and the debased savage. Based on his years as a bishop in the New World, Bartolomé de Las Casas (1474–1566) refuted sodomy as one of the justifications for the conquistadors to eradicate the indigenous population.[32] In Las Casas as in Erasmus Francisci's (1627–94) seventeenth-century encyclopedic manual on exotic lands, customs, and societies, the ancient Peruvians were presented as paragons of virtue who rigorously persecuted sodomites. According to the author, the Incan rulers seized sodomites' property, burned the sodomites to ashes, and even imposed the same punishment on family members if there was the slightest suspicion that they had known about the crime without denouncing their relatives.[33] As Francisci was only too ready to admit, ethnopoets like himself wanted to uplift morally degraded Europeans by holding up to them the mirror of exemplary humans.[34]

In the sixteenth century, in the period immediately after the conquest, portrayals of the Americas favored images that described natives in denigratory terms. In Johann Fischart's translation of Jean Bodin's (1529/30–96) *Daemonomania* (fr. 1580; 1591) into German, the author expediently juxtaposed German "innocence" in matters of sodomy with the depravity of both the Mediterranean lands and the New World: "When the Spaniards conquered the Occidental new islands, they also found such [amulets in the shape of a penis] which were carried around one's neck . . . an image of pederasty or buggery of a pedico and a *cynaedus* which was even more shameful." He added: "Because of the Germans' innocence with regard to this vice, I did not translate it."[35] Instead of censoring the reference altogether, Fischart tried to capture his reader's attention. By highlighting his omission, he claimed censorship, yet invited fantasies of the derided practice.

In fact, Bodin's original text was no more explicit than Fischart's translation of it.[36] But Bodin had gone on to express his repulsion at such behavior in a line that Fischart omitted in the German version: "Everybody will agree that this [sodomy] is an invention of the devil."[37] Whereas Bodin declared the practice successfully uprooted by the conquistadors and voiced a disgust about sodomy, presumed to be universal, Fischart ethnicized the sin and alluded to contamination of the conquering nation. Although the Spaniards had taken prevailing sins as justification for their eradication of indigenous peoples, others—the Dutch Estates notably, as Fischart lets us know—claimed that the Spaniards themselves were engaged in the same activities.[38]

By Fischart's time, German "innocence" in sodomitical matters had itself become a stock image. When Martin Luther lectured on the Old Testament story of Sodom, for instance, he claimed to have hesitated, because "the ears of the Germans have been innocent and free [*purae*] of this monstrosity up to this point." By introducing the subject matter in this way, he was sure to captivate his audience of students by implying that naming the story could initiate the actual behavior, even though it was never actually described, but instead portrayed negatively as a contagious disease. [39]

The Notion of German Innocence

Sexual sinfulness had a mutable geography. Its verbal continents followed the drift of rhetorical strategies. "Displacing a sexual practice by naming it geographically has its consequences," as Mark Jordan observes: "It sets boundaries not only on a practice, but on explanations for it." [40] Among other limitations, mapping illicit behavior onto foreign peoples implied that one's own group was innocent of the same behavior (unless infected by foreigners). Displacement was never absolutely effective, however. Rather, displacement had to be continually rehearsed. On a geographical plain, the rejected practices were therefore often placed at a safe distance, south of the Alps or outside Christianity, though close enough to evoke anxiety about potential intrusions.

Occasionally, knowledge surfaced that the sin of sodomy could not be located exclusively in foreign lands. Around 1506, for instance, the revered Alsatian humanist Jakob Wimpfeling (1450–1528) was accused of desiring his male students. According to an anonymous libeler, Wimpfeling exploited his students' ignorance in sexual matters. "A male virgin [Wimpfeling] takes pleasure in talking with virgins of the male sex": "be glad to live in Germany, where they do not know how to suspect such an evil" (*gaude te esse in Germania, ubi malum de his suspicari nescitur*). [41] Our libeler went a step further, though, when he linked Wimpfeling's diatribes against the female sex, conventional as they were in didactic writings of the period, with his assumed preference for young males. [42]

To be sure, in polemical writings of all genres, teacher-student relations frequently fell prey to suspicions of erotic intimacy—a suspicion that predates the advent of humanism. [43] Notions of intergenerational erotic activity between a mature man of superior position—the teacher—and a young man—the student—were useful items on the polemical agenda. [44] These images fit existing social as well as literary perceptions about the hierarchical nature of sexual activity, both between men and women and between members of the same sex.

Though clearly an import from foreign lands, the origin of Wimpfeling's particular "vice" is not stated explicitly. The *studia humanitatis* that Wimpfeling propagated do have a country of origin, however: Italy. In other words, in the context of this particular *libellus famosus*, Wimpfeling's behavioral shortcomings *in sexualibus* are reflected in his having perverted the right course of studies. Wimpfeling is strongly criticized for having abandoned sacred theology and having educated youths about moral philosophy instead, a topic for which, if we follow the defamer, students are unfit because of their age. Even the charge of heresy was in the air. The libeler portrayed Wimpfeling as a relentless critic of the Catholic Church and linked his critique to sodomitical sexuality. The humanist is vilified as a false prophet, a potential *alter Machometus*—"another Muhammad," with this name's manifold overtones of both religious and sexual heresy.[45]

In other contexts, harsher words were needed. In the same region, Alsace, and in the same year, 1506, when Johann Geiler von Kaisersberg (1445–1510) preached against the *bûbenketzer*—those "heretics" who commit sexual acts with boys—he observed, "it is deplorable [*ein arm ding*] that this vice invades our country from Latin countries [*vß welschen landen*]."[46] In order to persuade their readers, polemical writers fabricated an impression of imminent danger. *Die Welsch Gattung*, an anonymous pro-Imperial pamphlet in verse from the early sixteenth century, describes the ills of the German lands as an outcome of Italian influences.[47] Casting its net widely, touching on such themes as the inversion of divine truth, secret financial schemes, and moral depravities, this treatise warns against an Italianization of the German Empire; it mentions, among other sins, avarice and sodomy, the latter portrayed as an unnatural vice "which does not have natural lust in its action."[48] In keeping with the apocalyptic character of the text as a whole, "the sin against nature" serves as a prime proof that, ultimately, "sin cannot bear itself" and an example of the sin that deserves to call down God's wrath upon earth.[49] To fight this and other sins, the author calls on the secular authorities.[50]

In another "table talk," Martin Luther pontificated: "Turkey reigns in Germany, if not in terms of state power, at least in terms of [false] religion" (*et Turca regnat in Germania, si non potentia, tamen religione*).[51] In the same passage, he equated Reformed Germany with Lot (and matrimony), whose "soul was crucified day and night by the Sodomites."[52] This adaptation of an Old Testament narrative to contemporary confessional politics expressed the bond between Self (Lot) and Other (the inhabitants of Sodom). The passage imagines Lot as haunted by the unspecified sins of Sodom, his internal gaze fixated on sexual transgressions of the divine order.

Luther also issued warnings against "Italian customs" (*Welsche sitten*) espe-cially perilous for German youths that were supposedly spreading in Ger-many, imported by cardinals and propagated by the German courts.[53] The oxymoronic "Italian virtue" (*Welsche tugent*), to be read as "Italian scourges" (*Welschen plagen*), was deemed to be particularly dangerous. The sins' intru-sion was said to be invisible, like that of contagious diseases.[54] The fre-quently invoked "we," properly understood as Reformed Germany, is con-structed as a bulwark of martyrs in the defense of matrimony against those who defile this institution: heretics, Italians, Turks, and heathens.[55] Power-fully, writers thus attempted to enjoin their listeners to avoid sexual sins by invoking geographic, ethnic, cultural, and religious boundaries.

Verbalpolitik

Whenever they employed the defamatory as a mode of speech, early mod-ern men and women could draw from a wide array of expressions on dif-ferent stylistic levels, some of formulaic character, others highly artistic—a linguistic wealth that itself is a reminder of the power of defamation. Defamation was a practice replete with inventive language and neologisms, testifying to its significant role in early modern culture.

Felix Hemmerli conspicuously used Italianizing terms such as *macarelli sive busurones* to denote the derogatory expressions "buggers and sodomites." Recherché phrases like *macarelli sive busurones* bear the mark of their foreign origin and textually display the sexually infected air of *italianità*. To make sure his non-Italian readers understood, Hemmerli inserted a lengthy ex-planation of his terms. He also explained why he had to use such outlandish vocabulary, even though he assumed it would not be familiar to his read-ership: "*Macarelli* or *busurones* are Italian names for sodomitical men who sin against nature; because of the enormity of the crime this wicked act [*nephas*] does not have a word of its own in our Latin language, but only an ad-justed one [a loan word], although very old."[56] Sodomy required linguistic extravagance. Hemmerli reflects a common belief when he contends that languages lack words to express what is foreign to their speakers. What is more often claimed for the German language (by authors of the late fifteenth and sixteenth centuries) is here claimed for Latin, in this case, a deficit of words for sodomy. The cultural poetics of sodomy is treach-erous. *Busurones*, despite and because of its Italian derivation (*buzerar*), be-came quite a common German expression for men engaging in homosex-ual intercourse (and therefore would have been easily understood by his audience);[57] *macarelli*, however, derived from another Germanic language,

Dutch or Flemish, entered the fringes of the Italian lexicon only through the mediation of medieval Latin. One of the few Italian dictionaries to reference the term explains it as a regional expression for "procurer."[58]

Luther claims, for instance, that no native dialect in Germany had an indigenous expression for the phrase "Italian wedding," that is, sodomy with a strong insinuation of male-male sexual activity—adding "thank God."[59] Whereas, presumably, the German language steered clear of indigenous terms for sodomy, Luther claimed that the Church as an institution had created a "new Roman language." Necessarily, such a novelty perverted the original sense of God's word:[60] in the same treatise, this new language is described as "thieves' cant" (the German word for thieves' cant, *Rotwelsch*, implies a connection to Romance languages).[61] In this idiom (as opposed to the sacred and divine language), the pope's and cardinals' chastity, for example, has to be rendered as "the chastity of Sodom and Gomorrah" or "Italian buggers [*puseronen*]."[62]

Many authors elaborated on the sexual content of slanderous formulations. They transformed simple slurs into complex rhetorical condemnations and brought the sexual content of slander into high relief. Moreover, they constantly crossed linguistic boundaries in composites of slanderous words. Writers inserted imported terms into their texts in order to denote the supposedly foreign locus of male homosexual activities. Linguistically, the lexicon of sodomy associations referred most frequently to Latin and the Romance languages, especially Italian, and, more rarely, French. To make sure that their readers understood certain terms, authors like Felix Hemmerli, Martin Luther, Johann Fischart, and others listed synonyms.

Johann Fischart mixed German with Greek, Latin, and Italian elements when defaming illegitimate sexual acts in order to fashion his eulogy of normative sexuality in matrimony. In an exuberant German-language adaptation of François Rabelais's *Gargantua* (the chapter from which I quote here is an addition of the German poet to Rabelais's text),[63] the hero disdains a plethora of extramarital sexual activities, including adultery, oral intercourse, bestiality, and pederasty:

Noch vil minder kont er verdåwen des Platons Gartenbrüderisch Weibergemeynschafft [polygamous people] . . . Noch die Lesbische Lawdische Klingenbalierer vnnd Wadelsauger [women who perform oral intercourse], Buberonen, wie sehr es der Malevintisch Bischof de la Casa Sodomae rhůmet: [sodomitical men][64] noch alle Kysolacken [anus lickers], Pfitzidisser [urine drinkers?], Cotitto [dildo users?],[65] Fellrumer, die die Jungen durchs Maul wie die Wiesel werfen solten [people who practice fellatio and give birth through the mouth like a weasel],[66] Lidische Mittaggeyle Stielmelcker [masturbators], Geyßhirten in der Sonnen [men who practice

bestiality?], Siphniasserische Pfostenhalter vnd Cibeles Orden [masturbators?],
Noch das vnmenschliche, Stallstinckige Stafermo schône Fraw Geyßbergerin [peo-
ple who engage in heterosexual anal intercourse]."[67]

This list should not be regarded as simply a sixteenth-century compendium
of street slang; it demonstrates great erudition and displays literary-artistic
playfulness lacking in court documents or edifying texts. Many of the expressions listed contain highly learned riddles or exhibit far-fetched literary
allusions. Whereas *wadelsauger* (cocksucker) was easy enough to understand
and *buberonen* (derogatory for "pederast"), reminiscent of the German word
for "knave" and of the German-Italian *buseron*, could easily be decoded as denoting sodomites, a word like *Kysolacken* cannot be found in any sixteenth-
century glossary. This hybrid neologism copulated *kissos* for "anus" and *lack*
for "licker" verbally, presenting the German swearword "arslicker" in a foreign disguise.

These verbal components do not stay pure. One language contaminates
the other. It is hard to imagine a reader so polyglot that she or he would
have readily available all the information and glosses needed to decode
the subtle messages in this refined artistic slander. Verbal clusters ensure
that readers, uninformed as they might have been—and we still are—about
specific allusions to Greek literature, history, or mythology, would nevertheless get the gist of a slanderous attack à la Fischart. Indeed, one of the
pleasures of reading might have been to crack the macaronic concepts at
hand, a pleasure still available to us.[68]

In the period before the linguistic purity movements of the seventeenth
century, foreign words were sometimes valued as enriching the target language. Simon Roth (d. after 1567), author of the first dictionary of foreign
words used in German-speaking lands (1578)—interestingly enough titled
Teutscher Dictionarius (German Dictionary)—celebrated linguistic permeability
and the advent of verbal imports from different European languages as a
sign of German cultural efflorescence.[69] The stance of multilingualism was
challenged, however, by a competing stance that posited the German national and linguistic character as distinct and, hence, to be protected against
the onslaught of foreign words. According to the sixteenth-century theologian Johann Agricola (1494–1566), the Germans disregard their "national"
heritage not only in literature and history but also in their habits. They
"wear Italian [*welsche*], Spanish, and French clothes, have Italian cardinals,
French and Spanish diseases [e.g., syphilis] and also carry out Italian practices [*welsche practiken*]."[70] With breathtaking velocity Agricola shifts from
the world of words to that of material things, and from objects to the influx

of foreigners, only to end up with corrupted sexual behavior—all the topoi grouped together under the label "foreignness." This semantic entropy collapses the difference of logical categories, insinuating the sameness of potential threats from the outside, as if imported words were the causes of disease or the wearing of foreign luxury clothing induced sinful same-sex sexual behavior among men. A people's linguistic standard and their mores are correlated, Agricola posits. He offers a textual antidote in the form of German proverbs authored by exemplary ancestors that are to be handed down to a young generation of Germans.[71] In the case of Martin Luther and Johann Agricola, his close associate and opponent (later in life), terms associated with sodomy often formed the climactic telos of scattered observations about foreign societies, especially those of the Mediterranean. In their drive to *imitatio*, the author seems to suggest, the Germans might in turn get something unexpected and unwanted.

The anti-Italian thrust of sodomy accusations betrayed a deep-seated ambivalence about humanism as an import not only of words, but also of depraved manners.[72] "We the German beasts are to learn this new Latinity in these times from the Italians" (*Hanc etiam latinitatem novam Bestiae germanae ab Italis hominibus hoc seculo discemus*), Martin Luther wrote when signaling the danger of Germans losing their "right" Christian beliefs, but then continued to slander the pope in stark sexual terms.[73] The agents of depravity imported from foreign lands varied from text to text. As transgressors of imagined or real boundaries, mobile people were natural suspects. Though ultimately Satan was responsible, Luther offered the courtiers, the "impious soldier" (*impium militem*), the "voluptuous merchant" (*voluptuarium mercatorem*), and the "Carthusian monks from Italian monasteries" (*Carthusiani monachi ex monasteriis Italicis*) as perpetuating the spread of sodomy among the Germans.[74] Italian "epicurism"—a catch-all phrase for sexual license—had already "conquered a good part of Germany," he stated.[75] By singling out mobility itself as a cause for sexual perversion, Luther made "Germanness" an imagined fixum. Thus, threats of (foreign) sexual depravities, often epitomized by sodomy, were enunciated to mobilize an (indigenous) constituency to resist a perceived outside intruder.

The Rhetoric of Inversion

In early modern polemics, *inversio* or reversal, a rhetorical device that connects extremes, reigns supreme as a rhetorical move. As a rhetorical strategy, this mode of writing frequently turned traditional notions upside down. Symbolic inversion was "used to mark a boundary, between peoples, between categories of persons, between life and death."[76] As Cameron Mc-Farlane noted, "Inversion—and the chaos that will inevitably result from upsetting the order of things—is the structuring of almost all representations of the sodomite, the one element that holds together what can otherwise be quite disparate depictions."[77]

Either explicitly or implicitly, the linguistic code surrounding sodomy involved or implied its opposite, namely, the truth of the Gospels and the true evangelical spirit. Antithetical structures, common in late medieval theology, devotional literature, or literary satires, gained in vigor and rhetorical force during the Reform process.[78] In this context, *inversio* leads the reader from antitype to type or vice versa. While the most popular literary satires shunned sodomy, it became a newly salient and important part of the rhetorical matrix of opposites within the context of Reformation polemic.

Luther and other religious writers aligned *inversio* with another device, that of disclosure. When superimposing God's order on the world, Protestants intended to reveal a hidden truth about the lamentable state of human affairs. Uncovering the true nature of religious institutions lent authority to Reformers who exposed in writing what had previously been hidden or secret in the world. In the cosmos of his writings, Luther selected particular sites for *inversiones* regarding same-sex accusations: celibacy as opposed to matrimony, the institution of the monastery, as well as Rome as the center of gravity for the institutionalized Christian Church.

The monastery as a secluded location for pious devotion was discovered to be the most debauched of places, for instance. Its outward appearance of spirituality was presented as deceptive. A hypocritical monastic way of life was not only presented as worthy of condemnation but also as dangerous, because believers were seduced by its false appearance. According to Luther, monks and nuns who espouse chastity refuse to follow God's nature. They "cannot stay pure and have to stain themselves with mute sins [possibly masturbation or sodomy] or whoredom."[79] Tied to their vows of chastity, clerics were "forced" to commit the "mute sin" (without further specification) "against God's creation and His words: 'Be fruitful and multiply.'"[80] Luther greeted a new convert to the Reformed cause as a *defectorem Aldenburgensis Sodome*, a deserter from the Altenburg monastery, which had been equated with Sodom.[81]

One of the most important norms that sodomy repeatedly destabilized was matrimony. If Reformation theology proceeds from the assumption that all humans need to act on an innate sexual impulse, marriage emerges as the only legitimate outlet for man's and woman's sexual drive (though the naturalness of the urge to have sex should not be misread as celebrating human sexuality).[82] Contrary to Catholic dogma, Luther extended the command to procreate to all humankind, including those having taken clerical vows, as long as sexual activity was contained within the bounds of marriage. Luther thereby radicalized medieval theology on marriage as it had evolved since the twelfth century. Nonheteronormative sites were to be condemned: "It is one thousand times better . . . to marry than to sin like the devil in the monastery (as long as it is natural, couple by couple, husband with wife . . .)," writes Luther in one of his treatises on marriage. He inserts, "never mind what one does in monasteries, I don't know what, of which one should not talk."[83] The familiar, verbally explicit injunction not to speak is seconded here by an emphatic "I don't know," alluding to the outspoken metaphor of unspeakability as the traditional signifier for sodomy, not to mention the reference to "German innocence" with regard to sodomy.

In other contexts, Luther juxtaposed rightful marriages between men and women with incest, celibacy, and, last but not least, "abominable Italian weddings," that is, sodomitical relations with strong insinuations of male-male anal sexuality.[84] Strangely enough, these opposites are ordered along a continuum of sexual outlets with no radical division—not even verbal, since both terms, "Italian weddings" for sodomy and marital unions, invoke matrimony. "Infamous sodomitical misdeeds" and "unregulated lusts" are the devil's side of the coin, whereas "matrimony" emerges as a divinely ordained estate.[85] In the polemical wars of the Reformation, clerical marriage as advocated by the Reformers was played off against "Roman Sodom, Italian wedding, Venetian and Turkish brides and Florentine bridegrooms."[86]

Luther described a religious world turned upside down in the strongest sexual terms.[87] The main thrust of his defamatory impetus was directed at the institution of the papacy. In Luther's portrayal, the pope saw himself in the likeness of Christ—a blasphemy that the Reformer countered by exposing him as the living Antichrist who, according to exegetical tradition, would arise from the ranks of the Church: "impious and loathsome catamite, usurer, sacrilegist, most cruel tyrant" (*Impius ac sceleratus Cynaedus, Usurarius, Sacrilegus, cruentissimus tyrannus*).[88] Traditionally, since the debates waged during the era of Gregorian reforms (eleventh century), the Antichrist bore manifold inscriptions of pride, priapism, imminent punishment, heresy, and tyranny.[89] The Bohemian Jan Hus (c. 1370–1415), the Church reformer who had been burned at the stake and whom the Reformers honored as a precursor, had preceded Luther in identifying the pope as the Antichrist and Pope John XXIII as a "base murderer, a sodomite, a simoniac, and a heretic."[90]

As to the institution of the papacy, Luther claimed that during the Lateran Council of 1515 each cardinal was given papal permission to keep 5 *pusiones et Ganimedes* (five boys and ganymedes).[91] A sixteenth-century version in German introduced an element of realism into the utterance that was not evident in the Latin text: *"fünf Knaben zu Buhlen und Kämmerlingen"* (five boys as lovers and valets).[92] Rome was portrayed as a court and the pope himself was discovered to be "the pope of sodomites."[93] As the seat of a *Bubenschule*—a "school of knaves"—Rome will reproduce itself easily in the next generation.[94] The Roman clerics' assumed offenses were accentuated by the fact that they had given up all restraint and "publicly" (*palam*) lived their monstrous lives (*monstra*), while evangelical truth allowed Luther to publicly expose their indecency. In Luther's reading, the word *cephas* for the pope not only means "rock" (cf. Mt 16:18: "You are Peter, and on this rock I will build my church") but also connotes all of the following: " *'Cephas' est Apostolus, caput, princeps Apostolorum, impius, ebriosus, scortator, usurarius, tyrannus, impostor, simoniacus, Cynaedus."*[95]

Defamation based on connotations of sodomy followed conventional rhetorical patterns.[96] Enumeration—the listing of seemingly unrelated terms and concepts—was one of the primary devices used to introduce accusations of sodomy in prose texts of the early modern period.[97] Often, the *cynaedus* or sodomite was posited either at the list's forceful beginning or, as in the last example, at its climactic end.[98] What seem different categories to a modern reader were combined in such lists. Vilifying terms appear in decontextualized phrases and therefore remain vague, inviting the reader to fill in definitions and supply readings. Yet enumerations generate a context of their own—a context that exceeds the mere accumulation of verbal aggressions. Clearly, one word potentiates the other. Not accidentally, therefore, sodomy is frequently found at the elliptic end of these lists before they break off into silence.[99] Rhetorically, this structure implied that sodomy, whatever its exact meaning in each of these contexts, was the worst transgression of all.[100] Such structures constituted an important aspect of sodomy's prohibitive as well as productive relationship to language. Sodomy marked both rhetorical climax and the silence that followed.

Unlike didactic texts, polemical texts are invasive in nature. They tend to transgress the boundaries of integrity. Within the context of the Reformation, prohibitions against voicing the so-called unspeakable broke down on a large scale. In the polemical campaigns during the Reform, sodomy as a concept witnessed an inflation, especially between 1520 and 1555. Why sodomy? Why did sexual relations between men serve polemics so well? First, to ensure the success of his writings, Martin Luther exploited a repertoire of imagery that was well known before the Reformation. The Italian association with sodomy in the German mind was, as I have pointed out, all too well known and could easily be focused to express enmity against what figured as Rome. Second, and more generally, the practice of voicing political critique through a language of sexual depravity was well established. In addition, antimonastic writings had made the Holy Orders objects of ridicule. This third strand fed the anti-Catholic rhetorics of Protestant authors such as Luther. According to Hans-Jürgen Goertz, anticlericalism, especially an anti-Roman bias, united all Reform movements, Lutheranism, Calvinism, as well as the so-called radical Reformation. Anticlericalism was also taken up by the protesting peasants;[101] in their view, clerical chastity was the gateway to all kinds of sexual perversion.[102] Fourth, among all the so-called sins against nature, sodomy was particularly fit for polemical purposes: any kind of sexual activity between men and women could not match "less natural" forms of intercourse, masturbation was not a major cause for panic, and bestiality united an irrational animal and a human. By comparison, sodomy was a social sin. It could be construed as destructive to social relations and as contagious, especially since it involved the guarantors of patriarchal power and religious authority, men. Weaving a spider web of political associations around sodomy—illegal financial dealings, heretical practices, and illegitimate sexual doings among the powerful—therefore proved extremely useful to Protestant polemical writers.

7

Sodomy in the Reformation Pamphlet

In Reformation polemics the manifold inhibitions about speaking out on sodomy characteristic of an earlier period were largely put aside. During the conflicts over religious issues triggered by the Reforms, the traditions that had guarded the dissemination of licentious names and images in other literary media collapsed. The immediacy of the Protestant cause with its penchant for the apocalyptic left little space for deferral or forbearance, let alone rhetorical restraint. To rescue God's word from its Roman captivity legitimized and even demanded the starkest verbiage, or so many Reformers believed. During the period from 1520–55, the polemics reached levels of aggression that forestalled a rapprochement between the emerging confessions. Insinuations of sodomy, one of the utmost violations of the political and sexual order, thus became a regular feature of Protestant ideology in the early 1520s. No other medium contributed more to the wide circulation of images of Sodom than the pamphlet. Though pamphlet wars preceded the "Gutenberg Galaxy" (Marshall McLuhan), libelous texts now circulated more swiftly and in greater numbers, and access to these publications became more widespread.

After 1517 an army of Reform-oriented theologians, priests, and believers produced thousands of pamphlets advocating issues of religious, social, and political reform.[1] Significantly, pamphlets provided information as well as entertainment and moral teaching. According to Steven Ozment, "in the 1520s and 30s [the pamphlets] were basic tools of information, revolution and reaction by which individuals and groups attempted to preserve and/or reshape the societies in which they lived."[2] The years 1523 and 1524 marked an unprecedented peak in the production of this literature. In 1524 alone, twenty-four hundred pamphlets saw the light of day. Hans-Joachim Köhler stresses that after 1520 most pamphlets were in German, while before 1520 Latin publications dominated the market.[3] Though this high level of pamphlet production could not be sustained, other increases in polemical writing came in 1530 with the Diet of Augsburg and in the 1540s and 1550s with the Schmalkaldic War (1546/47) and the Church Council of Trent (1545–63). Not only did these tracts appeal to a mass audience, they were also marketed so that, as historians of reading have shown, they reached illiterate segments of the population. New copies were read to listeners aloud and broadsheets were hung on walls, ensuring that diverse groups of readers would be served.[4] It would be a mistake, however, to associate pamphlets as a medium entirely with the culture of the simple folk. There was a market for pamphlets published in Latin, and numerous documents testify to the fact that members of the learned elite took a keen interest in polemics. The pull of these publications was such that they tended to create an audience which united, at least rhetorically, a fractured pre-Reformation public.

Very few critics have mentioned, let alone analyzed, the Reformers' frequent invocation of the sins of Sodom in the wider context of the Reformation.[5] Yet suspicions of sodomy were important to the popular acceptance of the Protestant split from Rome. "If Reformation popular propaganda was so highly successful, it was because it relied so heavily on what was taken for granted in popular culture," as Robert W. Scribner pointed out.[6] Pamphlets brought sodomitical images to the fore and adapted them to the Reform's particular needs. In pamphlets printed between 1520 and 1555, sodomy became a stock image and consistent tool for vilification. Whether or not people gave full credence to the slurs and polemic images of pamphlets, polemicists connected their audience to the center of politico-religious decision making. In the words of Winfried Schleiner, one of the few scholars to address the cultural context of "homophobic slurs in renaissance cultural politics," these polemical myths "validated Protestantism."[7] Protestantism as an "imagined community," to use Benedict Anderson's phrase,[8] had to rely on an idiom which circumscribed the boundaries of its community of believers. Pamphlets served as this community's channel of communication, while polemics served to police the community's boundaries. Polemical writings thus fostered a sense of belonging among the Reformation's followers. Sodomiphobia contributed significantly to a "we-sentiment," and a "high symbolic integration."[9]

Modern critics have largely resisted theorizing and historicizing references to sodomy in the context of the Reformation. Before approaching the chronology as well as the function of sodomy slurs in sixteenth-century pamphlets, I will, therefore, first focus on responses among modern critics to one of Luther's most vitriolic publications.

No author's publications better testify to the centrality of polemics in general and sodomy slurs in particular than those of the great theologian and highly gifted polemicist, Martin Luther.[10] As the previous chapter showed, Luther's opulent sodomy-related vocabulary permeated many genres: sermons, Biblical commentaries, letters, recorded conversations, and so on. Furthermore, his writings connected the literary realms of Latin and German publishing. Often, his Latin writings were translated into the vernacular shortly after their publication, while his German writings were rendered in Latin.

Arguably, *Against the Roman Papacy, an Institution of the Devil* of 1545 is Luther's most ferocious publication. In this tract, he seized the timely opportunity to drive a rhetorical wedge between the papacy and the emperor. Charles V (1500–1558; r. 1519–58) had made religious concessions to the Protestant estates at the Diet of Speyer in 1544 in exchange for their support of his military efforts against the Turkish advance in Europe. Subsequently, the pope criticized the emperor in harsh words for leniency against a movement of heretics. A draft of a letter by Paul III (1534–49) not meant for publication ended up in the hands of Luther, who used it as a basis for *Against the Roman Papacy, an Institution of the Devil.*

In Luther's treatise, the theme of language features most prominently. The true evangelical message is played off against various linguistic caricatures. Pope Paul III, for instance, became a grammatically transgendered *Sanct Paul tertia* (note the feminine ending).[11] Rhetorical wavering between grammatical genders implied the pope's complete absence of theological authority. The apostle Paul—as opposed to the derided and feminized pope Paula—is quoted in this context as saying that "women should keep silence in the churches" (1 Cor 14:34). The Curia, governing body of the Catholic Church, was depicted as an assembly of sexually ambiguous monsters: "hermaphrodites, androgynes, catamites [*cynaedi*], buttfuckers [*pedicones*], and similar monsters of nature."[12] Switching from the vernacular to the Latin (*Erstlich antworte ich Latinisch*)—a device rarely deployed in texts like this one that were aimed at a broad circulation—Luther shrouded the sexually most explicit part of his treatise in Latin, the language of erudition, while claiming to address the papacy in the sacred language of Western Christendom.[13] This wavering between two languages emerges as analogous to the indeterminacy of sex, polemically projected onto the leaders of the Roman Church. The Holy See (misrepresented here as the throne where the future pope's male sex was investigated) was unveiled as the site of endless gender confusion (note the allusion to the myth of Popess Joan).[14]

Clearly, a physically and morally degenerate assembly like the curia could not claim spiritual authority over the Reformers. Therefore, hope for a Church council was in vain. The anatomical metaphor of the pope as the head of Catholic Christianity became itself inverted in this context. Following the practice of *inversio*, the anus had to represent the mind. "We" are supposed to understand the pope and his entourage by "looking into their posteriors," quite literally.[15] These images border on the obscene, yet locate indecency in what the defamed do, not in what the images themselves do, to paraphrase Jonathan Goldberg.[16]

In a study that must count as one of the most eloquent pleas for giving pamphlets the attention they deserve, *The Rhetoric of the Reformation*, Peter Matheson has devoted a long discussion to this treatise—a treatise many other critics have avoided. Indeed, if one is interested solely in the theology of the Reformation, there is little of dogmatic value in these pages. In equating the papacy with anality, illicit sexuality, and Satanism, however, this treatise reaches a new level of verbal vitriol, unparalleled even in an oeuvre like Luther's that is so replete with polemic. "Texts such as this . . . stretch and strain our categories to [the] breaking-point," writes Matheson. He proceeds to employ stark imagery himself when he characterizes the treatise's style as "the black ecstasy of language"[17]—a statement echoing a host of other critics. Kurt Stadtwald calls this treatise "repugnant," mentioning it only briefly.[18] Mark U. Edwards, Jr., remarks: "This treatise is the most violent and vulgar to issue from Luther's pen,"[19] a change in tone that this critic explains by pointing to the increasing political pressures on Luther and the changing nature of the movement itself, which had turned from proselytizing to consolidation. "This is not the thought of a theologically alert and creative mind, but is reliant, in a derivative way, on some of the worst anti-curial abuse of the fifteenth- and sixteenth-century German humanists," Matheson states when confronted with "barrow-loads of references to sodomy and bisexuality." Ultimately, this treatise signifies "an awesome warning against the abuse of polemic" itself.[20]

I am quoting so extensively to illustrate the particular rhetoric at work in these studies. It tends to place references to sodomy outside a cultural framework. Luther's treatise is thought to represent the fall from the heights of theological creativity into the abyss of common insult: "This is polemic which is well on the road to propaganda." Matheson's critical intervention—a shift from *propaganda*, the term conventionally used in Reformation studies, to *polemics*—urges the critic to construe injurious excess, the pamphlets' frequent rambunctiousness, as a "down-side" of the Reform process. What is more, according to *The Rhetoric of the Reformation,* "dark polemic,"[21] the rise of propagandistic fervor, is relegated to the second half of the sixteenth century.[22] By contrast, the early Reformation appears as dialogue-oriented. In fact, I would argue that our assumptions about late sixteenth-century pamphlets are still tentative. Previous studies on pamphleteers and their products have almost exclusively targeted the emergence of the Reform in the early 1520s. While many editions have made the early efflorescence of the "Reformed printing press" easily accessible, editions of pamphlets authored in the latter part of the century lag behind.

There is no doubt that Luther indulged his temper here more than in previous writings. It is indeed striking how the text's offensiveness has traveled well through the ages. I am taking issue with a rhetorical Othering of sodomy that precludes an analysis which goes beyond Luther's personal idiosyncrasies in his later life. As Matheson points out, Luther's deployment of polemical references is consistent with previous practice, his own and that of other Reformers. One of the legacies of early pamphleteering is the imagery of sodomy. Given their pervasive use since the early 1520s, images of sodomy were not a deviation from the course of true debate. They were part and parcel of Reformed polemic—an outcome of the radicalizing rhetoric of the early 1520s.[23] What is more, Sodom's occurrence in pamphlets follows a certain textual logic—a logic that needs to be recovered analytically. In other words, the difference between this tract and earlier ones is a difference of degree. Matheson's emphasis on the intellectual merits of pamphlets, therefore, disables him in approaching the characteristic features used to deploy tropes of sodomy in these writings.

References to sodomy in Luther are not a sign of discursive disorder, as Matheson claims. Such an interpretation by a modern critic perpetuates the particular rhetorical gesture with which sodomy or similar charges were enacted in the early modern period. Instead, I suggest analyzing the cultural matrix that made sodomy a sign of textual unruliness. It is noteworthy that sodomy enters the historian's lens only when its excessive presence makes oversight difficult. Thus, sodomy becomes the marker of the very excess it was supposed to signify in the first place. I want to reverse such rhetoricity on the part of historians and expose the logic with which sodomy was deployed. In this logic, sodomy, an extremely severe charge, was reserved for the top of the Church hierarchy. Sodomitical images were consistent with the "geography of perversion" the Reformers had inherited from humanists and had refined for their own purposes. Yet these slurs also follow a historical trajectory that needs to be explored.

War of Words, War of Religions

The dissemination of sodomy-related imagery was tied to the ups and downs of confessional conflicts between Protestants and Catholics. Pamphlets from the early years of the Reform (1517–21) seem reluctant to indulge in defamatory imagery associated with male-male sexuality.[24] Instead, they focus on the German lands' financial exploitation and circulate more conventional attacks on Rome, describing it as indulging in whoredom, corruption, simony, pomp, gluttony, or procurement. "Indecent, unnatural impurities" were named in general, but writers refrained from inserting more suggestive descriptions.

The step toward sodomy as a more forceful accusation was not a big one, however.[25] Roman clerics indulged in good food and drink, it was said, and a luxurious style of life necessarily would lead to sensual corruptions.[26] In one of his most famous dialogues (1520), Ulrich von Hutten quotes a character named Vadiscus as stating "that three things are in common usage in Rome, lust of the flesh, affluence of clothes, and pride." His interlocutor, Ernodlus, responds by hierarchizing this unholy trinity, ranking lust first; in the realm of the senses, he says, "they constantly invent new shameful sins. They scold those who only favor natural ways and call them boorish."[27] Because of their supposedly affluent style of living, clerics are portrayed as "effeminate," as deficient men, and as "weaklings."[28] Tellingly, such descriptions display the premodern paradigm of roguery and male libertinism where, as Randolph Trumbach has argued, deficient masculinity was not yet linked exclusively to suspicions of homosexual activity.[29] Rather, same-sex sexual activity was part of a whole spectrum of sexual outlets. Polemical discourse, however, tended to veer toward the extreme. What was implied in Hutten was made explicit in later pamphlets. Under the aegis of such a concept of depravity, the lustful sought ever new ways to satisfy their insatiable desires. Suspicions of sodomy were, therefore, not excluded. Importantly, sensual unruliness, including sodomy, appeared as an upper-class pastime—an argument well-suited for use against the papal court in Rome.

In the context of the Reform, polemic followed a path of radicalization that characterized much of the early development of the Reformation.[30] Once Luther had identified the pope as the Antichrist, the verbal floodgates were wide open. As a result, the Reformers amplified both the emotional and offensive value in polemical imagery. Yet the first steps in this direction were contested. In a 1521 treatise (*Super coelibatu*), Andreas Bodenstein, named Karlstadt (c. 1480–1541), describes the dangers of monastic celibacy by pointing rather graphically to masturbation and bestiality. This argument, couched in extremely strong language of those men and women who waste their semen, incurred Martin Luther's critique and Philipp Melanchthon's (1497–1560) discomfort—though Karlstadt had reserved his verbal vitriol for the Latin edition of his treatise only, while the German alluded to "sins that should not be expressed."[31] In the mid-1540s, offensive language, including suspicions of sodomy, had become more common. A Protestant who identified himself as "P.C.D." responded to "H.S.," a member of "the pope's camp." P.C.D. often used the adjective "sodomitical," when he castigated Catholics for obstructing the Protestant cause in the empire. He accused his opponent, H.S., of having published his own treatise "in locations in which the sodomitical Italian apostles . . . had first begun to dishonor, rob, burn, and kill the common man of the German nation." He juxtaposed "our fatherland" with "the sodomitical shrine in Rome," but added enigmatic details about how the Romans raised boys in their chambers and then sent them north to do harm. In his polemical view, the "Roman Sodomitical whore, your mother"—the Catholic Church—had conspired "to bring the vices of sodomy to Germany." Although the author criticized his opponent for having resorted to polemics, he endlessly repeated the highly charged formula of tyrant, Turk (or even *übertürckisch*), defrauder, and sodomite, though his treatise comprises only sixteen leaves.[32]

Usually, "conversations"—the most prominent type of pamphlet in the 1520s—featured one character who functioned as a messenger with whom the reader could identify.[33] As Germans, low-class observers, and paragons of Christian piety, these protagonists, named "Kunz" or "Hans" or simply "layman," served as a living "antithesis" to a "negative reference group" (Lawrence Stone). In Hutten's *Lament*, a German on his return from Italy gives a "firsthand" account of the events at the pope's court.[34] In another pamphlet, a supposedly authentic Italian addresses his fellow Italians and deplores the widespread sins of Sodom. This "Italian" voice advocates conversion to the truth of the Gospels.[35] Other pamphlets feature "authentic" documents. One pamphlet consists of a "papist manual," a supposedly original document, in which Catholic clerics are taught how to commit atrocities against the Christian faith.[36] In other cases, writers claim that a pamphlet's assertions could be experienced. "Experience will teach" those "who do not want to believe this," "how shamefully and repellently they [the supposedly spiritual prelates] live not only with women, but also (most of all the courtiers and the riff-raff at the pope's court) with their catamites [*Pusuronen*]," writes a mid-sixteenth-century polemicist.[37] In front of their print audience, popes readily talk about their sins, their heinous, idolatrous deeds, including their doings with women and boys. At rhetorically prominent junctures, that is, at the beginning and at the end of *Pasquillus,* for example, the devil reveals that he "especially liked very much the sodomitical abomination which is so common with you and your cardinals in Rome."[38]

As in other genres explored elsewhere in this book, pamphlets mostly presented illegitimate sexual activities with textual gestures of shame, disdain, and horror—means of inducing distance in anxiously close encounters between the Self and the Other. Seeking refuge in the German lands from Catholic persecution, Pasquillus, a comic stock figure of Protestant polemic, professes that while in Rome he "did as the Romans do; nevertheless, I was horrified by the shameful sin of sodomy."[39] He compares the strict prosecution of sodomites under antique Roman law (naming the *lex Iulia* specifically) to the new Rome, where sodomy had become common.[40] In various ways, Pasquillus distances himself from what he hastens to report and thus avoids a full-fledged description of the derided practice of sodomy.[41]

The pamphlets reviewed here offer anything but a picture of unified discourse administered by a central dogmatic institution. These writings originated within different strands of Protestantism and were disseminated in various ways; both theologians and laymen participated in making these slurs. Nevertheless, certain patterns, both in sodomy's imagery and its rhetorical presentation, permeate the rugged confessional landscape of sixteenth-century Germany and Switzerland.

Sexual and Social Strata

In polemical literature by Protestants, one of the highest violations of the divine and human order—sodomy—became identified with the highest ranks in the Catholic Church. In other words, the stratification of sexual (and other) sins was mapped on the stratification of Church offices. What once had been an accusation of the elites and directed to the elites, became, during the Reformation, an increasingly common way of denouncing ecclesiastical leaders, often targeting the upper echelons of the social hierarchy. Sodomy emerged as a sexual behavior characteristic of bishops, cardinals, and, most of all, popes.

In the early phase of the Reformation, when much of the discourse on sexuality revolved around the issues of celibacy and the marriage of priests, Reform-minded authors began to revile German Catholic bishops for promoting sexual impurity and prohibiting priests from redressing their "amoral state" through the "holy and pure state of matrimony."[42] According to Simon Reuter, "adultery, whoredom, and sodomitical sins" all derive from enforcing chastity on human beings.[43] Whereas bigamous men were barred from Church office, *sodomi* were not, lamented one interlocutor in a dialogue of 1525.[44] Arguments of rhetorical reversal like "The greatest and highest are the least when it comes to . . ." and the "pope as the head of all malice, ignominy, vice and evil" paved the way for sodomy accusations of this kind.[45] Metaphorically, Hutten called for decapitation, to save the body ecclesiastic from decay by a radical intervention.[46]

Thus, the dogmatic hierarchy of sins as developed by scholastic theology was turned against an institution that had espoused this edifice of beliefs over centuries. In later years, Popes Julius II, Leo X, Clement VII, Paul III, Julius III, Paul IV were all suspected of engaging in sex with young men at their court. "Isn't the pope with his . . . celibacy and dirty (*vnflätig*) chastity an archmaster of all sodomy, adultery, whoredom, and unchastity?" asked a Protestant who compared papal sinfulness to heretical movements in the history of Christianity, only to find that the popes, "the kings of Sodom," were even more depraved.[47] Erasmus Alberus's *New News from Rome* (*Newe zeittung von Rom*) of 1541 was "a family romance of sodomy": Pope Paul III (1550–55), surrounded by "innumerable knaves and pederasts" (*Buben und knabenschender on zal*), supposedly is a sodomite like his son, born by a whore.[48]

Sexual imagery focused specifically on the city of Rome and the Holy See as the site of all human vices. In a gesture of inversion, the holy city was exposed as an "inexhaustible mine of all evils and miseries."[49] "The pope and his sodomitical court following" became a stock phrase that was reiterated in endless variations.[50] Although some authors left unclear the sexual connotations, others delved into sexual innuendo. Homosocial contexts (the pope "with his tender little Junkers and painted dummies") often strongly implied that "Roman impurity" actually meant homosexual acts across lines of class and age.[51] In the chronicle of the city of Esslingen (1551), Dionysius Dreytwein relates the (hi)story of Pope Julius III, who elevated a boy from his entourage in order to please "his flesh's desire" (*seines fleischs begerlikeitt*). After having "florenced" him for a long time, he promoted this favorite to the rank of a cardinal—the "pope's whore," as the burghers of Rome supposedly called him.[52] In a treatise disseminated in both Latin and German, Philipp Melanchthon (1497–1560) endowed Rome, the center of Catholic Christianity, with layers of associations—the sexually licentious antique Rome as well as depraved Turkey. Under his pen, the ancient city was turned into a sewer with unbearably bad smells. One of the most widespread tropes with regard to sodomy—verbal horror—was transposed here to the realm of the senses with strong connotations of anal sexuality.[53] Although these passages often imply effeminacy, emasculation, and sexual submission in intercourse, sexual meanings were not always played out openly. In the guarded language of pamphlets, though replete with allusions to sexual acts, "Roman impurity" and "sodomy" are closely linked but not exactly equivalent.

In polemic, the differentiation among the highest ranks of the Catholic Church—portrayed as infested with sins that were difficult to name (and therefore difficult to understand)—and lower ranks that had committed lesser, heterosexual sins, served a distinct purpose. By this polemical move, monks, priests, and others were disentangled from loyalty to their Church superiors.[54] Ultimately, they were encouraged to leave Catholicism behind and join the ranks of the new religious community. Sodomy was linked to Catholics in Rome and Italy. By contrast, polemicists suspected plain German clerics of sustaining "monk whores" (Mönchshuren), with whom these monks had illegitimate offspring. Many Protestants found it only too obvious that Catholic clerics had formed such liaisons, and believed that their existence proved correct the Lutheran dogma of a licentious human nature that could not be shed, certainly not by a vow to remain chaste. With matrimony promoted as an order for all humankind, Protestant polemicists urged unchaste common clerics to legitimize their heterosexual unions. Thus, German Catholics were lured to convert to Protestantism.

Typically, pamphlets were called Vermanung (exhortatio), characterizing a mode of speech in which specific audiences were addressed spiritually. In a "Christian conversation" between an Augustinian and a Dominican monk of 1524, for example, the anonymous author tried to motivate monks to leave their monasteries. Not surprisingly, sodomy does not figure in this pamphlet. When it came to pastoral care, the rhetoric of Sodom was out of place.[55] Naturally, defamatory gestures toward the addressees would have undermined the genus persuasorium.[56]

In the context of the drive to win over Catholic clerics, the identification of Rome with Sodom served a distinct purpose: to make it easier for clerics to sever their ties with the center of Catholic orthodoxy. If Rome represented, as Protestant pamphlets held, the whore of Babylon, the Antichrist, and the new Sodom, then individual clerics were free to join the cause of Protestantism. The severity of the accusations and the starkness of the language, therefore, depended on the pamphlets' addressees.

Significantly, women are completely absent from this upside-down world of the defamed in the textual cosmos of Reformers. Almost no instance of defamation invoking same-sex sexual activities between women can be found in Luther's abundant writings or those of his contemporaries. On the rare occasions when the decried breaches of the divine sexual order involve both men and women, Luther used the double phrase of "mute sin and whoring."[57] Among hundreds of Reformation pamphlets that I have studied, I found only two defamatory remarks that, even by a long stretch of the imagination, may be said to hint at female-female sexuality.

With regard to nuns, Johann Eberlin von Günzburg (1483–1532), Luther's comrade-in-arms, mentioned "the unnamed sin as well as [sexual intercourse] with foul spirits."[58] Eberlin's abstract formula defied explicit description behind the veil of a highly conventional metaphor, though one that could be decoded, most likely either as masturbation or sexual acts between females. When exhorting nuns to leave their monastic institutions, the author, a more potent writer than most of his fellow polemicists with the exception of Luther, integrated a female voice in his text.[59] This nun advised other nuns to leave institutions that, as the author and his nun saw it, destroyed rather than bettered their hopes for spiritual salvation. If not satisfied within a legitimate union between husband and wife, nuns would have to seek sexual satisfaction in illegitimate ways.[60] In other words, nuns ought to marry.

Whereas Eberlin had his nun mention promiscuous sex with a "farmhand" (*stall knecht oder vych knecht*) in drastic terms, he only hinted at various less "natural" forms of sex, the "unnamed sin" of sodomy and sexual intercourse with evil spirits "as is now frequently discovered."[61] Such vague allusions to sexual acts were exceedingly rare in the large body of polemical publications, as were assertions of links between female homoeroticism and witchcraft, though Eberlin claimed a growing amount of evidence to support such an association. He radicalized notions about sexual doings behind convent walls that were proffered without insinuations of sodomy that had been made by such pre-Reformation teachers as Johann Geiler von Kaisersberg.[62] If readers knew Eberlin's identity (the text's first edition appeared anonymously), the fact that he had been a Franciscan lent credence to his suspicions of sexual doings among women. When proselytizing nuns to the cause of marriage, the Protestant Thomas Stör followed Eberlin in ranting against the dishonorable state of the "clerical sodomitical virgins" (*gaistlichen zodomitischen junckfrawen*).[63]

On the eve of the Reformation, defamation centered mostly on male power, political as well as intellectual power, religious authority and patriarchy,[64] a masculine realm from which women were *de facto* excluded despite highly popular imagery depicting the "woman on top," a reflection of the absence of women in lofty positions of power like those occupied by some women in France.[65] Note, however, that the ultimate battleground is all too often not sexual practice. Sodomy is a valued concept in the verbal exchanges among men promoting their competing aspirations to superiority, power, and intellectual precedence—an arena where defamation looms large and women are mostly confined to the antechamber.

Polemical Traditions

Neither Luther nor his fellow Reformers invented the explosive sexual imagery they deployed in their numerous polemical writings. Critiques of the Roman Catholic Church and the papacy were widespread on the eve of the Reformation, and many of them hinted at sodomy by invoking metaphors of unspeakability.[66]

In 1519 Martin Luther came across the Latin pamphlet *Julius exclusus* (later editions were also entitled *De obitu Julii*), composed shortly after Pope Julius II's death in 1513.[67] This and similar texts served as models for Luther's own pamphlets. In his view, this "very learned" piece was not the first to disclose the truth about "the Curia's monsters, but confirms what has long and everywhere been known."[68] In this pamphlet featuring several speakers, the former Pope Julius II (1503–13) arrives at St. Peter's gate in heaven only to find with great dismay that his keys do not fit. Starting from this symbolically charged comic situation, a long conversation unwinds in which the state of affairs in the papacy is relentlessly exposed.[69] St. Peter reveals that the former pope and his enormous entourage, with its extravagant display of wealth, reek of sodomy: "I am ashamed to say it and it annoys me to see that there is no part of your body that is not stained with visible signs of a horrific and shameful impurity that cannot be named."[70] The perceptibility of sins and the bodily signs of sinful behavior are an ongoing theme in this treatise. St. Peter comments, for instance, on the boys in the company of the former pope, intimating that they are Julius's erotic playmates. All these insinuations are mixed with highly informative digressions into Church history, Julius's biography, and warfare in northern Italy.[71]

The dialogue's effective use of an elevated style and of pseudo-dramatic scenes as well as the display of superior erudition have led many commentators to credit Erasmus with writing the piece.[72] Erasmus himself never claimed authorship; obviously, anonymity was one of the constant parameters for pamphlet literature. More importantly, a number of editions in the late 1510s testify to the piece's success even when the event that caused its publication—Pope Julius II's death—had lost its news value. Treatises like this anti-Roman polemic dating back to the period prior to the Reformation became models that were frequently imitated during the first decades of the Reformation. As Luther had wished, a German translation of *Julius exclusus* appeared circa 1520.[73]

The *Dialogus vere elegans* and its German translation, *Ein kleglich gesprech*, set for the different religious and political context of the year 1538, read like a counterpart to *Julius exclusus*.[74] The anonymous author claims to have eavesdropped on a conversation between Leo X (1513–21) and Clement VII (1523–34)—the two deceased Medici on the Holy See—and their chamberlain and messenger, Cardinal Spinola. Since both popes had died years before the piece was published, the dialogue was staged in hell, where Protestants suspected the popes to be.

Like his counterpart in *Julius exclusus*, the chamberlain, despite his Catholic credentials, was set in contrast to the depraved popes, thereby inviting the audience to sympathize with his reactions and commentaries. As in *Julius exclusus*, the popish protagonists openly confess their manifold wrongdoings in the course of a dialogue. As in *Julius exclusus*, the author mixed allusions to recent political issues (such as the English king Henry VIII's separation from Rome) with images of multiple depravities that culminated in the "unspeakable sin" of sodomy, which is effectively dramatized between the interlocutors. When Leo and Clement ask the chamberlain (who functions as a messenger of current affairs) about Pope Paul III and his son's current doings, they are informed that the latter, introduced as a sodomite (*busuron*), committed an act of "courtesy" (*hofflikeyt*)[75] on the bishop of Fano.[76] The term foregrounded the elitist associations of sodomy (*hoff* is "court"). Puzzled by an ambiguous term like "courtesy" (despite the preceding synonym of sodomite, *busuron*), one of the popes asks Spinola to explain the euphemism. He receives a cascade of circumlocutions replete with disgust: "the great tyranny, the most shameful sin that one could ever not only commit but even think. I myself am ashamed to name it, but wonder why God does not send fire from heaven because of it."[77] Interrupting the chamberlain's flow of words, Clement acknowledges that he finally comprehends and responds by asking: "It is a sin common to all of us, isn't it, Leo?" Leo answers that he conceivably would not be where he is—in hell—if he were not guilty of this vice.[78]

Many signals make the reader understand the (in)comprehensible, including a reference to the destruction of Sodom in Genesis 19. The fact that the two Medici popes are both Florentines provides an additional link to make the accusation credible. Moreover, the wordily constructed rejection of sodomy is juxtaposed with the commonality of the practice that they confess to, uniting two popes who followed one another in a genealogy of sins. After deliberating at length about the current state of Church affairs, both Leo and Clement thus calmly exit to endure their daily ritual of torture in hell.

Latin pamphlets such as *Julius exclusus* and *Dialogus vere elegans* were often translated into German. Denunciatory practices that had been reserved for the few thus became popularized on a grand scale. Accordingly, a great number of the pamphlets that appeared between 1520 and 1555 were disseminated in both German and Latin. During the Reform process with its high demand for printed information, translations often appeared in immediate succession. *Ein kleglich gesprech* appeared in the same year (1538) as its Latin model, *Dialogus vere elegans et lepidus*. When Martin Luther published *Against the Roman Papacy, an Institution of the Devil* in German in 1545, two independent Latin translations appeared in the same year, one by his close collaborator Justus Jonas (1493–1555) and another by an anonymous translator.[79]

When we compare German and Latin versions of the same text, German turns out to be an especially colorful, spiteful, and polemical linguistic medium of expression. Often, German texts elaborated on facts presented in Latin, emphasized the tone or exaggerated small details.[80] *Ein kleglich gesprech* (*A lamentable conversation*), a translation of *Dialogus vere elegans et lepidus* (*A truly elegant and witty dialogue*), for instance, added a suspicion of sodomy (*groß hauffen Cineden vnd Roß*, A3v) where in the Latin original a fictitious pope had characterized his rotten, extravagant court by referring to the upkeep of "dogs and horses" (*canes et equos*, A4r). In the German translation, the term *cineden* (catamites) replaced *canes* (dogs)—whether by a slip of the pen or deliberately is difficult to judge.[81]

Whereas German in the sixteenth century was less fit than Latin to express the subject matter of the arts and sciences, because of its "popular" qualities, it had a wide spectrum of polemical *colores rhetorici* at its disposal. German's relatively low level of standardization and its proximity to a host of dialects made it permeable to drastic expressions of all kinds. To add to the rhetoric of polemic in Latin, some polemicists therefore included German elements or words like *pusuron* that were geared toward having an effect on native speakers of German.[82]

As before the Reformation, sodomy in all its configurations evoked images of imminent danger.[83] In a confessional age that prided itself on having revived the study of the Bible, references to male-male sexuality could not be brought up without also referencing the destruction of Sodom and Gomorrah as told in Genesis 19.[84] Allusions to Genesis 19 engendered a sense of urgency that fit well with furthering the manifold causes propagated in pamphlet literature. These anxieties resonated with both lay and academic theology in which expectation of the world's imminent end was omnipresent.[85]

The noble Hartmuth von Cronberg (1488–1549) forewarns the Germans that if they do not turn to the Gospels, they will be punished even more than the inhabitants of Sodom and Gomorrah.[86] In passages like this, references to Sodom have no sexual specificity. Rather, the allusion to Sodom and Gomorrah reminds the readers of God's devastating retaliation for human behavior. In his pastoral letter to the new Protestant community of Zwickau, Wenzeslaus Linck (1483–1547) allegorized the Reform as the exodus from Sodom, an analogy positioned at the epistle's dénouement.[87] Linck tied "sodomitical mute sins" to praiseworthy matrimony by way of inversion. At the same time, these same sins, though clearly sexual, remain extremely vague in his description.[88] In a letter to his wife, Katherina von Bora (1499–1552), of July 1545, Luther likened even the city of Wittenberg, birthplace and revered haven of Protestantism, to *Sodoma*. Like Lot and his wife, Luther and his wife are to leave this urban hotbed of vice, where the vile round dance, revealing female attire, and illegitimate unions between the sexes outside of marriage prevail.[89]

One strand within pamphlet literature is akin to the genre of prediction or *prognosticatio*. Several pamphleteers adapted the literary formula of the most popular text in this genre, Johann Lichtenberger's *prognosticatio* (in which, among other predictions, Lichtenberger foresaw God's wrath because of same-sex sexual activities) to their own needs.[90] The fact that people "commit sins against nature" came itself to be a sign of the end of time: "Christians become so bold / That they begin impudent things / and turn their thoughts to mute sins."[91] In Martin Schrot's (d. before 1576) *Apocalipsis*, the pope's demise and the rise of Protestantism were linked to the pope's "sodomitical life."[92]

Millenarian writings of this kind became most virulent in the context of the Peasants' War of 1525. Hans Virdung's *Practica von dem Entcrist* predicted that God would single out Italian cities, especially Tuscan and Lombard ones, for destruction.[93] Some Protestant writers exploited popular familiarity with the genre in order to disseminate a message of moral improvement.[94] For Balthasar Wilhelm, the whole world had turned into a Sodom. This was a sign of the imminent end, a divine call to atone before God's wrath would strike humankind.[95] In an anonymous *Lamentation of the German Nation* (after Jeremiah) from 1526, the author compared all clerics to "the citizens of Sodom and Gomorrah who were destroyed by God with a thunder." Sodomites were positioned at the climactic end of a long list of socially degrading "professions," including "toilet cleaners, arsewipers, whorers, drunks, gamblers, rapists."[96]

Sodomy in a religious context added an apocalyptic layer to slander.[97] Moreover, it served as a focal point for a host of sins. In many instances, the cluster of wrongdoings associated with sodomy led to rather abstract contextualizations. Within other contexts, sodomy's sexual graphicness was exploited. In all instances, sodomy occupied the most elevated or, rather, the most abject symbolic space.[98]

Catholic Responses

Catholic writers were much less prone than Protestant pamphleteers to circulate suspicions of sodomy. This finding is consistent with David Bagchi's contention that the discourse of Catholic pamphleteers emphasized the legitimate authority of the Church; their discourse was reactive in nature and refrained from verbal excess.[99] As Germans, they probably shared beliefs that cast Italy as the land of sodomites. Catholic pamphleteers therefore exposed the Lutheran "heresy" without exploring the rich associations of illicit sex and particularly sodomy that were associated with the German words *ketzer* ("heretic" and "sodomite") or *ketzerie* ("heresy" and "sodomy").[100]

Commonly, these authors argued against Luther's dogmatic positions. Georg Witzel (1501–73), for example, refused to retort with counterabuse against his Protestant opponent, Justus Jonas. Instead, he contended that personal attacks were motivated by sheer desperation over the Protestant cause.[101] Of course, some Catholic polemicists were equally sharp-tongued in bad-mouthing Protestants. In *Wyder den Wittenbergischen Abgot Martin Luther* of 1524, the Franciscan Augustin von Alfeld (c. 1480–c. 1535) chastised Luther's followers by means of stark sexual language. He leveled charges such as unchastity, adultery, and rape against Protestants. Accusations of sodomy are largely absent from this pro-Catholic publication, though the author locates the new "evil Church" in the land of Sodom, Gomorrah, Seboym, Adama, and Segor—cities that God will destroy as he did once

before.[102] In his 1546 anonymous attack on Martin Bucer (1491–1551), Anton Engelbrecht (c. 1485–1558) portrayed Strasbourg's Reformer as a false
crusader against adultery who in truth defiled himself and his partners by
siring children with nuns and maids.[103] Even though Catholic writers used
sexual offenses as signifiers in a world that defied the divine order,[104] in
general their tone was less sexually vituperative.[105]

If Catholic writers vilified Luther by invoking a sexual register, they
usually exploited a different line of defamation, slurring Luther's excessive
heterosexuality. Thus, Simon Lemnius (d. 1550), a Protestant *manqué*, im-
pugned Luther's integrity by suggesting that in his marriage to Katherina
von Bora, it was the woman who was on top and that her husband, though
lecherous, could not satisfy Katherina's insatiable sexual drive. Tellingly, he
labeled his scathing caricature of Wittenberg *Monachopornomachia* or *Battle
of the Monks' Concubines* (1538).[106]

Disciplining Polemics

The sodomite was a versatile and unstable figure whose nebulous contours
served various functions and permeated different shades of Protestantism.
Ironically, the protean nature of this figure made it dispensable. Once the
different Protestantisms had consolidated, the sodomite as a stock figure of
Protestant polemic was laid to rest.

In the years following the Diet of Augsburg (1555), pamphlet literature
went into sharp decline and with it the images of Sodom that had been
so persistently circulated by this type of literature. By the later decades of
the sixteenth century, few publications rose to the propagandistic fervor
of the late Luther. In fact, Luther's *Against the Roman Papacy* of 1545 had
itself given rise to criticism among his supporters. Many felt Luther had
gone too far in his verbal rage.[107] A Catholic pamphleteer called Martin
Luther "Mortinus" (from Latin *mors*, "death," and in lieu of Martinus)—a
wailer and lamenter from a "raging city" (*in montibus ferriosis, Wüttenberg dictis*),
playing upon the phonetic similarity of *wütten*—to rage—and *Wittenberg*.[108]
Luther's verbal vitriol provoked criticism even among his followers.[109] In
a dialogue between a true follower of the Gospels (*evangelischer Christ*) and
a Lutheran, a derogatory expression for a false Protestant in this context,
published as early as 1524, Hans Sachs (1494–1576) had one interlocutor
named Hans say, "The Lutherans do nothing but insult clerics . . . how can
one find good in them and their teaching?"[110] After the mid-1520s, fear
of sectarianism among Protestant groups stimulated interest in control-

ling the output of pamphlets,[111] and their output decreased rapidly. Even when the confessional conflicts escalated again in the 1580s, the rhetoric of sodomy was more rarely invoked. It was because defamations carried sexual connotations (among other reasons) that their deployment decreased after the Reformation. Many factors contributed to this shift toward toning down verbal aggression. In a development that was far from linear, a state-controlled Protestantism gradually replaced the more diffuse religious regimes of an earlier period. The censorship of printers and print publications became another important means of enforcing the new climate of rhetorical restraint.[112]

Yet this new verbal regime, inimical to polemics, did not remain uncontested. In 1551 a Protestant writer under the pen name of Sigismund Cephalus argued vigorously against what he perceived as emerging tolerance among Protestants of Catholicism. In his view, such unwillingness to fight Satan and his forces constituted a breach of the divine command to disseminate the truth of the Gospels. Clearly, such a truth demanded rigorous, strong, vituperative language against the "princes of Sodom and the people of Gomorrah" (*fürsten von Sodom / vnd das volck von Gomorrha*). Starting with the treatise's title, Cephalus did not hesitate to provide his readers with ample linguistic evidence of such language. He criticized "the powerful" (*die gewaltigen*) for asking priests to reprimand Christians "abstractly" (*abstractive*), not individually or *ad personam*, that is, by disclosing a sinner's identity.[113] In the author's view, censoring priests equaled censoring the divine word. He refuted the Biblical reference his opponents used to bolster their argument, Matthew 5:22 ("whoever insults his brother shall be liable to the council"), by saying it was not applicable to the word of God. He defended the rich repertory of Protestant polemic against a perceived onslaught of control. His own language reflects the increasing abstraction with which polemical arguments were proffered. Although the sin of Sodom was listed, the sin's rhetorical register was strikingly mild compared to Luther's *Against the Roman Papacy, an Institution of the Devil*.

Of course, the polemical images that had helped to make the Reformation a successful crusade lived on in a variety of ways. Some passed on to publications other than pamphlets. Despite all attempts to control public speech, the stream of pamphlets never came to a complete halt. In addition, *Wissensliteratur* or collections of stories, published in the late sixteenth and seventeenth centuries, became the receptacle for some of the slurs discussed in this chapter.[114] Ironically, defamatory suspicions were thus reconfigured as knowledge of a higher order.

The transition to a new moral economy will be illustrated by an invective that, like few others, fueled the imagination of European societies in the age of confessionalization. Investigating the slur against the celebrated Italian writer and bishop Giovanni Della Casa (1503–56) allows me to recapitulate some of the constants of sodomy defamations. It also enables me to demonstrate the tremendous impact of pamphlets, since such a publication initiated the smear.

When at the beginning of the seventeenth century an English traveler, Thomas Coryat (1577?–1617), went on a grand tour of Europe, he also came to Zurich. There, he met with "Henry" (Heinrich) Bullinger, a descendant of the great theologian and successor of Huldrych Zwingli, Heinrich Bullinger, whose library "Henry" had inherited. Among other treasures in Bullinger's study, Coryat marveled at a great rarity, "one most execrable booke written by an Italian, one Joannes Casa Bishop of Beneventum in Italy, in praise of that unnaturall sinne of Sodomy." The volume is described in some detail: "This booke is written in the Italian tongue, and printed in Venice."[115] Yet our traveler felt compelled to explain why the collection harbored such a dangerous book as Della Casa's poems: "It came first to the hands of the man's grandfather aforesaid, who kept it as a monument of the abhominable impurity of a papistical Bishop, to which end this man also received it from his grandfather, keepeth it to this day."[116] Though the Venetian print was indeed hard to come by, the invective associated with it was not. According to Winfried Schleiner, the smear against Della Casa amounted to "one of the most often rehearsed commonplaces of Protestant propaganda."[117]

Not accidentally, *De laude sodomiae* or *De laudibus sodomiae*, "The Praise (or Defense) of Sodomy," was of Italian origin. What is more, a prominent representative of the old creed, the prelate and humanist Giovanni Della Casa (1503–56), was said to have authored what figured as a poetic apology of sodomitical sex. For many decades if not centuries, this "Defense of Sodomy" marked a literary transgression of the utmost severity in Protestant polemic. By dint of a poem, Della Casa was said to have "defended" a sexual practice that God had condemned vigorously. The *scandalum* was having authored and published such a piece, these writers claimed. Della Casa's imagined transgression thus served as a potent stimulus for his critics to represent sodomy through revulsion against the practice and its so-called defender. As late as Johann Heinrich Zedler's *Universal-Lexikon* (1743), one of the leading encyclopedias of the early Enlightenment, the entry on sodomy recapitulates the debate around Della Casa.[118]

What passed as *De laude sodomiae* was a poem from a collection of verses published in Venice in 1538.[119] The poem's title was not "The Praise of Sodomy," as Della Casa's detractors would have it, but *Il capitolo sopra il forno* or, simply, *Il forno*. *Il forno* was a metaphor whose erotic connotations are apparent even if one does not add that the "oven" was a well-known erotic image in Italian poetry of the times. Hiding the sexual content—anal intercourse—behind a veil of dubious pronouns and creating a masquerade of metaphorical transpositions, these verses fit easily within the tradition of erotically explicit poetry, where the sexually audacious demanded a particular aesthetic practice of veiled allusions. Here, one might conjecture, at the edge of conventionality, where sexual and linguistic transgressions intersected, lay the lure of the poet's interest in obscenity. An artistic poem like *Il capitolo sopra il forno* is far from advocating anything, let alone sodomy. This absence may be the mark of the aesthetic, but this circumspection offered no protection against polemics.[120]

Only fragmentary knowledge of Della Casa's "Defense of Sodomy" circulated throughout early modern Europe. When Johannes Sleidan (1506–56), the Reformation's "court" historian, published his *Commentaries on the state of religion and the republic* (1555), he decried the fact that Della Casa had not been ashamed (*nec enim puduit eum*) to publish a "booklet . . . full of ganymedes" (*libellum . . . plane cinaedum*) on an "atrocious deed more shameful than all others, but extremely known in Italy and in Greece" (*scelus omnium longe turpissimum, sed per Italiam nimis notum atque Graeciam*).[121] Whatever sex practice Della Casa circumscribed in his poem, this detractor took *Il forno* to be about sexual relations among men. In his universal "library" (*Bibliotheca*), Konrad Gesner (1516–65) mentions Giovanni Della Casa solely with reference to his poetical "Defense of Sodomy" and his role as censor, despite his authorship of a famous book of etiquette, *Il Galateo*, as well as of many other stylish writings in both Italian and Latin. He is listed as having penned an index of prohibited books and "a couple of Italian poems, printed in Venice [*in publicum Venetijs excusa*], in which he (oh heinous deed) extolled sodomy through praises."[122] Derisively, Johann Fischart (1541–90) mocked Della Casa as the bishop of Malevent rather than the bishop of Benevent that he was, exchanging "good" (*bene*) for "bad" (*male*).[123] Thomas Nashe (1567–1601) counts the fact that "Sodomitrie[124] a Cardinall commends" as proof of the fact that "there is no vice / Which learning and vilde knowledge brought not in."[125] In a different work, while again arguing against dangerous readings, the same author lumped Germans and Italians together, stating that "the posterior Italian and German cornugraphers sticke not to applaude and canonnize vnnaturall sodomitrie."[126] German legal manuals of the seventeenth century allude to Della Casa's poem while the authors expound the workings of the law on sodomy.[127] Seen through the lens of polemics, Della Casa's poem took on manifold guises, to be sure.

While enlightened literati of a later age made a point of publishing the incriminated poem together with their pleas to exonerate Della Casa (at least from the charge of praising sodomy, though not of the youthful misdeed of having published obscene poetry),[128] many of their late sixteenth-century forebears did not have access to these obscure verses other than in the context of slanderous gossip about them.[129] Before these editions, it must have been hard to get hold of a copy of *Il forno* to study its content, at least outside of Zurich, whence the whole propagandistic coup had been launched.

Over the course of centuries, Della Casa's poem has not divulged beyond all doubt the sexual practice it depicted as well as veiled—despite all the efforts summoned to extort its secret. Is *Il capitolo sopra il forno* about heterosexual or homosexual intercourse? Scholars and readers arrived at either the one or the other conclusion. More important than unequivocally answering this question or adding another chapter to this "sexual philology" is to point to the insistence of the question itself. For Della Casa, the slipperiness of his poetic play was warranted by the term sodomy. Theologically, both heterosexual and homosexual anal sex could be cast as *vicium sodomiticum*. After all, these sexual activities were one and the same in ignoring God's command to procreate. Yet the multilayeredness of the term sodomy in scholastic theology—usually subdivided into masturbation, anal intercourse between man and woman, homosexual intercourse, sexual intercourse with animals—came up against efforts, already manifest during the early modern period, to capture sodomy unambiguously, usually as male-male eroticism, and narrowly, especially in polemical passages. The attempts of critics to make unambiguous what Della Casa had left opaque purposefully manifest the desire to harmonize Della Casa's poem with powerful and polemical images of the foreign, in which the Italians (and Catholic prelates in particular) like Della Casa were thought to practice same-sex eroticism.

The origins of the smears regarding Della Casa's "Defense of Sodomy" can be traced with great accuracy. In the Swiss Confederacy in the year 1549, an Italian refugee, Pietro Paolo Vergerio (d. 1565), former bishop of Capodistria (Koper), published a pamphlet containing an annotated edition of one of the first Catholic indexes, authored by none other than Giovanni Della Casa in the same year. [130] Wordily pretending to be at a loss for words that might express the inappropriate "appropriately" (*con parole degne*), Vergerio accuses Della Casa by addressing him personally at the pamphlet's climactic end. Having commented at length on various items, he asks why obscene works do not appear in the index. At this juncture, at the rhetorical dénouement of his pamphlet, the piece's *peroratio* with its emotionally heightened tone, he discloses Della Casa's depravity by exposing him as an advocate of male-male sexuality. According to Vergerio, Della Casa composed "some . . . verses that were printed with your beautiful name on front . . . and you have spoken up to celebrate the praises, alas, I am ashamed to say it, but I will say it nevertheless, because my God wants me to and forces me so that I have to say it and reveal who are his foes, you have spoken up to celebrate (by your leave) the praises of sodomy," [131] adding that "this is widespread in all of Italy." [132] The accusation brands Della Casa, an educated Church official, as a heretic—heretics being, as I have shown, vilified as perpetrators of same-sex sexual acts.

With great verbosity, Vergerio invokes the topos of the unspeakable. Brilliantly, he delays any mention of sodomy and thereby inflates his own rhetoric considerably. In imitation of oral speech, he seems to hesitate several times, only to gather his courage and finally express the inexpressible. It is only God's command to speak out that causes Vergerio to give up restraint. Fighting for a divine cause required a verbal practice beyond the rules of the ordinary. Sodomy's status as an ultimate sin was marked by extravagant rhetoric and the prominent position it held in this tract. Della Casa's willingness "to praise sodomy" contrasted powerfully with Vergerio's verbose unwillingness to name "it."

In order to proselytize among his compatriots, Vergerio published the pamphlet in Italian without naming the location of its original publication (possibly Zurich), for most Italians had not yet taken (and for the most part never would take) the step that Vergerio was about to complete, that from Catholicism to a new creed. He himself never fully joined a particular form of Protestantism, and, not surprisingly, he was viewed with increasing suspicion by the Reformers themselves. Yet in singling out Della Casa as an exemplar of Catholic depravity, Vergerio was not without personal animus. After 1548 Della Casa, papal nuncio in Venice, headed the prosecution against Vergerio, the former papal legate to the German lands, for heretical tendencies—according to Anne Jacobson Schutte, "the first [inquisition] trial of a bishop for heresy." [133] The investigation into Vergerio's orthodoxy was first initiated in 1544 and finally resulted in Vergerio's escape to the lands north of the Alps in 1549. In Rhetia and on travels abroad, he joined the small but eminent group of Italian expatriates, all followers of the Gospel (spirituali), to whose leadership he aspired.[134] In fact, the 1549 tract was one of his first publications in his new role as a relentless critic of the Catholic church.[135]

It would be a mistake to turn Vergerio into a champion of freedom of expression and an opponent of censorship. In fact, while trying to impugn Della Casa's qualifications as a censor, this Catholic manqué approved of censorship in general. His accusation heralds a change of a larger magnitude: Within the context of the various Reforms, authors were increasingly held morally liable for the content of their writings, a concern which contributed significantly to the emergence of the category of the author and his oeuvre. Genre distinctions were leveled by this pressure to cohere on moral (and legal) grounds. Whereas medieval authors often wrote within the parameters of textual conventions valid for a particular milieu, early modern writers also had to conform to moral standards. Polemic in the context of the Reformation thus sheds new light on "the author" as auctor of texts and of actions.

It is surprising that another of Della Casa's writings never inspired the Reformed rhetoricians' furor. In Quaestio lepidissima an uxor sit ducenda, he had treated a common question among humanists, the question of whether one ought to marry or not.[136] Playfully (lepidissima) addressing a group of unmarried youths, the orator, presented as an expert in marriage (Nam et nos cum uxore fuimus, id quod non ignoratis, aliquot annos),[137] rehearses the whole arsenal of antifeminist topoi, only to argue, for the sake of the state, in favor of matrimony at the oration's surprising end. Martin Luther ranted against similar arguments taken from the Querelle des femmes in his writings on matrimony.[138] In a preface to a treatise on marriage, the Reformer lengthily castigated Sebastian Franck (1499–1542) for having included misogynistic verses in a collection of proverbs, reading the relevant lines as "proof" of Franck's utter lack of respect for his own mother.[139] To us, Della Casa's oration may well serve as a caveat against reading in the Reformed mode, that is, taking rhetorical stances for biographical facts. Historians who label sexual identity on the basis of literary evidence run the risk of misjudgment because of the anachronism of terms such as homosexual, heterosexual, or bisexual. Judging by his poems, commentators have labeled Della Casa a sodomite or, in modern parlance, a homosexual, while, judging by the Quaestio lepidissima, we might conjecture heterosexuality. This indeterminacy may be the reason why Schutte called the same man "a bisexual."[140] The willingness to pin down sexual identity by reference to literature gives evidence of a modernist bias some of whose roots lead back to the disciplining of publishing during the sixteenth-century Reforms.

We have a firsthand account of the tremendous shock value that Vergerio's revelations had for an audience of educated Protestants. In a letter to Heinrich Bullinger, Oswald Myconius (1488–1552), leader (*antistes*) of the Basel church, dramatically shared a piece of information he had learned during a recent conversation with the Italian émigrés Pietro Paolo Vergerio and Curio Celio Secundo (1503–69), namely, "that a certain papal legate [Della Casa] wrote in Italian against the German heretics. Among other things, he excuses the sin of Sodom on the occasion, praising it as a divine work [*opus divinum*]."[141] Apparently, the letter's author believed this piece of news to be sensational. Before disclosing the information, Myconius prescribed a physical posture deemed appropriate for the content of the message that was about to follow, a posture indicating bodily distress. Sodomy invaded the senses, or so it was suggested. The body's openings therefore had to be put on guard: "Plug your ears, focus your eyes."[142] In such a strained posture, reading the news must have metamorphosed into a physical act, not unlike penetration. The writer cast the sin that involves sexualized bodies into a rhetoric which elided the epistle as medium of communication: the letter simulated an encounter with strong physical overtones. No wonder then that the news itself reached its readers only in a distorted fashion.

Besides the calculated physicality of this passage, another rhetorical device is worth noting. Frequently, sixteenth-century writers craft facts and fictions about sodomy as unheard-of novelties. Again, Myconius: "In addition, it will please you to hear what, I believe, neither you nor anybody else has ever heard."[143] Let us not take this literally. It is a censorious move apt to silence sources of knowledge, polemics among them, that were available to sixteenth-century scholars and readers. We are dealing with a gesture signaling noninvolvement on the part of the writer, who presents himself as unable to conceive or know of such acts—ignorance unlikely in view of the writer's erudition. Tropes staging unfamiliarity were commonplaces with regard to sodomy, especially among Reformers who wanted to foster an image of a moral probity newly gained. Familiarity with the rhetorical gesture of disclosing a secret may in fact have helped to make Della Casa's "Defense of Sodomy" an early modern *cause célèbre* in scholarly conversations on same-sex sexual acts.

By the time of this meeting recorded in a letter, Vergerio had already composed his tract, which Myconius narrowed down to one element, a treatise "against that sodomite" (*contra Sodomitam istum*). Yet this piece of insult masquerading as information was far too precious in the war of the confessions to be kept to private conversations. Since Vergerio had published *Il catalogo* in Italian, Myconius asked him for a Latin translation. In a letter to Joachim von Watt of January 1550, Vergerio indeed speaks of a Latin and a German version of the pamphlet.[144] Yet even without these published translations, the invective made the rounds among the educated.

Polemics were an effective weapon and pamphlets an effective vessel for disseminating invectives. For one, because of the uproar his poem created, Della Casa never became a cardinal as he desired, or so historical legend has it. What is more, he retorted in the same vein. In an age of honor, offensive words induced offensive words. By means of a pamphlet (*Dissertatio adversus Paullum Vergerium*), Della Casa leveled stark accusations against his former fellow-bishop, Vergerio. He dismissed the accusation that he had praised sex with men, instead claiming that he had written about sex with women. The attacked poet and bishop also addressed the Germans (*Ad Germanos*) in an elegant Latin poem, defending himself against the charge of having authored indecent poetry. He pointed to his youth and argued that he had written the verses in jest—arguments of a *literatus* in both form and content, but arguments hardly apt to pacify the stir he had created.[145] Sodomy was anything but an appropriate topic for jest, at least north of the Alps.[146]

By the early 1540s, only a few years after the poem's publication in 1538, the onset of the Catholic Reform changed the moral climate in Italy also. In the following years, Della Casa refashioned himself as one of the Reform's staunch supporters.[147] Given his ecclesiastical rank and his new role as arbiter of Catholic dogma, circulating poetry of the licentious kind became inappropriate.[148] Yet the cross-Alpine polemical clash around Della Casa brought to the fore the different dynamics of literary discipline that governed Italian and German society. Both societies embarked on a road of ecclesiastical reform in the sixteenth century, but the thrust of changes following the Council of Trent hit Italian Catholics only after 1550. It is in this crucial period between the beginnings of the Reformation and the end of the Council of Trent that the polemical debate on Della Casa emerged.

The increasing rigidity with regard to the discourse on sexual matters became evident when, in 1559, Giovanni Della Casa (d. 1556), author of the Venetian index of 1549,[149] was himself indexed on the first such index issued in Rome. Under the rubric where selected publications by certain authors were prohibited (in other words, not all his publications were indexed), we find the entry: *Ioannis Casae poemata.*[150] The index's modern editors insist that the Roman censors in the 1550s were familiar with Vergerio's pamphlets against Della Casa, though the exact impact of Vergerio's crusade is hard to assess. Vergerio himself was quick to note the fact that his opponent, the late archbishop of Benevent, had become an object of concern to the gatekeepers of Catholic orthodoxy. He immediately reported his triumph in a letter to the head of the Reform in Zurich, Heinrich Bullinger.[151] In a Latin commentary on the new index of 1559 (the one that listed Della Casa), published in 1560, he reveled publicly in the Catholic censorship of Della Casa's works and remarked: "Even the Antichrist [i.e., the pope] realizes that horrible and abominable misdeed."[152]

The very terms of literariness underwent a significant change in the sixteenth century. Della Casa's poem had partaken of an elaborate literary-aesthetic code. But it went down in the annals as a piece of evidence. To Protestant literati, *Il capitolo sopra il forno* proved Catholic depravity—a depravity beyond all hope of return. Della Casa, the censor, became a living example of the satanic wolf in Catholic sheep's clothing. What was at issue was not sexual practice alone. It was the *publication* of a poem that stimulated the furor around Della Casa. At issue were the boundaries of public speech. Under a regime of enforced moral strictness in Reformed communities on all sides of the religious divides, public speech had to be governed by extreme caution. Talking about sodomy qualified as the violation of a decorum which gained new credibility in confessional competition. Furthermore, the demarcations between different modes of literary expression lost significance during that process—a process which the reception of Della Casa's *Il forno* shows. Every literary utterance, be it in Latin or German, in a play, a poem, or a sermon, could be measured against the standards of the new moral economy. The communicative niches that had made it possible for medieval writers to circulate their writings among a limited audience (thereby allowing them to be, for instance, more sexually explicit in certain contexts) lost their status as venues of expression. They were replaced by a more unified understanding of public speech whose boundaries were or were supposed to be policed by the guardians of confessional morality. In polemics, all differences between genres were leveled. Irony and jest were lost on these "new" readers. The poetic product, whatever its literary frame of reference, came to represent an author's moral integrity. Irony, satire, and similar modes of ambivalence were thus laid to rest. To be sure, such control was far from fully developed or perfect, but the full force of polemical debate hit many a writer. Thus, the relationship between a writer and his writings took on a new form. Now a writer's utterances were thought to reflect his beliefs. Increasingly, writers were held morally responsible for their writings.

Conversely, polemic emerges as a potent literary force in the early modern period. Sodomy as a term called for the courtroom, only rarely for a writer's poetic self-identification. The ubiquity of the disparaging anecdote testifies to the effectiveness of polemical slurs and the appeal of pamphlets and other publications circulating them. Polemics was part and parcel of the ancien régime's literary horizon. The manifold stories around Della Casa's poem also exemplify the increasing constraints on publications in the sixteenth century, especially after the cultural wars of confession had begun. Composed at a time when Italy was about to embark on the Catholic Reformation, the poem rose to be an emblem of these same religious conflicts and reform movements. The ultimate sin of sodomy was made to symbolize the ultimate depravity of Roman Catholics in general and of Roman Catholic bishops especially. In other words, the symbolic status of sodomy was such that a casual poem and its reference to sexual practice could be used to vilify a whole person, a whole country, a whole church.

8

The Close Encounter of Matrimony and Sodomy

"Marriage is the social institution whose regulatory functions ramify everywhere" in the early modern era, whereas "[s]odomy . . . fully negates the world, law, nature."[1] With these words, Jonathan Goldberg circumscribes a highly significant moment in the duet that unfolds between the distant relatives of the heterosexuality/homosexuality dichotomy, marriage and sodomy. The figure of speech at play in this passage is one encountered several times in the course of this study, *inversio*. The sexual appears as the inverse to the social. Whereas marriage's impact on the social can be traced, sodomy, according to Goldberg, evades categorization. Indeed, *inversio* has been invoked so often to describe the phenomenon known by that utterly confused name, sodomy,[2] that the term inversion itself came to circumscribe sexual acts between persons of the same sex—practitioners who in turn were labeled "inverts" (though after the period under consideration here).

To be sure, we cannot escape rhetoric. All we can do is to call attention to rhetoric's workings. Thus viewed, the trope by the name of *inversio* operates as a constraint on our ability to grasp the manifold dynamic relationships that group phenomena together, in the past as much as the present. The relationship between sodomy and marriage, as I will argue in the following, can also be cast as mutually constitutive in forms other than *inversio*. Not only did sodomy surface when marriage was talked about, but also a particular understanding of marriage gave shape to a particular understanding of sodomy. In other words, sodomy became legible through matrimony as much as matrimony achieved legibility through its supposed sexual opposite. During the early history of the Reform, marriage and sodomy formed a close alliance—a rhetorical wedding that was relatively novel, as Goldberg's quote suggests. Yet while numerous studies have focused on matrimony in the context of the Reformation, sodomy and its relation to legitimate sexual activity in marriage have by and large escaped critical attention. In other words, sodomy is traceable through marriage. What is more, matrimony was more than a social institution. It held a firm but multi-faceted place in the early modern imaginary of Reformation Germany and Switzerland. And this is where matrimony connected with sodomy most intimately.

✠✠✠

Matrimony has offered modern historians an exquisite laboratory for investigating how the sexes interacted or, from the perspective of textual critics, were supposed to interact. Regardless of whether researchers subscribed to a romantic view in which the Protestant propagation of marriage improved the lot of women, or the opposite view in which the Reformers' focus on marital life intensified the subjugation of the so-called weaker sex, marriage became the primary site of investigation that placed gender on the map of early modern German, and especially Reformation, history.[3] In a nuanced synthesis of great analytical force, Isabel Hull concludes that "[m]arriage was in fact the key social/sexual institution of the early modern period."[4] Unlike Hull, who canvassed a broad array of sexual practices, many historians of the Reformation have aligned themselves with that which is arguably central—marriage—without exploring the framework of social and discursive forces that was necessary to bestow this centrality on marriage in the first place. Yet how can we approach the so-called order of matrimony critically if we set marriage apart from the field of social and discursive forces in which it rests so uneasily?

Even the few historians who address the sexual margins in the context of the Reformation assert their lack of significance. Richard van Dülmen contended that "in German courts homosexuality was a marginal phenomenon."[5] To be sure, north of the Alps women who had sex with women almost never came to court, while men were only rarely prosecuted for same-sex sexual activities. As this book has shown, some of these court trials attracted a great deal of attention, however. They amounted to spectacles of crime, and court records reveal oral networks of informed "grumbling" in communities.[6] With regard to the Protestant discourse *in sexualibus,* Hull stated that Reformers were "so firmly fixed on marital or heterosexual sex, . . . that they had little to say about sodomy, bestiality, and masturbation."[7] In pamphlets, however, the close alliance of matrimony and sodomy fused what was perceived to be distant, foreign, secret, and heretical with that which was familiar, orthodox, and close to home. Yet it is the Reformers' restructuring of sexual discourse itself that left the terrain beyond legitimate sexuality so inaccessible. In Protestant writings about sexual matters, sodomy and the whole gamut of practices that one encounters in medieval *summae* came to be hidden behind differentiations separating legitimate sexual acts in marriage from illegitimate extramarital acts. It is not that Protestant writers had nothing to say about sodomy. Rather, they chose to deproblematize conjugal sexuality by throwing into relief the whole range of devilish doings outside of marriage.[8] As a result of such rigid juxtapositions, sexual discourse became even vaguer than prior to the Reformation.

After 1519 the debate on the celibacy of priests inaugurated a vehement discussion of the sexual order appropriate for the Reformed body social.[9] By reconsidering the sexual status of priests, Reformers continued a debate that had originated before the Reformation. The so-called *Reformation of the Emperor Sigismund* (*Reformatio Sigismundi*), an anonymous manifesto for church reform, written in Basel in 1439, most likely by a member of the lower clergy, stated that priests should be allowed to marry legally in order to avoid illicit sexual outlets: "Many priests have lost their livings because of women. Or they are secret sodomites. All the hatred between priests and laymen is due to this." And the manifesto concludes: "In sum: secular priests ought to be allowed to marry. In marriage they will live more piously and honorably, and the friction between them and the laity will disappear."[10]

The celibacy of priests figured as a marker of social and sexual distinction. In this and other statements, a priest's status within his parish was at stake. The multiple loyalties of priests summoned up considerable concerns—concerns that were also played out on the level of jokes and fabliaux. Priests were imagined as sexual transgressors, commonly as predators on their parishioners' wives but in more polemical texts and especially from a Protestant perspective, as sodomites. In the fantasies around the liminal position of the clergy, priests were, by virtue of sexual activity, thus denigrated or, rather, according to various critics, elevated to become members of the community of believers, just as fallible or prone to sexual activity as everybody else. Critiques of the clergy's corrupt behavior before and during the Reformation responded to what were often perceived as social evils, concubinage and adultery. The Protestant pamphleteer Johann Eberlin von Günzburg held that if they had wives, "many priests would stop being idlers and whore chasers. Instead they would marry, learn trades and live like pious fellow burghers and fellow Christians."[11] For Reformers, the marital union appeared to be synchronous with the divine and secular order, while people in monastic institutions supposedly violated this prescribed way to live.

Once the Wittenberg theologians had recognized that priestly celibacy was not founded on the Scriptures (1520/21), their arguments became more radical. They fleshed out the dire outcomes of a life against God's will and Nature's necessity, not only for the salvation of individual priests, but also for human society at large. In 1520 Andreas Karlstadt showed himself concerned about priestly masturbation and bestiality—practices he equated with idolatry.[12] Winfried Schleiner has called attention to the fact that Martin Luther's treatise on monastic vows (De votis monasticis) "invokes Sodom at least four times."[13] Eberlin claimed that one could experience daily how the "devilish prohibition to marry" encouraged fornication, adultery, incest, and sodomy among clerics.[14] In a pamphlet staging a "friendly conversation" between a Franciscan and a craftsman, the monk exclaims: "By God, we should have women in monasteries to avoid worse," and added "because of the mute sin" (potentially referring to masturbation but certainly referring to sodomy): "How can a monk or a nun be chaste if they drink and eat well without working?"[15] In a 1524 dialogue between two laymen and a monk, Hans Sachs exposed the hypocrisy of clerical vows, chastity among them. A certain Hans suspects that "although you [monks] refrain from sexual acts, you defile yourself in other inappropriate ways."[16]

Many voices in the rising wave of publications on marriage relied on an implicit or explicit opposition between marriage and sodomy/Sodom. When Luther mentions matrimony, especially in polemical contexts, allusions to the "unmentionable sin" or sodomy are frequently to be found in close proximity.[17] A letter of circa 1075 on clerical celibacy, allegedly by a bishop of Augsburg, Ulrich (Huldericus) (890–973), which gathered a substantial readership during the Reformation, authenticated the charge that the Catholic clergy had always indulged in adultery, rape, as well as sodomy (with boys), "though it is shameful to talk about it."[18] When defending his marriage, a newly wed priest resisted talking about the temptations of the flesh "more clearly" (deutscher ader klerer), since "everybody carries old Adam around."[19] In 1523 Simon Reuter echoed the Reformatio Sigismundi's concerns when he contended that bishops acted against God's will in their persecution of married priests, who have escaped the "adultery, whoredom, and sodomitical sins" that originated in celibacy.[20] In a poem published in 1562, Hans Sachs looked back to the history of the Church after the Council of Nicaea (325), when "against God and natural law" clerics had been barred from matrimony, and noted with satisfaction that many places in Germany had restored the natural, divine order. The poet stated that "sodomitical and horrible sins" (sodomitisch und grewlich sünd), just as adultery, rape, perjury, and murder, are the result if one prohibits men, be they members of the clergy or the laity, from living in matrimony.[21] Johannes Bugenhagen (1485–1558) hailed the departure of priests from "the land of the sodomites," welcoming them among the married.[22] Characteristically, sodomy's sexual connotations are rarely played out in these contexts. Yet these passages resonate with more obscene descriptions in the polemical theology treated in earlier chapters.

By advocating clerical marriage, Reformers redrew the boundary separating the sacred and the sexual.[23] If the absence of sexual activity among the clergy had previously signified the sacred, now celibacy contradicted God's will and humanity's corporeality, which was taken to be self-evidently libidinous; the sacred was supposed to cohabit with sexual activity in matrimony. Subsequently, theologians condemned behavior incongruous with marriage in toto: "For if we judge the tree by the fruits, I pray you, what fruits of single life may we recite? What filthiness, what bawdry, what adulteries, what fornications, what ravishings, what incests and heinous copulations may we rehearse? Who at this day liveth more unchaste or dishonest, than the rabble of priests and monks do?"[24] By advocating the marriage of priests, Reformers thus shifted the religious and cultural meanings of priesthood and marriage as well as of sexuality. As a result, a religiously exemplary life became compatible with sexual activity in marriage, even for priests. According to Reformation historiography, this "abolition of the celibate religious ideal" was one of the most sweeping changes brought about by the Reform, "especially as it affected moral reform and pastoral care."[25] It also initiated a major shift in the history of sexuality. In the eyes of the Reformers, one "sexual institution" was applicable to all social groups.

The Protestant reappraisal of human sexuality resulted first of all in extending the marital mode of life to groups that had formerly been excluded from marrying, namely, religious men and women. Subsequently, Reformed theologians did away with what they considered as impediments to marriage and made matrimony an even more inclusive institution. In conjunction with abolishing the sacrament of marriage as well as reevaluating canon law, the introduction of clerical marriage pointed to a new beginning in the politics of matrimony. The departure from the old sexual order finally manifested itself in civic ordinances intended to regulate marriage, among other matters. The competition of civic and ecclesiastical jurisdictions gave way to a more unified legal system. The councils of Basel, Schaffhausen, and Zurich instituted special courts for marital litigation in the late 1520s. Their ordinances gave legal and administrative expression to the changing theological framework of the discourse on marriage. Marriage had supposedly become a secular affair.[26]

The debate on the marriage of priests thus marked a transitional phase in the Reformation of the sexual order. Already by the beginning of the 1520s, the doctrine of a married priesthood moved toward the doctrine of universal marriage. The model of a body-sexual unified in its embrace of matrimony and its rejection of other forms of sexual life superseded the model of a society that applied different sexual expectations to clerics than to laypersons. To be sure, matrimony was seen as a necessity, not primarily a source of mutual enjoyment. It was God who commanded humans to live in matrimony, and human nature, understood as a profoundly fleshly state, left no other choice but to marry. As a sexual union, matrimony addressed the inescapable physical urges of both men and women—urges that, if not given a legitimate outlet, would surface in ways detrimental to Christian society, individual religious morality, and salvation. As a centerpiece of the new system of beliefs and practices, considerable attention was given to matrimony in the context of the new sexual order. The discourse on matrimony thus absorbed much of the pre-Reformation discourse on sexuality and sexual sins.

By the eve of the Reform, sodomy had come to hold a highly significant place in the imaginary, a place where notions of power and masculinity intersected with intensified religiosity and a revived interest in ancient literature. Protestant polemics then disseminated notions of same-sex sexuality on a grand scale in the years between 1520 and 1555. Yet a pre-Reformation discourse of manifold sins delving into layers of misbehavior such as sodomy was soon supplanted by a Protestant discourse of abstract didacticism that put forth a single dividing line between legitimate sexual behavior in marriage and illegitimate or "impure" sexual activities outside of marriage. Whereas before the Reform different pockets of discourse proffered multiple ways to speak the so-called unspeakable, in post-Reformation Germany a more unified discourse took shape. As a result of this shift, sodomy became an even more unintelligible term. Reformers actively reconfigured existing categories of sins. They crafted an idiom on sexual matters in which the illegitimate served as a backdrop for the main focal point, marriage.[27]

Matrimony as a subject of treatises underwent a remarkable career in sixteenth-century Germany.[28] The humanist Albrecht von Eyb (1420–75) was the first to publish a German book entirely devoted to marriage in 1472.[29] Only a few years later, publications on the holy union of husband and wife proliferated. The growing market for print publications shows that the public thirsted for small prose tracts of practical value to the common man. Pamphlets on matrimony counted among these useful publications for expanding readerships. The so-called *Sermo de matrimonio,* a tract of one sheet of paper, became the most popular text on marriage before the Reformation.[30] This anonymous compilation, previously circulated in manuscript form, provided "instruction," as its title advertised, on "how a husband should conduct himself and instruct his wife as to how the wife [should conduct herself] toward her husband."[31]

After the Reform, marriage, despite its loss of sacramental status, became a matter of great theological concern. Publications on matrimony emerged from the shadows of anonymous publications like the *Sermo.* Matrimony's newly increased significance is evidenced, among other things, by the fact that many Reformers followed the lead of Martin Luther and elaborated on questions of marital life in print. Moreover, these Protestant treatises absorbed themes that originally pertained to a different discourse— themes like sodomy. To be sure, these themes were not fully fleshed out. Yet, significantly, matrimony as a mode of life was cast in relation to other concepts. In Thomas Stör's treatise on marriage of 1524, a text very much indebted to Luther's *The Estate of Marriage* (1522), the individual believer is shown to be the battleground for the clash of oppositional forces described as chastity and its opposites. Whoever tries to dupe a person's sexual instincts is bound to defile him- or herself by "other forms of unchastity" *(andern geschlechten der vnkeüschait).*[32] Citing adulterers, knaves, and sodomites, Stör intended to deter his audience from joining their ranks: truly, he insists, these sinners will not enter heaven.[33] Other Protestant texts on marriage staged a juxtaposition between unruly, illegitimate sexuality and the well-ordered household in which husbands and wives appeared as guarantors of the civic order.[34] In one of his homilies, Johann Baumgarten (1514–78) depicted matrimony as a fortress against the doings of the devil, for example. In a list of misogamous heretics, sexual misdeeds were superimposed on religious heresies—a popular strategy of vilification. Though many of the sects listed—all of them "heretics, opponents and defilers of marriage"—could hardly have been familiar to the sermonizer's audience, this extraordinarily elaborate list must have resonated well with an audience raised on Protestant polemics against the Catholic Church: "sodomites, florentines, anabaptists, papists, priapists, couples married the Latin way [sodomites], monks, and nuns."[35] Whatever this list's intellectual benefits, it offered a locus for group identity by means of negative self-identification, drawing powerfully on antimonasticism as an ideological resource, and sodomy came to hold an important place in this context. Michael Caelius (d. 1559) published a sermon "against the invalid objections of many unmarried papists against the order of matrimony."[36] Despite the occasion, a wedding among nobles, he rehearsed the argument that celibate priests lived "against nature." He warned all those who commit adultery, fornication, or "mute sins" to repent. God will strike another Sodom and Gomorrah, and he will punish those who "not only ignore . . . but defile and desecrate" holy matrimony.[37] What is more, the sodomitical Other, be it the high ranks of the so-called Roman Church or Turks, were often imagined as active enemies of true Christians.[38]

During the Reform, the locations from which marital discourse was disseminated multiplied: homilies, wedding sermons, catechisms, marriage treatises of various kinds, Biblical dramas, and legal compilations provided information as well as guidance on issues pertaining to matrimony. In short, many Reformers addressed salient issues around this social institution in a host of publications. The Protestant community of all believers crystallized importantly around matrimony and its opposition to "institutionalized" unchastity. This growing body of Protestant literature spread a standard way of speaking about sex, a rhetoric of abstract didacticism. Such abstraction offered distinct advantages. In its "vagueness,"[39] marital doctrine addressed a plethora of social groups, nobles as well as burghers, artisans as well as professors. Notably, in the Protestant sexual discourse redefined as marital discourse, the exact contours of both legitimate and illegitimate sexual activity often remained undefined.

This is particularly evident in catechisms—those newly fashioned and broadly disseminated instructional tools for inculcating believers with the central tenets of the faith, the very foundation of the emerging confessions. While Protestant catechisms often avoid any mention of sodomy, castigating waste of semen and unchastity in general,[40] many Catholic catechisms of the sixteenth century give brief mention to the sodomitical sin, thereby perpetuating pre-Reformation lists of sinful behaviors.[41] This is all the more telling since Luther's 1519 manual for confession—like many catechisms based on the Decalogue—contained a reference to the "mute sin," while his later catechetical texts shunned such explicitness.[42]

In Protestant publications, the omnipresent bifurcation of sexual expression between legitimate marriage and extramarital illegitimacies grouped together categories of lust that had been differentiated in Catholic theology. In a wedding sermon held in Nuremberg in 1550, Johannes Mathesius briefly addressed man's "disorderly lusts" (vnordentliche[] begierden), claiming not only that "powerful great disorderly lust, indecencies, whoredom, adultery, Florentine impurities and Roman weddings [both strong allusions to sexual acts between men],[43] and other abominable offenses of which we do not want to speak are of the devil and have been introduced by evil natures," but also that these practices disrupt the marital union of husband and wife. [44] When addressing the sexual, many early modern commentators created clusters of oppositional structures of thought that were often overlapping, contradictory, or incoherent. Even though Heinrich Bullinger (1504–75) lamented that the confusion over the "right names" for vices caused a deluge of vices in his own "last, evil, dangerous time," he differentiated little more than his contemporaries, listing without further distinction adultery, whoredom, and "all kinds of impurity." [45]

Characteristically for post-Reformation discourse, religious authors like Bullinger invoked *sodomia* or sodomy without delineating its meaning. But this bifurcation also affected marital discourse. Because of the straitjacket of linguistic and conceptual binaries, many authors devoted little ink to explicating practicalities. The pragmatics of marital life and sexual activity in marriage were left aside in favor of ruminating about the rules writ large that regulate access to "the highest honor and holiest estate among men." [46] Such a lack of conceptual precision was exacerbated by a vague way of speaking about sex that reigned supreme after the Reformation, though it was rooted in pre-Reformation religious didacticism.

Composites of oppositions tend to obscure nuances and blur distinctions behind sharp dividing lines that separate the normative from its opposite. Genres of behavior available to pre-Reformation writers were collapsed when folded into these blinding dichotomies of relatively undifferentiated realms of sexual behavior. Rhetorical decorum surfaced in a variety of textual milieus, most notably court records. As examples in this book have illustrated, legal experts (like theologians before them) warned of the dangers of putting illegitimate sexual practices into words, especially after the end of the sixteenth century, when legal professionalism reached unprecedented heights. The fact that this cautious mode of enunciation filtered into a textual milieu predicated on explicitness (e.g., court documents) bespeaks a rhetorical standard whose dissemination coincided with a move toward centralization in the political realm.

Many Reformed forces collaborated to ensure that a rhetorical regime of sexual vagueness was established. Writers, ministers, and theologians had a vested interest in furthering a discourse that blinded their audience to sexual specifics. Aware of the power of language, Protestant authorities invested heavily in the surveillance of words spoken and written. Directed most of all at the caste of priests, this system of surveillance helped to "mainstream" sexual discourse. Such a rhetorical regime is therefore congruous with the increase in urban and territorial power which gave authorities the leverage to enforce acceptance, even if such implementation was handled only unsystematically.

During the processes of Reform, the advocacy of marriage and the enmity to sodomy had a distinct purpose, namely to forge an imagined community.[47] According to Peter Matheson, the Reformation "was primarily a paradigm shift in the religious imagination, not a structural reform, not even a doctrinal reform."[48] Legitimizing Reformed systems of belief, marital ideology and its companion piece, rejection of sodomy, was supposed to mobilize Protestant believers against the foes of the Gospels. Whatever their stance on the eucharist, Protestants of many different shades projected an image of themselves as staunch warriors in defense of matrimony—a stance only rarely taken up by Catholics.[49] Celebration of marriage as well as sodomiphobia were particularly successful as Protestant rallying points because both accorded with and could be mapped onto values held by communities before the Reformation. Ignorance of central beliefs and resistance to disciplining measures notwithstanding, marriage and sodomy therefore rose to great prominence in the symbolic social order in societies affected by the Reforms. If polemics against sodomites helped to sever ties with the Catholic clergy, the papacy, and the "Italian" church, the liberation of matrimony from its Roman captivity helped to create a sense of unity across social divides.

In recent historiography, sodomy's significance as a rallying point for the Protestant cause has been largely overlooked.[50] It was Lyndal Roper who first framed her magisterial study on the profoundly gendered politics of "civic righteousness" within the context of the dissolution of convents, prostitution, and perceptions about female homosexuality.[51] Subsequent studies have expanded Roper's focus on women. Following the shift from women's history to gender studies, analysts have started to investigate both sexes analytically, but, at the same time, they have paid increasing attention to the marital union of husband and wife, largely leaving aside matrimony's Others.[52] I want to argue that it is time to cast our critical net more widely and take up the original challenge of Roper's seminal work, a research project whose contours I can only sketch at this point.

By focusing on the changing institutional framework of Augsburg, Roper situates the drive to domesticate women and the concurrent discourse locally. Yet there remains an unresolved tension between the specificities of the locale in her account and the commonalities of the discourse of domestication after the Reform. While the emerging regime of a religiously inspired civic moralism in Augsburg may have been a result of social and political machinations specific to that locale, other urban communities experienced strikingly similar transformations. A civic regime based on the well-ordered household and the indissoluble marital union was also not limited to any particular social group. By arguing for matrimony's and sodomy's places in the imaginary, I do not mean to suggest that we should divide religious ideas from the ways in which these same ideas, like the relations between men and women, were regulated in the empire's treasure house of cities and territories. Yet it is important to remind ourselves that the distinction between matrimony and sodomy was, among other things, a potent ideology predicated on proliferating boundaries and dichotomies.

Outlining the imaginary more prominently in historical analysis helps to transform our understanding of the confessional landscape in early modern Europe. Due to scholarly reorientation toward "confessionalization" (*Konfessionalisierung*), Catholicism and Protestantism have emerged as kin movements whose long-term effects on society closely resemble one another. By moving the alliance of state and confessional formation center stage, researchers like Wilhelm Zeeden, Heinz Schilling, and R. Po-chia Hsia have systematically overcome the traditional divide between Protestant and Catholic scholars. The debate on marriage after the Reform reflects this shift toward a historiography that has increasingly foregrounded the similarity between the various confessions. In his study on marital litigation in Freiburg, Constance, and Basel, Thomas Max Safley concluded that "the Catholic Church could not offer reforms commensurate with those of the Protestants."[53] More recently, Joel Harrington has taken issue with a view of Protestantism as a willing, able helper in early modern state formation. He contends that claims about differences between the "Protestant and Catholic legal treatment of marital offenses" during the sixteenth century have been exaggerated.[54] Having studied the enforcement of marital discipline among Lutheran, Calvinist, and Catholic magistrates in the Palatinate, he found similar, if not shared social concerns and policies, independent of religious affiliation. In fact, all authorities sought to uphold sexual discipline and marital monogamy. Significantly, however, magistrates acted on a case-by-case basis—a finding that resonates well with the fact that there was no upsurge in executions or other punishments for sodomy after the Reform.

The discourse on matrimony (and the concomitant polemics against sodomy) was an almost exclusively Protestant discourse. Not only did it matter what was spoken, but also who spoke. As I have shown earlier, few Catholic pamphleteers joined in the chorus of sodomy allegations. Also, few Catholic theologians participated in the "flood" of sixteenth-century publications with regard to marriage, so much so that the celebration of matrimony appeared to be identified with the Protestant cause.[55] If we take the 1472–1620 holdings of what used to be West Berlin's State Library as a sample, only six texts on marriage were authored by Catholics, whereas more than sixty were penned by Protestant teachers and ministers.[56] In addition, many of the Catholic contributions on marriage were not indigenous but literary imports, translations of foreign-language models.[57] Conversely, viewed through a Protestant lens, the notion that the Reformers had restored marriage to its God-given place in society was so pervasive that it was useful as a polemical weapon against both Catholics and "deviant" sects like the Anabaptists.

What is more, it was only on the level of the *imaginaire* that marriage became universal or same-sex eroticism was universally rejected. Court records show that homosocial milieus in the sixteenth-century German lands allowed for sexual encounters. In social practice, marriage was contained. Many farmhands, servants, journeymen, and teachers never married or, following the "European marriage pattern," chose to do so only late in life.[58] Researchers have found relatively large numbers of single women in early modern German cities, before and during the Reformation.[59] Though exact figures are not available for the sixteenth century, it is safe to assume that a significant portion of the population entered the revered, divinely ordained state of matrimony late or never, despite increasing religious pressure to marry.[60] While Luther and other writers advocated marriage regardless of economic circumstances, arguing that God would provide his people (the married) with the means necessary to raise children, a community of believers united in their commitment to matrimony remained a lofty goal rather than becoming a palpable reality. But even if one was or remained single, one could still partake of marriage as an imagined institution or sodomy as Christianity's imagined foe. In future studies, we would be well-advised to start from ruptures between doctrine and social practice rather than to work within the framework of the universalism of marriage, which, at least to a significant degree, is the product of Protestant theology.

Conclusion

A joke would be my preferred way to conclude this book. Yet laughter is extremely hard to come by with regard to sodomy. Medieval and early modern comic tales or carnival plays subvert conventions on many accounts, but the rule that narratives ought to be limited to the intercourse of a man with a woman is not among them. Humor vanished when the sodomite entered. Martin Luther expressed the indecency of laughter when he had the "insolent sodomites" [*Puseronen*] laugh—on their path to damnation.[1] This absence of overt playfulness or humor documents the abject status assigned to same-sex sexual behavior, predominantly among men, in a particular culture at a particular time, the German-speaking lands in the age of Reform.

When we start to hear about the much condemned sexual acts between men (and, to a lesser degree, between women) from a variety of sources in the thirteenth century, it is because fundamental developments shaped the cultural context under consideration. Inspired by scholastic theology, religious educators increased their efforts to enforce a host of norms, some of them regulating sexual behavior, among the laity. Rulers, driven by new visions of the commonwealth, increasingly attempted to police sexual mores and punish offenders found to be transgressors. From the outset, secular and ecclesiastical concerns over sodomy, though different in character and often in conflict over individual cases, mutually reinforced each other. Whether religious beliefs or urban politics framed this interest in uprooting unorthodox sexual behavior, sodomy figured as a serious threat—an attitude that led to cruel executions of people convicted of same-sex behavior in cities of the empire after 1350. The term that Church reformers had launched in debates over reform of the clergy, the "sodomitical vice," thus rose to a matter of social as well as religious concern. These concerns over sexual "heresy" became especially prominent during

179

the Protestant Reformation. Importantly, the Reformers reconfigured the sexual imaginary—a reconfiguration that comprised sodomy as a crucial element. In doing so, the Reformers strongly relied on pre-Reformation images of Sodom. Yet they advocated matrimony as the only legitimate locus for sexual activity, while rejecting sexual transgressions, and sodomy especially, as that which was to be left behind once believers embraced evangelical beliefs. Three points serve to highlight sodomy's significance in this context: first, sodomy as a divisive concept; second, the rhetorics of sodomy; third, the social dimension of sodomy.

Sodomy was a highly divisive concept in all the contexts in which it appeared. Accusations of sodomy designated social, ethnic, geographic, or political boundaries. Though constantly shifting from text to text and context to context, these boundaries, once identified, were hard if not impossible to ignore. This divisiveness made suspicions of sodomy a useful (and dangerous) weapon in late medieval and early modern Europe—societies whose social stratification gained in complexity and whose populations became more mobile. In fact, notions of sodomy divided *and* connected people: the derision shed on perceived transgressions often enabled communities to develop a negative group identity and thus a sense of belonging.

When I started to work on this project, I expected to find vastly different representations depending on the genre in which an individual passage was articulated. As my work progressed, I realized how uniform many invocations of sodomy were in terms of wording, imagery, and rhetorics, despite different contexts, genres, functions or audiences. Such similarity is worth noting. Above all, the polemical was the appropriate mode for enunciating sodomy. Conveniently, defamation distanced the writer or speaker from the sexual practice. Polemics sifted into a variety of genres, enlivening texts as diverse as pamphlets and sermons. Defamation cases that led to court investigations show forms of verbal abuse that closely correspond to literary patterns of defamatory speech. At the same time, both oral and literary modes of vilification resonate with a scholastic taxonomy of sin in which same-sex sexual acts figured as one of the most serious of transgressions.

The pervasiveness of a certain rhetoric with regard to sodomy is not the full story. Importantly, specific rhetorical clichés reached different genres and milieus at different times. On a textual plain, sodomy occasioned euphemisms or censorship. It was, for instance, only after the mid-sixteenth century that urban judges adopted the warnings of pastoral theologians against suggestive enunciations of sodomy. This book, therefore, also documents change. After the middle of the sixteenth century, the discourse on sexual matters, including sodomy, became uniformly vague in a variety of genres.

Behind the rhetorical registers of disgust, there is, however, less uniformity in the conceptualization of homoeroticism across cultural boundaries than previously assumed. The German-speaking culture that was my focus here shows patterns of thinking and behaving that differ from what we know about fifteenth-century Italy (where sodomy occasioned laughter more readily than north of the Alps). We need to resist the temptation to regard one well-documented and well-researched example like the city of Florence as representative of all of early modern Europe. Many of the concerns were local, as were the ways in which same-sex eroticism was experienced, verbalized, and punished. Thus, this book illustrates the continuing importance of writing histories of sexuality from a local perspective.

What is there to learn about "how to do the history of (male) homosexuality," to pick up, once again, David Halperin's provocative formulation? The challenge of writing the history of sexuality today lies in leaving the well-trodden paths of writing about discourse; it lies in daring to imaginatively connect acts and words. I have, therefore, canvassed what many researchers treat separately, literary texts and court records, pamphlets and proceedings in insult cases. I have insisted that men tried for sodomitical acts had something in common with women who were charged with having sex with women, despite differences in patterns of persecution or popular responses to their plight. I have created an encounter between social and conceptual history on the grounds of rhetorics. Most of all, I have interpreted passages in which same-sex sexual behavior among men is clearly at issue alongside texts in which *sodomia* figures as a sign of destruction devoid of sexual content. I have done so because the concept of sodomy gained its force precisely in these rhetorical patterns, resonances, correspondences, echoes, and contradictions.

By reviving this forgotten early modern story, I want to thwart our obsession with telling histories that lead toward what is commonly, though rather obtusely, called modern sexuality. In the first volume of his fragments of a *History of Sexuality*, Foucault presents various stories of genealogical thresholds. We have tended to construe modernity—a term too often left unexplained—as the ultimate *telos* of historical processes. Historians of sexuality have responded to Foucault's visionary thesis by searching for the origins of a modern sexual system. What would modernity be if we did not have the premodern, or, more ambiguously, the early modern, to delimit it? Unlike the oppositional structures of sexual thought put into place in the early modern period, historiography's binaries often play themselves out on a temporal scale. I wonder, for instance, whether the birth of the "modern homosexual" is not even more complex than previously assumed. What if we expanded the groups and discourses usually cited to explain the emergence of "homosexuality" and took into account modes of articulation? In this regard, polemics may indeed prove to be an important source of inspiration for the formation of the category of male (and female) homosexual. Like few other ways of speaking, defamations invest the person with a distinct character—invectives that often link personhood and sexual activity.

If the particular *historia* told here teaches us anything, then it teaches us that the tensions and dichotomies exposed in this study might help us to disentangle some of the dichotomies of our own conditions. What we can learn from contemporary criticism and, more particularly, from queer studies is to question the binarism of thought which makes the late medieval/early modern serviceable by subjecting it to the either/or of alterity and modernity. Even if we have learned the lesson that history cannot easily be told as a story from thence to hence, however, we should not refrain from inserting temporality, the messy stuff from which history is made, into the equation. Rhetorical regimes had and have their chronologies. Sodomy fueled the imagination at certain, important historical junctures in the German lands. Different genres, contradictory messages, and overlapping discourses constituted what figured as matrimony or sodomy. Sex may be indeterminate and defy scholarly delineation, as recent definitions have it. Yet the historical specifics of this heterogeneity still warrant exploration.

Appendix / Sodomy Trials in Early Modern Germany and Switzerland

The following appendix lists chronologically the sodomy trials treated in this book. Date, location, name and number of offenders, as well as the penalties they received precede a mention of the source. The trials collected here are the result of years of research in mostly urban archives, predominantly in Switzerland and the south of Germany. The list is not exhaustive, however. Note also that in some cases sodomy is not the only transgression.

1277. Location unknown. Dominus de Haspisperch—burned.

From "Annales Basileenses," ed. Philipp Jaffé, in *Annales aevi suevici*, ed. Georg Heinrich Pertz, Monumenta Germaniae Historica: Scriptores 17 (Hannover: Hahnsche Buchhandlung, 1861), 201.

1367. Augsburg. Chuontz Metz—banished.

From A. Buff, "Verbrechen und Verbrecher zu Augsburg," in *Zeitschrift des Historischen Vereins für Schwaben und Neuburg* 4 (1877/78): 203.

1378. Munich. Heinrich Schreiber—executed?

From StadtA München, Zimelie 17, Ratsbuch III 1362–1384, 106r (124r).

1381. Augsburg. Five *ketzer* (Brother Hans Störzl, Brother Eberhart of St. Lienhart, two beghards, and one peasant)—burned.

From "Chronik des Burkard Zink," in *Chroniken der deutschen Städte*, vol. 5 (Augsburg, 2) (Leipzig: S. Hirzel, 1866), 26–27.

1399. Basel. Friedrich the cook—burned.

————. Friedrich Schregelin—banished.

From StABS, Ratsbücher A 3 (*Leistungsbuch* 2), 32v.

1400. Strasbourg. Johannes Rorer—burned.

————. Heinzmann Hiltebrant—fugitive.

From StALU, RP 1, 177v.

1408/09. Augsburg. Ulrich Frey, a chaplain—starved to death.

————. Jacob Kyss, a chaplain—starved to death.

————. Ulrich, a priest—starved to death.

————. Jerg Wattenlech, a Dominican—starved to death.

————. Gossenloher, a tanner—burned.

From *Chroniken der deutschen Städte*, vol. 4 (Leipzig: S. Hirzel, 1865), 111, 230–31, 317–18; *Chroniken der deutschen Städte*, vol. 5 (Leipzig: S. Hirzel, 1866), 67; *Chroniken der deutschen Städte*, vol. 22 (Leipzig: S. Hirzel, 1892), 54, 466–67; *Chroniken der deutschen Städte*, vol. 23 (Leipzig: S. Hirzel, 1894), 32 [dates, spelling of names, and the episode's details vary from chronicle to chronicle].

1414. Lucerne. Antoni Diener—hearing (see also 1422, 1433).

From StALU, RP 1, 270v.

1415. Basel. Offender unknown, record on the execution of a "heretic."

From StABS, Finanz G 4 (Wochenausgabenbücher IV), 146 (vgl. auch WAB IV, 260, 1426).

1416. Basel. Heinrich of Rheinfelden—investigation.

From StABS, Criminalia 31, R 1.

1418. Constance. Brother Hans and Brother Friklin—burned.

From *Die Chroniken der Stadt Konstanz*, ed. Philipp Ruppert (Konstanz: Selbstverlag, 1891), 388.

1422. Lucerne. Antoni Diener—hearing.

From StALU, RP 3, 77r.

1423. Lucerne. Offenders unknown, (sexual?) heresy in a clerical institution?—penalty?

From StALU, RP 3 (1423), 41r.

1427. Basel. Peter Keller—banished.

From StABS, Ratsbücher A 3 (*Leistungsbuch* 2), fol. 99r.

1431. Zurich. Hermann von Landenberg—burned.

From StAZ, Ratsbuch B VI.209, 193r–195v.

1433. Lucerne. Ludwig Walker and Antoni Diener—hearing.

From StALU, RP 1, 424r/v.

1434. Basel. Johann von Swyco—fugitive.

From G. Steinhausen, *Deutsche Privatbriefe des Mittelalters*, vol. 2 (Berlin: n.p., 1907), 138.

1441. Basel. Peter Koller—banished for attempted "heresy."

From StABS, Ratsbücher A 3 (*Leistungsbuch* 2), 122r.

1444. Rottweil. Katharina Güldin, a recluse, and one laywoman—investigation.

From Erzbischöfliches Archiv Freiburg, Liber conceptorum, B (1441–46), Sign. Ha 315, 131v.

1456. Regensburg. Mang Plaichknecht—penalty?

From Christine Reinle, "Zur Rechtspraxis gegenüber Homosexuellen," in *Zeitschrift für Geschichtswissenschaft* 44 (1996): 315–16, 323.

1457. Weissensee (near Erfurt). A priest and a Knight of the Teutonic Order—investigation.

From Hartung Cammermeister, *Die Chronik Hartung Cammermeisters*, ed. Robert Reiche (Halle: O. Hendel, 1896), 162.

1464. Einsiedeln. A sexton and a boy—burned.

From *Chronik der Stadt Zürich*, ed. Johannes Dierauer (Basel: A. Geering, 1900), 244.

1464. Constance. Brother Conradt and Ulrich Vischer—burned.

From Stadtarchiv Konstanz, B I.11, 250 (1464).

1471. Regensburg. Georg Semler, Fritz Röttel, Stefan Karl, and Andre Vetter—
decapitated.

From Reinle, "Zur Rechtspraxis," 323–26.

1474. Basel. Eighteen captured Lombard mercenaries—burned.

From Claudius Sieber-Lehmann, *Spätmittelalterlicher Nationalismus* (Göttingen:
Vandenhoeck & Ruprecht, 1995), 426–35 (appendix).

1475. Basel. Johannes Stocker—banished.

From Archives de l'ancien Evêché de Bâle, Porrentruy, A 85, Officialitas Basiliensis;
Basler Chroniken, vol. 2, ed. W. H. Vischer and H. Boes (Leipzig: S. Hirzel, 1880), 239,
275.

1477. Speyer. Katherina Hetzeldorfer—drowned.

From Stadtarchiv Speyer, 1 A 704/II, 12r–14r.

1482. Zurich. Richard Puller von Hohenburg and Anton Mätzler—burned.

From H. Witte, *Der letzte Puller von Hohenburg*, Beiträge zur Landes- und Volkskunde von
Elsass-Lothringen, vol. 4, issue 16–20 (Strasbourg: J. H. E. Heitz, 1895); Christine
Reinle, "Konflikte und Konfliktstrategien eines elsässischen Adligen," in *"Raubritter" oder
"Rechtschaffene vom Adel"?* ed. Kurt Andermann (Sigmaringen: Thorbecke, 1997), 89–113.

1482. Lucerne. Defamation case—no penalty.

From StALU, RP 5B, 366v (1482).

1484. Cologne. Johann Greffroide—posthumous investigation.

From B.-U. Hergemöller, "Die 'unsprechliche stumme Sünde' in Köln," in *Sodom und
Gomorrha* (Hamburg: MännerschwarmSkript, 1998), 99–144.

1488. Constance. Cristan Schriber—burned.

From Stadtarchiv Konstanz, B I.14, 283 (1488).

1489. Lucerne. Hans Zögg and Uli im Tann—burned.

———. A Benedictine monk—extradited.

From StALU, RP 7 (1489), 5r, 9r.

1490. Lucerne. Offender unknown—defamer banished for "heresy" defamation.

From StALU, RP 7, 85 (1490).

1490. Lucerne (territory). Herr von Hiltisrieden and Herr von Sempach
(defamation case)—defendant banished.

From StALU, RP 7, 94 (1490).

1493. Constance. Hans Bischoff and Hans Vogel—banished.

From Stadtarchiv Konstanz, L 843, 32 (1493).

1493. Fribourg. Jehan Ruaulx—burned.

From P. J. Gyger, *L'épée et la corde* (Lausanne: Faculté des Lettres, 1998), 308–9.

1499. Fribourg. Franciscan Hans Surer—extradited.

From Gyger, *L'épée et la corde*, 322.

1500. Lucerne. Jost Suter—burned for "heresy" (unspecified) and theft.

From StALU, RP 9, 27v (1500).

1504. Erfurt. Johannes Mathis (a priest)—banished from Thuringia.

From S. Oehmig, "Bettler und Dirnen, Sodomiter und Juden," in *Mitteilungen des Vereins für die Geschichte und Altertumskunde von Erfurt 56*, n.s. 3 (1995): 91; G. May, *Die geistliche Gerichtsbarkeit* (Leipzig: St. Benno, 1956), 192, 220.

1506? Strasbourg. A bottlemaker and Jerome—burned.

From Johann Geiler von Kaisersberg, *Die brösamlin doct. Keiserspergs vffgelesen*, trans. Johannes Pauli (Strasbourg: Johannes Grüninger, 1517), 7r.

1506. Lucerne. Heinrich Baltschmid, Felix Bluntschli, Caspar Noll, and Hans Honegger—burned.

From StALU, RP 9, 247v (1506).

1515. Zurich. Jacob vom Schloss—burned.

From StAZ, B VI.245 (*Rats- und Richtbuch 1513–1519*), 79r/v.

1515. Solothurn. Ulrich Conrad—investigation.

From StASO, DS (*Denkwürdige Sachen*) 33, 35r–36r (1515); StASO, Copiae 1524–1525, AB 2.9, 8; StASO, Missiven 1515–1519, AB 1.6, 83–85.

1518. Zurich. Hans Bröpstli—reprimanded for "groping" another man.

From StAZ, A 27.3 (*Kundschaften und Nachgänge 1500–1520*).

1519. Lucerne. Andres von Tschafel—broken on the wheel and burned.

From StALU, RP 11, 103v.

1519. Lucerne. Bonifaz Dorn—decapitated.

From StALU, RP 11, 86r (1519 Januar 27).

1519. Zurich. Blasius Hipold—burned.

From StAZ, B VI.245 (*Rats- und Richtbuch 1513–1519*), 232r–33r.

1520. Lucerne. Johannes Nusser—broken on the wheel.

From StALU, RP 11, 141r/v (Johannes Nusser) (1520).

1524. Solothurn. Ulrich Conrad versus Jost Zigerli and Bartholomaus von Spiegelberg (defamation)—settlement, no penalty.

From StASO, Copiae 1524–1525, AB 2.9, 253–57; StASO, Ratsmanual 1523–1525, A 1.12, 247–48, 254–58, 260–61, 263–67, 310–13; StASO, Ratsmanual 1523–1526, A 1.14, 68, 71–77, 91–93; StASO, Copiae 1524–1525, AB 2.9, 8.

1525. Solothurn. Hans Pröpstli—decapitated and burned.

From StASO, Vergichtbuch (*Ratsmanual rot 19*) 1478–1552 (Hans Pröpstli 1525), 166, 170–72.

1529. Augsburg. Wolff Keck—investigation.

From B.-U. Hergemöller, *Männer, "die mit Männern handeln," in der Augsburger Reformationszeit* (Munich: Forum Homosexualität, 2000).

1530. Schaffhausen. Hans Fritschi—decapitated.

———. Hans Räss—fugitive?

From StASCH, Justiz, D 1 (*Vergichtbuch*), 76r–77r.

1532. Lucerne. Balthasar Bär—drowned.

———. Balthasar Fölck—banished.

From StALU, RP 13, 169r–170r.

1532. Augsburg. Jacob Miller—decapitated.

——————. Berlin Wagner—decapitated.

——————. Hans Burckhart—released.

——————. Christoff Schmid—result unknown.

——————. Philipp Zeller—one hand cut off and banished.

——————. Michel Will—decapitated.

——————. Kunerl—fugitive?

——————. Sigismund Welser—fugitive.

From Hergemöller, *Männer.*

1533. Sankt Gallen. Conrat Mülibach—burned.

From StArchiv St. Gallen, Malefiz-Buch no. 192, 74–75; J. Rütiner, *Diarium 1529–1533,* vol. 1, part 2 (St. Gallen: Vadiana, 1996), 233–34.

1536/37. Münster. Franz von Alsten—decapitated.

From B.-U. Hergemöller, "Das Verhör des 'Sodomiticus' Franz von Alsten (1536/37)," *Westfälische Zeitschrift* 140 (1990): 31–47.

1537. Zurich. Andreas Pfister—banished.

From StAZ, A 27.8 (*Kundschaften und Nachgänge* 1536–1538).

1537. Zurich. Marx Anthon—burned.

——————. Hans Apfmotz—no punishment?

From StAZ, A 27.8 (*Kundschaften und Nachgänge* 1536–1538); StAZ, B VI 253 (*Rats- und Richtbuch*), 216r/v.

1537. Near Basel. Unnamed woman—executed for wearing men's clothing.

From *Basler Chroniken,* vol. 1 (Leipzig: S. Hirzel, 1872), 150.

c. 1537. Lucerne. Jörg Sigler—burned.

From StALU, Archiv 1, Personalien, AKT 113/1952 (not dated).

1538. Schaffhausen. Bonifacius Amerbach—burned.

From Staatsarchiv Schaffhausen, Justiz, D 1 (*Vergichtbuch*), 116r.

1539. Bern. A "pederast"—penalty unknown.

From Joachim von Watt, *Vadianische Briefsammlung,* vol. 5 (1531–1540), ed. Emil Arbenz, Hermann Wartmann (St. Gallen: Huber, 1903), 526–27.

1539. Strasbourg. Two heretics—burned.

From Sebald Büheler, Jr., "La chronique strasbourgeoise de Sébald Büheler," ed. Léon Dacheux, *Bulletin de la société pour la conservation des monuments historiques d'alsace,* n.s. 13 (1888); L. J. Abray, *The People's Reformation* (Ithaca, N.Y.: Cornell University Press, 1985), 190.

1540. Zurich. Uli Rügger—decapitated.

From StAZ, B VI.255 (*Rats- und Richtbuch* 1538–1544).

1540. Zurich. Hans Blatter—burned.

——————. Michel Vogel—oath of truce.

From StAZ, A 27.9 (*Kundschaften und Nachgänge* 1539–1540).

1541. Zurich. Ambrosius Suter versus Peter Sifrid (sodomy defamation)—oath of truce.

From StAZ, A 27.14 (*Kundschaften und Nachgänge* 1541–1543); StAZ, B VI.256 (*Rats- und Richtbuch* 1541–1549), 47v/48v.

1541/42. Zurich. Werner Steiner—house arrest.

From StAZ, A 27.10 (*Kundschaften und Nachgänge* c. 1530–1570); A 27.14 (*Kundschaften und Nachgänge* 1541–1543).

1545. Zurich. Jacob Müller—decapitated and burned.

————. Boy—banished?

From StAZ, A 27.15 (*Kundschaften und Nachgänge* 1544–1545); StAZ, B VI.257 (*Rats- und Richtbuch* 1545–1552), 11r/v.

1547. Zurich. Hans Appenzeller—penalty unknown.

From StAZ, A 27.16 (*Kundschaften und Nachgänge* 1546–1549).

1547. Freiburg. Agatha Dietschi—banished.

From StadtA Freiburg i.Br., C1 Criminalia C9 (1547) (Agatha Dietschi); K. Simon-Muscheid, "Frauen in Männerrollen," in *Arbeit—Liebe—Streit*, ed. Dorothee Rippmann, Katharina Simon-Muscheid, and Christian Simon (Liestal: Verlag des Kantons Basel-Landschaft, 1996), 102–21.

1561. Lucerne. Jakob Streulin and Georg Koch—oath of truce.

From StALU, COD 4435 (Turmbücher), 59r/v.

1561. Lucerne. Franz Kessler—banished.

From StALU, COD 4435 (Turmbücher), 197r.

1561. Zurich. Thöni Rüttiman—hanged.

From StAZ, A 27.13 (*Kundschaften und Nachgänge* c. 1530–1570); StAZ, B VI.259 (*Rats- und Richtbuch*), 26v.

1566. Solothurn. Jaggin Moser's son-in-law—fugitive.

From StASO, Ratsmanual, vol. 66 (1566), 297.

1567. Zurich. Rudolf Bachmann and Uli Frei—decapitated and burned.

From StAZ, A 27.26 (*Kundschaften und Nachgänge* 1566–1567); StAZ, B VI.259, 271r.

1567. Basel. Discussion of the case of two youths, imprisoned in Delsberg, whose adult sexual partner had been executed earlier.

From StABS, Missiven B 11, 184–85 (August 30, 1567); StABS, Straf- und Polizeiakten, C 15 (Widernatürliche Unzucht), undatiertes Rechtsgutachten [old call number: DX.10].

1572–75. Lucerne. Hans Portmann—investigation during which suspicions of sodomy are raised.

From StALU, COD 4445 (Turmbücher), 23r–32v, 388v–89r; COD 4450, 279r; RP 34 (1575), 86r; S. Grüter, *Geschichte des Kantons Luzern im 16. und 17. Jahrhundert* (Luzern: Räber, 1945), 140–47.

1577. Lucerne. Paul Leemann—investigation against a priest.

From StALU, AA1 F9 SCH 990 (September 5, 1577).

1579. Zurich. Wilhelm von Mühlhausen—burned.

From StAZ, A 27.35 (*Kundschaften und Nachgänge* 1579); StAZ, *Rats- und Richtbuch*, B VI.262, 202v–3v.

1583. Zurich. Two boys—investigation.

From StAZ, A 27.37a (*Kundschaften und Nachgänge* 1583).

1586. Zurich. Hans Heinrich Vogler versus Felix Müller—result unknown.

From StAZ, A 27.39 (*Kundschaften und Nachgänge* 1586).

1592. Zurich. Hans Herter von Benken—penalty unknown.

From StAZ, A 27.43 (*Kundschaften und Nachgänge* 1592–1593).

1595. Zurich. Five boys—fugitive.

From StAZ, A 27.44 (*Kundschaften und Nachgänge* 1594–1595), five young boys 1595.

1596. Sankt Gallen. Franciscus de Rouiere—burned.

From S. Krings, "Sodomie am Bodensee," *Schriften des Vereins für Geschichte des Bodensees und seiner Umgebung* 113 (1995): 22.

1599. Lucerne. Jakob Bachmann—banished.

From StALU, RP 46 (1599), 315r.

1609. Lucerne. Jephat Scheurmann—executed?

From StALU, COD 4500 (Turmbücher), 152r.

1629. Lucerne. Melchior Brütschli—executed.

————. Jacob Franck—fugitive?

From StALU, A1 F6 SCH 826, 1629.

1647. Basel. Elisabeth Hertner—put in an asylum.

From StABS, Criminalia 4 12.

1658. Basel. Jacob Fischer—flogging?

From StABS, Criminalia 31 F 1.

Notes

Introduction

1. I have used the third German edition, *Geschichten der romanischen und germanischen Völker von 1494 bis 1514* (Leipzig: Duncker & Humblot, 1885); trans. Philip A. Ashworth under the title *History of the Latin and Teutonic Nations from 1494 to 1514* (London: George Bell, 1887).

2. Ranke, "Vorrede," vii: "er [der Versuch] will blos zeigen, wie es eigentlich gewesen." This famous statement is often misunderstood as naive belief in the reliability of sources. In fact, the *History* represents an unprecedented foray into the method of doing history. In the appendix to *Geschichten*, Ranke published his groundbreaking *Zur Kritik neuerer Geschichtsschreiber*, a discourse accompanying his narrative that addresses methodology. The English translation of 1887 does not render this part. See also Wilhelm von Humboldt's similar statement in his 1821 talk "On the Historian's Task," which might have inspired Ranke (Georg G. Iggers and Konrad von Moltke, eds., *The Theory and Practice of History: Leopold von Ranke* [New York: Irvington Press, 1973], 6).

3. Ranke, *Geschichten*, 263–65; Ranke, *History*, 313–15. Translations are my own. I am indebted to Johannes Süßmann for having called my attention to Ranke's "moral reflection" passage. Sodomy functions here not only as a warning sign, but also as a boundary marker between the Latin and the German people whose entangled histories were the subject of Ranke's study.

4. Note the frequent references to males in the military in this context (Ranke, *Geschichten*, 263; *History*, 313). Women enter the discussion only with regard to the question of education (264; 314).

5. Ranke, *Geschichten*, 263: "Es liegt fern von mir, über die Gesinnung eines großen Volkes urtheilen zu wollen"; *History*, 313: "Far be it from me to pass judgment upon the temperament of a great nation."

6. Note the context of the aforementioned famous quote in Ranke's *Geschichten*, vii: "Man hat der Historie das Amt die Vergangenheit zu richten, die Mitwelt zum Nutzen zukünftiger Jahre zu belehren, beigemessen: so hoher Aemter unterwindert sich gegenwärtiger Versuch nicht: er will blos zeigen, wie es eigentlich gewesen"; preface to Iggers and Moltke, *Theory and Practice of History*, 137: "To history has been given the function of judging the past, of instructing men for the profit of future years. The present attempt does not aspire to such a lofty undertaking. It merely wants to show how, essentially, things happened."

7. Ranke, *Geschichten*, 263; *History*, 313. Interestingly enough, Ranke suggests that the imitation by Italians of ancient Greek and Roman sexual behavior reflects on their national character (263–64). Ranke concludes, as if addressing his German audience with a moral precept to be learned from history, "Der Grund der Nachahmung ist allezeit die Schwäche" (264); "The motive for imitation is always to be found in weakness" (314).

8. Jacob Burckhardt, *Die Kultur der Renaissance in Italien*, ed. Horst Günther (Frankfurt am Main: Deutscher Klassikerverlag, 1989), 422–27; trans. S. G. C. Middlemore under the title *The Civilization of the Renaissance in Italy* (London: Penguin, 1990), 271–74. See also Lionel Gossman, *Basel in the Age of Burckhardt: A Study in Unseasonable Ideas* (Chicago: University of Chicago Press, 2000), 439–53.

9. Of sexual depravities, he only mentions "illicit intercourse of the two sexes"; "unerlaubte[r] Verkehr der beiden Geschlechter" (Burckhardt, *Civilization*, 278; *Kultur*, 433)—that is, extramarital sex and prostitution—while treating adultery in literature and life at length (*Kultur*, 433–40; *Civilization*, 278–83).

10. Michel Foucault, *The History of Sexuality*, vol. 1 (New York: Vintage, 1980). Foucault was not alone: a number of scholars initiated this sea change in historical study. See, for example, Jeffrey Weeks, *Coming Out: Homosexual Politics in Britain, from the Nineteenth Century to the Present* (London: Quartet, 1977). See also Bernd-Ulrich Hergemöller's excellent introduction to the relevant historiography, *Einführung in die Historiographie der Homosexualitäten* (Tübingen: Edition diskord, 1999).

11. Gilles Deleuze, "Ecrivain non: un nouveau cartographe," *Critique* 343 (1975): 1212; Gilles Deleuze, *Foucault* (London: Athlone, 1988).

12. Foucault, *History of Sexuality*, 43.

13. See David M. Halperin, "Forgetting Foucault: Acts, Identities, and the History of Sexuality," *Representations* 63 (1998): 93–120.

14. Of all of Randolph Trumbach's publications, I am quoting only his most recent booklength study, *Sex and the Gender Revolution*, vol. 1, *Heterosexuality and the Third Gender in Enlightenment London* (Chicago: University of Chicago Press, 1998).

15. Theo van der Meer, *Sodoms zaad in Nederland: Het ontstaan van homoseksualiteit in de vroegmoderne tijd* (Nijmegen: SUN, 1995); van der Meer, "Sodom's Seed in The Netherlands: The Emergence of Homosexuality in the Early Modern Period," *Journal of Homosexuality* 34 (1997): 1–16.

16. Dirk Jaap Noordam, *Riskante relaties: Vijf eeuwen homoseksualiteit in Nederland, 1233–1733* (Hilversum: Verloren, 1995), 313: "een soort homoseksuelen."

17. E. William Monter, "Sodomy and Heresy in Early Modern Switzerland," in *The Gay Past*, ed. Salvatore J. Licata and Robert P. Petersen (New York: Harrington Park Press, 1985), 41–55; first appeared as "La Sodomie à l'époque moderne en Suisse romande," *Annales esc.* 29 (1974): 1023–33.

18. Michael Rocke, *Forbidden Friendships: Homosexuality and Male Culture in Renaissance Florence* (New York: Oxford University Press, 1996). See also Romano Canosa, *Storia di una grande paura: La sodomia a Firenze e a Venezia nel Quattrocento* (Milano: Feltrinelli, 1991). For Venice, see Elisabeth Pavan, "Police des moeurs, société et politique à Venise à la fin du Moyen Age," *Revue historique* 104 (1980): 241–88; Patricia H. Labalme, "Sodomy and Venetian Justice in the Renaissance," *Tijdschrift voor Rechtsgeschiedenis* 52 (1984): 217–55; Guido Ruggiero, *The Boundaries of Eros: Sex, Crime and Sexuality in Renaissance Venice* (New York: Oxford University Press, 1985).

19. Theo van der Meer, "Tribades on Trial: Female Same-Sex Offenders in Late

Eighteenth-Century Amsterdam," *Journal of the History of Sexuality* 1 (1991): 424–45; Randolph Trumbach, "London's Sapphists: From Three Sexes to Four Genders in the Making of Modern Culture," in *Third Sex, Third Gender: Beyond Sexual Dimorphism in Culture and History*, ed. Gilbert Herdt (New York: Zone Books, 1994), 111–36.

20. Valerie Traub, *The Renaissance of Lesbianism in Early Modern England* (Cambridge: Cambridge University Press, 2002).

21. Harriette Andreadis, *Sappho in Early Modern England: Female Same-Sex Literary Erotics 1550–1714* (Chicago: University of Chicago Press, 2001). The term *lesbian-like* derives from Judith M. Bennett, "'Lesbian-Like' and the Social History of Lesbianisms," *Journal of the History of Sexuality* 9 (2000): 1–24.

22. Michel Foucault, "Nietzsche, Genealogy, History," in *The Foucault Reader*, ed. Paul Rabinow (New York: Pantheon Books, 1984), 78.

23. Judith Butler, *Bodies That Matter: On the Discursive Limits of "Sex"* (New York: Routledge, 1993).

24. Halperin has rightly called attention to the qualification of textual genre which Foucault included in his description, "as defined by the ancient civil or canonical codes," yet fails to establish how we can "contrast" so easily what has such different origins, Christian normative writings and sexology ("Forgetting Foucault," 97).

25. Halperin, "Forgetting Foucault," 95.

26. I have taken this expression from Kathleen M. Davies, "Continuity and Change in Literary Advice on Marriage," in *Marriage and Society: Studies in the Social History of Marriage*, ed. R. B. Outhwaite (New York: Europa Publications, 1982), 60, 61.

27. Jonathan Goldberg, *Sodometries: Renaissance Texts, Modern Sexualities* (Stanford, Calif.: Stanford University Press, 1992), 18. Also, "sodomy is not a self-evident category in the Renaissance" (18).

28. Foucault, *History*, 101. Goldberg was not the first to take up this phrase, see G. S. Rousseau, "The Pursuit of Homosexuality in the Eighteenth Century: 'Utterly Confused Category' and/or Rich Repository," in *'Tis Nature's Fault: Unauthorized Sexuality during the Enlightenment*, ed. Robert P. Maccubin (Cambridge: Cambridge University Press, 1987), 137–68.

29. Lyndal Roper, introduction to *Oedipus and the Devil: Witchcraft, Sexuality and Religion in Early Modern Europe* (London: Routledge, 1994), 25.

30. Allen J. Frantzen, "The Disclosure of Sodomy in *Cleanness*," *PMLA* 111 (1996): 451 (emphasis mine).

31. See Cameron McFarlane, *The Sodomite in Fiction and Satire, 1660–1750* (New York: Columbia University Press, 1997); Vincent A. Lankewish, "Assault from Behind: Sodomy, Foreign Invasion, and Masculine Identity in the *Roman d'Enéas*," in *Text and Territory: Geographical Imagination in the European Middle Ages*, ed. Sylvia Tomasch and Sealy Giles (Philadelphia: University of Pennsylvania Press, 1998), 219.

32. Frantzen, "Disclosure of Sodomy," 452.

33. Rousseau, "Pursuit of Homosexuality," 136.

34. See chapter 3.

35. StAZ, B VII 21.2. For abbreviations, see bibliography.

36. See John Boswell's sobering remark in *Christianity, Social Tolerance, and Homosexuality: Gay People in Western Europe from the Beginning of the Christian Era to the Fourteenth Century* (Chicago: University of Chicago Press, 1980), 93 n. 2.

37. Mark D. Jordan, *The Invention of Sodomy in Christian Theology* (Chicago: University

of Chicago Press, 1997), 5. See also Karma Lochrie, *Covert Operations: The Medieval Uses of Secrecy* (Philadelphia: University of Pennsylvania Press, 1998), 180.

38. See, for instance, Carolyn Dinshaw, "Chaucer's Queer Touches/A Queer Touches Chaucer," *Exemplaria* 7 (1995): 77; Jordan, *Invention of Sodomy*, 2; Anna Livia and Kira Hall, "'It's a Girl!' Bringing Performativity Back to Linguistics," in *Queerly Phrased: Language, Gender, and Sexuality*, ed. Anna Livia and Kira Hall (New York: Oxford University Press, 1997), 12–13.

39. See the astute remarks in Louise O. Fradenburg and Carla Freccero, "The Pleasures of History," *GLQ* 1 (1995): 376–77.

40. Lisa Duggan, "The Discipline Problem: Queer Theory Meets Lesbian and Gay History," *GLQ* 2 (1995): 188; Allen J. Frantzen ("Between the Lines: Queer Theory, the History of Homosexuality, and Anglo-Saxon Penitentials," *Journal of Medieval and Early Modern Studies* 26 [1996]: 257, 282) has even spoken of hostility between current historicist practices and queer studies. See also his *Before the Closet* (Chicago: University of Chicago Press, 1998), 1–29.

41. See Raphael Samuel, "Reading the Signs, II: Fact-Grubbers and Mind-Readers," *History Workshop Journal* 33 (1993): 220–51, esp. 231–32.

42. Jordan, *Invention of Sodomy*, 8. See also Lochrie, *Covert Operations*, 191.

43. Jordan, *Invention of Sodomy*, 1.

44. David Sabean, *Power in the Blood: Popular Culture and Village Discourse in Early Modern Germany* (Cambridge: Cambridge University Press, 1984), 95.

45. Boswell, *Christianity, Social Tolerance, and Homosexuality*; Alan Bray, *Homosexuality in Renaissance England* (London: Gay Men's Press, 1982).

46. Samuel, "Reading the Signs, II," 220.

47. Roper, *Oedipus and the Devil*, 11.

48. Carlo Ginzburg, *History, Rhetoric, and Proof: The Menahem Stern Jerusalem Lectures* (Hanover, N.H.: University Press of New England, 1999), 1 (see also 57).

49. See Michel de Certeau, *The Writing of History* (New York: Columbia University Press, 1988). The debate continues to be waged in an either/or fashion. See Perez Zagorin, "History, the Referent, and Narrative: Reflections on Postmodernism Now," *History and Theory* 38 (1999): 1–24; Keith Jenkins, "A Postmodern Reply to Perez Zagorin," *History and Theory* 39 (2000): 181–200; Zagorin, "Rejoinder to a Postmodernist," *History and Theory* 39 (2000): 201–9.

50. Gabrielle Spiegel, *The Past as Text: The Theory and Practice of Medieval Historiography* (Baltimore: Johns Hopkins University Press, 1997); Roger Chartier, "L'histoire culturelle entre 'Linguistic Turn' et retour au sujet," in *Wege zu einer neuen Kulturgeschichtsschreibung*, ed. Hartmut Lehmann (Göttingen: Wallstein, 1995), 29–58; Roger Chartier, *On the Edge of the Cliff: History, Language, and Practices*, trans. Lydia G. Cochrane (Baltimore: Johns Hopkins University Press, 1996).

51. Robert Weimann, *Authority and Representation in Early Modern Discourse* (Baltimore: Johns Hopkins University Press, 1996), 191.

52. Bennett, "'Lesbian-Like' and the Social History of Lesbianisms," 1. See also Duggan, "Discipline Problem," passim. In "Forgetting Foucault," David Halperin has approached this discrepancy from a different angle. He rightly points to the "irony" (109) of reading *The History of Sexuality* as a guide to social history and not as a history of dis-

course, though some of Foucault's formulations on sexual practice (Foucault, 37, quoted by Halperin, 98, etc.) clearly paved the way for this misunderstanding or, shall we say, appropriation.

53. David M. Halperin, "How to Do the History of Male Homosexuality," *GLQ* 6 (2000): 87–124, esp. 90, 92, 97.

54. The concept of acting words owes much to Judith Butler, *Excitable Speech: A Politics of the Performative* (New York: Routledge, 1997).

55. From the vantage point of legal sources, sexual "heresy" cannot be subsumed under religious heresy. See also Matthias Lexer, *Mittelhochdeutsches Taschenwörterbuch,* 37th ed. (Stuttgart: A. Hiersemann, 1986), 107; *Sammlung schweizerischer Rechtsquellen, Die Rechtsquellen des Kantons Aargau,* part 2: *Landschaft,* vol. 8 (Aarau: Sauerländer, 1976), 798; *Sammlung schweizerischer Rechtsquellen, Die Rechtsquellen des Kantons Zug,* vol. 3: *Sachregister und Glossar* (Aarau: Sauerländer, 1985); Katharina Simon-Muscheid, "Frauen in Männerrollen," in: *Arbeit—Liebe—Streit: Texte zur Geschichte des Geschlechterverhältnisses und des Alltags,* ed. Dorothee Rippmann, Katharina Simon-Muscheid, and Christian Simon (Liestal: Verlag des Kantons Basel-Landschaft, 1996), 119.

56. Sedgwick, *Epistemology,* 36.

57. See Bernadette J. Brooten, *Love between Women: Early Christian Responses to Female Homoeroticism* (Chicago: University of Chicago Press, 1996), 193, 356.

Chapter One

1. "Annales Basileenses," ed. Philipp Jaffé, in *Annales aevi suevici,* ed. Georg Heinrich Pertz, Monumenta Germaniae Historica: Scriptores 17 (Hannover: Hahnsche Buchhandlung, 1861), 201: "Rex Rudolphus dominum Haspisperch ob vicium sodomiticum combussit" (King Rudolf had lord Haspisperch burned at the stake for the sodomitical vice). On this chronicle and its transmission, see Erich Kleinschmidt, "Die Colmarer Dominikaner-Geschichtsschreibung im 13. und 14. Jahrhundert," *Deutsches Archiv* 28 (1972): 371–496; Alfred Ritscher, *Literatur und Politik im Umkreis der ersten Habsburger: Dichtung, Historiographie und Briefe am Oberrhein* (Frankfurt am Main: Peter Lang 1992), 128–84.

2. The Von Habesbergs were lords over Sternberg, Irmelshausen, Lichtenberg, and Habichtsberg (Habesberg) near Meiningen, a collateral line to the counts of Henneberg and the *Burggrafen* of Würzburg (*Europäische Stammtafeln: Stammtafeln zur Geschichte der europäischen Staaten,* ed. Detlev Schwennicke, n.s. 16: *Bayern und Franken* [Berlin: J. A. Stargardt, 1995], table 144). The executed is likely to be identical with Hermann von Habesberg, younger brother to Berthold II of Sternburg, bishop of Würzburg (1274–87). Despite some territorial conflicts, Berthold is repeatedly mentioned in close association with King Rudolf. See Alfred Wendehorst, *Das Bistum Würzburg,* part 2: *Die Bischöfe von 1254 bis 1455,* Germania Sacra, n.s. 26 (Berlin: de Gruyter, 1969), 20–28. Hermann made an ecclesiastical career in Würzburg. See Alfred Wendehorst, *Das Bistum Würzburg,* part 4: *Das Stift Neumünster in Würzburg,* Germania Sacra, n.s. 26 (Berlin: de Gruyter, 1989), 297–98. According to the *Europäische Stammtafeln,* Hermann died between April 1, 1277, and March 2, 1278 (no mention of an execution). If this identification is correct, the *dominus de Haspisperch* was a cleric.

3. Thomas Aquinas, *Summa theologiae,* ed. Pietro Caramello, *Pars secunda secundae* (Turin: Marietti, 1986), 674–76 (quaest. 154, art. 11 and 12).

4. The author's name is not known. He signed as "Der Tugent schriber" (The virtuous writer). Helmut Tervooren and Thomas Bein, "Ein neues Fragment zum Minnesang und zur Sangspruchdichtung," *Zeitschrift für deutsche Philologie* 107 (1988): 4; Thomas Bein, "Orpheus als Sodomit," *Zeitschrift für deutsche Philologie* 109 (1990): 33–55; Gisela Kornrumpf, "Der Tugendhafte Schreiber," in *Die deutsche Literatur des Mittelalters: Verfasserlexikon,* 2d ed., ed. H. Wolfgang Stammler, Karl Langosch, and Burghart Wachinger, vol. 9 (Berlin: de Gruyter, 1995), cols. 1138–41. Also, see the discussion of Stricker in n. 7 and in chapter 3.

5. Quoted in Brigitte Spreitzer, *Die stumme Sünde: Homosexualität im Mittelalter mit einem Textanhang* (Göppingen: Kümmerle, 1988), 119.

6. Christian Meyer, ed., *Das Stadtbuch von Augsburg, insbesondere das Stadtrecht von 1276* (Augsburg: F. Butsch, 1872), 106–7. See also 71, which mandates that in executions because of *ketzerie* the executioner is not to receive extra remuneration, because "this tribulation concerns all of Christianity" ("wan ez gemeinlich der cristenheit not ist"). The city is known to have executed sexual "heretics" as early as 1381. King Rudolf of Habsburg (see above) granted the city of Augsburg the right to enact this code (1).

7. Hermann Knapp, ed., *Das Rechtsbuch Ruprechts von Freising (1328)* (Leipzig: R. Voigtländer, 1916), 71–72. Like the aforementioned Augsburg code, this compilation is influenced by the *Schwabenspiegel* and distinguishes what pertains to the ecclesiastical court and what to the secular court. According to J. Andreas Schmeller (*Bayerisches Wörterbuch* [Stuttgart: Cotta, 1827–37], col. 1604), *maendlaer* is a derogatory term for a man who penetrates boys or men. Stricker, a thirteenth-century didacticist and literary innovator, seems to have been the first to use the term, when he addresses sodomites (*sodomiten*) themselves in a poetic lament over same-sex behavior. See Spreitzer, *Die stumme Sünde,* 228–31, esp. 230.

8. Pope Gregory IX's bull *Vox in rama* of 1233, composed to support Konrad of Marburg's fight against heretics in the German lands, was an important step in linking sodomy and heresy. The orgiastic ritual imagined in this document included, among other things, same-sex couplings of men and women. See Bernd-Ulrich Hergemöller, *Krötenkuß und schwarzer Kater: Ketzerei, Götzendienst und Unzucht in der inquisitorischen Phantasie des 13. Jahrhunderts* (Warendorf: Fahlbusch, 1996), esp. 27–28.

9. Erich Meuthen, *Das 15. Jahrhundert* (Munich: Oldenbourg, 1980), 41–45, 141–43 (with bibliography).

10. Francis Robin H. Du Boulay, *Germany in the Later Middle Ages* (London: Athlone, 1987), 115–69.

11. Heiko A. Oberman, "The Gospel of Social Unrest: 450 Years after the So-called Peasants' War of 1525,'" in *The Dawn of the Reformation: Essays in Late Medieval and Reformation Thought* (Edinburgh: Clark, 1986), 158–59.

12. Boswell, *Christianity, Social Tolerance, and Homosexuality,* 333.

13. Brooten (*Love between Women*) has made clear that this assessment might have to be recast once one examines women-oriented women. Roman and Christian writers in antiquity unanimously disapproved of female homoeroticism.

14. Pierre J. Payer, *Sex and the Penitentials: The Development of a Sexual Code, 550–1150* (Toronto: University of Toronto Press, 1984); Frantzen, "Between the Lines."

15. Peter Damian, *Die Briefe des Petrus Damiani,* part 1, ed. Kurt Reindel (Munich: Monumenta Germaniae Historica, 1983), 284–330; "Letter 31" ["Book of Gomorrah"], in *Letters,* vol. 2, ed. Owen J. Blum (Washington, D.C.: Catholic University of America Press, 1990), 3–53.

16. James A. Brundage *Law, Sex, and Christian Society in Medieval Europe* (Chicago: University of Chicago Press, 1987); Jordan, *Invention of Sodomy.*

17. Robert Ian Moore, *The Formation of a Persecuting Society: Power and Deviance in Western Europe, 950–1250* (Oxford: Basil Blackwell, 1987), 10. On sodomites, see 92–97.

18. Jacques Chiffoleau, "Dire l'indicible: La catégorie du 'nefandum' du XIIe au XVe siècle," *Annales esc.* 45 (1990): 299; Kari Ellen Gade, "Homosexuality and Rape of Males in Old Norse Law and Literature," *Scandinavian Studies* 58 (1986): 124–41; Michael Goodich, "Sodomy in Medieval Secular Law," *Journal of Homosexuality* 1 (1976): 295–302; David F. Greenberg, *The Construction of Homosexuality* (Chicago: University of Chicago Press, 1988), 279–98.

19. Boulay, *Germany,* 4–16, 89–90, 100, 119.

20. See Dilwyn Knox, "*Disciplina:* The Monastic and Clerical Origins of European Civility," in *Renaissance Society and Culture: Essays in Honor of Eugene F. Rice, Jr.,* ed. John Monfasani and Ronald G. Musto (New York: Italica Press, 1991), 107–35.

21. Stadtarchiv München, Zimelie 17, Ratsbuch III 1362–84, 106r/124r; KR (Kammerrechnung) 1378, 40r. For a list of the trials, consult the appendix.

22. "Chronik des Burkard Zink," in *Chroniken der deutschen Städte,* vol. 5 (Augsburg, vol. 2) (Leipzig: S. Hirzel, 1866), 26–27. Under the same heading, Zink mentions that Augsburg's Jewish community was rounded up and had to pay a ransom of five thousand florins to the city. Seen against the backdrop of the "persecuting society," the chronicler's leap from people expelled from the urban community for sexual behavior to a religious minority is telling. On Zink, see Boulay, *Germany,* 5–6.

23. StABS, Ratsbücher A 3 (*Leistungsbuch* 2), 32v.

24. StALU, RP 1, 177v. Helmut Puff and Wolfram Schneider-Lastin, "Quellen zur Homosexualität im Mittelalter: Ein Basler Projekt," *Forum Homosexualität und Literatur* 13 (1991): 121–22.

25. StALU, RP 1, 177v: "vnd habent den noch sinen geschichten tůn frogen in der mosse, als man soliche belúmdete lúte billich froget."

26. See Gn 18:20–21: "Dixit itaque Dominus clamor Sodomorum et Gomorrae multiplicatus est et peccatum earum adgravatum est nimis. Descendam et videbo utrum clamorem qui venit ad me opere compleverint an non est ita ut sciam."

27. On the origins of inquisition trials in medieval canon law and their impact on secular jurisdiction in medieval Germany, see Günter Jerouschek, "Die Herausbildung des peinlichen Inquisitionsprozesses im Spätmittelalter und in der frühen Neuzeit," *Zeitschrift für die gesamte Strafrechtswissenschaft* 104 (1992): 328–60.

28. *Die Chroniken der Stadt Konstanz,* ed. Philipp Ruppert (Constance: P. Ruppert, 1891), 388.

29. StAZ, Ratsbuch B VI.209 (1431), 193r–95v. His partners were mostly thirteen and fourteen years of age. One of them was a noble, while the others were of lower class. Of those whose age was not mentioned, two of them were pupils and two others were called "boys" (*knab*). The record describes Landenberg's sexual activities in a descriptive and a narrative fashion, while the sentence gives expression to the horror associated with these acts: "grosse[] swerre[] vnmentschliche[] bosheit" (great, grave, inhuman malice). See also Ernst Diener, *Das Haus Landenberg im Mittelalter* (Zurich: F. Schulthess, 1898), 98–100; Julius Studer, *Die Edeln von Landenberg: Geschichte eines Adelsgeschlechts der Ostschweiz* (Zurich: Schulthess, 1904), 43–44; Alfred Zanger, "Wirtschaft und Sozialstruktur," in *Geschichte des Kantons Zürich* (Zurich: Werd, 1995–96), 414–15.

30. Christine Reinle, "Zur Rechtspraxis gegenüber Homosexuellen: Eine Fallstudie aus dem Regensburg des 15. Jahrhunderts," *Zeitschrift für Geschichtswissenschaft* 44 (1996): 323.

31. Ibid., 323–26, 307–22. See below for a more detailed analysis of the language that was used.

32. Three cases of sodomy (as opposed to six prosecutions for bestiality) survive from the fifteenth century. Stadtarchiv Konstanz, B I.11, 250 (1464); B I.14, 283 (1488): Cristan Schriber was burned at the stake for having committed "heresy with men, both actively and passively" ("kätzery mit mannen getriben vnd mit jm triben lassen"); L 843, 32 (1493): Hans Bischoff and Hans Vogel were banished to four miles from the city for "having acted dissipatedly like a woman and a man" ("vnfur als frowen vnd mann mit ain andern getriben"). See also Beate Schuster, *Die unendlichen Frauen: Prostitution und städtische Ordnung in Konstanz im 15./16. Jahrhundert* (Konstanz: Universitätsverlag Konstanz, 1996), 94.

33. Patrick J. Gyger, *L'épée et la corde: Criminalité et justice à Fribourg (1475–1505)* (Lausanne: Section d'histoire médiévale Faculté des Lettres, 1998), 308–9. The term used is *sodomitique pailliardise* (308).

34. *Chronik der Stadt Zürich*, ed. Johannes Dierauer (Basel: A. Geering, 1900), 244. Yet legal records are not our only source of information about sexual relations between men and between women. Sometimes, letters inform us about similar events. (See also *Deutsche Privatbriefe des Mittelalters*, vol. 2, ed. Georg Steinhausen [Berlin: Weidmannsche Buchhandlung, 1907], 138: "zu Basel ist eine brüdigüm gewest und ist fonden wordin mit eime knaben").

35. StASO, Vergichtbuch (*Ratsmanual rot 19*) 1478–1552 (Hans Pröpstli 1525), 166: "die werck vnnd kåtzery der sodomy." In other parts of the records, simply "heresy."

36. StA Schaffhausen, Justiz, D 1 (*Vergichtbuch*), 76r–77r.

37. StArchiv St. Gallen, Malefiz-Buch no. 192, 74. It follows a list of twelve men and the information available about them. At the end of the document, the above passage is repeated with minor variations.

38. For a complete list of the trials I have been able to unearth, see the appendix. The records are incomplete, however. Sometimes, we hear of trials that left no trace in the urban archive. Also, the state of the relevant historiography on criminal records does not allow for absolute numbers in most cities.

39. Wolfram Schneider-Lastin and Helmut Puff, " 'Vnd solt man alle die so das tuend verbrennen, es bliben nit funffzig mannen jn Basel': Homosexualität in der deutschen Schweiz im Spätmittelalter," in *Lust, Angst und Provokation: Homosexualität in der Gesellschaft*, ed. Helmut Puff (Göttingen: Vandenhoeck & Ruprecht, 1993), 86. See also Hans-Rudolf Hagemann, *Basler Rechtsleben im Mittelalter*, vol. 1 (Basel: Helbing & Lichtenhahn, 1981), 262–63.

40. Gerold Meyer von Knonau, *Der Canton Zürich, historisch-geographisch-statistisch* (St. Gallen: Huber, 1844–46), 139–40. See also Hans-Jörg Gilomen, "Innere Verhältnisse der Stadt Zürich, 1300–1500," in *Geschichte des Kantons Zürich* (Zurich: Werd, 1995), 382–86. On the courts, see Gilomen, 377. During the fifteenth century, the overall number of executions seems to have increased.

41. Marc Boone, "State Power and Illicit Sexuality: The Persecution of Sodomy in Late Medieval Bruges," *Journal of Medieval History* 22 (1996): 135–53.

42. Rocke, *Forbidden Friendships*. Bernd-Ulrich Hergemöller has given us an excel-

lent survey of repression across Europe; see his "Sodomiter—Erscheinungsformen und Kausalfaktoren des spätmittelalterlichen Kampfes gegen Homosexuelle," in *Randgruppen der spätmittelalterlichen Gesellschaft,* ed. B.-U. Hergemöller (Warendorf: Fahlbusch, 1994), 361–403.

43. Ruggiero, *Boundaries of Eros,* 109–13; Bariša Krekić, "'Abominandum crimen': Punishment of Homosexuals in Renaissance Dubrovnik," *Viator* 18 (1987): 337–45. See also Pavan, "Police des moeurs," 287–88; Canosa, *Storia di una grande paura.*

44. Reinle, "Zur Rechtspraxis," 325: "sunde der unkeusch, die man nennet die stumenden sunde wider die menschlichen nature, dergleich sunden . . . dorumb dan gott umb dergleich sunden vor die funff stett vertilget."

45. *Corpus iuris civilis* (part v, *novellae,* n. 77), ed. Christoph Heinrich Freiesleben (Neukölln: E. Thurneysen, 1775), cols. 1041–42 (*Edictum Iustiniani ad Constantinopolitanos de luxuriantibus contra naturam*).

46. For the city of Basel, Christoph Maier (*Regiment und Rechtschaffenheit: Regelungen des öffentlichen "Benehmens" in Basel, 1415–1460* [Lizentiatsarbeit, University of Basel, 1985], 85) points to the clergy's influence on urban legislation and moral politics.

47. See Jacques Chiffoleau, "'Contra naturam': Pour une approche casuistique et procédurale de la nature médiévale," *Micrologus* 4 (1996): 265–312.

48. For the scope of moral concerns in Basel, see Maier, *Regiment und Rechtschaffenheit,* passim.

49. *Rufbuch* of 1451, quoted from Claudius Sieber-Lehmann, *Spätmittelalterlicher Nationalismus: Die Burgunderkriege am Oberrhein und in der Eidgenossenschaft* (Göttingen: Vandenhoeck & Ruprecht, 1995), 384: "verbunden . . . , aller ir undertanen missetat und mutwillige, ouch uppige wort und werke, die wider kriestenliche ordenunge und die zehen gebote des allmachtigen gots . . . ze straffen."

50. For exceptions, see the introductory and the concluding sections of this chapter.

51. Goodich, "Sodomy in Medieval Secular Law"; Boone, "State Power and Illicit Sexuality," 139–40; Hergemöller, "Sodomiter," 367.

52. See, however, the exceptions of Augsburg, above, and Bamberg, below.

53. Kalocsa, Föszékesegyházi Könyvtár, Ms 629, fol. 198va/b: "Die schämleichen sünde pessern kayserleichew recht gar swêrleich mit dem fewr vnd halden, das das vngewitter vnd schelmig sterben dauon chömen."

54. Gerald Strauss, *Law, Resistance, and the State: The Opposition to Roman Law in Reformation Germany* (Princeton, N.J.: Princeton University Press, 1986), 70–71.

55. Roman law was more widely applied only after 1500, partially fueled by the Reformation; see James Q. Whitman, *The Legacy of Roman Law in the German Romantic Era: Historical Vision and Legal Change* (Princeton, N.J.: Princeton University Press, 1990), 3–4.

56. Ulrich Tenngler, *Laÿen Spiegel: Von rechtmässigen ordnungen in Burgerlichen vnd peinlichen regimenten* (Augsburg: H. Ottmar, 1509), S5r: "Item so ain mensch mit vihe / mann mit mannen / oder weyb mit weibs person vnkeüsch treiben / verwürcken damit ir leben das man sy gewonlich mit feür vom leben zum tod richt." This wording is inspired by the *Constitutio Criminalis Bambergensis* of 1507. For a translation, see the discussion of the *Constitutio Criminalis Carolina,* below.

57. StABS, Ratsbücher A 3 (*Leistungsbuch* 2), 99r (Peter Keller): "von des böses lümden wegen ketzerie, so er mit mannen vnderstanden hat ze vollebringende, ob es jm gestattet wer worden."

58. StABS, Ratsbücher A 3 (*Leistungsbuch* 2), 122r (Peter Koller).

59. StABS, Ratsbücher A 3 (*Leistungsbuch* 2), 99r: (Peter Keller, Burchart Zibol).

60. StABS, Ratsbücher A 3 (*Leistungsbuch* 2), 32r (1399). The banishment "enet dem Lampertzschen gebirge" was replaced by "vor der statt crützen leisten," outside of the city's legal district.

61. Other factors might have affected this outcome, like the fact that Schregelin stood in the city's employment.

62. Gyger, *L'épée et la corde*, 309.

63. Maria R. Boes, "The Treatment of Juvenile Delinquents in Early Modern Germany: A Case Study," *Continuity and Change* 11 (1996): 43–60.

64. Since most records do not give the exact age, but rather characterize youths by descriptive terms such as "boy," it is hard to indicate exactly at what age punishment became more likely.

65. Reinle, "Zur Rechtspraxis," 307.

66. *Die Peinliche Gerichtsordnung Kaiser Karls V. von 1532 (Carolina)*, ed. Arthur Kaufmann (Stuttgart: Reclam, 1996), 81 (*Straff der vnkeusch, so wider die natur beschicht*): "Item so eyn mensch mit eynem vihe, mann mit mann, weib mit weib, vnkeusch treiben, die haben auch das leben verwürckt, vnd man soll sie der gemeynen gewonheyt nach mit dem fewer vom leben zum todt richten." Translation after Louis Crompton, "The Myth of Lesbian Impunity: Capital Laws from 1270 to 1791," in *The Gay Past*, ed. Licata and Petersen, 18. See also John H. Langbein, *Prosecuting Crime in the Renaissance: England, France, Germany* (Cambridge, Mass.: Harvard University Press, 1974); Warren Johansson, "Sixteenth-Century Legislation," in *Encyclopedia of Homosexuality*, ed. Wayne R. Dynes, vol. 2 (New York: Garland, 1990), 1198–1200; Heinrich Mitteis, *Deutsche Rechtsgeschichte: Ein Studienbuch*, ed. Heinz Lieberich, 19th ed. (Munich: Beck, 1992), 334.

67. Bamberg's law code was taken up by other practitioners of the law in cities as well as principalities. See Ulrich Tenngler, quoted in n. 56 above; *Brandenburgische halßgerichtsordnung* (Nuremberg: n.p., 1516), 29v (art. 141).

68. Emil Brunnenmeister, *Die Quellen der Bambergensis: Ein Beitrag zur Geschichte des Strafrechts* (Leipzig: Engelmann, 1879), 269, 289–92; Langbein, *Prosecuting Crime*, 129–206; Strauss, *Law, Resistance, and the State*; Hartmut Boockmann, Ludger Grenzmann, Bernd Moeller, and Martin Staehelin, eds., *Recht und Verfassung im Übergang vom Mittelalter zur Neuzeit*, part 1 (Göttingen: Vandenhoeck & Ruprecht, 1998). With regard to the position of women, see Merry E. Wiesner, "Frail, Weak, and Helpless: Women's Legal Position in Theory and Reality," in *Gender, Church, and State in Early Modern Germany* (London: Longman, 1998), 84–93.

69. Rudolf Hagemann, *Aus dem Rechtsleben im alten Basel* (Basel: Basler Zeitung, 1989), 65.

70. Anton Philipp von Segesser, *Rechtsgeschichte der Stadt und Republik Lucern*, vol. 4 (Lucerne: n.p., 1858), 182, 198–202, 212–33; Christoph Lerch (*Die Rechtsgrundlagen für Frevel- und Malefizsachen in Solothurn seit dem Stadtrecht von 1604* [Diplomarbeit, n.d.], 42) argues against the code's implementation for the city of Solothurn.

71. See, however, StABS, Criminalia 4 12 (Elisabeth Hertner), 6r (1647).

Chapter Two

1. For a survey of the cases known for medieval and early modern Europe, see Bennett, "'Lesbian-Like' and the Social History of Lesbianisms"; Helmut Puff, "Female

Sodomy: The Trial of Katherina Hetzeldorfer (1477)," *Journal of Medieval and Early Modern Studies* 30 (2000): 47–49.

2. Erzbischöfliches Archiv Freiburg, *Liber conceptorum*, B (1441–46), Sign. Ha 315, 131v.

3. Ibid.: "vicium contra naturam quod sodomiticum appelatur."

4. Puff, "Female Sodomy" (includes an edition of the document).

5. Mentions of the family name in the mid-fifteenth century can be found in Helene Burger, *Nürnberger Totengeläutbücher*, vol. 2: *St. Lorenz 1454–1517* (Neustadt a.d.Aisch: Kommissionsverlag, 1967), 3, 8, 19, 278.

6. Stadtarchiv Speyer, 1 A 704/II, 14r (Hans Welcker's testimony), and 13r (Hetzeldorfer's own account). Since her "sister" does not show up in these records, one is led to assume that she was able to escape a trial, most probably by fleeing the city of Speyer.

7. Stadtarchiv Speyer, 12r (Elß Muter): "sie entmeydelt vnd vngeuerlich ij jar gebult hab."

8. Ibid., 12r: "sie [Hetzeldorfer] jr elicher mann wer."

9. Ibid., 12r. See the expressions "jrn willn, mit ir manlichkeit zu tryben" (12r).

10. Ibid., 13r: "Vnd sagt auch darnach, daz sie eyn instrument gemacht habe mit eym roden loschen ledder vnd fornnen mit baumwoll gefult vnd daruf eynn holts gestossen vnd eynn loch durch daz hölts gemacht mit eyner snwer dar dürch gezogen vnd also vmb sich gebunden vnnd da mit jr gefert mit den zweyn wibern vnd die jr swester sin soll geschaft."

11. The three-page document is working notes, covered with additions and corrections. Particularly telling is the addendum to the confession of Else Muter, who, because she confessed to having been seduced by Hetzeldorfer, was severely implicated. Scribbled on the left margins of the page and hard to decipher, these notes demonstrate how the officials repeatedly dug deeper when interrogating witnesses about their perception of Hetzeldorfer's sex.

12. Stadtarchiv Freiburg i.Br., C1 Criminalia C9 (1547), 4 (Vergicht Agatha Dietschi). Reprinted in Simon-Muscheid, "Frauen in Männerrollen," 119.

13. See, for example, Brigitte Eriksson, ed., "A Lesbian Execution in Germany, 1721: The Trial Records," in *The Gay Past*, ed. Licata and Petersen, 27–40; Rudolf M. Dekker and Lotte C. van de Pol, *The Tradition of Female Transvestism in Early Modern Europe* (London: Macmillan, 1989), 259–79; Mary Lindemann, "Die Jungfer Heinrich: Transvestitin, Bigamistin, Lesbierin, Diebin, Mörderin," in *Von Huren und Rabenmüttern: Weibliche Kriminalität in der Frühen Neuzeit*, ed. Otto Ulbricht (Cologne: Böhlau, 1995), 259–79. On this same case, see Jakob Michelsen, "Von Kaufleuten, Waisenknaben und Frauen in Männerkleidern: Sodomie im Hamburg des 18. Jahrhunderts," *Zeitschrift für Sexualforschung* 9 (1996): 226–27.

14. Bennett, "'Lesbian-Like' and the Social History of Lesbianisms."

15. Richard van Dülmen, *Theatre of Horror: Crime and Punishment in Early Modern Germany* (Cambridge: Polity Press, 1990), 80, 88–91; R. Liebenwirth, "Ertränken," in *Handwörterbuch zur deutschen Rechtsgeschichte*, ed. Adalbert Stammler and Ekkehard Kaufmann, 4th installment (Berlin: E. Schmidt, 1967), cols. 1009–10. On the case of a "lesbian" drowned in Geneva in 1568, see Monter, "Sodomy and Heresy," 46. According to William G. Naphy, however, drowning was the common form of execution in Geneva.

16. "Die Chronik des Fridolin Ryff," in *Basler Chroniken*, vol. 1 (Leipzig: S. Hirzel, 1872), 150. Reprinted in Simon-Muscheid, "Frauen in Männerrollen," 112–13.

17. Stadtarchiv Freiburg i.Br., C1 Criminalia 9 (1547). See also Sully Roecken and

Carolina Brauckmann, *Margaretha Jedefrau* (Freiburg i.Br.: Kore, 1989), 295–98. The case is also mentioned in Lindemann, "Jungfer," 268. The sources are published in Simon-Muscheid, "Frauen in Männerrollen," 113–21.

18. Dietschi's and Reuli's accounts differ with regard to the time when her wife found out she was a woman: according to Dietschi, within days after their wedding; according to Reuli, in the second year of their marriage.

19. Letter of April 16, 1548 (Stadtarchiv Freiburg, C1 Criminalia 9, 16): "hinder ainem weyden stock ain rüstung gemacht und damit, mit ir Anna, zů drey oder viermaln ketzerey getribenn" (she made an armor behind a willow tree with which she committed heresy three or four times with Anna) (Simon-Muscheid, "Frauen in Männerrollen," 119).

20. See Valerie Traub's nuanced discussion of the terms and their implications in "The (In)Significance of 'Lesbian' Desire in Early Modern England," in *Queering the Renaissance*, ed. Jonathan Goldberg (Durham, N.C.: Duke University Press, 1994), 66–70. See also Judith Brown, "Lesbian Sexuality in Medieval and Early Modern Europe," in *Hidden from History*, ed. Martin B. Duberman et al. (New York: NAL Books, 1989), 498–99; Mary Elizabeth Perry, *Crime and Society in Early Modern Seville* (Hanover, N.H.: University Press of New England, 1980), 125; Jacqueline Murray, "Twice Marginal and Twice Invisible: Lesbians in the Middle Ages," in *Handbook of Medieval Sexuality*, ed. Vern L. Bullough and James A. Brundage (New York: Garland, 1996), 199, 201, 203; Lindemann, "Jungfer," 269; Trumbach, "London's Sapphists," 122.

21. See below for a case in Erfurt. Also, in 1367 in Augsburg, Chuontz Metz, "neither man nor woman" ("weder man noch weip"), was banished (see Adolf Buff, "Verbrechen und Verbrecher in Augsburg in der zweiten Hälfte des 14. Jahrhunderts," *Zeitschrift des Historischen Vereins für Schwaben und Neuburg* 4 [1878]: 203).

22. "Quicumque incontinentia illa, quae contra naturam est, propter quam venit ira Dei in filios diffidentiae et quinque civitates igne consumpsit, deprehensi fuerint laborare, si clerici fuerint eiciantur a clero vel ad poenitentiam agendam in monasteriis detrudantur"; "Let all who are found guilty of that unnatural vice for which the wrath of God came down upon the sons of disobedience and destroyed the five cities with fire, if they are clerics be expelled from the clergy or confined in monasteries to do penance." Quoted in *Decrees of the Ecumenical Councils*, vol. 1, ed. Norman P. Tanner, S.J. (Washington, D.C.: Georgetown University Press, 1990), 217 (Latin) and *217 (English).

23. See Boone, "State Power and Illicit Sexuality," 141–42.

24. Thomas Füser, "Der Leib ist das Grab der Seele: Der institutionelle Umgang mit sexueller Devianz in Cluniazensischen Klöstern des 13. und frühen 14. Jahrhunderts," in *De ordine vitae: Funktionen und Formen von Schriftlichkeit im mittelalterlichen Ordenswesen*, ed. Gert Melville (Munich: Lit, 1996), 226–37.

25. Bernd-Ulrich Hergemöller, "Die 'unsprechliche stumme Sünde' in Kölner Akten des ausgehenden Mittelalters," *Geschichte in Köln* 22 (1987): 5–43; reprinted in Hergemöller, *Sodom und Gomorrha: Zur Alltagswirklichkeit und Verfolgung Homosexueller im Mittelalter* (Hamburg: MännerschwarmSkript, 1998), 99–144.

26. Cammermeister, *Die Chronik Hartung Cammermeisters*, ed. Robert Reiche (Halle: O. Hendel, 1896), 162; Stefan Oehmig, "Bettler und Dirnen, Sodomiter und Juden: Über Randgruppen und Minderheiten in Erfurt im Spätmittelalter und in der frühen Neuzeit," *Mitteilungen des Vereins für die Geschichte und Altertumskunde von Erfurt* H. 56, n.s. 3 (1995): 90.

27. Georg May, *Die geistliche Gerichtsbarkeit des Erzbischofs von Mainz im Thüringen des späten*

Mittelalters: Das Generalgericht zu Erfurt (Leipzig: St. Benno, 1956), 192, 220; Oehmig, "Bettler und Dirnen, Sodomiter und Juden," 91.

28. Emanuel von Rodt, *Die Feldzüge Karls des Kühnen*, vol. 1 (Schaffhausen: Hurter, 1843), 325. One of the Burgundian soldiers was apprehended, but escaped criminal prosecution by subordinating himself to clerical jurisdiction. Bribes were paid to ensure his release. We know of this through a complaint filed by the city of Bern. Since bribes were paid, particular interests must have been involved. A similar case is reported for Venice; see Ruggiero, *Boundaries of Eros*, 130–31.

29. Patrick J. Gyger, *L'épée et la corde*, 322.

30. Thomas D. Albert, *Der gemeine Mann vor dem geistlichen Richter: Kirchliche Rechtsprechung in den Diözesen Basel, Chur und Konstanz vor der Reformation* (Stuttgart: Lucius & Lucius, 1998), 193–95, 211. Records from the diocese of Chur have no such category.

31. StABS, Criminalia 31, R 1. See also Helmut Puff, "Localizing Sodomy: The 'Priest and Sodomite' in Pre-Reformation Germany and Switzerland," *Journal of the History of Sexuality* 8 (1997): 181–82, 188, 193–94.

32. The lengthy depositions are presented in a descriptive tone. The heading, with its reference to several legal categories, was added later—apparently to lend weight to the accusations against Heinrich. The depositions themselves elude labels. Whenever the witnesses were recorded to have alluded to male-male eroticism, circumscriptions such as "such behavior" were used. For a detailed analysis, see Helmut Puff, "Überlegungen zu einer Rhetorik der 'unsprechlichen Sünde': Ein Basler Verhörprotokoll aus dem Jahr 1416," *Österreichische Zeitschrift für Geschichtswissenschaften* 9 (1998): 342–57.

33. StABS, Criminalia 31, R 1, 1 (deposition of Heini Böpplin).

34. Ibid., 1–2.

35. Georg Boner, "Das Predigerkloster in Basel von der Gründung bis zur Klosterreform 1233–1429," *Zeitschrift für Basler Altertumskunde* 34 (1935): 137–43; Brigitte Degler-Spengler, "Die Beginen in Basel," *Basler Zeitschrift für Geschichte und Altertumskunde* 69 (1970): 5–83; 70 (1970): 29–118. A conflict between the bishop and the city council over Basel's constitution might have provided an extra stimulus for the investigation. See Christoph Maier, *Regiment und Rechtschaffenheit*, 5–29. It is precisely around this time that the council began its efforts to police the citizens on moral grounds.

36. See Franz Egger, *Beiträge zur Geschichte des Predigerordens: Die Reform des Basler Konvents 1429 und die Stellung des Ordens am Basler Konzil 1431–1448* (Bern: Peter Lang, 1991), 67, 119–20, 232.

37. Archives de l'ancien Evêché de Bâle, Porrentruy, A 85, Officialitas Basiliensis, 83 (*scultio*). On the document, the space for the monastery's name (where Stocker was to be banished) was left blank and never filled in: "hoc currendo anno . . . ad nephandissimum instigacionem inimici humani generis . . . detestabile vicium sodomiticum vicibus repetitis perpetrasse et exercuisse cum quodam iuvene tunc Basilee et in domo sue inhabitationis constituto nomine Johanne Müller de opido Bruck Constancii dyocesis."

38. Johannes Knebel, "Diarium," in *Basler Chroniken*, vol. 2, ed. Wilhelm Vischer and Heinrich Boes (Leipzig: S. Hirzel, 1880), 239.

39. Archives de l'ancien Evêché de Bâle, A 85/83, Depositio: "Lůg für dich, das er dich nit brut, als er die zwen andern knaben gebrütet hatt" (Watch out that he does not copulate you like he did with the other two boys). This warning corresponds with Knebel's *Diarium*. There, it is said that Stocker "was found [to live] in sodomitical sin with two students" ("fuit repertus in peccato sodomitico cum duobus scholaribus"). *Brüten*, here

"to copulate," is quite a drastic locution. At the same time, the teacher refused to divulge the boys' names to Müller.

40. Ibid.: "Er wer jm als holt alß keinem monschen vnd hett nÿe keins knaben als wol gelust jn zůminnen als jn. Vnd wenn er jnn dem kor wer gesin, so werent sin ougen nie ab jm komen."

41. Ibid., *Confessio spontania*: "vnd er hab sunst mit keynem andern mann oder knaben sollichs vnderstanden noch gethon."

42. Ibid.

43. Knebel, "Diarium," 239.

44. Archives de l'ancien Evêché de Bâle, A 85, Intercessionales (July 1, 1475): "derselb priester hinweg geschickt vnd schand vermitten solt sin."

45. Monter, "Sodomy and Heresy," 42.

46. Astesanus, *Summa Astesana* ([Strasbourg: J. Mentel, 1489]; I have used an edition at Universitätsbibliothek Basel: FNP IV 27 2o, liber secundus, Titulus 46, no page numbers indicated). For information on this manual, see Pierre Michaud-Quantin, *Sommes de casuistique et manuels de confession au moyen âge (XII–XVI siècles)* (Louvain: Nauwelaerts, 1962), 57–60.

47. This is the version told explicitly by Burkard Zink in *Chroniken der deutschen Städte*, vol. 5 (Leipzig: S. Hirzel, 1866), 67.

48. *Chroniken der deutschen Städte*, vol. 23 (Leipzig: S. Hirzel, 1894), 32; *Chroniken der deutschen Städte*, vol. 5, 67; *Chroniken der deutschen Städte*, vol. 4 (Leipzig: S. Hirzel, 1865), 111, 230–31, 317–18; *Chroniken der deutschen Städte*, vol. 22 (Leipzig: S. Hirzel, 1892), 466–67, 54: "die waren recht sodomiten" (they were sodomites). These accounts vary. See Bernhard Schimmelpfennig, "Religiöses Leben im späten Mittelalter," in *Geschichte der Stadt Augsburg*, ed. Gunther Gottlieb (Stuttgart: Konrad Theiss, 1985), 223; Helmut Brall, "Reflections of Homosexuality in Medieval Poetry and Chronicles," in *Queering the Canon: Defying Sights in German Literature and Culture*, ed. Christoph Lorey and John Plews (Rochester, N.Y.: Camden House, 1998), 89–105.

49. Ludwig Schmugge, "Stadt und Kirche im Spätmittelalter am Beispiel der Schweiz: Ein Überblick," in *Variorvm Mvnera Florvm: Festschrift für Hans F. Haefele zum 60. Geburtstag*, ed. Adolf Reinle, Ludwig Schmugge, and Peter Stotz (Sigmaringen: Thorbecke, 1985): 295–99.

50. See Peter Blickle, "Antiklerikalismus um den Vierwaldstättersee 1300–1500," in *Anticlericalism in Late Medieval and Early Modern Europe*, ed. Peter A. Dykema and Heiko A. Oberman (Leiden: E. J. Brill, 1993), 118–23.

51. StALU, RP 7, 9r; Anton Philipp von Segesser, *Rechtsgeschichte der Stadt und Republik Lucern*, vol. 2 (Lucerne: n.p., 1852), 450 n. 1, 749.

52. StALU, RP 7, 9r: "kätzerÿe getriben vnd verbrächt vnd jr zegel an einn andrn grîben haben, bitz jnen jr nattur komen jst."

53. Appeal to the pope in cases of sodomy is known from Venice: Pavan, "Police des moeurs," 279; Labalme, "Sodomy and Venetian Justice in the Renaissance," 239; Ruggiero, *Boundaries of Eros*, 130.

54. StALU, RP 6 (1489), 9r: "daz aber der gemein man nit gern thůt, danne man allewegen fürchttet, er könn vngestrafft darvon."

55. Ibid.: "damit dz vnrecht gestrafft werde vnd der gemein man dester glöubiger belibe. Dann wo sÿ vnrecht tůn söllten vnd ander lütt ouch dar zů bewegen vnd dar vmbe nit gstrafft werden, möchtte ein merckliche jrung vnder dem gemeinen volck jm

globen bringen" (so that offenses are punished and the common man remains all the more religious. If they commit crimes, move other people to such acts, and remain unpunished, this might bring about a considerable deviation from the faith among the people).

56. Franco Mormando, *The Preacher's Demons: Bernardino of Siena and the Social Underworld of Early Renaissance Italy* (Chicago: University of Chicago Press, 1999), 155–62.

57. Sieber-Lehmann, *Spätmittelalterlicher Nationalismus*, 145 n. 246 (Johannes Knebel).

58. Stadtarchiv Strassburg, AA 261, no. 29, 1r. Anthony Parmisan, Paul de Ferrer, Bartholome, Orlando, Tartailo, Caspar Zitilian, Synoty, Natal Albanesse, Marell de Bressa, Andrea de Treviso, Batain de Bressa, Beloy, Sixtus, Jan de Brengne, Peter de Parma, and Michel Thaberin all confess to having florenced or having been florenced.

59. Stadtarchiv Strassburg, AA 261, no. 29: "ee er ein wip genommen, hab er tusent malen geflorentzt." See also Sieber-Lehmann, *Spätmittelalterlicher Nationalismus*, 430.

60. Stadtarchiv Strassburg, AA 261, no. 29: "Item Jan de Brengne hett veriehen, do er ein knab wer, do wurde er in Belletz [Bellinzona] by x malen geflorentz von dem bôsen volck" (Jan de Brengne stated that, when he was a boy, he was florenced in Bellinzona about ten times by the evil people).

61. Sieber-Lehmann, *Spätmittelalterlicher Nationalismus*, 150–61.

62. Knebel, "Diarium," 70. See also Sieber-Lehmann, *Spätmittelalterlicher Nationalismus*, 62, 279–80.

63. Sieber-Lehmann, *Spätmittelalterlicher Nationalismus*, 145: "der Lamparten mortlichen, lasterlichen, uncristenlichen und unnaturlichen geschichten im Súntgowe."

64. See below for the Italian associations of sodomy.

65. Sieber-Lehmann, *Spätmittelalterlicher Nationalismus*, 145–46.

66. Ibid., 148.

67. The following paragraphs are based on Heinrich Witte, *Der letzte Puller von Hohenburg: Ein Beitrag zur politischen und Sittengeschichte des Elsasses und der Schweiz im 15. Jahrhundert sowie zur Genealogie des Geschlechts der Püller*, Beiträge zur Landes- und Volkskunde von Elsass-Lothringen, Vierter Band (Heft 16–20) (Strasbourg: J. H. E. Heitz, 1893); and Christine Reinle, "Konflikte und Konfliktstrategien eines elsässischen Adligen," in *"Raubritter" oder "Rechtschaffene vom Adel"? Aspekte von Politik, Friede und Recht im späten Mittelalter*, ed. Kurt Andermann (Sigmaringen: Thorbecke, 1997), 89–113. In the appendix of his study, Witte published the sources pertinent to my portrayal of Puller's life. Christine Reinle is preparing a new study, based on newly discovered sources.

68. Diebold Schilling, *Die Schweizer Bilderchronik des Luzerners Diebold Schilling 1513*, ed. Alfred A. Schmid et al. (Lucerne: Faksimile-Verlag, 1981), 118 (fol. 73v). In this illuminated manuscript, the murder is depicted in images, whereas the sexual acts themselves are not.

69. Witte, *Der letzte Puller von Hohenburg*, 33.

70. See Gilomen, "Innere Verhältnisse der Stadt Zürich," 323, 330–31, 346.

71. Ernst Gagliardi, *Dokumente zur Geschichte des Bürgermeisters Hans Waldmann*, vol. 1 (Basel: Adolf Geering, 1911), 270: "ein verräter, meineyder böswicht und knebenschinder." Krut was sentenced to death and drowned. See also Ernst Gagliardi, *Hans Waldmann und die Eidgenossenschaft des 15. Jahrhunderts* (Basel: Verlag der Basler Buch- und Antiquariatshandlung, 1912), 116–17.

72. For example, Denis the Carthusian, "Contra simoniam," in *Opera omnia*, vol. 39 (Tournai: Cartusiae de S. M. Pratis, 1910), 288: "simonia est spiritualis sodomia" (simony is spiritual sodomy). See also Dinshaw, *Getting Medieval*, 63–64.

73. Christian Dietrich, *Die Stadt Zürich und ihre Landgemeinden während der Bauernunruhen von 1489 bis 1525* (Frankfurt am Main: Peter Lang, 1985), 21–97.

74. Gagliardi, *Dokumente zur Geschichte des Bürgermeisters Hans Waldmann*, vol. 2 (Basel: Adolf Geering, 1913), 349–50.

75. Schilling, *Die Schweizer Bilderchronik*, 118–19, 214–17; Schilling, *Diebold Schilling's des Lucerners Schweizer-Chronik* (Lucerne: F. J. Schiffmann, 1862), 105–7; Gerold Edlibach, "Gerold Edlibach's Chronik," ed. Joh. Mart. Usterj, in *Mitteilungen der antiquarischen Gesellschaft in Zürich*, vol. 4 (Zurich, 1847), 177–86; *Code historique et diplomatique de la ville de Strasbourg*, vol. 1 (Strasbourg: Silbermann, 1845), 209–13; Diebold Schilling, *Luzerner Bildchronik*, ed. Robert Durrer and Paul Hilber (Geneva: Sadag, 1932), 64, 98–99; Schilling, *Berner Chronik des Diebold Schilling 1468–1484*, vol. 2, ed. Gustav Tobler (Bern: K. J. Wyss, 1901), 255–67; Valerius Anshelm, *Berner Chronik*, vol. 1 (Bern: K. J. Wyss, 1884), 214–21.

76. Schilling, *Chronik des Luzerner Diebold Schilling*, 99: "Der was dem ritter treffelich lieb, wann er hieß Anthoni, waz ein bartschârer, kond vast wol uff der luten und darzû singen" (He was dearly loved by the knight, since his name was Anthoni, he was a barber, could play the lute very well and sang with it).

77. In Lucerne in 1482, for instance, the year of Hohenburg's execution, two citizens reportedly forced a boy named Abrogast to admit openly that Richard von Hohenburg had "florenced" him. The case before the council was not about whether the allegation could be verified or not. It was about the fact that yet a third citizen, after having spoken to Abrogast, spread the news about the citizens' behavior toward the boy. Hans Müller and the young Lowertschi felt defamed by Peter Fassbind and took him to court. Fassbind's testimony was corroborated by the boy's testimony, and the case was dropped. See StALU, RP 58, 366v (1482).

78. Gagliardi, *Dokumente zur Geschichte des Bürgermeisters Hans Waldmann*, vol. 2, 190. See also Gagliardi, *Hans Waldmann und die Eidgenossenschaft*, 56.

79. See a 1466 case in which an overlord, Pfalzgraf Otto II, used accusations that Konrad von Murach, a noble, had committed "the unnamed sin with men against human nature" ("hanndell der vngenanten sunde mit mannespersonen zu vermischen wider menschliche natur") in conflicts over property rights (Emma Mages, "Die Rücknahme der Pfandschaft Tännesberg 1466: Das Verfahren gegen Konrad von Murbach wegen der 'ungenannten Sünde,'" *Zeitschrift für bayerische Landesgeschichte* 62 [1999]: 206).

Chapter Three

1. In the following, I distinguish between the Latin term *sodomia* and its English equivalent, *sodomy*. By the former, I refer to a wide range of sins often called "against nature"— as a rule, masturbation, nonvaginal intercourse between men and women, sodomy, and bestiality—while the latter denotes homosexual acts more narrowly in my usage. Medieval authors often oscillate between more wide-ranging and more narrowly defined meanings of a term. See, for instance, Anthony of Florence (d. 1459)—author of an influential *summa confessorum*, printed frequently north of the Alps—who calls the sins against nature the worst among the species of lust (encompassing masturbation, sodomy, "unnatural" intercourse between men and women, as well as bestiality). Though bestiality is considered to be graver than sodomy (following Thomas Aquinas), the author focuses almost exclusively on male homosexual intercourse by way of example. See

Anthony of Florence [Antoninus], *Summa,* part 2, titulus 5, capitulum 4 (Basel: Amerbach/Petri/Froben, [1511]), Q3r: "superlativum mali et peius dici non potest" (The utmost evil; one cannot express something more evil).

2. With regard to the inhabitants of Sodom, see Denis the Carthusian, "Enarratio in Cap. XVIII Genesis," in *Opera omnia,* vol. 1 (Monstrolii: n.p., 1896), 261. See also Johann Geiler von Kaisersberg, *Sermones funebres* (Lyon: J. Klein, 1504), e4v.

3. I used the following edition, *Speculum exemplorum omnibus christicolis salubriter inspiciendum: vt exemplis discant disciplinam* (Hagenau: Heinrich Gran, 1512) (VD-16 A:4352; *Verzeichnis der im deutschen Sprachbereich erschienenen Drucke des 16. Jahrhunderts* [Stuttgart: A. Hiersemann, 1983–]). The story features in the part of "newly written" *exempla* ("noviter conscripta"). Other editions are Deventer, 1481; Cologne, 1485; Strasbourg, 1487, 1490, 1495; Hagenau, 1519 (VD-16 A:4353). The inability to leave sin behind is repeatedly discussed with regard to sodomites; see Paul Wann, *Sermones dominicales per anni circulum* (Hagenau: Heinrich Gran, 1512), l4r.

4. Previous generations wrongly identified Aegidius Aurifaber as the compiler. See also Richard H. Rouse and Mary A. Rouse, *Preachers, Florilegia, and Sermons: Studies on the "Manipulus florum" of Thomas of Ireland* (Toronto: Pontifical Institute, 1979), 11–23, 26–42, 118ff; Wolfgang Brückner, "Exempelsammlungen," in *Enzyklopädie des Märchens,* vol. 4 (Berlin: de Gruyter, 1984), cols. 592–626. This collection was much criticized by theologians of a later generation, see Melchior Cano, *Opera,* vol. 2 (Rome: n.p., 1890), 263.

5. *Speculum exemplorum,* last page (no page number).

6. Anthony of Florence [Antoninus] reports the opinion that "such men are said to be more consumed by passion for other men than others for women." See his *Summa,* Q3: "Plus enim exardescere dicuntur huiusmodi homines in viros quam alij in mulieres." See also his point on the "tenacitas voluptatis" (clinging to lust).

7. Frantzen, "Disclosure of Sodomy," 452.

8. Elizabeth B. Keiser, *Courtly Desire and Medieval Homophobia: The Legitimation of Sexual Pleasure in "Cleanness" and Its Contexts* (New Haven, Conn.: Yale University Press, 1997); Frantzen, "Disclosure of Sodomy." For the German context, see Bernd-Ulrich Hergemöller, "Dietrich Koldes *Verclaringhe* und *Een prophetye gepreect by broeder Dierick van Munster:* Zur Arbeitsweise und Rezeptionsgeschichte des Christenspiegels," in *Vestigia Monasteriensia,* ed. Ellen Widder, Mark Mersiowsky, and Peter Johanek (Bielefeld: Verlag für Regionalgeschichte, 1995), 73–99; Christine Reinle, "Zur Rechtspraxis," 318–20; Sven Limbeck, "Plautus in der Knabenschule: Zur Eleminierung homosexueller Inhalte in deutschen Plautusübersetzungen der frühen Neuzeit," in *Erinnern und Wiederentdecken,* ed. Dirck Linck, Wolfgang Popp, and Annette Runte (Berlin: Verlag rosa Winkel, 1999), 57–64.

9. Regarding German, see Wolfgang Stammler, "Die 'bürgerliche' Dichtung des Spätmittelalters" and "Deutsche Scholastik," both in *Kleine Schriften zur Literaturgeschichte des Mittelalters* (Berlin: E. Schmidt, 1953), 82–87, 127–55; P. Egino Weidenhiller, *Untersuchungen zur deutschsprachigen katechetischen Literatur des späten Mittelalters* (Munich: Beck, 1965); Johannes Geffcken, *Der Bildercatechismus des funfzehnten Jahrhunderts und die catechetischen Hauptstücke in dieser Zeit bis auf Luther,* vol. 1: *Die zehn Gebote* (Leipzig: T. O. Weigel, 1855); Steven Ozment, *The Reformation in the Cities: The Appeal of Protestantism to Sixteenth-Century Germany and Switzerland* (New Haven, Conn.: Yale University Press, 1975), 16–46; Thomas N. Tentler, *Sin and Confession on the Eve of the Reformation* (Princeton, N.J.: Princeton University Press, 1977), 28–53; Uta Störmer-Caysa, *Gewissen und Buch: Über den Weg eines Begriffes in die deutsche Literatur des Mittelalters* (Berlin: de Gruyter, 1998).

10. Leonard E. Boyle, "The *Summa Confessorum* of John of Freiburg and the Popularization of the Moral Teaching of St. Thomas and of Some of His Contemporaries," in *St. Thomas Aquinas 1274–1974: Commemorative Studies*, ed. Etienne Gilson (Toronto: Pontifical Institute, 1974), 245.

11. Ibid.

12. Tentler, *Sin and Confession*, 53.

13. Berthold, *Die "Rechtssumme" Bruder Bertholds: Eine deutsche abecedarische Bearbeitung der "Summa Confessorum" des Johannes von Freiburg*, ed. Georg Steer et al. (Tübingen: Niemeyer, 1987), 4:2168: "Von vnchawschait chommen vil sund."

14. Johann Geiler von Kaisersberg, *Die siben hauptsünd* ([Strasbourg: J. Knoblauch, 1511]), g2v: "Das sibent vnd letst schwert da mitt der böß gaist vnder steet zů tödten den menschen in seiner seel / ist vnkeüschait / vnd ist dz swert dz nyemant vber sicht / dem auch nyemant entfliehen mag."

15. Ibid., g2v.

16. Ibid., k5v.

17. Note, the "unspeakable sin" is not the only application of the unspeakable in medieval literature. See, for instance, Michel Beheim (1416/21–1474/78), who wrote a poem "about the unspeakable praise of God" ("von dem unaussprechlichen lob gottes"), for instance (in *Die Gedichte des Michel Beheim*, ed. Hans Gille, Ingeborg Spriewald [Berlin: Akademie, 1970], 55). Yet usages of the term to denote the unspeakable divine, most commonly in mysticism, are contextually and doctrinally far removed from the negatively "unspeakable." See Matthias Lexer, *Mittelhochdeutsches Handwörterbuch*, vol. 2 (Leipzig: S. Hirzel, 1876), col. 1939; vol. 3 (Leipzig: S. Hirzel, 1878), col. 286; Jacob Grimm and Wilhelm Grimm, *Deutsches Wörterbuch*, vol. 11 (Leipzig: S. Hirzel 1936), cols. 1298–99, 1299–1301, 1411–12.

18. Keiser, *Courtly Desire*, 55. Many religious writers identified the "sin against nature" ("sunde tegen de natuer") as homosexual activity (Geffcken, *Bildercatechismus*, cols. 96, 155, 172). Geffcken's rendering of sources does not meet modern standards for editions of medieval texts. To date, only a few texts from his collection have been published more reliably. Therefore, I have used Geffcken but supplemented his study by original editions wherever I was able to locate them.

19. Quoted in Jordan, *Invention of Sodomy*, 151.

20. Hieronymus, "Liber interpretationis Hebraicorum nominum," in *Opera*, part 1: *Exegetica*, vol. 1 (Turnhout: Brepols, 1959), 85.

21. Guilelmus Alvernus, "Supplementum tractatus novi de poenitentia," in *Opera omnia*, vol. 2 (Paris: L. Billaine, 1674), 232 (cap. xix). William himself quoted Gregory the Great as a source in this context (Gregorius, *Moralia*, 33.13). See also Michael Goodich, *The Unmentionable Vice: Homosexuality in the Later Medieval Period* (Santa Barbara, Calif.: Dorset Press, 1979), 62; Keiser, *Courtly Desire*, 237 n. 23.

22. Quoted in Hergemöller, *Krötenkuß und schwarzer Kater*, 223.

23. See Denis, "Enarratio in Cap. XI Apocalypsis," in *Opera omnia*, vol. 14 (Monstrolii: n.p., 1901), 303: "Sodomia vero, muta vel caecitas, interpreta[n]tur" (Sodomy translates as muteness or blindness). Ludovico Maria Sinistrari, *Peccatum Mutum: The Secret Sin*, ed. Montague Summers (Paris, n.d.), 29.

24. See Weidenhiller, *Untersuchungen*, 120: "die [sin] wil ich hy nicht auzlegen."

25. Geiler von Kaisersberg, *Die siben hauptsünd*, g3r: "das da nützer geschwigen ist dann geredet / wölche vnkeüschait der teüfel selbs hasset."

26. Peraldus, *Summa de vitiis et virtutibus*, B3v: "non debet homo loqui de peccato isto."

27. For more on Berthold and his sermons, see the text below and nn. 47–49.

28. Martin von Amberg, *Der Gewissensspiegel*, ed. Stanley Newman Werbow (Berlin: E. Schmidt, 1958), 68: "Die [unchewsch wider die natur, stumme sunde] ist alzo snode an ir selber daz die lewte durch ir snedicheit willen von ir nicht mogen gereden."

29. Johannes Herolt, "Sermo LXXXV," in *Sermones discipuli* (Mainz: n.p., 1612), 488: "secundum Aug. est grauius omnibus aliis peccatis, propter quod mutum, vel indicibile dicitur, eo quod ipsum nominare pessimum est." According to Herolt, it is committed in four ways, masturbation, nonvaginal heterosexual intercourse, same-sex sexual acts, and bestiality. See also [Heinrich of Friemar], *Preceptorium* (Cologne: n.p., 1505), Ee 5v/Ee 6r: "This sin exceeds all others; therefore, one calls it mute or inexpressible because it is very shameful to name it" ("Et hoc peccatum est grauius omnibus alijs. propter quod mutum vel indicibile dicitur eo quod ipsum nominare turpissimum est"); Martin Luther, "Decem praecepta Wittenbergensi praedicata populo" (1516/17; published 1518), in *Werke: Kritische Gesamtausgabe* (hereafter *WA*), vol. 1 (Weimar: Böhlau, 1883), 489: "Sodomy which men commit with men and women with women but also men with women and women with men; these acts are too ignominious to be named" ("Zodomia, qua vir viro, mulier muliere abutitur vel etiam vir muliere et mulier viro, quae omnia turpiora sunt quam nominare liceat"); Weidenhiller, *Untersuchungen*, 50: "Though this sin is called against nature, it is also called the mute sin, because one should not talk about it" ("Und wie wol man dye nennet die sünd wider dye natur, so hayssenn sy doch auch dye stummen sünd, wann es ist nicht guet davon zu reden," cgm 121, fifteenth century).

30. Herolt, "Sermo LXXXV," *Sermones discipuli*, 489: "Item nec homo cogitare debet de tali peccato."

31. Ibid.

32. See Raimundus of Pennaforte, *Summa de paenitentia*, ed. Xaverius Ochoa and Aloisius Diez (Rome: Commentarium pro religiosis, 1976), col. 845 (lib. iii, tit. 34.44): "Item, quia non solum actus, sed etiam ipsa prolatio . . . polluit" (Not only the act itself pollutes but also . . . its mention). This sentence refers to all "vices against nature," including the one between man and woman, though Raimundus evades definitions in this context.

33. Raimundus, *Summa de paenitentia*, col. 845: "os loquentis, aures audientium, . . . polluit." For further references for this stance, see Hergemöller, *Krötenkuß und schwarzer Kater*, 294; Heinrich of Friemar, *Preceptorium*, Ee 5v/Ee 6r: ". . . ita ut os dicentis et aures audientium polluantur"; Herolt, "Sermo LXXXV," *Sermones discipuli*, 488: "os dicentis, et aures audientis polluuntur."

34. Stricker, *Die Klage* (in Spreitzer, *Die stumme Sünde*, 221): "si [the sin of sodomy among men] ist so gar unmuglich, / ein schameloser schamte sich, / solt er ez hören und sagen; / er mohte ez chûme vertragen" (male-male intercourse is so impossible that even a shameless person would be ashamed if he were to hear it named; he could hardly bear it). Stricker defines the sin as "daz si daz mit mannen begent, / da got die wip zû geschûf," "that they commit with men what God created women for" (220).

35. Weidenhiller, *Untersuchungen*, 50: "wann es laidigt güettige oren" (cgm 121).

36. Johann Geiler von Kaisersberg, *Der dreieckecht Spiegel* (Strasbourg: M. Schürer, n.d.), Cc5r. The Latin word is *scandalizare*. Jean Gerson (translated by Geiler) declared that the more a sexual act "deviates" from the order of nature, the more sinful it is. Gerson also defines "unchastity" lucidly as "By the penance of deadly sin, this commandment [the sixth commandment] prohibits men and women from committing carnal acts outside of

marriage," adding that the same rule "also prohibits all unchaste touches of the genitals (*geburd glider*) to all humans, whether married or not, where they do not respect the natural order instituted by nature or which nature teaches us." *Der dreieckecht spiegel*, Cc4v: "Durch diß gebot würt verbotten / bey pen der tod sünd / alle geselschafft oder fleischlich vermischung man vnd frawen außwendig dem gesatz der ee . . . Würt auch durch diß gebott verbotten allen mönschen sie seyend in der ee oder ledig / alle vnkeüsche anrierung der geburd glider / in welcher nit gehalten würt natürlich ordnung / so die natur ingesatzt hat / oder vns die natur lert." On the concept of the reader being angered, see also Klaus Berg and Monika Kasper, eds., *"Das bůch der tugenden": Ein Compendium des 14. Jahrhunderts über Moral und Recht nach der "Summa theologiae" II-II des Thomas von Aquin und anderen Werken der Scholastik und Kanonistik*, vol. 1 (Tübingen: Niemeyer, 1984), 411; M. A. van den Broek, ed., *Der Spiegel des Sünders: Ein katechetischer Traktat des fünfzehnten Jahrhunderts* (Amsterdam: Rodopi, 1976), 267 (discussed later in this chapter).

37. Weidenhiller, *Untersuchungen*, 120: "und sind gar grözze sünde wider die natur, von den der engel fleucht, wenn man davon redet" (they are great sins against nature from which the angel flees if one talks about them).

38. Ibid.

39. Martin von Amberg, *Der Gewissensspiegel*, 68: "wenn man von ir sündleichen rett so flichen die engel von den lewten alz verre und die styme mag erreichen."

40. Guilelmus Peraldus: "Novitas tante et inaudite turpitudinis quasi admirationem et dubitationem parit in audiente." Quoted in Hergemöller, *Krötenkuß und schwarzer Kater*, 244. See also John Baldwin, *The Language of Sex: Five Voices from Northern France around 1200* (Chicago: University of Chicago Press, 1994), 247 (Petrus Cantor).

41. Denis the Carthusian, "Enarratio in Cap. XVIII Genesis," in *Opera omnia*, vol. 1, 261: "velut admirans quod tam abominabilia scelera possent inter homines inveniri"; Herolt, "Sermo LXXXV," *Sermones discipuli*, 488: "Dominus quasi admirans et dubitans super tanto scelere" (see Gn 18:21). See also Hergemöller, *Krötenkuß und schwarzer Kater*, 244.

42. Guilelmus Peraldus, *Summae virtutum ac vitiorum* [*Summa de vitiis et virtutibus*], vol. 2 (Lyon: G. Rovillius, 1585), 45 (tom. 2, tract. 3, pars 1, cap. 3). See also Hergemöller, *Krötenkuß und schwarzer Kater*, 258.

43. *Dat licht der sele* (Lubeck, 1484), 31a (Geffcken, *Bildercatechismus*).

44. *Die Pluemen der Tugent des Hans Vintler*, ed. Ignaz V. Zingerle (Innsbruck: Wagner, 1874), 209: "snödeu uncheusch . . . , von der sich der teufel selber schamt" (revolting unchastity . . . of which the devil himself is ashamed).

45. Herolt, "Sermo LXXXV," *Sermones discipuli*, 489: "aliqui doemones abhorrent illud vitium propter nobilitatem naturae."

46. Geiler von Kaisersberg, *Die siben hauptsünd*, g3r: "wölche vnkeüschait [*sodomia*, unspeakable sin] der teüfel selbs hasset / vnd dar ab speüwet vnnd spricht pfey pfey" (which unchastity the devil himself hates; he spits because of it and exclaims 'pfey, pfey'). Johannes Herolt gives the example of a *mulier Sodomita* who, when masturbating, heard the devil exclaim "pfi, pfi, pfi" ("Sermo LXXXV," *Sermones discipuli*, 489).

47. Berthold of Regensburg, *Predigten*, ed. Franz Pfeiffer (Berlin: de Gruyter, 1965), 1:92: "Ir tiuvel . . . getorstet ir [the sin] nie keinen namen geben." See also 2:151–52: "manic tiuvel ist, der die selben sünde niht getar gerâten offenlichen; Her Nimrôt und her Astarôt, ir kundet ir nie keinen namen geben."

48. Ibid., 1:93: "Übernamen hât sie vil diu verfluochte sünde: keinen rehten namen mohte ir weder mensche noch tiuvel nie gegeben."

49. Ibid., 1:93. According to Bernd-Ulrich Hergemöller (*Krötenkuß und schwarzer Kater*, 279), the red sin is Berthold's individual coinage.

50. Tentler, *Sin and Confession,* 128.

51. Geiler von Kaisersberg, *Die siben hauptsünd,* g3r: "mit der ungenanten unkeüschait / darumb man die leüt verbrent" (the unnamed unchastity because of which people are burned at the stake).

52. "This sin makes the sinner mute when he should confess," explicates the Franciscan Dietrich Kolde (d. 1515) in his *Mirror for the Christian (Der Christenspiegel des Dietrich Kolde von Münster,* ed. Clemens Drees [Werl: Dietrich-Coelde, 1954], 141).

53. Keiser, *Courtly Desire,* 235 n. 9.

54. William of Auvergne, *Summa virtutum ac vitiorum* (Lyon, 1668), 11r: "Ideoque Sodoma bene 'muta' interpretatur, quia hoc peccatum reddet homines mutos in die iudicii" (*Sodoma* can be translated as "mute," because this sin renders people mute on the day of judgment). Quoted in Hergemöller, "Dietrich Koldes *Verclaringhe,*" 86. See also Hergemöller, *Krötenkuß und schwarzer Kater,* 257.

55. Geiler von Kaisersberg, *Der dreieckecht Spiegel,* Cc5r.

56. Wann, *Sermones dominicales,* m2r: "debet taliter ea [peccata] confessori dicere quod ipse noscat sufficienter speciem peccati commissi: modum et circumstantiam: nec retrahat eum pudor aut verecundia qui non retraxit ipsum ab opere" ([The sinner] shall confess these sins [sins against nature] to the confessor in such a way that the latter will recognize sufficiently the kind of the committed sin, its manner and circumstance. Shyness or shame which did not keep [the sinner] from the act shall not keep him [from confessing]). See also *Der Spiegel des Sünders,* 227, discussed later in this chapter.

57. Berthold of Regensburg, *Predigten,* 1:92: "'Wie bruoder Berhtolt, wie sol ich mich vor der sünde behüeten?' Des helfe mir der almehtige got, daz dû mîn niht verstêst."

58. See, for instance, Ulrich von Lichtenstein (d. c. 1275), *Der vrouwen buoch,* in Spreitzer, *Die stumme Sünde,* 234; Stricker, *Die Klage,* in Spreitzer, 234, 221.

59. Nikodemus Frischlin, *Facetiae selectiores* (Strasbourg: B. Jobin, 1600), 6r (*De rustico puero simplici et confitente sacerdoti*). See also a related story in which a soldier confesses having sex with a nun, but the father confessor misunderstands and thinks the soldier had sex with an animal. In Latin the story can be found in Heinrich Bebel, *Heinrich Bebels Facetien Drei Bücher,* ed. Gustav Bebermeyer (Leipzig: W. Hiersemann, 1931), 24; in the vernacular, in Jakob Frey, *Jakob Freys Gartengesellschaft (1556),* ed. Johannes Bolte (Tübingen: Bibliothek des Litterarischen Vereins, 1896), 45–46. A variant of the story whose subject is not sexual in Hans Wilhelm Kirchhof, "Ein Knabe beichtet," in *Wendunmuth,* ed. Hermann Österley, vol. 1 (Stuttgart: H. Laupp, 1869), 294.

60. In the boy's mind, the priest broke the seal of confession when he castigated parents for teaching their children trivia (the boy had ultimately disclosed his secret to the priest—information not at all trivial to the boy).

61. No single manuscript renders the text as a whole. The computation of page numbers is based on several manuscripts that cover parts of Ulrich's *summa.* Ulrich envisioned such partitioning of manuscripts. See also Gabriele Baptist-Hlawatsch and Ulrike Bodemann, "Ulrich von Pottenstein," in *Die deutsche Literatur des Mittelalters: Verfasserlexikon,* 2d ed., ed. Stammler, Langosch, and Wachinger, vol. 10 (1996), 10–17.

62. Besides Ulrich, the following writers belong to this group: Leopold Stainreuter (c. 1340–c. 1400), Nikolaus of Dinkelsbühl (c. 1360–1433), Thomas Peuntner (c. 1390–1439), and Thomas Ebendorfer (1388–1464).

63. See Isnard W. Frank, "Das lateinische theologische Schrifttum im österreich-ischen Spätmittelalter," in *Die österreichische Literatur: Ihr Profil von den Anfängen im Mittelalter bis ins 18. Jahrhundert (1050–1750)*, ed. Herbert Zeman (Graz: Akademische Druck- und Verlagsanstalt, 1986), 261–93; Thomas Hohmann, "'Die recht gelerten maister': Bemerkungen zur Übersetzungsliteratur der Wiener Schule des Spätmittelalters," in *Die österreichische Literatur*, ed. Herbert Zeman (Graz: Akademische Druck- und Verlagsanstalt, 1986), 349–66 (both have bibliographical references to previous studies).

64. Christiane Laun, *Bildkatechese im Spätmittelalter: Allegorische und typologische Auslegungen des Dekalogs* (Ph.D. diss., Munich University, 1979); Weidenhiller, *Untersuchungen*, 14–15; Ruth Slenczka, *Lehrhafte Bildtafeln in spätmittelalterlichen Kirchen* (Cologne: Böhlau, 1998), 25–63, 205–25, I.1–I.4 (illustrations). Tentler, *Sin and Confession*, 86, 111, 135; Rudolf Suntrup, Burghart Wachinger, and Nicola Zotz, "'Zehn Gebote' (Deutsche Erklärungen)," in *Die deutsche Literatur des Mittelalters: Verfasserlexikon*, 2d ed., ed. Stammler, Langosch, and Wachinger, vol. 10, cols. 1484–1503. Questions to ask oneself prepared the sinner for confession. See also Geiler von Kaisersberg, *Der dreieckecht Spiegel*, Ff1v; Geiler von Kaisersberg, "Von der beycht," in *Les plus anciens écrits*, ed. L. Dacheux (Colmar: M. Hoffmann, 1882), 55; Martin Luther, "Eine kurze Unterweisung, wie man beichten soll," *WA*, vol. 2 (1884), 63.

65. Kalocsa, Föszékesegyházi Könyvtár, Ms 629, fol. 198ra: "Die sybenden v̈bertreten das gepot natürleiches naygens. Vnd darczu die natur natürleich nayget, das sint die, die sich vermailigen mit dem laster, daz nicht zu nennen ist vnd dauon nicht wol zu reden ist. Vnd die wider die natur sünden vnd natürleiche v̈bung vnd masse verscheren, in welicherlay weyse vnd v̈bung das geschïcht."

66. Ibid., fol. 198ra: "Auch ist das laster der vir laster aines, die von ïrer schämleichait wegen hincz got schreyen vnd enczichleich götleiche rache piten" (This vice is one of four which cry to God in their shamefulness and each ask for divine vengeance).

67. Ibid., 199ra.

68. Ms. Kalocsa 629, fol. 198rb: "Darvmb so gab si got gar in schantpäre leyden, wann ïre weib verwandelten natürleichen nücz vnd v̈büng, wann ez vermailiget aine die andern. Also enczündeten sich auch die man gegen einander, also das ainer den andern vermailiget" (Therefore, God gave them up to shameful passions. Their women departed from natural intercourse, when one woman polluted the other. Then, men's passion for one another was sparked so that one man polluted the other). This argument was far from expressing a *locus communis*, though there is further evidence; see Sinistrari, *Peccatum Mutum*, 33; Brundage, *Law, Sex, and Christian Society*, 533–34. In *Altercatio inter virum et mulierem*, a fourteenth-century poem, woman defends herself against man's accusations of having caused all evils by pointing to the destruction of Sodom and Gomorrah (Hans Walther, *Das Streitgedicht in der lateinischen Literatur des Mittelalters* [Munich: Beck, 1920], 138). For a different treatment, see Hergemöller, *Krötenkuß*, 163.

69. Henricus Cornelius Agrippa, *Declamation on the Nobility and Preeminence of the Female Sex*, ed. Albert Rabil, Jr. (Chicago: University of Chicago Press, 1996), 71: "Men were the first to devote themselves to excesses against nature (witness Sodom and Gomorrah, cities at other times celebrated, which the sins of men caused to perish)." See also Sinistrari, *Peccatum Mutum*, 33.

70. Anthony of Florence, *Summa*, Q3r; Cgm 632 ("Anonyme Dekalogerklärung," 1469), in *Aberglaube für Laien: Zur Programmatik und Überlieferung spätmittelalterlicher Superstitio-*

nenkritik, ed. Karin Baumann (Würzburg: Königshausen & Neumann, 1989), 798 (a critical assessment of Baumann's editorial practice can be found in Störmer-Caysa, *Gewissen und Buch,* 326–27); Herolt, "Sermo LXXXV," *Sermones discipuli,* 489; Geiler von Kaisersberg, *Der dreieckecht Spiegel,* Cc5r; Geffcken, *Bildercatechismus,* cols. 44, 96; Luther, "Decem praecepta," 489. Note also the gender-neutral formulations used in religious discourse (*mensche, man,* etc.) that should be read as referring to men and to women, though men are usually foregrounded.

71. Ulrich calls this "the sin of which neither to write nor to read is enjoyable" ("sünde, von der weder zu schreyben noch zu lesen lust pringet"), in Kalocsa, 199ra.

72. Jean Gerson, "De confessione mollitiei," in *Oeuvres complètes,* vol. 8 (Paris: Desclée, 1971), 71: "Lector autem obscoenitatem materiae ac verborum excusatam habeat ob necessitatem docendorum remediorum."

73. Weidenhiller, *Untersuchungen,* 120 (*Confessionale*).

74. *Opera omnia,* vol. 39 (Tournai: Cartusiae S. M. de Pratis, 1910), 88 ("De speciebus luxuriae, et de ordine enormitatis earum").

75. See Tentler, *Sin and Confession;* Hervé Martin, *Le métier de prédicateur en France septentrionale à la fin du moyen âge (1350–1520)* (Paris: Cerf, 1988), 386–88; Keiser, *Courtly Desire,* 60–62; Frantzen, "Disclosure of Sodomy."

76. See, for example, Berg and Kasper, eds., "*Das bůch der tugenden,*" 411–12. This manual's anonymous author states explicitly that material on unchastity was excluded, though the authorities (*meister*) write of it quite extensively, because the uneducated reader might either be angered or learn from and emulate described actions. This passage has no equivalent in the Latin sources which fed this German manual. The author's section on the sixth commandment is equally characterized by extreme brevity (371).

77. *Aberglaube für Laien,* ed. Baumann, 632. In one of the first and very influential *summae confessorum,* Raymond of Pennaforte "warned that even hearing about sodomy could be the occasion of sin" (Frantzen, "Disclosure of Sodomy," 455; Frantzen cites Brundage, *Law, Sex, and Christian Society,* 399). In Brundage, note further references to Robert of Flamborough. Gerson (as translated by Geiler von Kaisersberg) stated that "indecent" words or images are one of the reasons why humans fall into sins against nature (Geffcken, *Bildercatechismus,* col. 44).

78. Gabriele Baptist-Hlawatsch, *Das katechetische Werk Ulrichs von Pottenstein* (Tübingen: Niemeyer, 1980), 144–49 (Ulrich's preface to his *summa*); Helmut Puff, "'Allen menschlichen nuczlichen': Publikum, Gebrauchsfunktion und Aussagen zur Ehe bei Ulrich von Pottenstein," in *Text und Geschlecht: Mann und Frau in Eheschriften der frühen Neuzeit,* ed. Rüdiger Schnell (Frankfurt am Main: Suhrkamp, 1997), 176–96.

79. Martin von Amberg, *Der Gewissensspiegel,* 33. Twenty-one manuscripts are known to exist, most of them from the fifteenth century.

80. The first edition (n.p., n.d.) appeared in Augsburg in Günther Zainer's printshop (c. 1476). Like many Augsburg printers, Zainer specialized in vernacular publications. The print has neither title page nor page numbers (Hain 14945). I used the edition in Basel's University Library, Inc. 237. Three further editions appeared in Augsburg until 1482. For a modern edition, see van den Broek, *Spiegel.* See 3–4 for information on the four print editions.

81. Hans-Jörg Künast, "Entwicklungslinien des Augsburger Buchdrucks von den Anfängen bis zum Ende des Dreißigjährigen Krieges," in *Augsburger Buchdruck und Ver-*

lagswesen: Von den Anfängen bis zur Gegenwart, ed. Helmut Gier and Johannes Janota (Wiesbaden: Harrassowitz, 1997), 12, 21; Künast, *"Getruckt zu Augspurg": Buchdruck und Buchhandel zwischen 1468 und 1555* (Tübingen: Niemeyer, 1996).

82. I quote from the original but include references to the modern edition. See van den Broek, *Spiegel,* 282.

83. Van den Broek, *Spiegel,* 12–15. Van den Broek names Hugo Ripelin of Strasbourg, *Compendium theologicae veritatis;* Jean Gerson, *Opusculum tripartitum;* Antoninus Florentinus, *Summa confessionis;* and Matthew of Cracow, *Tractatus de modo confitendi et puritate conscientiae;* but also Heinrich von Langenstein, *Erchantnuzz der sund.*

84. Van den Broek, *Spiegel,* 13–14.

85. Such overlaps are common in this type of literature. Authors of didactic texts recognized recapitulation as an important component of moral learning, while rhetoricians advocated that one treat a subject matter from different perspectives (*pluribus modis tractare*). The manuscript of a short catechism from Basel lists *sodomia* under the sins of *luxuria* and also under the rubric "crying sins" (*peccata clamantia*). See also Basel UB, F VIII 15, 90r–97r; Paul Wann, *Sermones de septem vitijs criminalibus eorumque remediis* (Hagenau: Heinrich Gran, 1514), sermon 55.

86. Van den Broek, *Spiegel,* 224. The term sodomy appears only this once. For the sake of brevity, I will employ it in my reading.

87. The Latin terms in question are *fornicatio, meretricium, adulterium, stuprum, sacrilegium, incestus,* and *peccatum contra naturam.*

88. In discussions of sexual sins, references to sodomy are often posited at a prominent last position (Martin von Amberg, *Der Gewissensspiegel,* 68). The Low German *Eyn speyghel des cristen ghelouen* lists breaches of the sixth commandment according to severity: "This [same-sex sexual activity] is the greatest and foulest sin which one can do. It is called the sin against nature" ("Dyt is de aldermeyste unde de aldervulste sunde, de man doen mach, unde is geheten sunde tegen de natuer"; Geffcken, *Bildercatechismus,* col. 96). The author also lists the severe punishment that men and women deserve who act against nature (as he does not do with other sinners): They ought to be burned at the stake, in order for other cities to avoid God's wrath—as evidenced in Sodom and Gomorrah (col. 96).

89. Van den Broek, *Spiegel,* 224.

90. Van den Broek, *Spiegel,* 224–27. In this context, "unnatural" sexual intercourse between husband and wife makes two appearances (225, 226).

91. Van den Broek, *Spiegel,* 227: "Vil vnnd ander mer von diser súnde der vnkeusch zeschreiben not wåre: das ich von kúrtze vnderwegen lassen můß" (It would be necessary to write much more about this sin of unchastity from which, for the sake of brevity, I have to refrain). Note that both women and men, husbands and wives are specifically addressed in this context. Some small catechetical texts circumvent any mention of sins against nature. They focus entirely on marital sexuality. See "Peniteas cito," in *Bildercatechismus,* by Geffcken, col. 194; "Spiegel Christlicher walfart" (Strasbourg, 1509), in *Bildercatechismus,* col. 183; Rudolf Langenberg, *Quellen und Forschungen zur Geschichte der deutschen Mystik* (Bonn: P. Hanstein, 1902), "Eine Laienregel des XV. Jahrhunderts," 91, "Dekalog-Erklärung aus der Groote-Handschrift zu Münster," 171; Martin von Amberg, *Der Gewissensspiegel,* 52; Weidenhiller, *Untersuchungen,* 46 (cgm 121, 319v), 67 (clm 8729, 18r/v), 113 (cgm 324), 157 (cgm 458, 31v), 151 (cgm 509, 349r), 193 (cgm 1004, fifteenth century).

92. Van den Broek, *Spiegel*, chapter 34, "Das sibend gebot," 266–71. No cross-reference ties the two passages together. The colophon makes it clear that we are dealing with a compilation of several smaller texts ("booklets," or *búchlin*).

93. Van den Broek, *Spiegel*, 267: "von den stinckenden sunden vnd vnmenschlichen die in maniger weiß leider vil teufelhafftig menschen mit in selber vnd andern menschen oder tieren wider die natur begeen" (on the stinking and inhuman sins against nature which unfortunately many devilish men commit in manifold ways with themselves, other humans, or animals). The author simplifies canonical distinctions of specific sexual acts (e.g., it is unclear who the sexual partners among humans are). Only in a later passage does the teacherlike voice address both sinning men and women.

94. Brother Berthold's widely available legal *summa* (c. 1400) distinguished between "great," "mediocre" (*mittel mässig*), and "small mortal sins." In this alphabetically arranged handbook of canon law, an adaptation of John of Freiburg's (d. 1314) Latin *summa*, sodomy (*sodomey*) was listed under the gravest sins together with murder, simony, religious heresy, bestiality ("unchastity with animals"), incest ("unchastity with relatives"), and perjury (Berthold, "*Rechtssumme*," 4:2070–71 [S 61]). Quoting Thomas Aquinas, Brother Berthold holds that only bestiality is graver, yet asserts that sodomy is by far more severe than fornication, rape, adultery, incest, or sex with clerics (4:2160–62).

95. One anonymous catechism divided the sins against nature according to "acts with oneself, with others or however it occurs" ("so man sündet wyder dy natur, es wer mit im selbs oder andern oder wy das geschäch"; Weidenhiller, *Untersuchungen*, 76). Another manuscript leaves out masturbation and mentions only "the sin of the Sodomites with people or animals, that is the mute sin against nature" ("Sodomiter sündt mit lewten oder tyren, das ist dy stument sündt wyder dy natur"; Weidenhiller, *Untersuchungen*, 62). A similar text mentions only masturbation and sodomy "with young or old men" ("Dye stummen sünd: Wann ein mensch mit ym selber sündet. Item der mit mannes pildung, iungen oder allten sündet"; Weidenhiller, *Untersuchungen*, 50).

96. Van den Broek, *Spiegel*, 267–68.

97. The names of the five cities are Sodom, Gomorrah, Adamae, Seboim, and Segor.

98. Van den Broek, *Spiegel*, 268. Frequently, sodomy was characterized by its disastrous consequences on humankind—a causal connection first claimed in Justinian's *novellae*. See Nikolaus von Dinkelsbühl-redactor, "Von den czehen poten ain tractat," in *Aberglaube für Laien*, ed. Baumann, 631–32; Cgm 632 ("Anonyme Dekalogerklärung," 1469), in *Aberglaube für Laien*, ed. Baumann, 798; Marquard of Lindau, *Die zehe gebot* (*Straßburg 1516 und 1520*): *Ein katechetischer Traktat*, ed. Jacobus Willem van Maren (Amsterdam: Rodopi, 1980), 74a; Denis the Carthusian, "Enarratio in Capit. XVIII Genesis," in *Opera omnia*, vol. 1, 260–61; Hans Folz, "Beichtspiegel," in *Die Reimpaarsprüche*, ed. Hanns Fischer (Munich: Beck, 1961), 192; Geffcken, *Bildercatechismus*, cols. 44, 96, 133, 155, 172; Geiler von Kaisersberg, *Der dreieckecht Spiegel*, Cc5v; Georg Wickram, "Die sieben Hauptlaster," in *Sämtliche Werke*, ed. Hans-Gert Roloff, vol. 8 (Berlin: de Gruyter, 1972), 197; *Der grosse Seelentrost: Ein niederdeutsches Erbauungsbuch des vierzehnten Jahrhunderts*, ed. Margarete Schmitt (Cologne: Böhlau, 1959), 197–98.

99. Invocations of *sodomia* frequently occurred in the context of eschatological references. Later in this chapter, in Nikolaus of Dinkelsbühl and Erasmus, I present other instances of *bipartitio* in the context of discussions of *sodomia*.

100. At this juncture, two other authorities, viewed as complementary, enter the picture, canon law and imperial law (van den Broek, *Spiegel*, 267).

101. Van den Broek, *Spiegel*, 268–69: "wee dir man oder weib. der du die gifften ding treibest vnd andern menschen da von sagest oder sy das lerest. dann du bist dar durch ein glide vnnd iaghundt des teufels." The passage in which the sinner is personally addressed is reminiscent of Peter Damian's *Liber Gomorrhianus* (*Die Briefe des Petrus Damiani*, part 1, 298, 313–14).

102. Van den Broek, *Spiegel*, 267: "das nicht die reinen oren vnd keuschen hertzen der vnschuldigen menschen die der vergiften sünden nit wissent. dar durch hieinn ein wissen nemen vnd geergert werden" (so that the pure ears and chaste hearts of innocent people, ignorant of these poisonous sins, do not gain knowledge thereof or are angered).

103. Butler, *Excitable Speech*, 131.

104. William of Auvergne, *Summa*: "non est aliquis, qui ipsum [ignomiae peccatum] audeat nominare in praedicando." Before, *passio ignominiae* is introduced for the sins of Sodom. Quoted in Hergemöller, "Dietrich Koldes *Verclaringhe*," 85.

105. Keiser, *Courtly Desire*, 55.

106. Nikolaus of Dinkelsbühl-redactor in *Aberglaube für Laien*, ed. Baumann, 632; Wann, *Sermones dominicales*, m1v; Martin Luther, "Vorlesungen über 1. Mose von 1535–45," in *WA*, vol. 43 (1912), 56–57. See also Brundage, *Law, Sex and Christian Society*, 534; Tentler, *Sin and Confession*, 89.

107. Meffret, *Sermones Meffret. alius Ortulus regine de tempore pars Estiualis* (n.p., n.d.), sermo 77; Leonardus de Utino (b. 1400), *Quadragesimale de legibus seu anime fidelis* (Lyon: n.p., 1494), T2v–T5v; Heinricus Herp [Herpf] (c. 1400/1410–77), *Speculum Aureum de preceptis diuine legis* (Basel: J. Froben, 1496), s7v–s8v, E2v–E4r, E8r–E8v. With regard to sermons from northern France between 1350 and 1520, Martin has concluded that "sodomy and bestiality occupied preachers significantly less than adultery, concubinage or the 'excesses' within marriage" (*Le métier*, 381).

108. See Johannes Nider, *Praeceptorium divinae legis* (n.p., n.d.; Hain 11781), sixth commandment, G: "Predicanda autem de hoc vicio publice debet quilibet cautus esse et tamen in genere de ipso loqui taliter tam quod qui rei sunt ex hoc ualeant cognoscere culpam suam sed species et modos huius turpitudinis non expedit coram populo particulariter explicare" (Who preaches on this sin publicly must be cautious and talk about it in such a fashion that those who are guilty should recognize their guilt. But he proceeds not to expound the different kinds of this disgrace in detail before the people).

109. See Geiler von Kaisersberg, *Der dreieckecht Spiegel*, Cc4v; Martin Luther, "Decem praecepta," 489.

110. Quoted in *Aberglaube für Laien*, ed. Baumann, 632: "Wann hat er sich nicht geschambt, do er dy sundt tet, vil minner sol er sich schamen, so er sich peÿcht." See also Geiler von Kaisersberg, *Der dreieckecht Spiegel*, Cc5r.

111. Gerson, "De confessione mollitiei," in *Oeuvres complètes*, vol. 8 (1971), 71: "confessor sit solers et circumspectus circa inquisitionem hujusmodi peccatorum." Though the treatise is on masturbation, Gerson states at the outset that his treatment also touches on a violation "against the laws of nature . . . with another person" ("et consequenter illam [saniem] quae contra naturae jura transit in personam alteram").

112. Denis the Carthusian, "Summa de vitiis et virtutibus," in *Opera omnia*, vol. 39, 88: "De hoc vitio non nisi cum ingenti cautela est praedicandum atque in confessione interrogandum."

113. Herolt, "Sermo LXXXV," *Sermones discipuli*, 490: "Sed sciendum est, quod valde caute est loquendum in sermonibus de illo pessimo vitio, et etiam confessor debet se

caute habere de hoc vitio in confessione, ne alicui scandalum, vel occasionem peccandi praebeat."

114. Raimundus, *Summa de paenitentia*, col. 845: "inter omnia crimina, de isto credo circa interrogationes cum cautela et timore loquendum."

115. Berthold of Regensburg, *Predigten*, 1:92: "Ich verbiute dir halt bî gote, daz dû niemer dar nâch gefrâgest! Und ir priester, ir sult niemer dar nâch gefrâgen in der bîhte, noch nieman den andern umb einigez wort" (I prohibit you [a sinner who had asked the sermonizer what he meant by the sin without a name], by God, from asking after that. And you priests, you shall never ask after that in confession, nor nobody else for a single word).

116. Frantzen, "Disclosure of Sodomy," 454–55. Early medieval handbooks of penance (until the mid-eleventh century) and *summae confessorum* (since the twelfth century), though connected, testify to different theological visions of penance.

117. The so-called unspeakable is not the only topic that religious writers and theologians took as an occasion to issue warnings against the dissemination of doctrine. Yet because of sodomy's status as one of the worst sins, warnings were issued frequently and fervently in this context. Berthold of Regensburg warned against using misogynous passages from the Bible in (vernacular) preaching—"Nota hic caute loquendum ne scandalizes" (Note, speak cautiously in this instance to avoid scandal) (Berthold of Regensburg, *Sermones*, Fribourg/CH, Couvent des Cordeliers, cod. 117, vol. 2, fol. 63va/b). See also Richard Koebner, "Die Eheauffassung des ausgehenden Mittelalters," in *Archiv für Kulturgeschichte* 9 (1911/12): 316; Charles Schmidt, *Histoire littéraire de l'Alsace à la fin du XVe et au commencement du XVIe siècle*, vol. 1 (Paris, 1879; reprint: Hildesheim: Olms, 1966), 437; Thomas-Marie Charland, *Artes praedicandi: Contribution à l'histoire de la rhétorique au moyen âge* (Paris: J. Vrin, 1936), 338; Marcus von Weida, *Spigell des eblichen ordens*, ed. Anthony van der Lee (Assen: Van Gorcum, 1972), 40, 60–61; Rüdiger Schnell, "Geschlechtergeschichte und Textwissenschaft: Eine Fallstudie zu mittelalterlichen und frühneuzeitlichen Ehepredigten," in *Text und Geschlecht*, 160–61.

118. Geiler von Kaisersberg, *Der dreieckecht Spiegel*, Cc4v. "Chaste, pure, innocent ears" ought not "to gain knowledge of and would be offended by things that they did not know before" (Cc4v/Cc5r: "auff das nit die keüschen reinen vnschuldigen oren bekenntniß der ding / die sie vor nit gewüßt hond / gewinnen / vnd geergeret werden").

119. Johann Geiler von Kaisersberg, *Die brösamlin doct. Keiserspergs vffgelesen*, trans. Johannes Pauli (Strasbourg: J. Grüninger, 1517), 7v: "Ja sprechen sie man solt nichts dauon reden man lernt es." Unlike other authors at the time, Geiler uses *bube* (both "knave" and "boy") interchangeably with *knabe*. See also *Deutsches Wörterbuch*, vol. 2, col. 459. For *bube* as "rascal," see chapters 6 and 7.

120. Geiler von Kaisersberg, *Die brösamlin doct.*, 7v: "Wer es vor nicht gewißt hat / der lernt es nitt von dißen worten die er von mir gehôrt hat" (Who did not know it before will not learn it from the words I have spoken).

121. Geiler von Kaisersberg (*Die brösamlin doct.*) cites several authorities in order to back his move, St. Paul's letter to the Romans and an undated decision by the general chapter of the Dominicans. Jean Gerson, whose influential devotional writings Geiler translated and in many ways his prime influence, may also have served as a source of inspiration in this respect. See Louis Mourin, *Jean Gerson: Prédicateur français* (Bruges: De Tempel, 1952), 121, 237–38, 409.

122. Geiler von Kaisersberg, *Die brösamlin doct.*, 7r.

123. See Gerson, "De confessione mollitiei," in *Oeuvres complètes*, 8:71–75.

124. This message is reiterated by the sermon's end, the story (*exemplum*) of Pelagius, the handsome young martyr who defended his virginity against a heathen ruler's ardent, and ultimately vengeful, desire. See Geiler von Kaisersberg, *Die brösamlin doct.*, 7v–8v. Johannes Pauli (c. 1455 until after 1530), Geiler's translator, retold this story in a 1522 collection of tales (*Schimpf und Ernst*, ed. Johannes Bolte, part 1: *Die älteste Ausgabe von 1522* [Berlin: H. Stubenrauch, 1924], 380–81). See also Jordan, *Invention of Sodomy*, 10–28 (on earlier accounts and, especially, Hrothswita of Gandersheim's verse passion).

125. Geiler von Kaisersberg, *Die brösamlin doct.*, 7r.

126. Ibid.: "da hab ich vor dreissig iaren wider das laster geschruwen / also treffenlich vnnd also genow / das man es het mögen mercken / also dz ein gůter fründ auch ein gelerter zů mir sprach. Lieber herr doctor es ist genůg von dem ding." This episode is also mentioned in C. Schmidt, *Histoire littéraire de l'Alsace*, 439; as well as in Keiser, *Courtly Desire*, 56.

127. Erasmus, "De ratione studii," ed. Jean-Claude Margolin, in *Opera omnia*, I-2 (Amsterdam: North-Holland, 1971), 83.

128. Ibid., 142: "Hoc exemplum verbosius exposui, quo facilius in caeteris" (I elaborated on this example at greater length [since it] is easier in other cases).

129. Anthony T. Grafton, *Defenders of the Text: The Traditions of Scholarship in an Age of Science, 1450–1800* (Cambridge, Mass.: Harvard University Press, 1991), 38. The name *Alexis* itself became something of a code word; see, for instance, Jakob Wimpfeling's treatise *Adolescentia*. In it, he introduces a poem by Jean Gerson on the "vain trust and pride which originates in beauty of the body" ("Contra vanam fiduciam et superbiam ex pulchritudine corporis provenientem") of a young man loved by Octavian: *Pulcher Alexi, decor tuus urget . . .* Then, in his commentary, he references Virgil. (*Jakob Wimpfelings Adolescentia*, ed. Otto Herding [Munich: W. Fink, 1965], 267). See also the allegations against Christopher Marlowe. An informer reported that Marlowe had called "St John to be Our Saviour Christ's Alexis. I cover it with reverence and trembling that is that Christ did love him with an extraordinary love." Quoted in Bray, *Homosexuality in Renaissance England*, 64, which also contains an enlightening discussion of the signification of Alexis (64–65).

130. Erasmus ("De ratione," 139 and passim) speaks of "utility" (*utilitas*) in this context.

131. Ibid., 142.

132. Ibid., 142: "Haec, inquam, si praefetur . . . nihil opinor turpe veniet in mentem auditoribus, nisi si quis iam corruptus accesserit."

133. Ibid., 142: "venenum." See also Berthold of Regensburg, *Predigten*, 92.

134. Alan Bray, "Homosexuality and the Signs of Male Friendship in Elizabethan England," *History Workshop Journal* 29 (1990): 1–19.

135. Hermann Torrentinus, *Bucolica. P. Virgilij Maronis cum verborum contextu in poetices tyrunculorum subleuamen* ([Cologne: Quentel, 1503]), B1v.

136. *Epistolae obscurorum virorum aliaque aevi decimi sexti monimenta rarissima*, ed. Ernst Münch (Leipzig: J. C. Hinrichssche Buchhandlung, 1827), 154.

137. Gerhard Lorichius, "Dem Edlen und Ehrnvesten / Eberhardten Růden von Collenbergk," in Jörg Wickram, *Sämtliche Werke*, vol. 13: *Ovids Metamorphosen*, part 1 (Berlin: de Gruyter, 1990), 26: "Dann die Teutsch sprach ist ghar unedel und Tôlpisch / ist aller edelen sprachen zier ohn."

138. Ibid., 21, 25–26.

139. Ralph J. Hexter, *Ovid and Medieval Schooling: Studies in Medieval School Commentaries on Ovid's "Ars Amatoria," "Epistulae ex Ponto," and "Epistulae Heroidum"* (Munich: Arbeo-Gesellschaft, 1986), 74–75.

140. The antidote metaphor is used by Lorichius in Wickram, *Sämtliche Werke*, vol. 13: *Ovids Metamorphosen*, 28.

141. Ibid., 18.

142. Thomas Bein, "Orpheus als Sodomit," *Zeitschrift für deutsche Philologie* 109 (1990): 33–55.

143. Similar obfuscations abound when this Greek myth is treated in the period's translated literature in German (Limbeck, "Plautus," 24, 28, 43).

144. Lorichius in Wickram, *Sämtliche Werke*, vol. 13: *Ovids Metamorphosen*, 548: "Sint er sein weib jetz hat verlorn / So soll er meiden alle weib."

145. Jörg Wickram, "Dem Edlen unnd vesten Wilhelm Böckle von Böcklinsaw," in *Sämtliche Werke*, 13:5: "ich deß Lateins gar unkundig binn."

146. Ibid., 5–6, 9. See also Brigitte Rücker, *Die Bearbeitung von Ovids "Metamorphosen" durch Albrecht von Halberstadt und Jörg Wickram und ihre Kommentierung durch Gerhard Lorichius* (Göppingen: Kümmerle, 1997).

147. Medieval and early modern translators adopted widely differing attitudes toward their model texts depending on who their audience was or how much authority was attributed to a particular text or author. When Albrecht von Eyb (1420–75) translated the comedies of Plautus (c. 250–c. 184 B.C.) for a textbook on morals (*Spiegel der Sitten*, 1474; first printed 1511), he completely censored the Roman poet's allusions to male-male desire (in the case of heteronormative puns, he was less squeamish). As Sven Limbeck has shown, this is not because Albrecht von Eyb did not "get it." His lecture notes from his student years in Italy illustrate that not only did he understand the sexual innuendos of Plautus's comedies very well, but he also was familiar with many texts on homoerotic themes that circulated among Italian literati of the time. Yet while he copied erotically explicit Latin texts, their usage for a German audience was out of the question (Limbeck, "Plautus," 27–31). When Arigo, to pick a counterexample, translated Giovanni Boccaccio's (1313–75) *Il Decamerone* (1348–53)—a fifteenth-century translation reprinted in the sixteenth century—his text obfuscated the double entendres of *novella* V.10 (with a protagonist who, though married, chases young men erotically) merely by the ineptness of a verbatim translation. See Adelbert von Keller, ed., *Decameron von Heinrich Steinhöwel* (Stuttgart: Litterarischer Verein, 1860). I have compared this edition with *Cento Nouella Johannis Bocatij* (Strasbourg: Paul Messerschmidt, 1561).

148. Lorichius in Wickram, *Sämtliche Werke*, vol. 13: *Ovids Metamorphosen*, 549: "Die gedacht Sodomitisch sünd ist warlich grausamer dann bei seiner eygenen mutter oder schwester schlaffen. Dann wie wol auch solch INCAESTUS wider die natur ist / so ist doch dise stümmende sünde der natur vil meher zu entgegen."

149. Ibid., 548.

150. Ibid., 549.

151. Ibid., 550: "Was kan der natur mehr zu wider sein / dann sich der weiber wöllen pflegen und keyn kinder wöllen zeugen?"

152. Ibid., 550.

Chapter Four

1. Joachim von Watt [Vadian], "Peter Kunz an Vadian: Bern 1539. Januar 27," in *Vadianische Briefsammlung*, ed. Emil Arbenz and Hermann Wartmann, vol. 5: 1531–40 (St. Gallen: Huber, 1903), 526–27.

2. Possibly, Kunz approached Watt as someone able to give expert advice. In 1533 he had acted as the plaintiff's representative in the trial of Conrad Mülibach, a weaver of no fixed abode who was tried for having had sex with other males in and around St. Gallen over the course of many years. See StArchiv St. Gallen, Malefiz-Buch no. 192, 74. Johannes Rütiner's *Diarium* mentions Mülibach, though as Iacob, not Conrad Mulibach (*Diarium 1529–1539*, vol. i.1, ed. Ernst Gerhard Rüsch [St. Gallen: Vadiana, 1996], 233–34).

3. Watt, *Vadianische Briefsammlung*, 526.

4. Ibid., 526. See Alan Bray, "Homosexuality and the Signs of Male Friendship in Elizabethan England," in *Queering the Renaissance*, ed. Jonathan Goldberg (Durham, N.C.: Duke University Press, 1994), 47.

5. In a treatise of 1545, Luther once used a Germanized *Pedasterey* (in *WA*, vol. 54 [1928], 213). See also Joseph Cady, "'Masculine Love,' Renaissance Writing, and the 'New Invention' of Homosexuality," in *Homosexuality in Renaissance and Enlightenment England*, ed. Claude J. Summers (New York: Haworth Press, 1992), 14 (with regard to Francis Bacon). For further seventeenth-century references for England, see Bray, *Homosexuality in Renaissance England*, 65, 126 n. 25. For the eighteenth century, see George E. Haggerty, *Men in Love: Masculinity and Sexuality in the Eighteenth Century* (New York: Columbia University Press, 1999).

6. StALU, A1 F9 SCH 990, 1577 September 5. See Andreas Schmidinger, *Das Entlebuch zur Zeit der Glaubensspaltung und der katholischen Reform* (Schüpfheim: n.p., 1972), 150–53.

7. StALU, COD 4435 (*Turmbücher*), 198r (1561).

8. StArchiv St. Gallen, Malefiz-Buch, no. 192, 74–75.

9. StALU, A1 F6 SCH 826, 1629 (Melchior Brütschli, Jacob Franck): "do seige des Joglis frauw vss der nebendstuben kommen, vnd den Jocoben (Jacob Franck) gewaltigen gehudlet vnd geseit waz er aber anfange." Faced with a bad reputation, Jacob Franck fled the territory of Lucerne, while his partner, Melchior Brütschli, was arrested and sentenced to death.

10. StAZ, A 27.26 (*Kundschaften und Nachgänge 1566–1567*), Rudolf Bachmann/Uli Frei 1567.

11. Stadtarchiv Augsburg, Strafamt, Urgichten, December 4, 1533, Michel Will; June 11, 1532, Philipp Zeller; April 4 and 8, 1532, Jakob Miller. When the schoolteacher Zeller was first interrogated about same-sex sexual activities, he pointed to the fact that he was married. Jakob Miller explained his having engaged in same-sex acts by saying that his wife had been sick for ten years. When he was about twenty years old, he had sex with another youth. According to Miller, Sigismund Welser promised to marry one of his sex partners to a maid; Michel Will had married an artisan's widow with whom he had several children, all the while having sex with other men. After having squandered her wealth, he left the city before the proceedings started. The court records are now edited in Bernd-Ulrich Hergemöller, *Männer, "die mit Männer handeln," in der Augsburger Reformationszeit* (Munich: Forum Homosexualität und Geschichte, 2000), 46–47, 49, 60–61, 67.

12. Lyndal Roper, *The Holy Household: Religion, Morals and Order in Reformation Augsburg* (Oxford: Oxford University Press, 1989), 255.

13. StALU, COD 4435 (*Turmbücher*), 197v (1561). See also StAZ, A 27.35 (*Kundschaften und Nachgänge* 1579), Wilhelm von Mühlhausen: "zum füdlj [ass] jnhin minnen."

14. StALU, COD 4445 (*Turmbücher*), 37v (1572). According to Claus Heid, Hans Ackermann said about Hans Portmann: "Da habe er mitt jm wöllen handlen wie mitt einer frowen."

15. StALU, COD 4435 (*Turmbücher*), 59r (1561). Jakob Streulin stated that a boy named George approached him in a vineyard where they were both working and said: "Hett ich ein hüpsch meytli." When he asked whether they "wanted to do something" ("wend wir [es] mit einandren machen"), Streulin answered somewhat ambivalently, "why not?" ("es gillt mir glych"). "He took down his pants; Georg lay on his back and pushed a little into his ass [which they repeated] thereafter in bed" ("Hab dhosen abhin glon, sÿg Görgo jm vff den ruggen glegen, hab jm ein wenig hinder jnhin gstossen vnd dem nach jm bett ouch einmal").

16. StALU, COD 4435 (*Turmbücher*), 197r (1561): "mir ein gůtte feiste fud, rette er, jch hab keine, biss mir eyne."

17. StALU, COD 4435 (*Turmbücher*), 197v (1561).

18. StASO, Vergichtbuch (*Ratsmanual rot 19*) 1478–1552 (Hans Pröpstli 1525), 170. The guard followed up on the suspect's supposed lover and, much to his dismay, met a woman who denied any intention of a rendezvous with Pröpstli.

19. Ibid., 171. Apparently, the innkeeper remained suspicious (the house's doors were locked at the time).

20. By responding thus, he indicated that he had understood the other's intent. StASO, Vergichtbuch (*Ratsmanual rot 19*) 1478–1552 (Hans Pröpstli 1525), 172b/c.

21. Roper, *Holy Household*, 255–58; Hergemöller, *Männer*.

22. Hans Bröpstli, StAZ, A 27.3 (*Kundschaften und Nachgänge* 1500–1520), July 1518, 1: "Er . . . hab ouch der maß vnd gestalt wiß oder weg sin lebenlang jn sinen sin noch gmut nie gesecyt, jnn hab ouch sin leben lanng nie angefochten vnd den bösen willen oder gelust nie gehept mit keinem mans bild derglichen sachen zupflegen."

23. Ibid.: "So es kalt wer."

24. Ibid.; StAZ, A 27.16 (*Kundschaften und Nachgänge* 1546–1549), Hans Appenzeller 1547, confession, 1.

25. StAZ, A 27.16 (*Kundschaften und Nachgänge* 1546–1549), Hans Appenzeller 1547.

26. StASO, *Denkwürdige Sachen* (DS) 33, 35b. Jakob vom Schloss in his confession (1515).

27. Stadtarchiv Augsburg, Strafamt, Urgichten, June 11, 1532, Philipp Zeller; Urgichten, April 4, 1532, Jakob Miller.

28. StABS, Criminalia 31 F 1 (Jacob Fischer 1658): "er nicht gewußt hette, was es were, wüßte auch noch nicht was es außweiße vnd bedeüte." See also StAZ, A 27.3 (*Kundschaften und Nachgänge* 1500–1520), Hans Bröpstli.

29. See StABS, Criminalia 31 F 1: "da Wüest allweg den anfang gemacht"; Johannes Rütiner, *Diarium 1529–1539*, Kommentarband, ed. Ernst Gerhard Rüsch (St. Gallen: Vadiana, 1996), 233 (Jakob Mülibach 1533): "Et hoc didicisse ab illo redemptore willer zwilcken, rubro naso, confessus" ([He] confessed to have learned this from the leaseholder Willer Zwilck, called red nose). See also the discussion of Jephat Scheurmann later in this chapter.

30. StAZ, A 27.44 (*Kundschaften und Nachgänge* 1594–1595), 5 junge Knaben 1595: "Vnd als er . . . darby anzeigt, das er [das] by synem meister nit gelerth, habe er jme geandtwortet, habe es frylich bÿ jme nit sondes by niemad [anders] dan Ůlj Somerowern, der der glÿche . . . gehandlet, gelerth." The genealogical approach to sodomy resonates with elite culture. Stories of Orpheus and other mythological figures provided answers to the question of who had first invented this sexual practice: authors sometimes appropriated ancient myths to confer nobility upon the pedigree of sodomitical actors. See chapter 3.

31. StALU, Archiv 1, Personalien, AKT 113/937 (1590).

32. StAZ, A 27.39 (*Kundschaften und Nachgänge* 1586), Hans Heinrich Vogler: "es schade nützit."

33. StASO, Vergichtbuch (*Ratsmanual rot* 19) 1478–1552 (Hans Pröpstli 1525), 166.

34. Since Fribourg lies on the border between the regions where German is spoken and those where French is the idiom, Bär thus indicated that his partner was a native speaker of French.

35. StALU, RP 13, 169r–170r (Balthasar Bär/Balthasar Fölck): "derselb weltsch hab jnn disß anfangs gelert vnd gesagt, die weltschen chügen [cf. Middle High German *(ge)bîwen*, "to have sex"] allso."

36. StALU, COD 4500 (*Turmbücher*), 152r (1609), J. Scheurmann. As a dignitary, he showed himself to be familiar with ways of argumentation among jurists that respected limited responsibility of juvenile delinquents.

37. StASO, Vergichtbuch (*Ratsmanual rot* 19) 1478–1552 (Hans Pröpstli 1525), 170–71. The same defendant might even have sought out a *walchen knaben* (Italian boy) as a sexual partner who served in a household (171).

38. Bröpstli; especially interesting is StAZ, A 27.14 (*Kundschaften und Nachgänge* 1541–1543), Ambrosius Suter/Peter Sifrid 1541.

39. StAZ, A 27.14 (*Kundschaften und Nachgänge* 1541–1543), Suter/Sifrid 1541: "svnnder das jm villicht jm throum vorgschwäpt, er lēge bÿ siner frowen, die er dickermals gebētten, baß zů jm zeruckhen."

40. StAZ, A 27.8 (*Kundschaften und Nachgänge* 1536–1538), Andreas Pfister 1537: "jnn thrungkner vnd schimpffiger wyß."

41. StAZ, A 27.3 (*Kundschaften und Nachgänge* 1500–1520), 1518, 3: "Vnd hab er das jm schlaff gethon, so laß er jms nach."

42. StAZ, A 27.13 (*Kundschaften und Nachgänge* c. 1530–1570), Thöni Rüttiman 1561; StALU, A1 F6 SCH 826, Jacob Franckh (1629). See also Stefanie Krings, "Sodomie am Bodensee: Vom gesellschaftlichen Umgang mit sexueller Abartigkeit in spätem Mittelalter und früher Neuzeit auf St. Galler Quellengrundlage," *Schriften des Vereins für Geschichte des Bodensees und seiner Umgebung* 113 (1995): 22. In a case of bestiality from Lucerne, the defendant listed a host of reasons to explain his actions. His wife was a witch, he stated, and had led him to commit the act. But he also reported that an evil spirit had appeared in the shape of a handsome boy and of a dog to seduce him in this way. StALU, Archiv 1, Personalien, AKT 113/2093 (1573).

43. StAZ, A 27.39 (*Kundschaften und Nachgänge* 1586), Hans Heinrich Vogler. Vogler stated, "(leider vß Jngëben deß bößen geists) doch jnn einem vnuerdachten můt angeforderet, synenn schandtlichen můtwillen mitt jme zevolfüren."

44. StAZ, A 27.26 (*Kundschaften und Nachgänge* 1566–1567), Rudolf Bachmann/Uli Frei 1567: "Sunst [Jamer vnd leid] jm sÿnn gmüt nie berüret."

45. StASCH, Justiz, D 1, 76r: "vncristenliche vnd kätzersche werch mit enandern getriben vnd gebrucht."

46. Gadi Algazi, "'Sich selbst vergessen' im späten Mittelalter: Denkfiguren und soziale Konfigurationen," in *Memoria als Kultur*, ed. Otto Gerhard Oexle (Göttingen: Wallstein, 1995), 387–427. In seventeenth-century Lucerne, defendants in cases of sodomy excused their sexual acts by the phrase, "I had forgotten myself" or "I had forgotten God." See StALU, A1 F6 SCH 826, 1629 (Melchior Brütschli, Jacob Francke); StALU, A1 F6 SCH 826, 1670, 1676, 1677 (cases of bestiality where this phrase is used). See also Roper, *Oedipus and the Devil*, 3; Marc Breitenberg, *Anxious Masculinity in Early Modern England* (Cambridge: Cambridge University Press, 1996), 12.

47. In cases of sex with animals, defendants are also recorded to have come forward themselves. When Peter Lysentaler turned himself in for having committed sex with a cow in his youth, his self-accusation hardly mitigated the punishment he received, decapitation (StALU, Archiv 1, Personalien, AKT 113/1253).

48. StASO, Vergichtbuch (*Ratsmanual rot* 19) 1478–1552 (Hans Pröpstli 1525), 166: "Deßgelichen habe er mitt anndren, by denen er gelegen, vnnderstanden gelyche sünd zübegan, dann das si jm das abgeschlagenn."

49. Hans Bröpstli, StAZ, A 27.3 (*Kundschaften und Nachgänge* 1500–1520), July 1518, 4.

50. StASO, Vergichtbuch (*Ratsmanual rot* 19) 1478–1552 (Hans Pröpstli 1525), 171.

51. Rütiner, *Diarium 1529–1539*, 233.

52. StASO, Vergichtbuch (*Ratsmanual rot* 19) 1478–1552 (Hans Pröpstli 1525), 172a/b.

53. StAZ, A 27.16 (*Kundschaften und Nachgänge* 1546–1549), Hans Appenzeller 1547.

54. StAZ, A 27.37a (*Kundschaften und Nachgänge* 1583), 2 Knaben 1583, 1.

55. StALU, COD 4500 (*Turmbücher*), 152r (1609): "Wie er [Scheurmann] es auch glychergstalt von Vincentz Chünen dem glaser gesehen, daß er es midt ettlichen iungen knaben vnnd sÿ es midt ime getriben."

56. See StALU, COD 4445 (*Turmbücher*), 32v (1572): "Deßglÿchen habe der Ackerman ghört, das [Portman] jm Emmenthal eim knaben ouch allso thůn wöllen, der by jm glegen. Mitt dem habe er gmacht, das er ab dem beth jm entrünnen müßen vß der kammer."

57. StAZ, A 27.13 (*Kundschaften und Nachgänge* c. 1530–1570), Thöni Rüttiman, 3.

58. See, for instance, StAZ, A 27.3 (*Kundschaften und Nachgänge* 1500–1520), July 1518, 4.

59. See StALU, COD 4445 (*Turmbücher*), 37v (1572). Hans Ackerman said that Hans Portman was "a fierce man" ("ein hefftiger man").

60. StASO, Vergichtbuch (*Ratsmanual rot* 19) 1478–1552 (Hans Pröpstli 1525), 170–71: "Vnnd alls jnn die gesellen fragtten, warumb er vffgestanden, sagtte er, es wåre nitt gůtt by jm zůligenn."

61. Rütiner, *Diarium*, 233.

62 StALU, COD 4435 (*Turmbücher*), 198r (1561).

63. See also chapters 1 and 2.

64. StALU, A1 F9 SCH, 1577 September 5: "zum ersten ist der Herr [Leemann] jnn eines nachpuren huß . . . über nacht bliben . . . hatt er by einem knaben söllen ligen. Hatt sich der knab klagt, ër habe die gantze (nacht) vnnd sunderlich vor mitter nacht ghein rüw ghan, sunders habe stetz über jnn gwellen; Wolfensberg dar bÿ grett man sölle das bett bscheüwen. Do hatt man funden das vnß nit gfalt."

65. StAZ, A 27.8 (*Kundschaften und Nachgänge* 1536–1538), Andreas Pfister von Affoltern 1537, *Kuntschafft*.

66. StALU, COD 4435 (*Turmbücher*), 59r (1561).

67. See, for example, StAZ, B VI.245 (*Rats- und Richtbuch* 1513–1519), 79r (Jacob vom Schloß 1515); StAZ, A 27.10 (*Kundschaften und Nachgänge* c. 1530–1570), Werner Steiner (1542); StAZ, A 27.14 (*Kundschaften und Nachgänge* 1541–1543), 1541 VI 21.

68. StAZ, A 27.44 (*Kundschaften und Nachgänge* 1594–1595), 5 junge Knaben 1595: "Die knaben geandtwort, . . . [er] bruche aber andere sachen, so sy nit dörffind melden." Whether it was the perpetrator who had told them to remain silent or whether they had decided to remain silent themselves is unclear.

69. StALU, A1 F6 SCH 826, 1629 (Melchior Brütschli, Jacob Francke).

70. StAZ, A 27.44 (*Kundschaften und Nachgänge* 1594–1595), 5 junge Knaben 1595.

71. StALU, COD 4445 (*Turmbücher*), 37v (1572).

72. StAZ, A 27.39 (*Kundschaften und Nachgänge* 1586), Hans Heinrich Vogler: "gschreyg."

73. StAZ, B VI 245 (*Rats- und Richtbuch* 1513–1519), Jacob vom Schloß 1515, 79r.

74. See StAZ, A 27.3 (*Kundschaften und Nachgänge* 1500–1520), Hans Bröpstli.

75. StALU, COD 4445 (*Turmbücher*), 29v–32v, 37v.

76. StALU, A1 F9 SCH 990, 1577 September 5 (Pfarrer Leemann).

77. Only rarely can individuals crying out be named. See, for example, StAZ, B VI 245 (*Rats- und Richtbuch* 1513–1519), 79r/v (Jacob vom Schloß 1515): "Vnd machte der knab söllichs so lutrüf, daz er genanter Jacob vom Schloß deßhalb von Soloturn müßde wichen" (the boy was so vocal that aforesaid Jacob vom Schloss had to leave Solothurn).

78. StAZ, A 27.37a (*Kundschaften und Nachgänge* 1583), 2 Knaben 1583.

79. StALU, COD 4450, 165r/v (Paulus Leemann).

80. Leemann portrayed the farmers as rebellious, a stereotype surely meant to play into urban concerns about rural unrest. See Sebastian Grüter, *Geschichte des Kantons Luzern im 16. und 17. Jahrhundert* (Lucerne: Räber, 1945), 17–26; Roland Müller, "Der schweizerische Bauernkrieg von 1653," in *Bauern und Patrizier: Stadt und Land im Ancien Régime*, ed. Silvio Bucher (Lucerne: Lehrmittelverlag Luzern, 1986), 104; Anton Gössi, "Das Werden des modernen Staates: Luzern von 1550–1650," in *Renaissancemalerei in Luzern 1560–1650: Ausstellung im Schloss Wyher, Ettiswil* (Lucerne: Lehrmittelverlag Luzern, 1986), 17.

81. StALU, RP 3 (1423), 41r: "Für vns ist kon, wie im gotzhuß Sant Vrban grob sachen von ketzerÿe wegen vnder den München fürgangen" (We have heard how on clerical territory in St. Urban vile heretical things have occurred among the monks).

82. StALU, RP 6, 84v; StALU, RP 7, 5r, 9r (1489). See also Anton Philipp von Segesser, *Rechtsgeschichte der Stadt und Republik Lucern*, vol. 2, 650. For a fuller description, see chapter 2.

83. This measure is all the more surprising in light of the interdict against Lucerne in 1572 as retaliation for the city's execution of two clerics. See Gössi, "Werden des modernen Staates," 20.

84. Alois Steiner, "Luzern als Vorort der katholischen Eidgenossenschaft vom 16. bis zum 18. Jahrhundert," in *Bauern und Patrizier*, 96–103; Gössi, "Werden des modernen Staates," 18–19.

85. See StAZ, B VI.245 (*Rats- und Richtbuch* 1513–1519), 79r/v (Jacob vom Schloß 1515).

86. StAZ, A 27.13 (*Kundschaften und Nachgänge* c. 1530–1570), Thöni Rüttiman 1561. The formulation *geflorenntzt* appears only in the *Rats- und Richtbuch* B VI.259, 26v.

87. StAZ, A 27.14 (*Kundschaften und Nachgänge* 1541–1543): Ambrosius Suter/Peter Sifrid 1541.

88. StAZ, 27.14 (*Kundschaften und Nachgänge* 1541–1543), Suter/Sifrid 1541. See also chapter 5 on defamation. In fact, to call into question the other party's intentions in bringing up allegations was a strategy used by the accused to taint testimony. When Hans Heinrich Vogler was accused in court of having made sexual advances to a fellow shoemaker apprentice, he explained the other's accusation by referring to "envy and hatred" (*vß nÿd vnd haß*) (StAZ, A 27.39 [*Kundschaften und Nachgänge*], Hans Heinrich Vogler 1586).

89. When the case was summarized for the *Rats- und Richtbuch*, same-sex eroticism was not mentioned.

90. StAZ, A 27.35 (*Kundschaften und Nachgänge* 1579), Wilhelm von Mühlhausen 1579.

91. See Gerd Schwerhoff, *Köln im Kreuzverhör: Kriminalität, Herrschaft und Gesellschaft in einer frühneuzeitlichen Stadt* (Bonn: Bouvier, 1991), 195.

92. Especially interesting is the case of Jacob vom Schloß, 1515 in StAZ, B VI.245 (*Rats- und Richtbuch* 1513–1519), 79r/v.

93. See StALU, COD 4500 (*Turmbücher*), 152r (1609).

94. StAZ, A 27.9 (*Kundschaften und Nachgänge* 1539–1540), Ulrich Vogler, 2.

95. Puff and Schneider-Lastin, "Quellen zur Homosexualität im Mittelalter," 122–24. See also chapter 1.

96. StAZ, A 27.9 (*Kundschaften und Nachgänge* 1539–1540), Ulrich Vogler 1540. He pleaded forgiveness and cited his father, family, and youth as support for his plea, which was granted.

97. As a rule, death penalties were recorded in the *Rats- und Richtbuch*.

98. StAZ, A 27.3 (*Kundschaften und Nachgänge* 1500–1520), July 1518, 5. Should he be brought to court again in this matter, his punishment would be much more severe, they stated.

99. Knonau, *Der Canton Zürich*, 155. Thomas Weibel ("Der zürcherische Stadtstaat," in *Geschichte des Kantons Zürich*, vol. 2 [Zurich: Werd, 1996], 52) mentions 569 executions for the sixteenth century.

100. StALU, RP 13, 169r–70r (Balthasar Bär/Balthasar Fölck, 1532).

101. StALU, RP 46 (1599), 315r (Jakob Bachmann).

102. StALU, Archiv 1, Personalien, AKT 113/90 (1531); AKT 113/132; AKT 113/161 (1606); AKT 113/334 (1564, 1558); AKT 113/373 (1555); AKT 113/579 (1601); AKT 113/904 (1583); AKT 113/928 (c. 1595); AKT 113/937 (1590); AKT 113/956 (1563); AKT 113/962 (c. 1550); AKT 113/964 (1574); AKT 113/978 (1566); AKT 113/1033 (1577); AKT 113/1103 (1604); AKT 113/1151 (1604); AKT 113/1180 (1550); AKT 113/1253 (1573); AKT 113/1341 (1592); AKT 113/1412 (1607); AKT 113/1806 (1573); AKT 113/1844 (first half of sixteenth century); AKT 113/1863 (c. 1550); AKT 113/1901 (1594); AKT 113/1963 (1594); AKT 113/2055 (1580); AKT 113/2076 (1575); AKT 113/2115 (1572); AKT 113/2159 (1601); AKT 113/2241 (1596); AKT 113/2251 (1571); AKT 113/2266 (1570); AKT 113/2270 (1582); AKT 113/2283 (1580).

103. StALU, Archiv 1, Personalien, AKT 113/1952 (c. 1537). He confesses to having attempted to have sex with a boy and to having had sex with a man whose wife was said to be an Anabaptist.

104. Kasimir Pfyffer, *Der Kanton Luzern, historisch-geographisch-politisch geschildert* (St. Gallen: Huber, 1858), 19, 379.

105. In 1626 Hans Walther von Castanea, son of a wealthy merchant, was urged by his kin to flee the city in order to avoid being prosecuted for sodomy and other charges. Urban authorities took Castanea's escape for a confession of guilt and sentenced him to death in absentia. Yet the charges were so vague that they seem to have been fabricated. The whole scandal was related to conflicts over the inheritance of Hans Georg von Castanea and his business. See StALU, Archiv 1, Personalien, AKT 113/302; Kurt Messmer and Peter Hoppe, *Luzerner Patriziat: Sozial- und wirtschaftsgeschichtliche Studien zur Entstehung und Entwicklung im 16. und 17. Jahrhundert* (Lucerne: Rex-Verlag, 1976), 344–46, 348.

106. Rocke, *Forbidden Friendships*, 12–13, 97–111.

107. Greenberg, *Construction of Homosexuality*; Trumbach, *Sex and the Gender Revolution.*

108. Isabel V. Hull, *Sexuality, State, and Civil Society in Germany, 1700–1815* (Ithaca, N.Y.: Cornell University Press, 1996), 1. I am using the term differently, though, because in this context I am less concerned with how "sexual behavior is shaped and given meaning through institutions" (Hull, 1).

109. See StAZ, A 27.8 (*Kundschaften und Nachgänge 1536–1538*), Marx Anthonÿ 1537. Accused of having engaged in sexual relations with a twelve-year-old, an Italian was seized after a couple of weeks of traveling with this boy through Switzerland.

110. Hull, *Sexuality, State, and Civil Society*, 44.

111. Helmut Puff, "Acts 'Against Nature' in the Law Courts of Early Modern Germany and Switzerland," in *The Moral Authority of Nature*, ed. Lorraine Daston and Fernando Vidal (Chicago: University of Chicago Press, forthcoming).

112. Egidio Bossi demonstrates the viciousness of raping men by asserting that even to read about it is dishonorable. Therefore, legal texts speak of the crime so "obscurely" that one can hardly detect its meaning. Egidio Bossi, *Tractatus varii, qui omnem fere criminalem materiam excellenti doctrina complectuntur* (Lyon: Haeredes Iacobi Iunti, 1562), 339: "Tit. de stupro detestabili in masculos." In Johann Heinrich Zedler's *Universal-Lexikon* (1743), the laws themselves "abhor to speak clearly on the matter." See Johann Heinrich Zedler, *Grosses vollständiges Universal-Lexikon*, vol. 38 (Leipzig, 1743; reprint, Graz: Akademische Druck- und Verlagsanstalt, 1962), col. 329: "Wie denn auch disfalls die Gesetze selbsten einen Abscheu haben, die Sache klar anzudeuten und auszudrücken" (With regard to this [offense], the laws themselves abhor expressing the matter clearly). In this encyclopedia, a receptacle of early modern knowledge, the article on sodomy is subdivided into masturbation, sodomy with other humans (the dominant example thereof is pederasty), and bestiality, but only the second kind is presented as inappropriate for writing and reading: "How these different acts are committed, is appropriate neither for us to describe nor for shameful eyes to read" ("Wie aber eine und andere Art derselben vollbracht werden, stehet weder uns zu beschreiben, noch auch schamhafftigen Augen zu lesen, zu"; col. 329). See chapter 3 for similar arguments in pastoral theology.

113. StAZ, A 27.35 (*Kundschaften und Nachgänge 1579*), Wilhelm von Mühlhausen 1579. See StAZ, A 27.37a (*Kundschaften und Nachgänge 1583*), 2 Knaben 1583, 1; StAZ, A 27.39 (*Kundschaften und Nachgänge 1586*), Hans Heinrich Vogler 1586; StAZ, A 27.43 (*Kundschaften und Nachgänge 1592–1593*), Hans Herter von Bencken 1592; StAZ, A 27.44 (*Kundschaften und Nachgänge 1594–1595*), 5 junge Knaben 1595; StAZ, A 10 (*Bestialität und Sodomiterei 1561–1765*) has many more examples (mostly seventeenth century). StALU, A1 F6 SCH 826, Jephat Scheurmann (1609); StALU, A1 F6 SCH 826, 1619; StASO,

Vergichtbuch und Thurn Roedel 1600–1613, 375, 390–98, 403–11 (cases of bestiality). See also Krings, "Sodomie am Bodensee," 19, for St. Gallen in a case of bestiality committed by Jacob Grüter, 1607. See David Warren Sabean, "Soziale Distanzierungen: Ritualisierte Gestik in deutscher bürokratischer Prosa der Frühen Neuzeit," *Historische Anthropologie* 4 (1996): 216–33.

114. StABS, Criminalia 31 F 1: "sein mannlich glid c.v. in den hindern Leib getruckt."

115. Puff and Schneider-Lastin, "Quellen zur Homosexualität im Mittelalter"; StALU, Archiv 1, Personalien, AKT 113/213 (1468) in a case of bestiality: "das nit notturfftig ist hier ze ertzellen" ("which we need not relate here") with regard to Brüchi's sex act with a horse.

116. StALU, A1 F6 SCH 826, J. Scheurmann (1609): "wegen ettwas grober, ja züvor vnerhorter, vnd mitt höchster Reuerentz zů mellden, sodomitischer handlûng."

117. Stadtarchiv Augsburg, Strafamt, Urgichten, 4 June 1532, Bernhard Wagner: "das grewlich vbel vnd laschter wider die natur für sich selbs vnnd bey anderen; Daruore sich menigklich wisse zu verhietenn" (Hergemöller, *Männer,* 57).

118. StAZ, B VI.245 (*Rats- und Richtbuch* 1513–1519), 232r–33r (Bläßj Hipold, 1519); StAZ, B VI.255 (*Rats- und Richtbuch* 1538–1544) (Uli Rügger, 1540); StAZ, A 27.15 (*Kundschaften und Nachgänge* 1544–1545) (Jacob Müller 1545); StAZ, A 27.13 (*Kundschaften und Nachgänge* c. 1530–1570) (Hans Mötsch n.d.) (bestiality); StAZ, A 27.35 (*Kundschaften und Nachgänge* 1579), Wilhelm von Mühlhausen 1579; StAZ, B VI.262 (*Rats- und Richtbuch*), 203r/v (Wilhelm von Mühlhausen 1579).

119. StAZ, A 27.43 (*Kundschaften und Nachgänge* 1592–1593), Hans Herter von Bencken 1592: "Damit des orts von vnns weder ze lüzel noch zevill gehanndlet." The request is particularly interesting in light of the fact that the vogt of Kyburg held judicial authority in criminal matters. The final sentence was not recorded. The fact that the *Richtbuch* does not list Herter means that he probably was not executed.

120. Ibid.: "Vnd wiewoll man ine gezygen vnd lümbden habe, das er mit ernanten personen kätzeryg getriben, ouch er vnd dieselben vff einanderen glegen, als wan sy die lyblichen werch begen welten, sige dach das weder von ime nach anderen gar vnd gantz nit dan allein mit angryffung der gmechten beschechen." That family circumstances were taken into consideration is clear from the case of Heini uff dem Bühl (StALU, RP 9, 183r [1505]). For erotic games with young boys and intercourse with cattle, he was not sentenced to death but asked to go on a pilgrimage to Rome to atone. His wife and children had pleaded for mercy on his behalf.

121. Ibid.: "sam sy by wyben glegen weren." Cf. Lv 18:22: "You shall not lie with a male as with a woman; it is an abomination."

122. See Francisca Loetz, *Mit Gott handeln: Von den Zürcher Gotteslästern der Frühen Neuzeit zu einer Kulturgeschichte des Religiösen* (Göttingen: Vandenhoeck, 2002).

123. StAZ, B VI.257 (*Rats- und Richtbuch* 1545–1552), 11r: "Vnnd vmb söllich vncristenlich, schandtlich, lasterlich, gräwel mûtwillen bübery vnnd kätzery . . . wider Göttlichs, Cristenlichs vnnd menschlichs gsatz ouch wider die natur, alle eer vnd erbarkeÿt verruchtlich, üppigklich vnnd schanndtlich begangen." See StAZ, A 27.15 (*Kundschaften und Nachgänge* 1544–1545), Jacob Müller 1545.

124. StAZ, A 27.8 (*Kundschaften und Nachgänge* 1536–1538), Hans Apfmotz 1537. See also StAZ, A 27.13 (*Kundschaften und Nachgänge* c. 1530–1570), Thöni Rüttiman.

125. StAZ, B VI.259 (*Rats- und Richtbuch*), 271r: "schanndtliche, vnchristenliche vnd vnnatürliche werch."

126. Ibid.: "Vmb sölliche schanndtliche vnchristennliche / vnnatürliche kätzeryg, groß vbel vnnd mißthůn." See also StAZ, A 27.35 (Kundschaften und Nachgänge 1579), Wilhelm von Mühlhausen 1579 and StAZ, B VI.262 (Rats- und Richtbuch), 202v–3v.

127. Formulas were common in other cases besides sodomy, but the rhetoric was particularly stringent in sodomy cases, see StAZ, A 27.13 (Kundschaften und Nachgänge c. 1530–1570), Hans Mötsch, n.d.; StAZ, A 27.13 (Kundschaften und Nachgänge c. 1530–1570), Joder Hottinger, n.d.; StAZ, A 27.13 (Kundschaften und Nachgänge c. 1530–1570), Thöni Rüttiman 1561; StAZ, A 27.45 (Kundschaften und Nachgänge 1596), Hans Meÿhoffer von Landsberg 1596.

128. StAZ, A 27.44 (Kundschaften und Nachgänge 1594–1595) 5 junge Knaben, 1595: "Wie nun die knaben züget das schilt knëcht" [crossed out: "Jnen sÿn mëndlich glid mit Reuerentz zů melden zum hindern yn hüge"]. Replaced by: "sÿnen schantlichen můtwillen gegen jnnen fürnämmen wellen."

129. In one case, the Book reflected the exact wording of the proceedings, since these same proceedings had already adopted the language of moral rectitude (StAZ, A 27.15 [Kundschaften und Nachgänge 1544–1545], Jacob Müller 1545).

130. For context, see Heinzpeter Stucki, "Das 16. Jahrhundert," in Geschichte des Kantons Zürich, vol. 2 (Zürich: Werd, 1996), 225–26.

131. See above for cases of sodomy. Cf. StASO, Vergichtbuch und Thurn Roedel 1553–1579, 284–85 (Peter Heini 1565), a case of bestiality; StASO, Vergichtbuch und Thurn Roedel 1553–1579, 582–85 (Niggli Gruber 1578), for bestiality; StASO, Vergichtbuch und Thurn Roedel 1583–1587, 158 (Marti Winistorff 1587) for bestiality; StABS, Straf und Polizei C 15 1625, for bestiality. The term was applied widely, among other things, for black magic. See, for instance, Beat R. Jenny, Graf Froben Christoph von Zimmern (Lindau: J. Thorbecke, 1959), 85.

132. Modern linguists of German have rarely studied this interesting class of words. See, however, Hermann Paul, Deutsche Grammatik, vol. 5: Wortbildung, 4th ed. (Halle a.d. Saale: Max Niemeyer, 1959), 27–29; Hans Wellmann, Deutsche Wortbildung: Typen und Tendenzen der Gegenwartssprache (Düsseldorf: Schwann, 1975), 194–95.

133. Peter Stallybrass and Allon White, The Politics and Poetics of Transgression (Ithaca, N.Y.: Cornell University Press, 1986), 3.

134. See also Johannes Geffcken, "Beichte nach den zehn Geboten, aus einer Handschrift der hamburger Stadtbibliothek," in Bildercatechismus (Leipzig: T. O. Weigel, 1855), col. 87; Paul Rebhun, Haußfried: Was für Ursachen den Christlichen eheleuten zubedencken (Nuremberg: D. Gerlatz, 1569), G6r. Further examples can be found in Kurt Gärtner and Gerhard Hanrieder, eds. Findebuch zum mittelhochdeutschen Wortschatz (Stuttgart: S. Hirzel, 1992); Jakob Grimm and Wilhelm Grimm, Deutsches Wörterbuch, vol. 24 (Leipzig: S. Hirzel, 1936) col. 448–49; Friedrich Staub and Ludwig Tobler, eds., Schweizerisches Idiotikon: Wörterbuch der schweizerdeutschen Sprache (Frauenfeld: Huber, 1881), 1:7.

135. StAZ, B VI.245 (Rats- und Richtbuch 1513–1519), 232r–33r (Bläßj Hipold 1519); StAZ, A 27.16 (Kundschaften und Nachgänge 1546–1549), Hans Appenzeller 1547; StASO, Vergichtbuch und Thurn Roedel 1583–1587 (Marti Winistorff 1587), 156–58.

136. StAZ, A 27.8 (Kundschaften und Nachgänge 1536–1538), Hans Apfmotz 1537; StAZ, B VI.253 (Rats- und Richtbuch), 216r/v.

137. StAZ, A 27.35 (Kundschaften und Nachgänge 1579), Wilhelm von Mühlhausen 1579.

138. Earlier instances are reported from Lucerne. StALU, RP 11, 103v: Andres

Tschafel (1519); StALU, RP 11, 141r/v: Johannes Nusser (1520). At the end of the sixteenth century, St. Gallen recorded cases of sodomy and bestiality in a similar way (Krings, "Sodomie am Bodensee," 14–15).

139. StALU, COD 4530 (*Turmbücher*), 165v (1637).

140. Yet there are also a number of differences. The term *sodomy* was used in Lucerne throughout the sixteenth century. See also Solothurn, StASO, Vergichtbuch (*Ratsmanual rot* 19) 1478–1552 (Hans Pröpstli 1525), 166. In Zurich, the term was in use at the beginning of the century but reappeared only during the last two decades of the same century. StAZ, A 27.44 (*Kundschaften und Nachgänge* 1594–1595), 5 junge Knaben. If the sixteenth-century records in Zurich contain the term *sodomy* at all, this wording usually appears in the headings that introduce the documentation. These short summaries of a case were added later, presumably in the seventeenth century, when the archive was systematically ordered. See StAZ, A 27.26 (*Kundschaften und Nachgänge* 1566–1567), Rudolf Bachmann/Uli Frei 1567; StAZ, A 27.35 (*Kundschaften und Nachgänge* 1579), Wilhelm von Mühlhausen 1579. Krings, "Sodomie am Bodensee," 19, notes that the term's usage follows a similar chronology in records from St. Gallen.

141. StAZ, A 27.10 (*Kundschaften und Nachgänge* c. 1536/1542) and A 27.14 (1541). See also Diethelm Fretz, "Steineri fata," *Zwingliana* 4, no. 12 (1926, no. 2): 377–84. On Steiner, see Franz Karl Stadlin, *Der Topographie des Kantons Zug erster Theil*, vol. 4: *Die Geschichte der Stadtgemeinde Zug* (Lucerne: n.p., 1824), 353–63; Wilhelm Meyer, *Der Chronist Werner Steiner 1492–1542: Ein Beitrag zur Reformationsgeschichte von Zug* (Stans: Ad. & P. von Matt, 1910); Willy Brändly, "Jodocus Müller (Molitor)," *Zwingliana* 7, no. 5 (1941): 319–30; Willy Brändly, "Die Zuger Humanisten," *Innerschweizerisches Jahrbuch für Heimatkunde* 8–10 (1946): 206–20; Willy Brändly, "Peter Kolin von Zug," *Zwingliana* 9, no. 3 (1950, no. 1): 150–76; Joachim Staedtke, "Heinrich Bullingers Bemühungen um eine Reformation im Kanton Zug," *Zwingliana* 10, no. 1 (1954, no. 1): 24–47; Jean-Pierre Bodmer, "Werner Steiners Pilgerführer," *Zwingliana* 12 (1964): 69–73; Jean-Pierre Bodmer, "Werner Steiner und die Schlacht bei Marignano," *Zwingliana* 12, no. 4 (1965, no. 2): 241–47; Richard Feller and Edgar Bonjour, *Geschichtsschreibung der Schweiz vom Spätmittelalter zur Neuzeit*, vol. 1, 2d ed. (Basel: B. Schwabe, 1979), 172–74.

142. StAZ, A 27.10 (*Kundschaften und Nachgänge* c. 1530–1570), Steiner's undated confession (1541): "Er [Hans Kern] sölte jm sin mandlich glid jnn sin hand nemmen, so welte er [Steiner] jnn leren gryffenn oder daran rybenn, das es jm glich alls wol thätte, alls wann er [Kern] by einer frowenn lege" (He should take his male member in his hand. He [Steiner] wanted to teach him [Kern] how to grab and rub it, in order to make him feel as well as if he were lying with a woman).

143. Steiner was twenty-five years of age. Kern, who was about to marry, must have been roughly of the same age, given the average age at marriage.

144. Even in his final confession, Steiner denied having acted as Kern's confessor (StAZ, A 27.10 [*Kundschaften und Nachgänge* c. 1530–1570]).

145. In his confession, Steiner stated that he gave the presents "upon [Kern's] fervent request" ("vff sin pittlich begär"; ibid.).

146. See Alan Bray, "To Be a Man in Early Modern Society: The Curious Case of Michael Wigglesworth," *History Workshop Journal* 41 (Spring 1996): 155–65.

147. Interestingly, he shared this incident with Kern, presumably to arouse the latter's interest. Kern then told the authorities. StAZ, A 27.10 (*Kundschaften und Nachgänge* c. 1530–1570), Werner Steiner (c. 1536/42): "er were jnn einer Badstubenn by jm gesin

vnnd jnn der glust also ankommen dermassenn, das es jm zu herzenn gienge vnnd vff-stieß, das er meinte er mûste sich erbrâchen."

148. According to Sal. Rordorf-Gwalter ("Die Geschwister Rosilla und Rudolf Rordorf," *Zwingliana* 3, no. 6 [1915]: 191), Steiner was the author of a Protestant treatise on matrimony. I have not been able to locate this text.

149. See Rordorf-Gwalter, "Die Geschwister Rosilla und Rudolf Rordorf," 190–91, on the ties of friendship between the Steiners and the Pellicans.

150. StAZ, A 27.14 (*Kundschaften und Nachgänge* 1541–1543), Heinrich Bullinger, Konrad Pellikan (June 1541). [Kern to Bullinger] "Antwurte der Kern, er seite nit das er mit sinem brûder kêtzeret hette; es wer aber arckwônig vnnd niemer hüpsch by nacht am bett den arm vber einen zeschlachen."

151. StAZ, A 27.10 (*Kundschaften und Nachgänge* c. 1530–1570), Werner Steiner (c. 1536/42): "Doch nie dheins florenzens nit gedacht" ([He] never thought of florencing).

152. StAZ, A 27.14 (*Kundschaften und Nachgänge* 1541–1543), letter of council in Schwyz to the council of Zurich (June 18, 1541). See also the letter of June 23, 1541.

153. StAZ, A 27.10 (*Kundschaften und Nachgänge* c. 1530–1570), Werner Steiner's confession (1541/42). A further plea for mitigation was denied.

154. Monter, "Sodomy and Heresy," 46. In Sweden, the Law Committee, responsible for legal reform, turned down proposals that included mention of this sin (1696–1734), though an earlier law book had a sodomy statute. In November 1699 the committee's chairman gave the following reasoning: "that it seems inadvisable to mention sodomitic sins; rather it would be better to pass over them in silence as if unaware; should it go so far that such acts are committed, then due punishment should be meted out" (Jonas Liliequist, "State Policy, Popular Discourse, and the Silence on Homosexual Acts in Early Modern Sweden," *Journal of Homsexuality* 35 [1998]: 18).

155. StABS, Criminalia 4 12, Elisabeth Hertner (1647), 6r. The statement features Biblical references to circumscribe the offense in question, Genesis 19 and St. Paul's Letter to the Romans (1:26).

156. Ibid., 6v: "daß soviel möglich diß laster in stille vnd geheimb gehalten vnd vnder daß gemeine volck nicht aúßgebracht werde, damit nicht etliche wúndersame leüth vnder júngen oder alten personen zú erkúndigúng dises laster veranleÿtet, vnd hierdúrch dise schandtliche missethat, entweders jn der statt oder aúf der landtschafft je lenger je mehr aúßgebreittet wúrde."

157. StALU, COD 4530 (*Turmbücher*), 166v (1638).

158. Krings, "Sodomie am Bodensee," 21–22. For a case in eighteenth-century Hamburg, see Jakob Michelsen, "Von Kaufleuten, Waisenknaben und Frauen," 216. See also Zedler, *Universal-Lexikon*, vol. 38, col. 331: "niemahlen [soll] aber in den Urtheln dasjenige, so Aegerniß geben möchte, öffentlich abgelesen werden" (One shall never read from the sentences what could scandalize).

159. Sweden witnessed a shift toward a politics of silence similar to the German lands. See Liliequist, "State Policy," 20. For Hamburg during the eighteenth century, see Michelsen, "Von Kaufleuten, Waisenknaben und Frauen," 216–20. For a case of bestiality, see Pierre Olivier Lechot, "Puncto Criminis Sodomiae: Un procès pour bestialité dans l'ancien Evêché de Bâle au XVIIIe siècle," *Schweizerische Zeitschrift für Geschichte* 50 (2000): 123–40.

160. StALU, RP 46 (1599), 315r (Jacob Bachmann).

161. Today canton Neuchâtel. StABS, Polizeiakten C 15, undatiertes Rechtsgutachten, adds the information that this man was from Valengin.

162. StABS, Missiven B 11, 184–85 (August 30, 1567): "Jungling . . . welche vor drigen jaren uss anstifftung eines ubellthätigen . . . mitt einandern unnküscheit getriben." The approximate age is mentioned in StABS, Straf- und Polizeiakten C 15.

163. According to StABS, Straf- und Polizeiakten C 15, undatiertes Rechtsgutachten.

164. StABS, Missiven B 11, 184–85 (August 30, 1567): "unnd diewyl wir unns keiner sollichen derglychen gethat, das die by unns fürganngenn sye, erinnern konden."

165. StABS, Straf- und Polizeiakten C 15, undatiertes Rechtsgutachten.

166. Quoted from Hagemann, *Aus dem Rechtsleben im alten Basel*, 9. See also *Basilea Latina*, ed. Alfred Hartmann (Basel: Lehrmittelverlag des Erziehungs-Departements, 1931), 60: "Conswetudine magis quam lege scripta vtuntur."

167. StABS, Missiven B 11, 185.

168. A couple of years after the Delsberg case was discussed in Basel in 1573, Bonifacius Amerbach, an astute jurist from Basel, lamented that local customs and the judges' discretionary powers still determined the outcomes of court cases. See Hagemann, *Aus dem Rechtsleben im alten Basel*, 17. See also Hans Thieme, "Die beiden Amerbach," in *Ideengeschichte und Rechtsgeschichte: Gesammelte Schriften* (Cologne: Böhlau, 1986), 1:429.

169. StABS, Straf- und Polizeiakten C 15: "durch offentliche landtkundige sichparliche Straff der böß gaist villicht anlaß habe Jnn ettlicher hertzen, so sonst an sölliche grewliche Sünd nie gedacht hetten, seinen samen zerströwen. Dan vill wäger [better] diß Laster gentzlich zuverhälen vnd vnderzudrucken dan weytter lauttpreche zumachen. Derwägen es auch die Stummende Sünd nitt vbel genent werden, daß durch seinen rechten Namen ergernüß geben werde."

170. How destructively and how arbitrarily the early modern state apparatus could weigh on its subjects can be illustrated by the exceptional case of Kyburg, a region in the hinterland of Zurich. Between 1694 and 1698, 22 of 24 men were executed for sodomy—the document uses the term *sodomia* for male homoeroticism and *bestialitas* for bestiality—a wave of persecution that ended only when the landvogt Johann Conrad Heidegger had been replaced. StAZ, B VII 21.2. See also Erich Wettstein, *Die Geschichte der Todesstrafe im Kanton Zürich* (Winterthur: H. Schellenberg, 1958), 80–83.

Chapter Five

1. Richard Trexler, "Correre la Terra: Collective Insults in the Late Middle Ages," *Mélanges de l'Ecole Française de Rome: Moyen Age, Temps Modernes* 96 (1984): 845–902; Peter Burke, "The Art of Insult in Early Modern Italy," *Culture and History* 2 (1987): 68–79; Peter Burke, "Insults and Blasphemy in Early Modern Europe," in *The Historical Anthropology of Early Modern Italy* (Cambridge: Cambridge University Press, 1987), 95–109; Jean Delumeau, ed., *Injures et blasphèmes* (Paris: Editions Imago, 1989); Daniel R. Lesnick, "Insults and Threats in Medieval Todi," *Journal of Medieval History* 17 (1991): 71–89; Jane Kamensky, *Governing the Tongue: The Politics of Speech in Early New England* (New York: Oxford University Press, 1997). See below for further bibliographical references.

2. Bray, *Homosexuality in Renaissance England*, 58–80; Eve Kosofsky Sedgwick, *Between Men: English Literature and Male Homosocial Desire* (New York: Columbia University Press, 1985); Goldberg, *Sodometries*; Winfried Schleiner, "'That Matter Which Ought Not to Be

Heard Of': Homophobic Slurs in Renaissance Cultural Politics," *Journal of Homosexuality* 26 (1994): 41–75; McFarlane, *The Sodomite in Fiction and Satire*; Dinshaw, *Getting Medieval*.

3. McFarlane, *The Sodomite in Fiction and Satire*, 19.

4. Raphael Samuel, "Reading the Signs, I," *History Workshop Journal* 32 (1992): 92.

5. Cynthia B. Herrup, *A House in Gross Disorder: Sex, Law, and the 2nd Earl of Castlehaven* (Oxford: Oxford University Press, 1999), 37.

6. Since I am relying in part on trial records, my source base is slanted toward those of high social standing (who had the means to take their offenders to court) and toward egregious cases rather than loose talk or quarrels among lower-class individuals.

7. Dyan Elliott, *Fallen Bodies: Pollution, Sexuality, and Demonology in the Middle Ages* (Philadelphia: University of Pennsylvania Press, 1998), 81.

8. See chapters 6 and 7.

9. Damian, *Die Briefe des Petrus Damiani*, part 1, 287: "Sodomiticae igitur immunditiae cancer ita per clericalem ordinem serpit"; "Letter 31" ["Book of Gomorrah"], in *Letters*, 2:6: "The befouling cancer of sodomy is, in fact, spreading . . . through the clergy." See also Jordan, *Invention of Sodomy*, 45–66.

10. "Humberti Cardinalis libri iii. adversus simoniacos," in *Libelli de lite*, vol. 1, Monumenta Germaniae Historica (Hannover: Hahnsche Buchhandlung, 1891), 174; "Pseudo-Udalrici epistola de continentia clericorum," in *Libelli de lite*, 1:256, 258; "Manegoldi ad Gebehardum liber," in *Libelli de lite*, 1:338, 363, 366; "Walrami et Herrandi epistolae de causa Heinrici regis conscriptae," in *Libelli de lite*, vol. 2 (1892), 287, 289; "Arnulfi Sagiensis archidiaconi postea episcopi Lexoviensis invectiva in Girardum Engolismensem episcopum," in *Libelli de lite*, vol. 3 (1897), 95; "Gerhohi praepositi Reichersbergensis libelli selecti," in *Libelli de lite*, 3:160, 170; Gerhoch of Reichersberg, "De investigatione Antichristi," in *Libelli de lite*, 3:324; "Defensio pro filiis presbyterorum," in *Libelli de lite*, 3:581. See Boswell, *Christianity, Social Tolerance, and Homosexuality*, 217; Anne Llewellyn Barstow, *Married Priests and the Reforming Papacy: The Eleventh-Century Debates* (Lewiston, N.Y.: Mellen, 1982), 105–55; Rolf Lenzen, "Sodomitenschelte: Eine Invektive des Serlo von Bayeux?" in *Arbor amoena comis: 25 Jahre Mittellateinisches Seminar in Bonn*, ed. Ewald Könsgen (Stuttgart: Franz Steiner, 1990), 189–92; Erwin Frauenknecht, *Die Verteidigung der Priesterehe in der Reformzeit* (Hannover: Hahnsche Buchhandlung, 1997), 274–75. For context, see Ian S. Robinson, *Authority and Resistance in the Investiture Contest: The Polemical Literature of the Late Eleventh Century* (New York: Manchester University Press, 1978).

11. "Wido Episcopus Ferrariensis de scismate Hildebrandi," in *Libelli de lite*, 1:536 (and 558). See Bernd Schütte, "'Multi de illo multa referunt': Zum Lebenswandel Heinrichs IV," in *Arbor Amoena Comis*, ed. Könsgen, 147. See also "Annales Sancti Disibodi," ed. Georg Waitz, in *Annales aevi suevici*, ed. Georg Heinrich Pertz, Monumenta Germaniae Historica: Scriptores 17 (Hannover: Hahnsche Buchhandlung, 1861), 10.

12. F. Pagnotti, "Nicollò da Calvi e la sua *Vita d'Innocenzo IV*, con una breve introduzione sulla istoriografia pontificia nei secoli XIII e XIV," *Archivio Storico della R. Società Romana di Storia Patria* 21 (1898): 103; Hergemöller, *Krötenkuß und schwarzer Kater*, 121. See also Philipp of Novara, *The Wars of Frederick II against the Ibelins in Syria and Cyprus*, ed. John L. La Monte (New York: Columbia University Press, 1936), appendix ii.

13. Bernd-Ulrich Hergemöller, "Ludwig der Bayer, Friedrich der Schöne, Friedrich von Tirol—Verwirrungen und Verwechslungen," *Capri: Zeitschrift für schwule Geschichte* 1 (1991): 31–41. See also C. Stephen Jaeger, *Ennobling Love: In Search of a Lost Sensibility* (Philadelphia: University of Pennsylvania Press, 1999); Klaus van Eickels, *Vom inszenierten Kon-*

sens zum systematisierten Konflikt: Die englisch-französischen Beziehungen und ihre Wahrnehmung an der Wende vom Hoch- zum Spätmittelalter (Stuttgart: Thorbecke, 2002).

14. Jean Coste, ed., Boniface VIII en procès: Articles d'accusation et dépositions des témoins (1303–1311) (Rome: "L'erma" di Bretschneider, 1995), 52–53, 117–19.

15. Ibid., 151–52, 301, 384, 491–93, 530–32, 536–38.

16. Malcolm Barber, The Trial of the Templars (Cambridge: Cambridge University Press, 1978); Alan J. Forey, The Military Orders: From the Twelfth to the Early Fourteenth Centuries (London: Macmillan, 1992), 225–39; Anne Gilmour-Bryson, "Sodomy and the Knights Templar," Journal of the History of Sexuality 7 (1996): 151–83; Hergemöller, Krötenkuß und schwarzer Kater, 330–405.

17. Chiffoleau, "Dire l'indicible," 297, 303–4; James A. Brundage, "Politics of Sodomy: Rex vs. Pons Hugh de Ampurias (1311)," in Sex in the Middle Ages, ed. Joyce E. Salisbury (New York: Garland, 1991), 239–46; Chiffoleau, "'Contra naturam,'" 302–4.

18. Brundage, Law, Sex and Christian Society, 473.

19. See Chiffoleau, "Dire l'indicible," 299.

20. See David Teasley, "The Charge of Sodomy as a Political Weapon in Early Modern France: The Case of Henry III in Catholic League Polemic, 1585–1589," Maryland Historian 18 (1987): 17–30.

21. Harry J. Kuster and Raymond J. Cormier, "Old Views and New Trends: Observations on the Problem of Homosexuality in the Middle Ages," Studi medievali, 3d ser., 25 (1984): 603–4. For sexual insult in Scandinavia, see Kari Ellen Gade, "Homosexuality and Rape of Males," 132–41; Folke Ström, nid, ergi and Old Norse Moral Attitudes (London: Viking Society for Northern Research, 1974); Preben Meulengracht Sørensen, The Unmanly Man: Concepts of Sexual Defamation in Early Northern Society, trans. Joan Turville-Petre (Odense: Odense University Press, 1983), 27–32; Brall, "Reflections of Homosexuality."

22. Berthold, "Rechtssumme," 3:1696.

23. StALU, COD 1256/1 (Regierungsverordnungen), 125 (1395): "Vmb grob zureden: Du hast ein Kuh gehigt."

24. Ibid., 228–29 (1421).

25. StALU, RP 1, 270v (1414). A later reader, probably around 1600 and possibly the famous city scribe from Lucerne, Renward Cysat, annotated the word pûlscherûnet with the following explanation: "daz ist ein Sodomit, daz er gesodomitet hab mit man" (that is a sodomite who sodomized with men). Apparently, pûlscherûn (in the original source used as a verb), a word of bowdlerized Italian, was not commonly understood anymore.

26. StALU, RP 1, 270v (1414).

27. StALU, RP 3, 77r (1422) and RP 1, 424r (1422). The word was again commented upon by a late sixteenth-century scribe (probably Renward Cysat): "that is a sodomite who sins man with man, per anum."

28. StALU, RP 3, 77r (1422), and RP 1, 424r (1422); StALU, RP 3, 77r: "So wellen wir daz besser globen, sonder jnn für ein biderbman han. Den eid het er getan, darumb so sol er uss der lumden sin." RP 1 (1422), 424r. See also Anton Philipp von Segesser, Rechtsgeschichte der Stadt und Republik Lucern, vol. 2, 649–70: "wannt er erzelt het, wie im ein dieb ze Meilan zûgerett, er wer ein pulscherun. Daz verret er vnd slûg den, daz man sy mûst scheiden."

29. With regard to peace as a goal of urban politics, see Susanna Burghartz, Leib, Ehre und Gut: Delinquenz in Zürich Ende des 14. Jahrhunderts (Zurich: Chronos, 1990); Schwer-

hoff, *Köln im Kreuzverhör;* Peter Schuster, *Der gelobte Frieden: Täter, Opfer und Herrschaft im spätmittelalterlichen Konstanz* (Konstanz: Universitätsverlag, 1995).

30. StALU, RP 1, 424r/v (Ludwig Walker 1433).

31. Berthold, "*Rechtssumme,*" 3:1586: "mit worten oder mit priefen" (L25).

32. Ms. Vienna ÖNB, Series nova 3616, 6v: "Wo dj lewt zue sam chomen als bej hofelen vnd bej wirtschaftenn, so ist jr maiste red, das ains dem anderenn mindert sein ere vnd seinen guten lewmt." See also Berthold, "*Rechtssumme,*" 1586.

33. Ms. Vienna ÖNB, Series nova 3616, 7r: "schlachens halts an dj kirch thur oder werffens den lewten jn dj hewser. Oder sie werffens auf der gassen vonn jnn, darumb das sie funden vnd gelesenn werdenn vnd den menschenn zue schaden chomen."

34. Ibid., 8r: "dj da machent vnd tichtenn lyedle vnd dj singen dar jnn der mensch geschent wirt vnd dar jnn des menschen guter lewmt geschennt vnd gemindert wirt . . . , jnn vil landen vnd jnn vil stetenn [getragen werden]."

35. See Günter Schmidt, *Libelli famosi: Zur Bedeutung der Schmähschriften, Scheltbriefe, Schandgemälde und Pasquille in der deutschen Rechtsgeschichte* (Ph.D. diss., University of Cologne, 1970), 11–12, 147–49, 230–33; Thomas A. Fudge, *The Magnificent Ride: The First Reformation in Hussite Bohemia* (Aldershot: Ashgate, 1998), 186–226. Fudge has given extensive treatment to songs as vehicles of communication in the context of Hussitism. According to him, they are "a form of witness, sign of solidarity, polemical device and expression of militarism" (210).

36. Otto Hupp, *Scheltbriefe und Schandbilder—ein Rechtsbehelf aus dem 15. und 16. Jahrhundert* (Munich: G. J. Manz, 1930); Gherardo Ortalli, "*. . . pingatur in Palatino . . .*": *La pittura infamante nei secoli XIII–XVI* (Rome: Jouvance, 1979); G. Schmidt, *Libelli famosi,* 21, 76–130; Fudge, *Magnificent Ride,* 226–51.

37. See Ulinka Rublack, "Anschläge auf die Ehre: Schmähschriften und -zeichen in der städtischen Kultur des Ancien Régime," in *Verletzte Ehre: Ehrkonflikte in Gesellschaften des Mittelalters und der Frühen Neuzeit,* ed. Klaus Schreiner and Gerd Schwerhoff (Cologne: Böhlau, 1995), 391–411.

38. Hergemöller, "Die 'unsprechliche stumme Sünde,'" 5–43.

39. As early as the mid-fourteenth century, civic authorities in northern Germany had prohibited the use of anonymous letters that "were thrown in people's houses or other locations" ("We breue screue, vnde de in der lude hus eder an andere stedde worpe, . . . dene wel men vor enen vnrehten man hebben" [Braunschweig, before 1349]; quoted in G. Schmidt, *Libelli famosi,* 228).

40. Hergemöller, "Die 'unsprechliche stumme Sünde,'" 34: "Do ind hedde deme pastoir ouch den selven man genoempt Der sulchen oeveldeit mit yeme begangen hedde Ind dat were eyn rych selich man Ind hedde wyff ind kyndere (pleige zo raide zo gain Ind were eyn mit van den oeversten)."

41. StALU, RP 7, 94 (1490): "er wer ein kåtzer vnd hett ketzerie mit sinem knecht, so dann erstochen worden ist, getriben." See also Elisabeth Wechsler, *Ehre und Politik: Ein Beitrag zur Erfassung politischer Verhaltensweisen in der Eidgenossenschaft (1440–1500) unter historisch-anthropologischen Aspekten* (Zurich: Chronos, 1991), 183.

42. In addition to the following case, see also Jordanus (1301/4) in Thomas Füser, "Der Leib ist das Grab der Seele," 230–32. The proceedings against Jordanus closely resemble those against the canon E. from Hildesheim.

43. L. Rockinger, ed., "Briefsteller und formelbücher des eilften bis vierzehnten jahrhunderts," *Quellen zur bayerischen und deutschen Geschichte* 9 (1863): 328–29.

44. For German territories, see Lyndal Roper, "Will and Honour: Sex, Words, and Power in Augsburg Criminal Trials," in *Oedipus and the Devil*, 65–66; Roper, "Blood and Codpieces," in *Oedipus and the Devil*, 108–20; Schwerhoff, *Köln im Kreuzverhör*, 316. For other parts of the world, see Jim A. Sharpe, *Defamation and Sexual Slander in Early Modern England: The Church Courts at York* (York: Bothwick Institute of Historical Research, [1980]), 65; Mary Beth Norton, "Gender and Defamation in Seventeenth-Century Maryland," *William and Mary Quarterly*, 3d ser., 44 (1987): 3–39; Laura Gowing, "Language of Insult in Early Modern London," *History Workshop Journal* 35 (1993): 1–21; Laura Gowing, *Domestic Dangers: Women, Words, and Sex in Early Modern London* (New York: Oxford University Press, 1996).

45. For individual cases of sodomy accusations across early modern Europe and the new world, see Peter N. Moogk, "'Thieving Buggers' and 'Stupid Sluts': Insults and Popular Culture in New France," *William and Mary Quarterly*, 3d ser., 36 (1979): 539; Stefanie Siegmund, *From Tuscan Households to Florentine Ghetto: The Construction of a Jewish Community, 1560–1610* (Ph.D. diss., American Theological Seminary, 1995), 255; Robin Briggs, *Witches and Neighbors: The Social and Cultural Context of European Witchcraft* (New York: Penguin, 1996), 224. Of fifty-eight cases of insults that were prosecuted in Venice by the *Avogaria di comun* between 1500–1625, five featured "bugger" (*buzerar/buzerona*) and two *bardassa* for "dissolute/sodomite." See Elizabeth A. Horodowich, *Blasphemy, Insults and Gossip in Renaissance Venice* (Ph.D., University of Michigan, 2000), 29–31, 62.

46. Lynn Hunt, *The Family Romance of the French Revolution* (Berkeley: University of California Press, 1992), 89–123; Jill H. Casid, "Queer(y)ing Georgic: Utility, Pleasure, and Marie-Antoinette's Ornamented Farm," *Eighteenth-Century Studies* 30 (1997): 304–18.

47. Rainer Walz, "Schimpfende Weiber: Frauen in lippischen Beleidigungsprozessen des 17. Jahrhunderts," in *Weiber, Menschen, Frauenzimmer: Frauen in der ländlichen Gesellschaft 1500–1800*, ed. Heide Wunder and Christina Vanja (Göttingen: Vandenhoeck & Ruprecht, 1996), 196–97; Chris Wickham, "Gossip and Resistance among the Medieval Peasantry," *Past and Present* 160 (August 1998): 11, 15–16. See also Heinrich-Richard Schmidt, "Pazifizierung des Dorfes: Struktur und Wandel von Nachbarschaftskonflikten vor Berner Sittengerichten 1570–1800," in *Kirchenzucht und Sozialdisziplinierung im frühneuzeitlichen Europa*, ed. Heinz Schilling (Berlin: Duncker & Humblot, 1994), 96–97; P. Schuster, *Der gelobte Frieden*, 88.

48. StALU, RP 7, 85 (1490).

49. See chapter 2 (Burgundian mercenaries, 1474) and chapter 6.

50. Wechsler, *Ehre und Politik*, 236: "Der künig von Frankrich hat mich siben vnd zwenzig jar erzogen vnd ich wil im lieber dienen dann den arsbruttern vnd der bischof von Wallis ist ein arsbrutter vnd ein verlogner mann; er hat einen knaben gehan, den hat er ouch geflorenzet vnd hat zu wegen bracht (het), das er bapst wer worden, so het er den zers durch den sessel henken, damit er die esel geritten hab, ob er nicht ouch gehört hab, wann einer bapst were, das einer thun mus. Vnd die Lamparter syen arsbrutter vnd ketzer vnd er wol inen nit dienen, vnd der bapst sol des küngs müssig gan vnd sol wiewasser gesegnen, vnd der kung sye im lieber dann Sampeter, vnd wenn er schon für den himmel komen, so müsse er in lan."

51. Emil Usteri, *Marignano: Die Schicksalsjahre 1515/1516* (Zürich: Kommissionsverlag Berichthaus, 1974), 249–50.

52. Arnold Esch, "Mit Schweizer Söldnern auf dem Marsch nach Italien," *Quellen und Forschungen aus italienischen Archiven und Bibliotheken* 70 (1990): 434–35. Some Swiss merce-

naries seized on the opportunity to commit such acts themselves; see StAZ, A 27.13 (*Kundschaften und Nachgänge* c. 1530–1570), Thöni Rüttiman 1561.

53. Esch, "Mit Schweizer Söldnern," 435.

54. Ernst Gagliardi, "Mailänder und Franzosen in der Schweiz 1495–1499: Eidgenössische Zustände im Zeitalter des Schwabenkriegs," *Jahrbuch für schweizerische Geschichte* 39 (1914), 122*: "Hanns Bek hatt geredt, Lienhart von Grünenmatt hab geredt, die von Bern hankten sich an arßbruter und nämen gelt von inen, und sie söllen den <römschen küng> [deleted and replaced by:] die süwen in hindern küssen."

55. Gagliardi, "Mailänder und Franzosen," 122*: "wenn er ein Berner [sei], so sig er ein Lamparter und, mit Urlob, ein Arsbruter."

56. StAZ, A 27.3 (*Kundschaften und Nachgänge* 1500–1520), July 1518, 4: "Thonj Balthassar hete geredt vff menig, ja jung Bröpsstlj fügt wol jn das welschland, dann er ist ein ars bruter."

57. StAZ, A 27.35 (*Kundschaften und Nachgänge* 1579), Wilhelm von Mühlhausen 1579: "Vnnd wie nun er züg [Marti Gauser] samot einem weltschen bj jm Wilhelmen am beth gelegen, hette er den weltschen vber vßhin trucken wellen vnnd darbj gredt, das er gloube, der weltsch welle jnne zum füdlj [ass] jnhin minnen."

58. StALU, COD 4435 (Turmbücher), 197r (1561): "du wallch, du bist ein schelm dieb vnd böswicht."

59. Ibid.: "hests mit dem walchen, so hest alls gwüss ein stütten ghÿtt."

60. StAZ, B VI.245 (*Rats- und Richtbuch* 1513–1519), 79r/v: "Wölle ouch einen yeden biderman gewarnet haben, daz er sine kind niendert vnder die welschen, weder frantzoßen, sofoy noch ander schick, dann es sige jr großer flyß, daz sy vns tütschen vnsere kind also beschissint vnd sölich schantlich lasterlich sünd harvß ouch vnder vns bringint." See also StASO, DS (*Denkwürdige Sachen*) 33, 35r.

61. See the classic article by Max Gluckman, "Gossip and Scandal," *Current Anthropology* 4 (1963): 307–16. See also James C. Scott, *Domination and the Arts of Resistance: Hidden Transcripts* (New Haven, Conn.: Yale University Press, 1990).

62. StASO, DS (*Denkwürdige Sachen*) 33, 35r–36r (1515). See also StAZ, B VII.245 (*Rats- und Richtbuch* 1513–1519), 79r/v; StASO, Copiae 1524–1525, AB 2.9, 8.

63. Niklaus Conrad was *Schultheiss* (mayor) in 1494, 1495, 1498, 1499, 1502, 1503, 1506, 1507, 1510, 1511, 1514, 1515, and 1519. See also Gagliardi, "Mailänder und Franzosen," 200*, 210*. Kurt Meyer, *Solothurnische Verfassungszustände zur Zeit des Patriziats* (Olten: Dietschi, 1921), 357–58; Hans Sigrist, "Benedikt Hugi der Jüngere, Niklaus Conrad, zwei Lebensbilder," *Jahrbuch für solothurnische Geschichte* 22 (1949): 36–79; Silvan Freddi, *Das Kollegiatstift St. Ursus in Solothurn: Von den Anfängen bis 1520: Ursprung—Innere Organisation—Verhältnis zur Stadt* (Lizentiatsarbeit, University of Zurich, 1995), 214–15.

64. StAZ, B VI.245 (*Rats- und Richtbuch* 1513–1519), 79r, Jacob vom Schloß 1515.

65. StASO, Missiven 1515–1519, AB 1.6, 83.

66. Ibid., 85.

67. See the discussion of canon E. from Hildesheim, above, and Puller von Hohenburg (chapter 2).

68. See the statute *Der eim an sin ere redt*, Bürgerarchiv, "Wyss Buech," E I 61, 14.

69. StASO, Ratsmanual 1523–1526, A 1.14, 68, 71: "Er [Zigerli] wüsse einen brütloff . . . Es sÿe die allte brütt ["bride," here derogatory for bedmate, whore; note the feminine ending] von Büren vnnd Herr Ůlrich hinder der kilchen etc." Also in StASO,

Ratsmanual 1523–1525, A 1.12, 247, 254. In both copies the abbreviation *etc.* expressed something apparently deemed inappropriate to be put in writing.

70. Klemens Arnold, "St. Ursus in Solothurn," in *Die Weltlichen Kollegiatstifte der deutsch- und französischsprachigen Schweiz*, ed. Guy P. Marchal, Abteilung 2, Teil 2 of *Helvetia Sacra* (Bern: Francke, 1977), 516–17.

71. StASO, Copiae 1524–1525, AB 2.9, 254. In 1529 Solothurn authorities passed a statute against vilifying others as "heretics" ("Glaubensmandat . . . ," in *Rechtsquellen des Kantons Solothurn*, vol. 2, ed. Charles Studer [Aarau: Sauerländer, 1987], 198). Jost Zigerli was chaplain, a rank positioned below the canons.

72. This aspect of conflicts of honor is stressed by Michael Frank, "Ehre und Gewalt im Dorf der Frühen Neuzeit: Das Beispiel Heiden (Grafschaft Lippe) im 17. und 18. Jahrhundert," in *Verletzte Ehre*, ed. Schreiner and Schwerhoff, 323.

73. Whereas Zigerli had verbally abused Conrad without the defamed being present, Spiegelberg had called him a sodomite in Conrad's presence.

74. StASO, Ratsmanual 1523–1525, A 1.12, 260. Interestingly, in the proceedings against Spiegelberg, it is the council that uses the same argument of the *malefitzisch* character of the case to make the witnesses speak. See StASO, Ratsmanual 1523–1525, A 1.12, 312. With regard to the definition of *malefitzisch*: On Bernese territory, those offenses that "concerned the blood" were listed as robbery, arson, murder, rape, sodomy, and theft ("Berechtigung Berns über Trachselwald und über das Landgericht Ranflüh [1392 März 11]," in *Die Rechtsquellen des Kantons Bern*, part 1: *Stadtrechte*, vol. 3, ed. Hermann Rennefahrt [Aarau: Sauerländer, 1945], 298). See "Die Handveste von Zofingen," in *Die Rechtsquellen des Kantons Aargau*, part 1: *Stadtrechte*, vol. 5, ed. Walter Merz (Aarau: Sauerländer, 1914), 62 (1363). See also a seventeenth-century definition of *malefitzisch* offenses from St. Gallen: murder, manslaughter, assistance to manslaughter, sodomy, witchery, suicide, incest, flight from criminal persecution, rape, theft (with malign intent and above ten florins), perjury, or violence against parents (*Die Rechtsquellen des Kantons St. Gallen*, part 3: *Rechte der Landschaft*, vol. 1, ed. Ferdinand Elsener [Aarau: Sauerländer, 1951], 141 [1669]).

75. Ernst Haefliger, *Solothurn in der Reformation* (Solothurn: Gassmann, 1945), 134.

76. StASO, Copiae 1524–1525, AB 2.9, 253–57; StASO, Ratsmanual 1523–1525, A 1.12, 247–48, 254–58, 260–61, 263–67, 310–13; StASO, Ratsmanual 1523–1526, A 1.14, 68, 71–77, 91–93; StASO, Copiae 1524–1525, AB 2.9, 8.

77. In Constance, for instance, one man who had falsely accused another of having had sexual intercourse with a cow was burned at the stake, the punishment the slandered person would have received if the accusation had been found correct (Stadtarchiv Konstanz, Schultheiß Coll A I 8/1, 179 1/2 [1494]).

78. "Trostungsbuchstrafen" (1419), in *Die Rechtsquellen des Kantons Bern*, part 2: *Rechte der Landschaft*, vol. 2, ed. Hermann Rennefahrt (Aarau: Sauerländer, 1937), 69.

79. "Rechte und Freiheiten des Amtes im Eigen," in *Die Rechtsquellen des Kantons Aargau*, part 2, vol. 2, ed. Walter Merz (Aarau: Sauerländer, 1926), 9 (before 1313); "Trostungsbuchstrafen," in *Die Rechtsquellen des Kantons Bern*, part 2, vol. 2, 69 (1419); "Freistätte im Pfarrhaus," in *Die Rechtsquellen des Kantons Bern*, part 2, vol. 2, 149 (1522); "Die Stadtsatzung von Bern von 1539," in *Die Rechtsquellen des Kantons Bern*, part 1, ed. Welti, 327; "Das Stadtbuch von Schaffhausen," in *Die Rechtsquellen des Kantons Schaffhausen*, part 1, vol. 2, ed. Karl Schib (Aarau: Sauerländer, 1967), 3 (1385); "Glaubensmandat . . . ," in *Rechtsquellen des Kantons Solothurn*, vol. 2, ed. Charles Studer (Aarau: Sauerländer, 1987), 198 (1529);

"Entscheid der eidgenössischen Sendboten," in *Rechtsquellen des Kantons Solothurn*, vol. 2, 253 (1534).

80. "Die zweite Stadtsatzung (1604 V. 20./30.)," in *Die Rechtsquellen des Kantons Aargau*, part 1: *Stadtrechte*, vol. 5: *Das Stadtrecht von Zofingen* (Aarau: Sauerländer, 1914), 263.

81. Hans Conrad Peyer, *Verfassungsgeschichte der alten Schweiz* (Zurich: Schulthess Polygraphischer Verlag, 1978), 19. For an in-depth discussion of the notion of "Germanness" in polemical contexts, see the following chapter.

82. See Claudius Sieber-Lehmann, introduction to *In Helvetios—Wider die Kuhschweizer: Fremd- und Feindbilder von den Schweizern*, ed. Claudius Sieber-Lehmann and Thomas Wilhelmi (Bern: Paul Haupt, 1998), 53–54.

Chapter Six

1. Rüdiger Krohn, "Erotik und Tabu in Gottfrieds 'Tristan': König Marke," in *Stauferzeit: Geschichte, Literatur, Kunst*, ed. Rüdiger Krohn, Bernd Thum, and Peter Wapnewski (Stuttgart: Klett-Cotta, 1979), 362–76; Spreitzer, *Die stumme Sünde*; Sven Limbeck, "Mittelalter," in *Frauenliebe—Männerliebe: Eine lesbisch-schwule Literaturgeschichte in Essays*, ed. Alexandra Busch and Dirck Linck (Stuttgart: Metzler, 1997), 290–95; Tilmann Walter, *Unkeuschheit und Werk der Liebe: Diskurse über Sexualität am Beginn der Neuzeit in Deutschland* (Berlin: de Gruyter, 1998), 273; Brall, "Reflections of Homosexuality," 89. As chapter 3 showed, this does not apply to religious manuals.

2. For France, see Rebecca E. Zorach, "The Matter of Italy: Sodomy and the Scandal of Style in Sixteenth-Century France," *Journal of Medieval and Early Modern Studies* 26 (1996): 581–609. For context, see Lionello Sozzi, "La polémique anti-italienne en France au XVIe siècle," *Atti della Accademia della Scienze di Torino: Classe di Scienze Morali, Storiche e Filologiche* 206 (1972): 99–190. On German nationalism of the period, see Larry Silver, "Germanic Patriotism in the Age of Dürer," in *Dürer and His Culture*, ed. Dagmar Eichenberger, Charles Zika (Cambridge: Cambridge University Press, 1998), 38–68 (with bibliographical notes).

3. Sven Limbeck, " 'Sacrista'—'Hypocrita'—'Sodomita': Komödiantische Konstruktion sexueller Identität in Mercurino Ranzos 'De falso hypocrita,' " in *Exil, Fremdheit und Ausgrenzung in Mittelalter und früher Neuzeit*, ed. Andreas Bihrer, Sven Limbeck, and Paul Gerhard Schmidt (Würzburg: Ergon, 2000), 91–112.

4. Fedja Anzelewski, *Dürer: Werk und Wirkung* (Erlangen: Karl Müller, 1988), 54–55. The title is Dürer's own. On Orpheus and sodomy, see chapter 3.

5. Hutten, "Sendschreiben," in *Des teutschen Ritters Ulrich von Hutten auserlesene Werke*, ed. Ernst Münch (Leipzig: Georg Reimer, 1822), 18: "Jn Wälschland schämt' ich mich fürwahr jedesmal, ein Teutscher zu seyn, so oft im Gespräche mit Jtalienern auf die Verfolgung Reuchlins die Rede fiel, und jene mich fragten, ob denn die mönche in Teutschland so viele Gewalt hätten?"

6. See, for instance, Conrad Celtis's "Public Oration Delivered in the University of Ingolstadt," in *Selections from Conrad Celtis*, ed. Leonard Forster (Cambridge: Cambridge University Press, 1948), 52–53.

7. Ingrid D. Rowland, "Revenge of the Regensburg Humanists, 1493," *Sixteenth Century Journal* 25 (1994): 307–22.

8. Rowland, "Revenge," 311: "Horres Itale podicum fruator / . . . Pedicas: tremulumque crissitantes / Amplexu foves impio lacunas / Nec te fingere sobrium pudesas /

Infoelix: temulente: mentularum / Masturbator iners: et irrumator." "Pathic," from the Latin *pathicus,* is a derogatory term for a man who desires to be penetrated.

9. *WA, Briefwechsel,* vol. 1 (Weimar: Böhlau, 1930), 542: "impudicae mulieres ac prostituti pueri" (October 16, 1519).

10. Ibid., 542: "palliis, indulgentiis, bullis, nugis, gerris, quo sancti patres sua scorta et cynaedos alant."

11. As further proof of Italian immorality, he inserted a conversation with an Italian Dominican into the letter. Confronted about the "immodicam licentiam Romanam, qua christianus populus premeretur et mores polluerentur" (the immodest sexual licence, through which Christendom [is] plagued and morals [are] polluted), the Dominican supposedly responded with composure and equanimity. According to this monk, divine providence and God's will are impenetrable—an answer far from satisfying to a rigorous northern intellectual on the eve of the Reformation ("Crotus Rubeanus an Luther," in *WA, Briefwechsel,* vol. 1 [1930], 542).

12. "De matrimonio D. Felicis Malleoli Hemerlini," in *Septimum volumen tractatuum doctorum iuris* (Lyon: Dionysius de Harsy, 1535), 200vb. On the wording, see the discussion later in the chapter. On Hemmerli, see Katharina Colberg, "Felix Hemmerli," in *Die deutsche Literatur des Mittelalters: Verfasserlexikon,* 2d ed., ed. Stammler, Langosch, and Wachinger, vol. 3 (1981), cols. 989–1001.

13. Kurt Stadtwald, *Roman Popes and German Patriots: Antipapalism in the Politics of the German Humanist Movement from Gregor Heimburg to Martin Luther* (Geneva: Droz, 1996), 60–68.

14. Ibid., 196. The author traces the origins of pamphlet wars among humanists and the birth of antipapalism to the mid-fifteenth century. See also Hans-Jürgen Goertz, *Pfaffenhaß und groß Geschrei: Die reformatorischen Bewegungen in Deutschland 1517–1529* (Munich: Beck, 1987), 52–68.

15. *WA, Tischreden,* vol. 5 (Weimar: Böhlau, 1919), 468: "Nemo potest persuaderi tantam esse malitiam, nisi adhibeat testes oculos, aures et experientiam" (the entry is not dated). See also "Ratschlag eines Ausschusses etlicher Kardinäle Papst Paul III" (1538), in *WA,* vol. 50 (1914), 307: "Die selben unzucht haben wir jnn keiner andern Stad nicht gesehen, So doch Rom aller Stedte ein Spiegel und Vorbilde sein solt" (In no other city have I seen the same unchastity, though Rome should be a model for all cities). This is a German translation of a passage from a Catholic reform paper, originally not intended for publication but signed by Gasparo Contarini and others. It was edited with a gloss by Luther that comments on the text and supposedly reveals Catholic depravities: "Hie bekennen sie recht, Aber es ist kein sunde zu Rom, sondern grosse ehre gegen der Welsschen und Römisschen keuscheit" (Here, they state how it is. Yet it is no sin in Rome but a great honor with regard to the Italian and Roman chastity) (*WA,* vol. 54 [1928], 213). See also Richard Marius, *Martin Luther: The Christian between God and Death* (Cambridge, Mass.: Harvard University Press, 1999), 82.

16. Robert W. Scribner, "Anticlericalism and the Reformation in Germany," in *Popular Culture and Popular Movements in Reformation Germany* (London: Hambledon Press, 1987), 243–56; Scribner, "Antiklerikalismus in Deutschland um 1500," in *Europa 1500: Integrationsprozesse im Widerstreit,* ed. Ferdinand Seibt and W. Eberhard (Stuttgart: Klett-Cotta, 1987), 368–82; Goertz, *Pfaffenhaß und groß Geschrei,* 52–68; Thomas A. Brady, Jr., "'You Hate Us Priests': Anticlericalism, Communalism, and the Control of Women at Strasbourg in the Age of the Reformation," in *Anticlericalism,* ed. Dykema and Oberman, 167–

207; Hans-Jürgen Goertz, "Kleruskritik, Kirchenzucht und Sozialdisziplinierung in den täuferischen Bewegungen der Frühen Neuzeit," in *Kirchenzucht und Sozialdisziplinierung im frühneuzeitlichen Europa*, ed. Heinz Schilling (Berlin: Duncker & Humblot, 1994), 183–98. In literature on the subject, sodomy as a means of defamation is either not mentioned or underestimated, with the notable exception of Roper, *Holy Household*, 17–20, 255–58.

17. Michael Goodich, "Sodomy in Ecclesiastical Law and Theory," *Journal of Homosexuality* 1 (1976): 427–28; Hendrikus Johannes Kuster, *Over Homoseksualiteit in Middeleeuws West-Europa* (Ph.D. diss., Universiteit Utrecht, 1977), 39–60; Goodich, *Unmentionable Vice*, 10, 17–18; Kuster and Cormier, "Old Views and New Trends," 601–7, 610; Brundage, *Law, Sex, and Christian Society*, 536–37; Boulay, *Germany*, 200–204; Greenberg, *Construction of Homosexuality*, 280–92, 286; Jeffrey Richards, *Sex, Dissidence, and Damnation. Minority Groups in the Middle Ages* (London: Routledge, 1990), 138–40.

18. Martin Luther, "Vom Kriege wider die Türken" (1529), in *WA*, vol. 30.2 (1909), 142: "Denn so blind und unsynnig ist beide Bapstum und Türcke, das sie beyde die stummen sunde unverschampt treiben als ein ehrlich loblich ding. Und die weil sie den Ehestand nicht achten, . . . eitel Welsche hochzeit und florentzische breute bey yhn sind" (Both the papacy and the Turks are so blind and without reason that they commit the mute sin shamelessly as an honorable, praiseworthy affair. While they do not honor matrimony, . . . Italian weddings and Florentine brides are common among them). There is more on sodomy than the passage I just quoted; see further below on p. 142; also Luther, "Heerpredigt wider den Türken" (1529), in *WA*, vol. 30.2, 191; "Vermahnung an die Geistlichen" (1530), in *WA*, vol. 30.2 (1909), 337; "Warnung an seine lieben Deutschen" (1531), in *WA*, vol. 30.3 (1910), 303; "Ratschlag," in *WA*, vol. 50 (1914), 307; "Auslegung des 101. Psalms" (1534–35), in *WA*, vol. 51 (1914), 236–37, 262; *WA, Tischreden*, vol. 1 (1912), 464 (first half of the 1530s).

19. Martin Luther, "Wider Hans Worst" (1541), in *WA*, vol. 51 (1914), 549.

20. "Predigten des Jahres 1538," in *WA*, vol. 46 (1912), 216: "Ein iglich land hat sein laster." The Biblical reference is used here to replace a mention of sodomy, but Luther added with polemical venom "that in Italy cardinals and bishops perpetrated [this sin] with joy and with impunity" ("Ut in Italia impune et Bischöfe und Cardinäle thuns mit freuden"; 217). There are references to Sodom on the same page. See also "Diui Pauli apostoli ad Romanos Epistola" (1515–16), in *WA*, vol. 56 (1938), 184–85. Rom 1:24–25 is associated with masturbation above all. See also *WA*, vol. 57 (1939), 138.

21. "Predigten," in *WA*, vol. 46 (1912), 217: "Apud nos germanos tamen non fit mit rhum und ehre, sed mit schanden, quod wird einer an gesehen fur ein buben" (Among us Germans, [this sexual act] occurs not in glory and honor, but in shame, so that [the offender] will be regarded as a rascal).

22. *Epistolae obscurorum virorum*, ed. Ernst Münch, 198: "sunt in . . . Bohemia haeretici . . . In Saxonia potatores . . . Et Romae Curtisani . . . Sodomitici Florentiae."

23. Johann Fischart, *Aller Practick Großmutter* ([Strasbourg: B. Jobin, 1572]), fol. J6v: "Jungheern in Teutschland / Bischof in Italien / geadelte in Osterreich / Döcterlein vnd Practicanten zu Speir . . . Sodomiter zu Florenz."

24. Luther, "Brief an den Kardinal Erzbischof von Mainz" (1530), in *WA*, vol. 30.2 (1909), 411; see also n. 3.

25. Rudi C. Bleys, *The Geography of Perversion: Male-to-Male Sexual Behaviour Outside the West and the Ethnographic Imagination 1250–1918* (London: Cassell, 1996).

26. "Satirische Umdichtung auf den Papst" (1546), in *WA*, vol. 60 (1980), 178.

Another version of the text skips the pope's name: "du heilige jungfraw S. Bapst" (178). This passage is positioned at the very end of the text. The poem appeared anonymously. Most titles, including that of the *editio princeps*, claim falsely that the pamphlet was printed in Rome. See also Luther, "Wider das Papsttum zu Rom, vom Teuffel gestiftet" (1545), in *WA*, vol. 54 (1928), 214, 218, 223, 233.

27. Eve Levin, *Sex and Society in the World of the Orthodox Slavs 900–1700* (Ithaca, N.Y.: Cornell University Press, 1989), 199.

28. Sozzi, "La polémique anti-italienne."

29. Bray, *Homosexuality in Renaissance England*; Stephen Orgel, *Impersonations: The Performance of Gender in Shakespeare's England* (Cambridge: Cambridge University Press, 1996), 39; Winfried Schleiner, "Burton's Use of *praeteritio* in Discussing Same-Sex Relationships," in *Renaissance Discourse of Desire*, ed. Claude J. Summers and Ted-Larry Pebworth (Columbia: University of Missouri Press, 1993), 167–78. On the association of Islam with sodomy in general, see Hergemöller, *Krötenkuß und schwarzer Kater*, 134, 142–53, 169, 299–301, 382–83, 400–401. According to Martin Luther, Muhammad permitted men to have sex with boys and women (implied here: not their own wives). See Martin Luther, "Verlegung des Alcoran Bruder Richardi, Prediger Ordens" (1542), in *WA*, vol. 53 (1920), 304: "Es sey nicht wider die Natur, sich mit Knaben und Weibern vermengen" (It [is] not against nature, to have intercourse with boys and women). The Koran has no such provisions. Luther inserted this piece of information into his source, Brother Ricardus's treatise on Islam. See Luther, "Heerpredigt wider den Türken" (1529), in *WA*, vol. 30.2 (1909), 191: "Sihe unter diesem heiligen schein der Türcken ligen verborgen, ia unverborgen, so viel ungehewrer schrecklicher grewel, nemlich, das sie . . . solch Welsch und Sodomitisch unkeuscheit treiben, das nicht zu sagen ist für züchtigen leuten" (Underneath this semblance of sainthood [allusion to the German word for halo], lie hidden, or rather unhidden, so many horrendous abominations: namely, they . . . commit such Italian and sodomitical unchaste acts which should not be named in front of virtuous people). They are said to also violate matrimony and be blasphemers, murderers, tyrants, robbers—transgressions they deem to be virtues. This is a rare commonality between Luther and his Catholic opponent, Augustin von Alfeld, who counted Muhammad under the "persecutors of the state of matrimony" (*die verfolger des eelichen standts*) (Alfeld, *Wyder den Wittenbergischen Abgot Martin Luther* [Münster: Aschendorff, 1926], 35).

30. Van der Meer, "Sodom's Seed in The Netherlands," 2. See also Pieter Spierenburg, *The Broken Spell: A Cultural and Anthropological History of Preindustrial Europe* (New Brunswick, N.J.: Rutgers University Press, 1991), 272; Boone, "State Power and Illicit Sexuality," 142.

31. Goldberg, *Sodometries*; Richard C. Trexler, *Sex and Conquest: Gendered Violence, Political Order, and the European Conquest of the Americas* (Ithaca, N.Y.: Cornell University Press, 1995).

32. This argument was published in German in 1597 as an appendix to a translation of Las Casas's *Brevissima relación* of 1552 (excerpted from other works of his). I have used Bartolomé de Las Casas, *Warhafftiger vnd gründlicher Bericht / Der Hispanier grewlich: vnd abschewlichen Tryannrey von jhnen in den West Jndien / die newe Welt genant / begangen* (Oppenheim: Theodor de Bry, 1613), 149–50. On earlier editions, see VD-16 C:1232–33. See also Bartolomé de Las Casas, "Ganz Kurzer Bericht über die Zerstörung Westindiens" (1552), in *Werkauswahl*, ed. Mariano Delgado, vol. 2, trans. Ulrich Kunzmann (Paderborn: Ferdinand Schöningh, 1995), 25–138. (On the European dissemination, see 38–44.) The fact that Las Casas's text was so widely disseminated in Dutch, English, French, and German

speaks to the anti-Catholic slant of these publications which exposed the Spaniards as despots.

33. Erasmus Francisci, *Neu=polirter Geschicht= Kunst= und Sitten=Spiegel ausländischer Völcker* (Nuremberg: J. A. Endter, n.d.), 396, 398 (*Der Sodomiten Straffe*).

34. Francisci, *Neu=polirter Sitten=Spiegel,* book 2, 283. In the "Preface to the Reader," (fol.) (2v), Francisci argues that reading about the fates of the Biblical Sodomites could motivate the readers to improve, just as reading about foreign cultures would.

35. Johann Fischart, *Vom Außgelasnen Wütigen Teüffelsheer Allerhand Zauberern / Hexen vnnd Hexenmeistern / Vnholden / Teufelsbeschwerern / Warsagern / Schwartzkünstlern / Vergifftern / Augenverblendern / etc.* (Strasbourg: B. Jobin, 1591), 178, col. a: "Als die Spanier die Occidentalischen Newen Insulen einnamen / haben sie deßgleichen auch gefunden / daß man für das Gespenst vnnd Vngeheur am Halß ein Bild von der Pederastia oder Buberonigkeit eines Pediconis vnnd eines Cynaedi hat getragen / welchs noch schantlicher / vnd bei den Teutschen jhrer dieses lasters vnschuld halben nit vertolmetschen steht." See also Gerhild Scholz Williams, *Defining Dominion: The Discourses of Magic and Witchcraft in Early Modern France and Germany* (Ann Arbor: University of Michigan Press, 1995), 86, 184–85.

36. Jean Bodin, *De la demonomanie des sorciers* (Paris: Jacques du Puys, 1580), 145v: "Et quand les Espagnols se firent maistres des Isles Occidentales, ils trouuerent aussi qu'on portoit pendu au col vne image de Pederastie d'vn Pedicon, & d'vn Cynede, pour contrecharme, qui estoit encores plus villain. Aussi ces peuples là estoient fondus en Sodomies & ordures detestables, & en toutes sortes de Sorceleries, & qui ont esté tous extermines par les Espagnols."

37. Ibid.: "Chacun sera d'accord que c'est vne inuention diabolique."

38. Fischart, *Vom Außgelasnen Wütigen Teüffelsheer,* 178.

39. Martin Luther, "Vorlesungen über 1. Mose von 1535–45," in *WA,* vol. 43 (1912), 55: "Ac ego quidem non libenter versor in hoc loco, quod aures Germanorum adhuc innocentes et purae sunt ab hoc portento." See also 43:56: "Honor sit auribus innocentibus, non enim libenter haec tracto, et tamen cavendum nobis est, ne tales scandalosi sermones incautam et alioqui pronam ad peccatum aetatem abripiant et evertant. Ubi enim sic vivitur et docetur, ac vicia in mores abeunt, ibi, inquit graviter Seneca, remedii locus non est" [Seneca, ep. 39] (Honor to innocent ears. I do not like to treat this [sin]. We have to watch out so that offensive speech and sermons do not sweep away [our] careless age—an age disposed to sin. Where one lives and teaches thus and vices become customs, there, Seneca states sternly, is no place for a remedy).

40. Jordan, *Invention of Sodomy,* 7.

41. Jakob Wimpfeling, *Briefwechsel,* vol. 2, ed. Otto Herding and Dieter Mertens (Munich: W. Fink, 1990), 574–79; "Forte virgo es et cum virginibus te conversari delectat masculini generis" (577). The letter is transmitted only as a copy. This copy bears no indication of where or when the letter was written. See also Wimpfeling's letters to Pope Julius II and Bishop Albrecht of Strasbourg (both 1506) in which he sought to clear himself of similar accusations (559–67). There, Wimpfeling names his defamer as a certain Franciscus Schatzer of Rottweil. According to the editors of his letters, it is unclear whether the above *libellus famosus* is Schaczer's or somebody else's personal attack.

42. Ibid.

43. The milieu of emerging scholasticism, for example, produced a number of polemical critiques that linked the exclusively male environment of the school with erotic activities between men and adolescents (Boswell, *Christianity, Social Tolerance, and*

Homosexuality, 248–56). See also the controversy about the sin of Brunetto Latini, Dante's teacher: John Boswell, "Dante and the Sodomites," *Dante Studies* 112 (1994): 33–51. For the Renaissance, see Giovanni dall'Orto, "'Socratic Love' as a Disguise for Same-Sex Love in the Italian Renaissance," in *The Pursuit of Sodomy: Male Homosexuality in Renaissance and Enlightenment Europe*, ed. Kent Gerard and Gert Hekma (London: Harrington Park Press, 1989), 33–65; Leonard Barkan, *Transuming Passion: Ganymede and the Erotics of Humanism* (Stanford, Calif.: Stanford University Press, 1991); Alan Stewart, *Close Readers: Humanism and Sodomy in Early Modern England* (Princeton, N.J.: Princeton University Press, 1997).

44. See, for instance, the accusation against the magician Georg Faustus by Johannes Trithemius circulated in a letter dated August 20, 1507, and addressed to Johannes Virdung. According to Trithemius, Faustus served as a teacher in Kreuznach after Franz von Sickingen had intervened on his behalf. Faustus had to flee when it became known that he was having sex with his students ("nefandissimo fornicacionis genere cum pueris voluptari cepit") (Frank Baron, *Faustus: Geschichte, Sage, Dichtung* [Munich: Winkler, 1982], 128).

45. Wimpfeling, *Briefwechsel*, 577. See also Jacques de Vitry, *Historia orientalis* (Douai: B. Bellerus, 1597), 1:18: "latenter vitium sodomiticum hostis nature [Mahomet] in populo suo introduxit" ([Muhammad], the enemy of nature, secretly introduced the sodomitical sin to his people). For other examples linking Muslims to the host of sins associated with Sodom, see Johannes Wolff, "Beichtbüchlein" (1478), in *Drei Beichtbüchlein nach den zehn Geboten aus der Frühzeit der Buchdruckerkunst*, ed. Franz Falk (Münster: Aschendorff, 1907), 19; Luther, "Verlegung," 304; Alfeld, *Wyder den Wittenbergischen*, 34–35.

46. Geiler von Kaisersberg, *Die brösamlin doct.*, 7v: "es ist ein arm ding das das laster vß welschen landen kummet in vnser land."

47. Friedrich Waga, ed., *Die Welsch-Gattung* (Breslau: M. & H. Marcus, 1910).

48. Ibid., 242: "ein laster, das nit hat / Natürliche lüst inn der gethat," with references to the crying sin and Genesis 19.

49. Ibid.: "Das sünd sich selbs nit leiden mag."

50. See also Paracelsus [Theophrast Bombast von Hohenheim] and his claim that Germans emulate the Italians and try "to turn us Germans into Italians": "die Teutschen . . . machen aus uns Teutschen walen." Juxtaposed to Germany ("die wir doch Teutsch, mit den Walen gar kein commercium"), *welsch* is identified here with *Italia* ("Herbarius," in *Sämtliche Werke*, part 1, ed. Karl Sudhoff and Wilhelm Matthießen, [Hildesheim: Olms, 1996], 2:3). In the anonymous Reformation pamphlet "Ich kan nit vil neues erdenken" (c. 1518–20; in *Satiren und Pasquille aus der Reformationszeit*, 2d ed., ed. Oskar Schade [Hannover: C. Rümpler, 1863], 1:14), the author addresses the *Teutschen Franzosen*, "German Frenchmen."

51. *WA, Tischreden*, vol. 4 (1916), 669. Note the analogy that he suggests between *Epicurismus* from Italy and the impact of Turkey on Germany. On images of the Turks in the context of the Reformation, see Carl Göllner, *Tvrcica*, vol. 3: *Die Türkenfrage in der öffentlichen Meinung Europas im 16. Jahrhundert* (Baden-Baden: Valentin Koerner, 1978), 173–215.

52. *WA, Tischreden*, vol. 4 (1916), 669: "Wir mussen Loth sein, cuius anima cruciabatur dies ac noctes a Sodomitis." See also Luther, "Vom Kriege wider die Türken," 142 (ironically): "welch ein öffentliche herrliche Sodoma die Türckey sey" (what a public and wonderful Sodom is Turkey).

53. Luther, "Wider Hans Worst," 549: "das nu auch Welsche sitten sich in Deudschen landen beginnen zu pflantzen."

54. Luther, "Auslegung des 101. Psalms" (1534–35), 262: "Es reissen jtzt auch Welsche tugent jnn Deudsch land (sonnderlich jnn Regimenten). Niemand sihets, niemand wehrets, darnach wenn wirs nicht mehr leiden wollen und gern gesteuret hetten, so werden die rauppen jnn allen blettern sitzen, und wird heissen, zu lange geschlaffen" (Currently, Italian virtues catch on in Germany, especially among rulers. Nobody notices it, nobody fends it off. By the time we do not want to suffer this anymore and would have liked to control it, the caterpillars will populate all the leaves. One will say, slept too long). See also 236: "Das haben herein bracht die Curtisanen und Lands knechte, wie sie es zu Rom und im Welschen lande gesehen und gelernt haben. Mit dem selben Welschen regiment werden auch die Welschen plagen und unglück komen. So ist es denn aus mit Deudsch land und wird Fuit heissen" (Courtiers and mercenaries have imported what they have seen and learned in Rome and Italy. 'Italian' rules will bring Italian plagues and disaster [over Germany]. Then, Germany will be finished and one will [have to] say: over and done with).

55. WA, Tischreden, vol. 4 (1916), 669; Luther, "Vom Kriege wider die Türken," 142.

56. Hemmerli, De matrimonio, 200vb: "Dicuntur autem macarelli sive busurones viri sodomitae contra naturam peccantes in Italica lingua quoniam propter criminis enormitatem hoc nephas horrendum in nostro latino non habet proprium vocabulum sed accomodatum: licet sit antiquissimum." To make doubly sure his readers understood, Hemmerli added a Biblical (Gn 37:2) and a legal (Justinian's law code) reference to sodomy.

57. See Luther, "Warnung an seine lieben Deutschen," 303: "die Bepstlichen und Cardinalisschen keuscheit und heisst auff Welsch Puseronen, nemlich die Sodomitische und Gomorrische keuscheit" (the chastity of popes and cardinals which in Italian is called Puseronen, namely, the chastity of Sodom and Gomorrah).

58. Vocabolario della lingua italiana, vol. 3 (Rome: Istituto della Enciclopedia italiana, 1989), 2. See also Salvatore Battaglia, ed., Grande dizionario della lingua italiana, vol. 9 (Turin: Unione tipografico-editrice torinese, 1997), 347, s.v. maccherèlla; which is explained as ruffiana. See also Charles Du Fresne Du Cange, Glossarium mediae et infimae latinitatis, vol. 4 (Paris: Didot, 1845), 269. Macarelli is related to the French maquerel, maquereller, maquellerie (maquerelie) (procurer, to prostitute onself, procuration). Etymologically, it is not a Romance word. Ironically the French terms are linguistic imports from a Germanic language, the middle Dutch makelâre, "courtier." See Paul Robert, ed., Le Grand Robert de la langue Française (Paris: Le Robert, 1985), 6:236; Altfranzösisches Wörterbuch, ed. Adolf Tobler and Erhard Lommatzsch, vol. 5 (Wiesbaden: Franz Steiner, 1963), col. 1104–5; Dictionnaire de l'anciennce langue française et de tous les dialectes du IXe au XVe siècle, ed. Frédéric Godefroy (1888; New York: Kraus Reprint, 1961), 5:159; Dictionnaire de la langue française du seizième siècle, ed. Edmond Huguet (1934; Paris: Didier, 1961), 5:136. A sixteenth-century reader of the 1535 edition of De matrimonio at Basel's university library picked up on the manifold ways that Hemmerli calls attention to the words for sodomite in his text. In a copy of the print that is hardly marked, he not only underlined the vituperative remarks, but also rewrote in his own hand the gloss "Macarelli vt Busurones" on top of the column.

59. WA, Tischreden, vol. 3 (1914), 630–31 (1538): "Nuptiae Italicae . . . nulla materna lingua in Germania de illo scelere Dei gratia aliquid novit."

60. "Wider das Papsttum," in WA, vol. 54 (1928), 211ff, esp. 274.

61. Ibid., 218, 222, 224, 227.

62. "Warnung an seine lieben Deutschen" (1531), in *WA*, vol. 30.3 (1910), 303. See above for quotation.

63. On Fischart, see also Mikhail M. Bakhtin, *Rabelais and His World* (Bloomington: Indiana University Press, 1984), 63–64.

64. On Della Casa, see chapter 7.

65. According to Lewis Richard Farnell, Kotytto was the name of a Thracian goddess "whose rites were notoriously obscene" and might have included the use of an artifical penis (*The Cults of the Greek States* [Oxford: Clarendon, 1909], 5:87).

66. On the weasel, see *Physiologus*, a late antique manual of animals widely used as a textbook in the German-speaking lands (Otto Seel, ed., *Der Physiologus* [Zurich: Artemis, 1960], 20–21).

67. Quoted in Pia Holenstein, *Der Ehediskurs der Renaissance in Fischarts "Geschichtklitterung"* (Bern: Peter Lang, 1991), 122–25.

68. Bakhtin, *Rabelais*, 110. R. Howard Bloch has recently argued that the French fabliaux seduce their audience into sexual pleasures by means of linguistic impropriety ("Modest Maids and Modified Nouns: Obscenity in the Fabliaux," in *Obscenity, Social Control, and Artistic Creation in the European Middle Ages*, ed. Jan M. Ziolkowski [Leiden: Brill, 1998], 293–307). In this sixteenth-century context, pleasure derives from invoking the obscene when refuting illicit sexuality.

69. Simon Roth, preface to *Ein Teutscher Dictionarius* (Augsburg: Michael Mayer, 1571). See also William Jervis Jones, *Sprachhelden und Sprachverderber: Dokumente zur Erforschung des Fremdwortpurismus im Deutschen (1478–1750)* (Berlin: de Gruyter, 1995).

70. Quoted in Michael Giesecke, *Der Buchdruck in der frühen Neuzeit* (Frankfurt am Main: Suhrkamp, 1991), 894: "Denn wir Deutschen tragen nu forthyn Welsche / Hispanische vnd Frantzosische kleidung / haben Welsche Cardinal / Frantzosische vnd Hispanische kranckheiten / auch Welsche practiken."

71. On this text and its dissemination, see Robert W. Scribner, "Luther's Anti-Roman Polemics and Popular Belief," *Luther-Jahrbuch* 57 (1990), 106–7.

72. For France, see Zorach, "The Matter of Italy," 589–90; Sozzi, "La polémique anti-italienne," 122; Winfried Schleiner, "Linguistic 'Xeno-Homophobia' in Sixteenth-Century France: A Page from Early Modern Gay Philology" (forthcoming).

73. "Ad librum eximii Magistri Nostri Magistri Ambrosii Catharini, defensoris Silvestri Prieratis acerrimi, reponsio" (1521), in *WA*, vol. 7 (1897), 718.

74. Luther, "Vorlesungen über 1. Mose von 1535–45," 55; "Auslegung des 101. Psalms," 236.

75. Luther, *WA, Tischreden*, vol. 4 (1916), 669: "Es will ein Epicurismus werden, der ist aus Italia komen et occupat bonam partem Germaniae."

76. Barbara A. Babcock, introduction to *The Reversible World: Symbolic Inversion in Art and Society*, ed. Barbara A. Babcock (Ithaca, N.Y.: Cornell University Press, 1978), 27.

77. McFarlane, *The Sodomite in Fiction and Satire*, 33–34.

78. In a cycle of woodcuts of 1521, the *Passional*, Lucas Cranach (1472–1553) developed these models into a highly successful iconography. He juxtaposed images of the debauched life of the pope, Christ's representative on earth but in fact the Antichrist, to images of the true Christ (David Kunzle, "World Upside Down: The Iconography of a European Broadsheet Type," in *The Reversible World*, ed. Babcock, 62; Scribner, "Luther's Anti-Roman Polemics," 99–103).

79. Luther, "Vom ehelichen Leben" (1522), in *WA*, vol. 10.2 (1907), 277: "sie nicht reyn bleyben und mit stummen sünden oder hurerey sich besuddeln müssen." See also 294; and Luther, *WA, Tischreden*, vol. 4 (1916), 408 (1539).

80. Luther, "Grund und Ursach, daß Klosterleben unchristlich sei" (1528/31), in *WA*, vol. 59 (1983), 100–101: "Das sye zu vnmuglicher keuscheyt vnd stummen sünden zwingen wider gottes geschöpfft vnd wort Gene. 1: 'Wachsset vnd meeret euch.'"

81. "Luther an Spalatin in Kolditz" (July 22 or 23, 1523), in *WA, Briefwechsel*, vol. 3 (1933), 115. See also Johannes Bugenhagen, *Von dem ehelichen stande der Bischoffe vnd Diaken / an Herrn Wolffgang Reyssenbusch / der Rechte Doctor vnd / Preceptor zu Lichtemberg Sant Anthonius ordens*, trans. Stephan Roth (Wittenberg: J. Klug, 1525), A3v.

82. See chapter 8 for a fuller exploration of Reformed ideas on sexuality and matrimony.

83. Luther, "Der Wiener Artikel wider Paulum Speratum" (1524), in *WA*, vol. 15 (1899), 132–33: "Es ist tausent mal besser . . . zu der ehe greyffen, denn teufflisch sundigen ym kloster (Es sey schon naturlich par und par, man mit weyb, wil geschweygen das man ynn den klöstern anfacht, ich weys nicht was, davon nicht zu reden ist), damit yhr gelub der keuscheyt viel schendlicher und schwerer zerbrochen wird."

84. Luther, *WA, Tischreden*, vol. 1 (1912), 464: "Wenn ich bey mir selbs bin, danck ich vnserm Herrn Gott pro vera agnitione nuptiarum, prasertim cum confero illud cum incesto coelibatu papistarum et abominandis nuptiis Italicis etc." Rendered also as: "gegen dem gottlosen, schändlichen, ehelosen Leben im Papstthum und gegen den gräulichen welschen Hochzeiten." See also 2:138–39.

85. "Vorlesungen über 1. Mose von 1535–45," in *WA*, vol. 43 (1912), 451: "[Matrimony] Est ergo divina coniunctio" (see the reference to the devil's "vagas libidines et infanda scelera Sodomitica" in this context [452]).

86. "Vermahnung an die Geistlichen" (1530), in *WA*, vol. 30.2 (1909), 337: "Römische Sodoma, Wellsche hochzeit, Venedische und Türckische breute und Florentzische breutgam."

87. Scribner, *For the Sake*, 37–58; Scribner, "Luther's Anti-Roman Polemics"; Peter Matheson, *The Rhetoric of the Reformation* (Edinburgh: Clark, 1998), 125.

88. Luther, "Ad librum eximii Magistri Nostri Ambrosii Catharini," 742.

89. Hans Dieter Rauh, *Das Bild des Antichrist im Mittelalter: Von Tyconius zum deutschen Symbolismus* (Münster: Aschendorff, 1973).

90. Heiko Oberman, "Hus und Luther: Der Antichrist und die zweite reformatorische Entdeckung," in *Jan Hus: Zwischen Zeiten, Völkern, Konfessionen*, ed. Ferdinand Seibt (Munich: Oldenbourg, 1997), 319–46. See also Fudge, *Magnificent Ride*; Dinshaw, *Getting Medieval*, 63.

91. *WA, Tischreden*, vol. 4 (1916), 290. Another manuscript has *puserones* instead of *pusiones*.

92. Ibid. According to Luther, Pope Leo X later revoked the statute (which may explain to the contemporary reader why it cannot be located).

93. *WA*, vol. 54 (1928), 227–28: "der Sodomiten Bapst." See also "Warnung an seine lieben Deutschen" (1531), in *WA*, vol. 30.3 (1910), 304.

94. *WA*, vol. 54 (1928), 213: "Römische Bubenschule"; and "seine Bubenschule, Huren- und Hermaphroditen" (233). *Bube* denotes both "knave" and "boy" in this period. As a rule, Luther uses *knabe* for the latter. Contextually, the first translation is appropriate (see above for further examples in which *bube* means "knave").

95. *WA*, vol. 7 (1897), 718 (1521).

96. The link between sodomite and usurer in the above quote, for example, was common in late medieval pastoral theology. See chapters 2 and 3 for the connection between sodomy and tyranny in the context of charges against the Burgundians.

97. For example, *WA*, vol. 54 (1928), 224. See also *WA*, vol. 30.3 (1910), 303; and Matheson, *Rhetoric of the Reformation*, 122.

98. See "Vom ehelichen Leben" (1522), in *WA*, vol. 10.2 (1907), 276; "Vorlesung über den 1. Brief des Johannes" (1527), in *WA*, vol. 20 (1898), 664: "Abstinete ergo a fornicatione, adulterio, Sodomitica pollutione" (Therefore abstain from fornication, adultery, sodomitical pollution) (see also context); "In epistolam S. Pauli ad Galatas Commentarius ex praelectione D. Martini Lutheri collectus" (1535), in *WA*, vol. 40.1 (1911), 68–69, 246. See above for more examples.

99. "Von den Schlüsseln" (1530), in *WA*, vol. 30.2 (1909), 461: "Cortisanen, officiale, Sodomiten, Puseronen und dergleichen"; "Artikel wider die ganze Satanschule und alle Pforten der Hölle" (1530), in *WA*, vol. 30.2 (1909), 422, 426.

100. This structure need not surprise us since it echoes features of handbooks of penance, which were themselves informed by Church dogma (chapter 3).

101. See Goertz, *Pfaffenhaß und groß Geschrei*, passim, esp. 84–90, 114–18, 184, 247; Geoffrey Dipple, *Antifraternalism and Anticlericalism in the German Reformation* (Brookfield, Vt.: Ashgate, 1996); Peter A. Dykema and Heiko A. Oberman, eds., *Anticlericalism*.

102. Martin Luther, *Offenbarung des Endtchrists* (Wittenberg: n.p., 1524); [Lactantius Fabricius?], *Ware Abcontereytung vnnd vergleichung des Bapstumbs / Mit andern grössesten Ketzereien* (n.p., n.d. [after 1546]), e1v.

Chapter Seven

1. Hans-Joachim Köhler, *Bibliographie der Flugschriften des 16. Jahrhunderts*, part 1: *Das frühe 16. Jahrhundert (1501–1530)*, 2 vols. (Tübingen: Bibliotheca Academica, 1991); Mark U. Edwards, Jr., *Luther's Last Battles: Poltitics and Polemics, 1531–46* (Ithaca, N.Y.: Cornell University Press, 1983); Johannes Schwitalla, *Deutsche Flugschriften 1460–1525: Textsortengeschichtliche Studien* (Tübingen: Niemeyer, 1983); Hans-Joachim Köhler, "Die Flugschriften der frühen Neuzeit: Ein Überblick," in *Die Erforschung der Buch- und Bibliotheksgeschichte in Deutschland*, ed. Werner Arnold et al. (Wiesbaden: Harrassowitz, 1987), 307–45; Miriam Usher Chrisman, *Conflicting Visions of Reform: German Lay Propaganda Pamphlets, 1519–1530* (Atlantic Highlands, N.J.: Humanities Press, 1996); Johannes Schwitalla, *Flugschrift* (Tübingen: Niemeyer, 1999).

2. Steven Ozment, "The Social History of the Reformation," in *Flugschriften als Massenmedium der Reformationszeit*, ed. Hans-Joachim Köhler (Stuttgart: Klett-Cotta, 1981), 177.

3. Hans-Joachim Köhler, "Erste Schritte zu einem Meinungsprofil der frühen Reformationszeit," in *Martin Luther: Probleme seiner Zeit*, ed. Volker Press and Dieter Stievermann (Stuttgart: Klett-Cotta, 1986), 244–81, esp. 249–51. According to Frédéric Hartweg, 150 publications in German were printed in 1518, a figure that rose to 990 for the year 1524 ("Die Rolle des Buchdrucks für die frühneuhochdeutsche Sprachgeschichte," in *Sprachgeschichte: Ein Handbuch zur Geschichte der deutschen Sprache und ihrer Erforschung*, vol. 2, ed. Werner Besch, Oskar Reichmann, and Stefan Sonderegger [Berlin: de Gruyter, 1985], 1420).

4. Schwitalla, *Deutsche Flugschriften*, 17; Robert W. Scribner, "Flugblatt und Analpha-betentum: Wie kam der gemeine Mann zu reformatorischen Ideen?" in *Flugschriften als Massenmedium der Reformationszeit*, ed. Hans-Joachim Köhler, 65–76; Scribner, *Popular Culture*, 54–62.

5. See the notable exception of Walter, *Unkeuschheit und Werk der Liebe*, 129–30, 139–40. There are mentions in passing with regard to Protestant ideology in general in Lyndal Roper, "Was There a Crisis in Gender Relations in Sixteenth-Century Germany?" in *Oedipus and the Devil*, 43–44; and Schleiner, "That Matter," 48. Quotes with references to sodomy appear in the following studies (although the authors do not comment): Edwards, *Luther's Last Battles*, 4; Goertz, *Pfaffenhaß und groß Geschrei*, 82; Stadtwald, *Roman Popes and German Patriots*, 189.

6. Scribner, *For the Sake*, 94.

7. Schleiner, "That Matter," 67.

8. Benedict Anderson, *Imagined Communities: Reflections on the Origin and Spread of Nationalism*, rev. ed. (London: Verso, 1991).

9. Goertz, *Pfaffenhaß und groß Geschrei*, 247.

10. Scribner, "Luther's Anti-Roman Polemics," 95. See also Birgit Stolt, *Wortkampf: Frühneuhochdeutsche Beispiele zur rhetorischen Praxis* (Frankfurt am Main: Athenäum, 1974).

11. Martin Luther, "Wider das Papsttum zu Rom, vom Teufel gestiftet" (1545), in *WA*, vol. 54 (1928), 287. See also 54:214–15, 218, 221, 223, 274: "Sanct Paula tertius," "S. Paula tertius fraw Bepstin," "Paula tertius," "Sanct Paula," "die heilige Jungfraw," "der schalck Paula" (with reference to *pederastey* on the same page).

12. "Wider das Papsttum," 287: "Hermaphroditae, Androgyni, Cynedi, Pedicones et similia Monstra in natura." See also *Against the Roman Papacy, an Institution of the Devil, 1545*, trans. Eric W. Gritsch, in *Luther's Works*, ed. Helmut T. Lehmann, vol. 41 (St. Louis, Mo.: Concordia, 1966), 257–376: "hermaphrodites, androgynites, cynoideans, pedicones, and similar monsters in nature" (362). This translation renders the original almost illegible despite a footnote explaining the terms as a "list of sexual perverts." See also Luther, "Wider das Papsttum," 222: "da sind des Römischen stuels Cardinel und gsind, Hermaphroditen, a parte ante viri, a parte post mulieres" (There they are, the Holy See's cardinals and riff-raff: hermaphrodites, from the front men, from behind women).

13. Ibid., 287. Most other Latin parts are quotations; see 215, 240–41, 243, 258, 264, 274–75, 279.

14. See Alain Boureau, *The Myth of Pope Joan* (Chicago: University of Chicago Press, 2001).

15. "Wider das Papsttum," 218: "lassen uns in jren hindern sehen, das wir sie kennen mügen." See also 212, and this treatise's counterimage of Christ as the true head of the Church (243 and passim).

16. Goldberg, *Sodometries*, 4.

17. Matheson, *Rhetoric of the Reformation*, 199, 202.

18. Stadtwald, *Roman Popes and German Patriots*, 25, 195.

19. Edwards, *Luther's Last Battles*, 185.

20. Matheson, *Rhetoric of the Reformation*, 212, 214.

21. Ibid., 212, 183, 196.

22. Matheson's use of the term propaganda is characterized by a certain ambivalence. Having first criticized its usage, he adopts the term later in his study, though not without reservation. Following Miriam Chrisman ("From Polemic to Propaganda: The

Development of Mass Persuasion in the Late Sixteenth Century," *Archive for Reformation History* 73 [1982]: 175–95), Matheson detects a transition from polemic to propaganda in the mid-sixteenth century. This is the change at stake in his discussion of Luther's treatise.

23. In Luther's writings, once the pope is identified as the Antichrist, he musters the starkest sexual imagery. See Martin Luther, "Epitoma responsionis ad Martinum Luther (per Fratrem Silvestrum de Prierio). 1520," in *WA*, vol. 6 (1888), 328. At the end of his preface, Luther provides his reader with a list of people who populate the Holy See, including "ganymedes" (*cynaedi*).

24. See, for example, Martin Luther, "Condemnatio doctrinalis librorum Martini Lutheri per quosdam Magistros Nostros Lovanienses et Colonienses facta. Responsio Lutheriana ad eandem condemnationem. 1520," in *WA*, vol. 6 (1888), 193. In his response to doctrinal statements issued by the Universities of Leuven and Cologne, Luther satirically introduced the term *hermaphroditae* in commenting on the canon *Omnis utriusque sexus*, thereby ridiculing the canon without linking the term to the theologians and professors themselves.

25. See Martin Luther, "Epitoma responsionis" (1520), 329.

26. See *Drey ding findt man tzu Rhom* ([Leipzig: M. Landsberg, 1519]), A2r/v; Kunz von Oberndorff [Urbanus Rhegius?], *Dialogus ader eyn ghespreche / wieder Doctor Ecken Büchlein* ([Braunschweig: Hans Dorn, 1521]), B2v; Johann Römer, *Das ist der hochthuren Babel id est Confusio Pape* ([Strasbourg: Matthias Schürer Erben, 1521]), J3v; Martin Bucer, *Eyn schoner dialogus vnd gesprech* ([Wittenberg: Johann Rhau-Grünenberg, 1521]), A2r; Haug Marschalck, named Zoller, *Von dem weyt erschollen Namen Luther* (Strasbourg: [Erfurt: J. Loesfeld], 1523), a2v.

27. Ulrich von Hutten, *Eyn lustiger vnd nuczlicher Dialogus [Vadiscus, 1520]* (Strasbourg: B. Beck, 1544), d4v: "Darumb sagt auch der Vadiscus / daz drey ding zů Rom in gmeynem brauch seyen / Der wollust des fleyschs / überfluß der kleyder / vnd stoltz des gemůts. Erno. Fürwar seind die hefftig im brauch da / die vnkeüscheyt regiert aber sunderlich da / inn welcher sy stets neüwe schandtliche sünd erdencken / vnd die so sollichs alleyn der natur nach brauchen / verspotten / vnd beürisch heyssen."

28. Hutten, "Sendschreiben," in *Des teutschen Ritters*, 31–32: "weil sie nicht einmal eigentlich Männer sind, jene Zärtlinge, Venus- und Bacchussklaven, jene einzig dem Müßiggang, und der Unthätigkeit mehr als je ein Weib ergebene Gesellen, die jeder Männertugend bar."

29. Randolph Trumbach, "The Birth of the Queen: Sodomy and the Emergence of Gender Equality in Modern Culture, 1660–1750," in *Hidden from History*, ed. M. B. Duberman, Martha Vicinus, and George Chauncey, Jr. (New York: NAL Books, 1989), 129–40; Trumbach, "Erotic Fantasy and Male Libertinism in Enlightenment England," in *The Invention of Pornography*, ed. Lynn Hunt (New York: Zone Books, 1993), 253–82. See also his *Sex and the Gender Revolution*, vol. 1: *Heterosexuality and the Third Gender in Enlightenment London*.

30. See also contemporary voices that criticize the verbal venom spilled over issues of the Reform. Anton Zimmermann in *Vom vbeln der Eyde / so ynn offenlichen gerichten geschehen* ([Erfurt: J. Loersfeld], 1523), G3v, claims to quote a popular argument ("eyn gemeyne rede / vnther dem volck") that "the new priests and authors are biting, arrogant, sharp, and impatient" and therefore lead to discord ("Die newen prediger / vnd buchschrieber synt beyssig / hochfertig / spitzig vnd vngedultig / welche art vnd weiße vom geist Gottis nicht seyn moge nach kond / dan solche spitzige wort vnd schreiben / brengt nicht

mher dan auffrore vnd zwytracht"). Andreas Osiander expressed his reluctance to participate in verbal feuds. By laying bare the priests' unchristian attitude, Osiander hoped to win his readers for a more benign view of his own writings (Osiander, *Verantwortung des Nürmbergischen Catechismi / Wider den vngelerten zenckischen Sophisten / Hansen Mayr zu Jngelstat* [Nuremberg: L. Milchtaler, 1539], B2v).

31. Andreas Bodenstein, named Karlstadt, *Super coelibatu, monachatu et viduitate* (Wittenberg: Nikolaus Schirlentz, 1521), c2r/v. In the revised edition of the same year by the same title, he introduced no changes to this passage (D4v). Cf. Andreas Bodenstein, *Von gelubden vnterrichtung* (Wittenberg: [Nickel Schirlentz], 1521), E4r: "Item weyl solche grawsame sunde / die nit wol zu sagen seind / von Nonnen vnd Monichen beschehen. Die auch erger seind den gemeyne vnkeuscheit vnd ehepruch / vnd geschehen derhalben / das sie starcker natur vnd zu vnreynigkeit / vast woll geneygt. Wer es tausent mal besser / das sie sich verenderten / dann das sie solche grewliche sunde zu thuen benottigt werden" (Nuns and monks commit such horrendous sins—sins that cannot be expressed appropriately and are worse than common unchastity or adultery. These sins occur because they are of a strong nature and prone to impurity. It would be one thousand times better to change than to be moved to such a horrendous sin). See also Philipp Melanchthon, *Melanchthons Briefwechsel*, vol. T1: *Texte 1–254 (1514–1522)*, ed. Richard Wetzel (Stuttgart-Bad Cannstatt: Frommann Holzboog, 1991), 319–20 (end of July, 1521), 384–85 (November 21?, 1521); Martin Luther, "Luther an Melanchthon," in *WA, Briefwechsel*, vol. 2 (1931), 373–74 (August 3, 1521). Luther objected on theological grounds, arguing that Karlstadt's (Bodenstein's) reference to Onan was misleading. See also Stephen E. Buckwalter, *Die Priesterehe in Flugschriften der frühen Reformation* (Gütersloh: Gütersloher Verlagshaus, 1996), 79–112, esp. 84–93. Buckwalter argues that, despite theological differences, both Luther and Karlstadt arrived at similar conclusions regarding clerical celibacy. Moreover, Karlstadt's radicalism in this question helped Luther to transform his own position.

32. P. C. D. *Antwort. Auff den Sendbrieff / so H. S. . . . geschriben hatt* (n.p., n.d. [c. 1546]): "die Sodomitische Wålsche Apostlen" (A1v); "dein Sodomitisch Hailgthumb zů Rom / mit hülff jrer knaben / die sie zů Rom in kamern aufferzogen / vnd vns volgents für beyßschaff inn teutschland geschickt" (A2v); "ewer můtter die Rômisch Sodomitisch Hůr / vber alle straff vnd warnung / in jrem allerlåsterlichsten vnd vbertürckischen wandel nun ob XXVI Jaren verhart" (A2v); "eüwer Sodomittischer Persianer / der Bapst zů Rhom" (A2v); "[the papists with] jrem schandtlichen bracht vnd vnraines Sodomittisch leben" (A4v); "die Welschen Sodomiten" (B1r); "so die Sodomitischen laster in Teütschland bringen" (B3v); "Hie solt du wissen das es schendtlicher vnd vbler dann es die blůthůnd / ertzketzer / Abgôttische Sodomiten / die Romanisten / zů disem mordt / verwůstung vnnd zwang Teütscher nation / auch zů erhaltung jhres vbermåssigen prachts / vnd Persianischen waichen lebens / nit außgeben noch gepraucht werden kan / noch mag" (B4v). See also C2r, C4r/v, etc.

33. In "Ain schöner dialogus oder gesprech so ain prediger münch Bembus genant und ain burger Silenus mit ainander haben" (in *Satiren und Pasquille*, ed. Schade, vol. 3) a fool takes on that role. In an aside, he defames clerics as "sodomitical rascals" (*sodomitische[] bůbe[]*) (214). In "Ein wegsprech gen Regensburg" (in *Satiren und Pasquille*, ed. Schade, 3:159–95) it is a servant, Kůnz.

34. Ulrich von Hutten, *Clag und vormanung* ([Strasbourg: J. Schott], n.d.), c1v: "Was Hutten zů Rom gesehen hab"; Ulrich von Hutten, *Eyn lustiger vnd nuczlicher Dialogus*.

35. Civilius [Mathias Flaccius Illyricus?], *Ein freidige vermanung zu klarem vnd öffentlichem bekentnis Jhesu Christi* (n.p., 1550). Italy is constantly equated with *Sodoma*. Yet the treatise concludes by saying that the punishment for Italy will be even more severe, because the Italians act in contempt of God.

36. *Der Papisten handtbüchlein fleissig zu mercken* (n.p., 1546), esp. A2r.

37. [Lactantius Fabricius?], *Ware Abcontereytung*, g1r: "Wer dises nicht glauben wölt/ der beschawe eyn kleyne zeit / der vermeynten geystlichen Prelaten höfe vnd haußhaltung / so wirt es jnen die erfarung leren / wie schandtlich vnd vnflåtig sie / aber nicht alleyn mit weibern / sondern auch (vorab die Curtisanen vnd des Bapsts hofgesind) mit jren Pusuronen leben."

38. *Pasquillus: New Zeytung Vom Teuffel* (n.p., 1546), C2r, C4r, A2v: "ich bin ein freundt vnd liebhaber aller Abgötterey vnd falschen gottes dienst / Ja ich lieb vnd lob vor allen dingen falsche verfürersiche lere / lügen / mord / vnd vnzucht / Jnn sonderheit gefelt mir hertzlich wol der Sodomittisch grewel / der dann bey dir vnd deinen Cardinåln zu Rom vnd anderst wo gemein ist etc."

39. Alphonsus Aemilius Sebastus, *Pasquillus* (n.p., n.d.), B1v/B2r: "Pas. Ja weil ich zů Rom was / da lebt ich nach der Römer art vnnd brauch. Wiewol ich nichts minder allwegen / von dem schendtlichen laster der Sodomiterey / ain scheüch vnd grawen gehabt hab."

40. Ibid., C1r. The treatise was written in Latin, obviously to appeal to a more educated audience, but was translated into German afterward.

41. Ibid., C1r: "Jch wil auch nit melden / was sy für hůrerey / Ehbruch / vnd Sodomitische vnzucht treiben / welchs ja bey jnen kain schand mehr / so fast ist es inn ain gemain brauch bey yederman kommen" (I also do not want to tell about their committing fornication, adultery, and sodomy, which is not shameful among them so much so that it has become a common custom among everybody). Note a similar rhetorical move in Hieronymus Rauscher's *Ein nützliches gesprech eines Christlichen Fursten mit seynen Reten* ([Magdeburg: Christian Rödinger], n.d.), A4r: "they [the Catholic clerics] lead an indecent sodomitical life which it is a shame to tell" ("Auch neben dieser falschen lehre füren sie ein vnzuchtig Sodomitisch leben welches ein schand ist zu erzelen").

42. *Epistell des heyligen Bischoffs Hulderici czu Augspurg wyder die Constitution vnnd ansatzung. von der keuscheit und Enthaldung der priesterschaft* (n.p., [1521?]), A2r, B1r. This "historical" document was directed at the contemporary Church. (See chapter 8, n. 18, for more bibliographic information concerning this document.)

43. *Ein Christliche frage Simonis Reuters vonn Schlaytz / an alle Bischoffe / vnnd anndere geystliche auch zum teil weltliche regenten / Warumb sy doch: an priestern: vnnd andern geistlich geferbten leuten / den elichen standt nicht mügenn leyden* (n.p., 1523), A2v: "eebrecherey hůrerey vnd den Sodomitischen sundenn (welche alle auß gezwungener keuscheit zůhalten kummen)."

44. "Ein wegsprech gen Regenspurg zůins concilium," in *Satiren und Pasquille*, ed. Oskar Schade, 3:189.

45. [Martin Bucer], *Gesprech biechlin neüw Karsthans* ([Strasbourg: Matthias Schürer, 1521]), A4v, C1v. See also "Ein wegsprech" (in *Satiren und Pasquille*, ed. Schade, 3:159–95), in which two interlocutors comment on a whole procession of clerics on their way to a Church council.

46. Hutten, *Eyn lustiger vnd nuczlicher Dialogus*, f2v.

47. [Lactantius Fabricius?], *Ware Abcontereytung*, e1v, b4v: "Jst aber der Bapst mit seinen

genanten geystlichen Coelibat / vnd vnflåtigen keuschheyt / nicht eyn ertzmeyster aller Sodomei / Eebruchs / Hůrerei / vnd vnkeuschheyt?"

48. Erasmus Alberus, "Ein Te Deum laudamus von Bapst Paulo dem Dritten," in *Satiren und Pasquille*, ed. Schade, 1:45. On the meaning of *bube*, see my remark in chapter 6.

49. Hutten, *Eyn lustiger vnd nuczlicher Dialogus*, n2r: "Dise statt Rhom ist . . . ein vnerschöpffliche grůb alles übels vnnd jamers."

50. Hiob Gast, *Ein Trostpredige vnd Christenliche trewe vermanung* (Nuremberg: L. Milchtaler, 1540), B3v: "Der Babst aber sampt seinem Sodomitischen hoffgesinde."

51. *Newe zeytung auß Rom. Vom newen Babst Paulo / dem Vierdten dises namens / in disem M.D.LV. Jare erwelet* (n.p., 1555), A3v: "bey seinen zarten Jůnckerlein / vnnd geschmůrten Olgötzen; Römische vnzucht."

52. Adolf Diehl, ed., *Dionysius Dreytweins Esslingische Chronik (1548–1564)* (Tübingen: H. Laupp, 1901), 172: "Dasselb ein lange zeitt mitt ime gethreiben, nemlich geflorentzt, zulest dennselben knaben zu einem cardynall gemacht, das die burger sagtten, wan man in sach: 'Das ist die basts hur.'" This anecdote has strong resonances with Josef Nadler's tirades (see chapter 5), especially since the link to animals is also present here.

53. *Eine Schrifft Philip. Melanth. newlich latinisch gestellet / Wider den vnreinen Bapsts Celibat / vnd verbot der Priesterehe. Verdeudtscht durch Justum Jonam* (Wittenberg: J. Klug, 1541), C1r.

54. See Martin Luther, "Vermahnung an die Geistlichen" (1530), in *WA*, vol. 30.2 (1909), 337. Luther, "Warnung an seine lieben Deutschen" (1531), in *WA*, vol. 30.3 (1910), 303.

55. Martin Luther, "An die Herrn deutschs Orden, daß sie falsche Keuschheit meiden und zur rechten ehelichen Keuschheit greifen, Ermahnung" (1523), in *WA*, vol. 12 (1912), 232–44, esp. 237 (note the comparison with the sins of the Sodomites). See also *Ain Christenlicheslustigs gesprech / das besser . . . seye auß den Klöstern zůkommen / vnd Eelich zůwerden / dann darinnen zůbeleyben* (n.p., 1524).

56. See Hartmuth von Cronberg, *Drey Christliche schrift* (Wittenberg: M. Lotter, [1522]).

57. Luther, "Vom ehelichen Leben," in *WA*, vol. 10.2 (1907), 277, 294. An analysis strongly suggests that the two concepts are themselves gendered. Potentially, we are supposed to read that the mute sin is a male sin, whoring a female sin.

58. See n. 61 for the quotation. On Eberlin see Richard G. Cole, "Reformation Pamphlet and Communication Processes," in *Flugschriften als Massenmedium*, 148–49; Ozment, "Social History of the Reformation," 192–97.

59. In Eberlin's "Syben frumm aber trostloß pfaffen klagen ire not" (*Ausgewählte Schriften*, ed. Ludwig Enders, vol. 2 [Halle a.d. Saale: Max Niemeyer, 1900], 59–64, esp. 60–61), this nun's counterpart, an "authentic" Catholic priest from the cock's bishopric, speaks on sexual sins. Yet, whereas this protagonist becomes involved in manifold heterosexual transgressions, he only hears of masturbation and sodomy (*knabenschanden*) through an erudite monk's sermon. Though he thanks God for not having defiled himself in this way, nevertheless his fantasy is greatly stimulated by the sermon's words.

60. For the polemical campaign against the monastic ideal of chastity and the debate about clerical marriage in the context of the early Reformation, see chapter 8.

61. Johann Eberlin, *Ein klägliche klag an den christlichen Römischen Keyser* (n.p., [1521]), C3v; Johann Eberlin von Günzburg, "Der III. bundtgnoß: Ein vermanung aller christen das sie sich erbarmen vber die klosterfrawen," in *Ausgewählte Schriften*, vol. 1 (1896), 25: "[ein kind] sich mit schand vnd sünd eim nachgültigen stall knecht oder vych knecht

vnderwerffe, ja wo es do by blibe vnd nit ergers volgte der vngenanten sünd, auch mit bösen gaysten, wie laider jetz an vilen orten erfunden wirt." See also Eberlin, "Wie gar gfarlich sey. So ein Priester kein Eeweyb hat" (1523), in *Ausgewählte Schriften*, 2:34. If one were to assume that such practices were to take place between fellow nuns, the text resisted such an interpretation by portraying the convent as a place of mutual hatred rather than a spiritual community of women. In other writings, Eberlin again warned against the dangerous estate of nuns without hinting at this form of eroticism ("Eyn freundtlichs zuschreyben an alle stendt teutscher nation" [n.p., 1524]). Couples of monks and nuns populate Eberlin's polemical writings frequently; see, for example, "Die ander getreue Vermahnung," in *Ausgewählte Schriften*, vol. 3 (1902), 33, 36. For Eberlin and the evolution of his anticlerical crusade in the context of his reception of Protestant ideas, see the excellent study by Geoffrey Dipple, *Antifraternalism and Anticlericalism in the German Reformation*.

62. Johann Geiler von Kaisersberg, *Ain gaistliche bedeütung des Häßlins / wie man das in dem pfeffer bereyten sol* ([Strasbourg: J. Knoblauch, 1511]), e3v.

63. Thomas Stör, *Der Ehelich standt vonn got mit gebendeyung auffgeseczt* (n.p., 1524), A4v. For European languages and literatures other than German, see Judith Brown, *Immodest Acts: The Life of a Lesbian Nun in Renaissance Italy* (New York: Oxford University Press, 1986), 3–20; Claude J. Summers, "English Literature: Renaissance," in *The Gay and Lesbian Literary Heritage*, ed. Summers (New York: Henry Holt, 1995), 224; Guy Poirier, *L'homosexualité dans l'imaginaire de la Renaissance* (Paris: Champion, 1996), 122–23; Katharine Park, "The Rediscovery of the Clitoris: French Medicine and the Tribade, 1570–1620," in *The Body in Parts: Fantasies of Corporeality*, ed. David Hillman and Carla Mazzio (London: Routledge, 1997), 184–87.

64. The latter, in my reading, refers to notions around gender, matrimony, and hierarchy, whereas by "power" I mean people who hold office or influential positions.

65. Natalie Zemon Davis, "Women on Top," in *Society and Culture in Early Modern France* (Stanford, Calif.: Stanford University Press, 1975), 124–51; David Price, "When Women Would Rule: Reversal of Gender Hierarchy in Sixteenth-Century German Drama," *Daphnis* 20 (1991): 147–166.

66. See, for instance, one of the widely disseminated reform treatises from the mid-fifteenth century, the *Reformatio Sigismundi* (Heinrich Koller, ed., *Reformation Kaiser Sigismunds* [Stuttgart: A. Hiersemann, 1964]). See chapter 8 for more on this treatise.

67. See a letter by Wilhelm Nesen to Bruno Amerbach from 1518 about the same treatise: "O unspeakable times, O Rome, you haven for all manner of evil! Someone has finally arisen from the clique of zealots who has portrayed him a little more distinctly with his descriptions, than anyone who has reviled Julius, but with great respect, in a most Christian manner, and most ingeniously" (Alfred Hartmann and Beat Rudolph Jenny, eds., *Die Amerbachkorrespondenz*, vol. 2 [Basel: Verlag der Universitätsbibliothek, 1943], 118–19; translation quoted after Stadtwald, *Roman Popes and German Patriots*, 86).

68. "eruditissimus ille dialogus Julii et Petri . . . quandoquidem monstra romana Curiae non tam revelat ipse primus, quam confirmat jam diu ubique, heu, cognita . . ." (quoted from *Epistolae obscurorum virorum*, ed. Ernst Münch, 418).

69. A more thorough description can be found in Stadtwald, *Roman Popes and German Patriots*, 80–87.

70. *Von dem gewalt vnd haupt der kirchen / ein gesprech* (n.p., n.d.), A4v: "Jch scham michs zu sagen / vnd verdrüsst mich dy ich so gar kein teyl an deinem leib sihe / das nit mit

mercklichen zeichen einer erschrocklichen vnd schantlichen vnkeüscheit (nit zu nennen) befleckt ist."

71. I have used *Iulius. Dialogus viri cuiuspiam eruditissimi festiuus sane ac elegans* (n.p., n.d.). Also published as Erasmus von Rotterdam, "Dialogus, Iulius exclusus e coelis," in *Ausgewählte Schriften*, ed. Werner Welzig, vol. 5 (Darmstadt: Wissenschaftliche Buchgesellschaft, 1968), x–109 (Latin and modern German translation); Desiderius Erasmus, "Julius Excluded from Heaven," in *The Praise of Folly and Other Writings*, ed. Robert M. Adams (New York: Norton, 1989), 142–227.

72. Most recently, Jozef IJsewijn has argued convincingly against this widely held opinion, citing philological as well as ideological reasons (he concedes that Erasmus might have provided the piece's core content or that, if indeed Erasmus authored the piece, it was significantly changed during the printing process). See his "I rapporti tra Erasmo, l'umanesimo italiano, Roma e Giulio II," in *Erasmo, Venezia e la cultura padana nel '500,* ed. Achille Olivieri (Rovigo: Minelliana, 1995), 123–29. I will not delve into the discussion of the treatise's authorship since it is of little import for my discussion here. Whether Erasmus is the actual author or not, the contemporary rumor that he had penned this vicious attack on the papacy certainly helped its popularity (on this point see IJsewijn, "I rapporti tra Erasmo," 124).

73. *Von dem gewalt vnd haupt der kirchen / ein gesprech* (n.p., n.d.).

74. The title of *Dialogus vere elegans* is in fact very close to *Iulius. Dialogus . . . festiuus sane ac elegans*, an edition of *Julius exclusus*.

75. The Latin has *facetia*.

76. About this incident see Schleiner, "That Matter," 56; Anne Jacobson Schutte, *Pier Paolo Vergerio: The Making of an Italian Reformer* (Geneva: Droz, 1977), 190.

77. *Ein kleglich gesprech* (n.p., 1538), a4r: "die größten tyranney / das schendlichst laster / das man ye / ich sag nit thun / sonder erdencken möcht / für mein person scheme ich michs zu sagen / vnnd verwundert mich / warumb nit Got das fewer von himel herab sendet / vnnd brant"; *Dialogus vere elegans* (n.p., 1538), A4v: "facinus crudelißimum et scelus abominandum, quale nunquam non dico fieri, sed ne excogitari quidem debuisset, adeo ut me pudeat narrare, mirorque, cur Deus non ignem de coelo in illum exurendum iaculetur."

78. *Ein kleglich gesprech*, a4v: "Clemen. . . . Es ist ein laster uns allen preuchlich / ists nit war Leo? LEO Also wer es nit / villeicht wer ich ytzo nit dieser ort." *Dialogus*, a5r: "CLE. . . . uitium illud peculiare nobis omnibus est. Non ita est Leo? LEO. Vtinam non esset, forsan hic iam non adessem."

79. M. Luther, *Contra papatum Romanum, a diabolo inventum, D. Doct. Mar. Luth. E germa. latine redditum, per Iustum Ionam* (n.p., 1545); *Adversus papatum Romae a Sathana fundatum* (n.p., 1545).

80. Compare, for example, *Julius exclusus* and *Von dem gewalt vnd haupt der kirchen / ein gesprech*. Here, of course, the time lag needs to be taken into consideration. Whereas the Latin text was published after Julius's death in 1513, the German text was released in quite a different political and religious climate, at a time when the religious conflicts had become much more acute.

81. *Dialogus vere elegans et lepidus; Ein kleglich gesprech.*

82. *Adversus papatum; Contra papatum.* By contrast, a Latin pamphlet like the *Dialogus vere et elegans* was embedded in a more elaborate paratext than its German counterpart (*Ein kleglich gesprech*). In fact, the treatise's presentation used an erudite code, which was rare

with German polemical literature. Note the title, but also the publication's structure: a poem "To the reader" prefaces the actual dialogue in addition to two highly ambitious poems. Latin texts were likely to present factual elements more accurately. In *Dialogus*, the Popes Leo and Clement were introduced as the tenth and seventh of their name, while the German characterized them solely by their first names. While the Latin title claimed that the text was news from Bologna, the German said it was "sent from Italy."

83. For pre-Reformation examples, see, for example, Jean-Etienne Genequand, "Quelques 'Petites Annales bourguignonnes' à Genève," in *Publications du Centre d'Etudes burgundo-médianes* 14 (1972), 51; Malachias Tschamser, *Annales oder Jahrs-Geschichten der Baarfüseren*, ed. A. Merklen (Colmar: n.p., 1864), 1:723 (1511).

84. See *Vrsprung vnd Vrsach diser Auffrur / Teutscher Nation* (n.p., n.d.), title iullustration; *Ratschlag eins ausschus etlicher Cardinel* (Wittenberg: Hans Luft, 1538), D4v; Michael Höfer, *Wes man sich in disen gefehrlichen zeyten halten / vnd wie man dem zorn Gottes . . . zuuorkommen soll* (Nuremberg: J. v. Berg/U. Neuber, 1546), B4v; Georg Major, *Ewiger Göttlicher / Allmechtiger Maiestat Declaration* (n.p., n.d.), D1r/v. For images of destruction, see also "Ein wegsprech," in *Satiren und Pasquille*, ed. Schade, 3:189; and this pamphlet's later edition, "Der Huren-wirt," in *Satiren und Pasquille*, ed. Schade, 3:286; "Ain schöner dialogus oder gesprech," in *Satiren und Pasquille*, ed. Schade, 3:214. In the late Middle Ages, knowledge about the five destroyed cities was available, for instance, through John Mandeville's widely popular *Voyages and Travels*. There, readers found a description of the Dead Sea's "impure" waters and the ruins reminding people of God's wrath.

85. Paul A. Russell, *Lay Theology in the Reformation: Popular Pamphleteers in Southwest Germany 1521–1525* (Cambridge: Cambridge University Press, 1986).

86. [title page not preserved], HAB Wf 435.9 Theol. (44), a2r. Unlike the inhabitants of Sodom, Germans have the Bible's account of Sodom's destruction. If they do not repent, they therefore will be punished more severely.

87. W. Linck, *Ein schöne Christliche Sermon von dem außgang der kinder Gottes auß des Antichrists gefengknüß* (n.p., 1524), D1r: "außgang auß Zodoma." See also C1v, D1r–D2r, D3v–D4r. The exodus from Sodom precedes the whole community's entry into matrimony, presented here as pure (as opposed to defiled) and orderly (as opposed to disorderly). This argument has a long and venerable pedigree leading back to Apc 11:8. See Denis the Carthusian, "De laude et commendatione vitae solitariae," in *Opera omnia*, vol. 38 (1909), 326.

88. Linck, *Ein schöne Christliche Sermon*, D4r: "zodomitische[] stummende[] sünden" (sodomitical mute sins); D1v: "zodomitische[] vnreinigkeit / welche ein sonderliche frucht ist der abgötterey" (sodomitical impurity which comes from idolatry). See also my earlier point that pastoral discourse minimized sexual and defamatory explicitness.

89. Martin Luther, *WA, Briefwechsel*, vol. 11, no. 4139 (July 28, 1545) (Weimar: Böhlau, 1948), 148–52. A thorough account of the proximity between polemic and apocalyptic visions of the end of time is found in Edwards, *Luther's Last Battles*, 97–114. "To leave Sodom" is a more frequently used standard expression among Reformers, alluding to Gn 14:8, 17. See Andreas Osiander, "Brief an Johannes Brenz" (1533), in *Gesamtausgabe*, ed. Gerhard Müller and Gottfried Seebaß, vol. 10 (Gütersloh: Gütersloher Verlagshaus, 1997), 906 (here referring to Nuremberg).

90. See Joseph Grünbeck, *Spiegel der naturlichen himlischen vnd prophetischen sehnungen aller trubsalen* (Leipzig: W. Stöckel, 1522).

91. *Vom Ende der Welt* (Frankfurt am Main: H. Gülfferich, n.d.), F1v: "Die Christen

werden also vermessen / Das sie vnzemlicher ding beginnen / Vnd auff die stummen sund sinnen"; "Die wider natur vnkeuscheit treiben" (B4r).

92. Schrot, *Apocalipsis* (n.p., n.d.), A4r: "Du hast zůRom vnd anderstwa / Jn teütsch vnd welschen landen da. [/] So Sodomisch gelebet . . . Drumb hat dich gstirtzet Gott der Her" (You [pope] have lived in Rome and elsewhere in German and Italian lands so sodomitically . . . This is why the Lord has brought you down).

93. Hans Virdung, *Practica von dem Entcrist* ([Speyer: J. Schmidt, 1523]), 7v.

94. See Leonhard Reynmann, *Practica vber die grossen vnd manigfeltigen Coniunction der Planeten* (Nuremberg: H. Hölzel, 1523).

95. Balthasar Wilhelm, *Practica oder Prenostication auff tzůkunfftig tzeythe / auss der heyligen schrifft getzogenn* (n.p., [1524]), A2r, B1v, B2v.

96. *Beclagung Tütscher Nation* ([Schlettstadt: Nikolaus Küffer, 1521] 1526), a3r/v: "glyßner / stalknecht / muldier tryber / eselknecht / roßhůter / kůhirten / katzenfaher / müßfallen macher / rattenfaher / kuchenbuben / mistfůrer / sprachhaußfeger / arßwischer / hůrer / froßen / schleckmyler / suffer / bůben / spiler / iunckfrawenschender / burger Zodome vnd Gomorre / die da got vorzyten mit dem dunder verderbt hat / vmb der grosse sünd willen / das sind vnser herren / vnser brôbst vnser dechet / lermeyster / vnser Custodes / vnser canonicen / vnser pfarhet / vnd vicarien." Cf. the Latin original, *Lamentationes Germanicae nationis.* See also Johann Eberlin von Günzburg. "Die ander getreue Vermahnung (1523)," in *Ausgewählte Schriften*, 3:34. In this passage, Eberlin outlined the future destruction of monasteries as a result of the horrible crimes committed in them. Hans Sachs, "Disputation zwischen einem chorherren und schuchmacher" (1524), in *Werke*, ed. Adelbert von Keller et al. (Hildesheim: Olms, 1964), 22:10.

97. See, for instance, Luther, "Epitoma responsionis," 329: "Nunc vale, infoelix, perdita et blasphema Roma" (Farewell, unhappy, lost, and blasphemous Rome). See also Luther's commentary on Dan 11:36 in *WA, Deutsche Bibel*, vol. 11.2 (Weimar: Böhlau, 1960), 179 annotation to *Frawenliebe*.

98. It would be a fascinating intellectual endeavor to study the polemical imagery developed south of the Alps and compare it to polemics north of the Alps, thus introducing a comparative angle into the study of slanderous imagery. See Ottavia Niccoli, *Prophecy and People in Renaissance Italy* (Princeton, N.J.: Princeton University Press, 1990), 131.

99. David N. Bagchi, *Luther's Earliest Opponents: Catholic Controversialists, 1518–1525* (Minneapolis, Minn.: Fortress Press, 1991).

100. A brief reference in *Iohanens Fisher, Sacri sacerdotii defensio contra Lutherum (1525)*, ed. Hermann Klein Schmeink (Münster: Aschendorff, 1925), 26. In a letter, Nikolaus Ellenbog (1481–1543), an erudite monk, compared the departure of nuns from a women's monastery to the Exodus of Lot from Sodom who, like these nuns, stayed pure of the Sodomites' vice (*Nikolaus Ellenbog, Briefwechsel*, ed. Andreas Bigelmair and Friedrich Zoepfl [Münster: Aschendorff, 1938], 297–98 [July 25, 1531]).

101. Georg Witzel, *Von der Christlichen Kyrchen: wider Jodocum Koch / der sich nennet / Justum Jonam* (Leipzig: N. Schmidt, 1540), B1r, B3v, D3r, F4v, V2r. A similar stance is expressed by Thomas Murner, see *Thomas Murner im Schweizer Glaubenskampf*, ed. Wolfgang Pfeiffer-Belli (Münster: Aschendorff, 1939), 2, 20, 32, 70, etc. See also Witzel's "Antwort auf Martin Luthers letzt bekenete artickel, unsere gantze religion und das concili belangend" of 1538 in *Drei Schriften gegen Luthers Schmalkaldische Artikel von Cochläus, Witzel und Hoffmeister*, ed. Hans Volz (Münster: Aschendorff, 1932), 108–9. As a married priest, Witzel took

an intermediate position. He criticized Luther for doing away with virginity. At the same time, he disapproved of Catholicism's rigidity toward married clergy, in contrast to their leniency with whorers and sodomites: "Sind scheflin gegen allerley fornicarien, Sodomiten etc. und lewen gegen die conjugaten" (They are lambs against fornicators, sodomites, etc. and lions against the married).

102. Alfeld, *Wyder den Wittenbergischen*, 32. See also Walter, *Unkeuschheit und Werk der Liebe*, 135–36.

103. Anton Engelbrecht *"Abconterfeyung Martin Butzers"* (*1546*), ed. Werner Bellardi (Münster: Aschendorff, 1974), 72–73, 82–83.

104. See, for instance, "Aufzeichnungen eines Basler Karthäusers aus der Reformationszeit 1522–1532," in *Basler Chroniken*, vol. 1, ed. Wilhelm Vischer and Alfred Stern (Leipzig: S. Hirzel, 1872), 427–89; "Die anonyme Chronik aus der Reformationszeit," in *Basler Chroniken*, vol. 7, ed. August Bernoulli (Leipzig: S. Hirzel, 1915), 272–74.

105. Conrad Wimpina, Johann Mensing, Wolfgang Redorffer, and Rupert Elgersima, *Gegen die bekanntnus Martini Luthers auff den yetzigen angestellten Reychßtag zů Augspurg* ([Leipzig: V. Schumann, 1530]); *Bericht: Welches die rechte wahre vnnd allgemain Kirchen Gottes sey / ausser welcher niemand die Seligkait erlangen kan* (Wien: n.p., 1560).

106. Simon Lemnius, *Monachopornomachia*, in *Lemnius und Luther: Studien und Texte zur Nachwirkung ihres Konflikts* (*1538/39*), ed. Lothar Mundt (Bern: Peter Lang, 1983), 2:257–315. Lemnius was intimately familiar with Protestant strategies of defamation. A Swiss by birth, he had become a promising student of Philipp Melanchthon in Wittenberg in the early 1530s. He angered Luther by publishing a volume of slanderous Latin epigrams that the Reformer understood, not altogether wrongly, as targeting himself. Subsequently, he had to flee in order to avoid prosecution—another example of how seriously the powerful took defamation. For other Catholic writers and the context of this conflict, see Mundt, *Lemnius und Luther*, 1:45–56, 1:105–40.

107. Luther, "Wider das Papsttum," 200–201. See also Edwards, *Luther's Last Battles*, 163–64.

108. Quoted in *Luthers Briefwechsel* (Weimar: Böhlau, 1935), no. 4139, 152. For Catholic critiques of Luther's polemical form of argumentation, see Edwards, *Luther's Last Battles*, 30, 44–67.

109. Matheson, *Rhetoric of the Reformation*, 200. With reference to a study by Miriam Chrisman ("From Polemic to Propaganda"), Matheson develops a similar chronological framework.

110. Hans Sachs, "Eyn gesprech eynes evangelischen Christen mit einem Lutherischen" (1524), in *Werke*, 22:79: "Die Lutherischen können nichts, dann die gaistlichen schmähen, . . . wie kann dann etwas guts hindter in und irer leer stecken?"

111. See Johann Eberlin von Günzburg, "Mich wundert, dass kein Geld im Land ist (1524)," in *Ausgewählte Schriften*, 3:161–70.

112. Michael Schilling, *Bildpublizistik der frühen Neuzeit: Aufgaben und Leistungen des illustrierten Flugblatts in Deutschland bis um 1700* (Tübingen: Niemeyer, 1990), 154–70, 201–45. Rudolf Hirsch, "Pre-Reformation Censorship of Printed Books," *Library Chronicle* 21 (1955): 100–105; Ulrich Eisenhardt, *Die kaiserliche Aufsicht über Buchdruck, Buchhandel und Presse im Heiligen Römischen Reich Deutscher Nation, 1496–1806* (Karlsruhe: C. F. Müller, 1970); G. Schmidt, *Libelli famosi*, 197–309. For a specific territory, see Esther-Beate Körber, *Öffentlichkeiten der Frühen Neuzeit: Teilnehmer, Formen, Institutionen und Entscheidungen öffentlicher Kommunikation im Herzogtum Preußen von 1525 bis 1618* (Berlin: de Gruyter, 1998), 352–58.

Künast, "Getruckt zu Augsburg," 200–216; Arnd Müller, "Die Zensurpolitik der Reichsstadt Nürnberg," Mitteilungen des Vereins für Geschichte der Stadt Nürnberg 49 (1949): 82–85.

113. Sigismund Cephalus [?], Warer Grundt vnnd beweisung / das die vnrecht handlen / die jren Predigern verbieten / das Antichristisch Bapstumb mit seinen greweln zustraffen (Magdeburg: Christian Rödinger, 1551), E4r, A2v, B4v. See also Georg Major, Ewiger Göttlicher Allmechtiger Maiestat Declaration (n.p., n.d.), D1v; Joachim Mörlin, Von dem Beruff der Prediger (Eisleben: U. Gaubisch, 1555).

114. Hans Sachs presented his critique of the papacy in the form of a chronicle, authenticated by various historical sources. See Hans Sachs, "Johannes, der 12 bapst des namens, mit seinem gottlosen leben und endte" (1558), in Werke, vol. 8, 648–51. See also Hans Wilhelm Kirchhof, Wendunmuth, ed. Hermann Österley (Stuttgart: H. Laupp, 1869), 1:449 ("Von der römischen keuschheit"); Theodor Zwinger, Theatri Humani Vitae Volumen Quintum (Basel: Henricpetri, 1604), 2:2303.

115. Coryat's Crudities (Glasgow: J. MacLehose, 1905), 2:109. On Della Casa, see Giovanni della Casa's Poem Book "Ioannis Casae Carminum Liber," ed. John B. Van Sickle (Tempe, Ariz.: Arizona Center for Medieval and Renaissance Studies, 1999), 1–27.

116. Coryat's Crudities, 2:110. Coryat does not state whether he had been familiar with the story prior to his visit in Zurich. Nor do we know whether he actively engaged the text by reading these highly artistic Italian verses. Heinrich (Henry) Bullinger clearly deemed the little book of poems one of the literary "monuments" through which he wanted to bond with a foreign traveler from another Protestant country.

117. Schleiner, "Burton's Use of praeteritio," 164.

118. Zedler, Universal-Lexikon, vol. 38, col. 328.

119. Giovanni Della Casa, Le terze rime (Usecht: J. Broedelet, 1726), 3–7. A partial English translation may be found in Schleiner, "Burton's Use of praeteritio," 165–66; Schleiner, "That Matter," 52–53. Antonio Santosuosso, The Bibliography of Giovanni della Casa: Books, Readers, and Critics 1537–1975 (Florence: L. S. Olschki, 1979), 30.

120. Another Italian poem by the title "In lode della pederastia" (In praise of pederasty), authored by Francesco Beccuti (il Coppetta) (1509–53), did not attract the attention that critics lavished on Della Casa's poem (Francesco Coppetta Becutti and Giovanni Guidiccioni, Rime, ed. E. Chiorboli [Bari: Laterza, 1912], 283–86). Beccuti refrained from contesting the condemnation of same-sex desire. Despite the title's lure, the poem is replete with double entendres, just like Della Casa's. Through the lens of a false eulogy, "the beautiful and noble art" ("questa bella e nobil arte") of a sexual practice against nature (pederasty) reveals its true nature, its lack of grace, immoderation, and antifeminism. Like another poem by the same author, Contro la pederastia (Against pederasty; Rime, 287–91), "In praise of pederasty" amounts to a personal invective in verse (the name of the addressee is mentioned in both poems).

121. Johannes Sleidan, Ioan. Sleidani, De Statu Religionis et reipublicae, Carolo Quinto, Caesare. Commentarii (1555), 362r. I used Sleidan, De statu religionis et reipublicae Carolo Quinto Caesare commentarii, ed. Johann Gottlob Boehm, vol. 3 (Frankfurt am Main: Varentrapp/Wenner, 1786), 154.

122. Conrad Gesner, Bibliotheca, ed. Georg Simler (Zurich: Christoph Froschauer, 1574), 335: "Ioannes de Casa, Romani pontificus legatus, scripsit catalogum haereticorum, cui respondit Vergerius. Praeterea impurissimus hic nebulo edidit poemata quaedam Italica in publicum Venetijs excusa, in quibus (proh scelus) Sodomiam laudibus extollit."

123. Holenstein, Der Ehediskurs der Renaissance, 122: "der Malevintisch Bischof de la

Casa." See chapter 6 for full treatment of this passage. According to Franco Mormando, Benevent was a region known for its proclivities to magic (*Preacher's Demons*, 68).

124. Goldberg, *Sodometries*, xv.

125. Nashe, "Summers Last Will and Testament," in *The Works of Thomas Nashe*, ed. Ronald B. McKerrow, vol. 3 (London: Bullen, 1905), 277–78.

126. Thomas Nashe, "The Praise of Red Herring," *Works of Thomas Nashe*, 177. For further evidence, see Schleiner, "Burton's Use of *praeteritio*," 164–67.

127. Christophorus Crusius, *Tractatvs de indiciis delictorum specialibus*, part 2 (Frankfurt am Main: Wolfgang Hoffmann, 1635), 152; Benedikt Carpzov, *Practica imperialis saxonicae rerum criminalium*, ed. Johann S. F. Böhmer (Frankfurt am Main: Franciscus Varentrapp, 1758), 229 (in the context of *quaestio 76, De poena Sodomiae*).

128. Gilles Ménage, *Anti-Baillet ou critique du livre de Mr. Baillet, intitulé "Jugement des savans"* (La Haye: Louis & Henry van Dole, 1690), vol. 2, 338, 355–82; Clarmund, *Vitae*, 7, 105–6, 108–11; Nikolaus H. Gundling, "Ioannes Casa an παιδεραςίασ [paiderasias] crimen defenderit," in *Observationes selectae ad rem litterariam spectantes*, 2d ed. (Halle: Renger, 1737), 1:120–36 (plus a copy of the poem on six additional pages). See also Gundling, "De Ioannis Casae monumentis latinis iudicium," in *Observationes*, 2:229–45; Pierre Bayle, *Dictionnaire historique et critique*, 5th ed. of 1740, vol. 4 (Geneva: Slatkine, 1995), s.v. Vergerius, 435–36. German translation in Pierre Bayle, *Historisches und Critisches Wörterbuch: Nach der neuesten Auflage von 1740 ins Deutsche übersetzt*, ed. Johann Christoph Gottsched, vol. 4 (Hildesheim: Olms, 1997), 440–47; Johann Georg Schelhorn, *Apologia pro Petro Paulo Vergerio Episcopo Ivstinopolitano adversus Ioannem Casam Archiepiscopum Beneventanvm accedvnt qvaedam monvmenta inedita* (Ulm: Lieberkühn, 1760), 32. This whole discussion has been excellently documented in Schleiner, "Burton's Use of *praeteritio*," 164–67; and Schleiner, "That Matter," 49–58. In the following, I have focused on the time and place where the invective originated.

129. In 1710 Adolf Clarmund (*Vitae clarissimorum in re literaria virorum*, part 9 [Wittenberg: C. G. Ludwig, 1710], 7) calls for a scholar traveling to Italy to get hold of the poem's edition and find out by way of textual criticism whether it was authored by Della Casa or not. Apparently, he had been writing about *Il forno* without having had access to a copy of it.

130. Pietro Paolo Vergerio, *Il catalogo de libri, li qvali nvovamente nel mese di maggio nell'anno presente M.D.XLVIIII. sono stati condannati, & scomunicati per heretici, Da M. Giouan. della Casa legato di Vinetia* (n.p., 1549). Other pamphlets by Vergerio repeated the slur, see, for instance, P. P. Vergerio, *A gl'inqvisitori che sono per l'Italia: Del catalogo di libri eretici, stampato in Roma nell'Anno presente* ([Tübingen], 1549), 14v; *Postremus catalogus haereticoum Romae conflatus, 1559* (Pforzheim: Corvinus, 1560), 8r/v. The 1549 index was edited by J. M. Bujanda, René Davignon, and Ela Stanek in *Index de Venise, 1549, et Milan, 1554* (Sherbrooke: Centre d'études de la Renaissance, 1987), 383–93. On the index, see Gottfried Buschbell, *Reformation und Inquisition in Italien um die Mitte des 16. Jahrhunderts* (Paderborn: Ferdinand Schöningh, 1910), 31–32; Paul F. Grendler, *The Roman Inquisition and the Venetian Press, 1540–1605* (Princeton, N.J.: Princeton University Press, 1977), 86–89. On Vergerio, see Friedrich Hubert, *Vergerios publizistische Thätigkeit nebst einer bibliographischen Übersicht* (Göttingen: Vandenhoeck & Ruprecht, 1893); A. Hauser, *Pietro Paolo Vergerios protestantische Zeit* (Ph.D. diss., University of Tübingen, 1980); Ugo Rozzo, ed., *Pier Paolo Vergerio il Giovane, un polemista attraverso l'Europa del Cinquecento* (Udine: Forum, 2000).

131. Vergerio, *Il catalogo* (n.p., 1549), k6r: "In alcuni uostri uersi, che sono stampati col uostro bel nome in cima, et . . . voi hauete tolto a celebrar le laudi, oime mi uergogno a dirlo, ma lo dirò pure, perciò che il mio Signore uuole, et mi sforzza, che io lo debba dire, et palescare quali siano gli suoi auersarij, Tolto hauete a celebrar (per gratia uostra) le laudi della Sodomia."

132. Ibid., k6r: "questa è cosa notoria in tutta la Italia."

133. Schutte, *Pier Paolo Vergerio*, 217.

134. Buschbell, *Reformation und Inquisition*, 103–54; Schutte, *Pier Paolo Vergerio*, 139–265. Both authors agree that the inquisition trial against Vergerio was fair and that it would be wrong to assume that Della Casa prosecuted the bishop as a personal enemy. For Vergerio's time as expatriate, see Frederic C. Church, *The Italian Reformers 1534–1564* (New York: Columbia University Press, 1932).

135. Hauser, *Vergerios protestantische Zeit*, 78.

136. Giovanni Della Casa, "Quaestio lepidissima an uxor sit ducenda," in *Prose*, ed. Arnaldo di Benedetto (Turin: Unione tipografico-editrice torinese, 1991), 53–139. See Detlef Roth, "'An uxor ducenda': Zur Geschichte eines Topos von der Antike bis zur Frühen Neuzeit," in *Geschlechterbeziehungen und Textfunktionen: Studien zu Eheschriften der Frühen Neuzeit*, ed. Rüdiger Schnell (Tübingen: Niemeyer, 1998), 171–232.

137. Della Casa, "Quaestio," 54.

138. Luther, "Vom ehelichen Leben" (1522), in *WA*, vol. 10.2 (1907), 292–94.

139. Martin Luther, "Vorrede," in Johann Freder, *Ein Dialogus dem Ehestand zu ehren geschrieben* (Wittenberg: Nickel Schirlentz, 1545), B1r/v.

140. Schutte, *Pier Paolo Vergerio*, 191.

141. Oswald Myconius to Heinrich Bullinger (December 2, 1549), StAZ, E II 336, 308: "Legatus quidam papalis scripsit Italice contra haereticos Germaniae interque alia per occasionem excusat peccatum Sodomae laudatque opus divinum adpellat." "Opus divinum" is a quote from *Il forno*: "questo mestier divino" (Della Casa, *La terze rime*, 4).

142. Oswald Myconius to Heinrich Bullinger (December 2, 1549), StAZ, E II 336, 308: "Obtura aures, oculos tantum sine percurrere, quod dicam."

143. Ibid.: "Praeterea placet audire, quod nunquam vel tu vel alius quispiam, credo, audivit unquam."

144. Joachim von Watt [Vadian], "Petrus Paulus Vergerius an Vadian: Basel 1550, Januar 20," in *Vadianische Briefsammlung*, vol. 6 (1908), 827.

145. Della Casa, "Dissertatio adversus Paullum Vergerium," in *Opere di Monsignor Giovanni della Casa* (Venice: Angiolo Pasinelli, 1752), 3:103–16; Della Casa, "Ad Germanos," in *Opere*, 1:295–97. Mario Richter, *Giovanni della Casa in Francia nel secolo XVI* (Roma: Edizione di storia e letterature, 1966), 46.

146. Catholic polemicists did not have to wait too long before an analogous literary scandal surfaced in the camp of the Protestants. Theodor de Bèze, the famous Calvinist theologian, was discovered to be the author of a poem on whether to love a woman or a man, cast in the tradition of Virgil's second Eclogue. See Schleiner, "That Matter," 47.

147. Buschbell, *Reformation und Inquisition*, 22–35.

148. Many post-1538 editions of Della Casa's poetry do not contain the poem in question, for example, *Rime, et prose di M. Giovanni della Casa* (Venice: Marc'Antonio Bonibelli, 1616). This omission might be due to an act of censorship by the author or his editors, though this is hard to prove. The 1752 edition of the *Opere* does not contain the poem in question. Significantly, the *Terze rime* were also disseminated in pamphlet

form from Holland, a popular printing place for literature considered obscene. See the preface to Giovanni Della Casa, *Le terze rime piacevoli* (Benevent: n.p., 1727), 1–6, which responds to the slurs against Della Casa. On the editions of *Rime piacevoli*, see Klaus Ley, *Giovanni della Casa (1503–1556) in der Kritik* (Heidelberg: Winter, 1984), 8–9.

149. Vergerio, *Postremus catalogvs*, 8r: "conscripsit eius mandatu primum . . . Catalogum." Vergerio wrongly makes this the first index altogether.

150. J. M. de Bujanda, *Index de Rome 1557, 1559, 1564: Les premiers index romains et l'index du Concile de Trente* (Sherbrooke: Centre d'études de la Renaissance, 1990), 770. The index is divided into authors whose writings were all prohibited and those authors who had produced certain prohibited texts. In addition, there were prohibited anonymous texts.

151. Vergerio, Letter to Heinrich Bullinger (May 16, 1559), StAZ, E II 356a, 707–8.

152. Vergerio, *Postremus catalogvs*, 8v: "Sentit enim Antichristus horribile illud atque abominabile scelus."

Chapter Eight

1. Goldberg, *Sodometries*, 16. The author quotes Bray's *Homosexuality in Renaissance England* as a reference for the second part of the statement.

2. See McFarlane, *The Sodomite in Fiction and Satire*, 33–34.

3. See Merry E. Wiesner, "Reassessing, Transforming, Complicating: Two Decades of Early Modern Women's History," in *Gender, Church, and State in Early Modern Germany* (London: Longman, 1998), 200–203.

4. Isabel Hull, *Sexuality, State, and Civil Society*, 30.

5. Richard van Dülmen, ed., *Kultur und Alltag in der Frühen Neuzeit* (Munich: Beck, 1990), 1:195 (my translation).

6. Scott, *Domination and the Arts of Resistance*, 138.

7. Hull, *Sexuality, State, and Civil Society*, 21.

8. On Catholic moral theology, see Pierre Hurteau, "Catholic Moral Discourse on Male Sodomy and Masturbation in the Seventeenth and Eighteenth Centuries," *Journal of the History of Sexuality* 4 (1993): 23.

9. This debate has been traced from a historical perspective by Marjorie Elizabeth Plummer, *Reforming the Family: Marriage, Gender and the Lutheran Household in Early Modern Germany, 1500–1620* (Ph.D. diss., University of Virginia, 1996), 30–180; and from a theological perspective by Stephen E. Buckwalter, *Die Priesterehe in Flugschriften der frühen Reformation* (Gütersloh: Gütersloher Verlagshaus, 1996).

10. Heinrich Koller, ed., *Reformation Kaiser Sigismunds* (Stuttgart: A. Hiersemann, 1964), 152: "Aber sehent an, was groß ubels teglich auffstat gegen weyben und dochtern, des mancher priester umb sein leyb kumen ist, welicher sich vor der werlt doch erberglichen treyt; so sein sye aber heimlich sodomiten, dye bestethentz. Sehent an, alle feintschafft zwyschen der priesterschafft und den weltlichen ist davon komen, und ist mer gotlicher teglich gesundet dann totlich, und umb das sol man einem yetlichem weltlichem priester erlauben und geben ein eekint zü weybe; dye sollen sich erberglichen und geystlichen halten und tragen, als hyenach stet, so verlesche alle feintschaft, dye zwyschen in und den leyen were." Translation from Gerald Strauss, *Manifestations of Discontent in Germany on the Eve of the Reformation* (Bloomington: Indiana University Press, 1971), 14–15. This passage is derivative of earlier texts and reform treatises; see Hermann Heimpel, "Reformatio Sigismundi, Priesterehe und Bernhard von Chartres," *Deutsches*

Archiv für Geschichte des Mittelalters 17 (1961): 526–37. References to sodomy were censored in the process of transmitting texts via manuscripts and prints. With few exceptions, the *Reformatio*'s redactors elided the original reference to "secret sodomites" among priests. One mid-fifteenth-century scribe rewrote the passage by keeping the reference to secrecy but cut out the allusion to sodomy—an intervention which left the passage almost unintelligible (Koller, 152 [K-version]). Yet the vulgate version, from which twelve manuscripts and all prints were disseminated after 1440, skipped the passage altogether. It cited only the command for priests to marry. Only one redactor of yet another branch, well-versed in theological questions, reinserted a reference to sodomy in the context of the *Reformatio*'s discussion of priestly celibacy (before 1449), independently from the original, though consonant with the original's intent. He quoted a short twelfth-century poem in defense of clerical marriage and against efforts by the church to enforce celibacy (Koller, 153, with commentary on 152). Yet by leaving the two-liner untranslated, he veiled the reference nevertheless.

11. Johann Eberlin von Günzburg, "Die ander getreue Vermahnung," in *Ausgewählte Schriften*, 3:36: "Dan wurden vil pfaffen auffhören müsickgenger sein vnnd huren iager. Aber wurden eheweyber nehmen, vnd handtwerck lernen, vnd sich neren, vnd üben, wie fromme mitburger vnnd mitchristenn zu stündt."

12. See chapter 7. See also Buckwalter, *Priesterehe*, 85–86, 101. Buckwalter argues that Melanchthon and Luther objected to Karlstadt's radicalization of their own critique of celibacy on exegetical grounds and because they took offense at his breach of sexual decorum ("Gewiß fanden Melanchthon und Luther Karlstadts Interpretation des Moloch-Opfers in Lev 18:21 und Lev 20:2–5 als Hinweis auf die sexuelle Selbstbefriedigung Anstoß erregend und exegetisch unhaltbar" [101]). Yet the *Epistola divi Hulderichi* and other texts familiar to the Reformers circulated similar images.

13. Martin Luther, "De votis monasticis" (1521), in *WA*, vol. 8 (1889), 564–669; Schleiner, "That Matter," 58.

14. Johann Eberlin, *Wie gfarlich sey: So ein Priester kein Eeweyb hat* (n.p., 1522), B2v: "als man yetzt leyder sicht / Hůrery / Eebruch / werck mit blůt verwunnten / ya Sodomi were / nymmer so gemeyn worden / wer das teuflisch verbot der Ehe nit auffgelegt worden / den Pfaffen / Mûnchen vnnd Nunnen." (see also *Ausgewählte Schriften*, 2:34).

15. *Eyn freüntlichs gesprech* (n.p., n.d.): "wôlt got daß wir weyber in Clôstern hetten / darmit ergers würd vermyden durch der stummenden sünd willen. Wie kann ain Münch oder Nunne keüsch sein / vnd wôllen wol essen vnd trincken darzů / vnd nit arbayten."

16. Hans Sachs, "Eyn gesprech von den scheinwercken der gaystlichen und iren gelübdten" (1524), *Werke*, 41: "[Hans] ob ir euch gleich der naturlichen werck enthalt, besudelt ir euch doch in andre unzimliche wege."

17. Martin Luther, "An die Herren deutsch Ordens" (1523), in *WA*, vol. 12 (1891), 237; "Predigten über das erste Buch Mose" (1523/24), in *WA*, vol. 14 (1895), 471; "Fastenpostille" (1525), in *WA*, vol. 17.2 (1927), 62; "Katechismuspredigten" (1528), in *WA*, vol. 30.1 (1910), 76; "Matth. 18–24 in Predigten ausgelegt" (1537–40), in *WA*, vol. 47 (1912), 321–22. See, for example, *WA*, vol. 10.2 (1907), 276–77, 294; vol. 14 (1895), 471; vol. 20 (1898), 664; vol. 30.2 (1909), 142, 191, 337; vol. 40.1 (1911), 246; vol. 42 (1911), 177–78; vol. 43 (1912), 57, 112, 451–52; vol. 46 (1912), 216–17; vol. 50 (1914), 640; vol. 51 (1914), 550; *Tischreden*, vol. 1 (1912), 464; *Tischreden*, vol. 4 (1916), 669.

18. *Epistell des heyligen Bischoffs Hulderici*, A2r, B1r. Published by Martin Luther as *Epistola divi Hulderichi Augustensis Episcopi, adversus constitutionem de Cleri Coelibatu, plane referens Apos-*

tolicon Spiritum (Wittenberg: [M. Lotter d.J.], 1520), based on a print of 1515. Other Protestant editions include two by Matthias Flacius Illyricus, *Epistola S. Hvlrici Episcopi* (Magdeburg: n.p., 1550); and *Des h. Hulrichs etwa vor sechshundert jaren Bischoffs zu Augspurg schrifft wider das ehelos leben der Priester* (Augsburg: n.p., 1553). An edition of the Latin original can be found in Frauenknecht, *Verteidigung der Priesterehe*, 203–15: "patrum scilicet uxores subagitare, masculorum ac pecudum amplexus non abhorrere" (205), and "ut neque adulteria, neque incestus neque masculorum, pro pudor! turpissimos amplexus . . . casta clericorum coniugia" (212). On interest in this treatise during the Reformation, see 194–202. In Eberlin's "Wie gar gfarlich sey. So ein Priester kein Eeweyb hat" (1523) (*Ausgewählte Schriften*, 2:34), the author cites "bishop Ulrich's epistle" as evidence for the fact that a pope invented the celibacy of priests against the letter of the Gospels— a practice that according to him leads to sexual illegitimacies of all kinds, including sodomy.

19. Bartholomäus Bernhardi, *Das die Priester Ee weyber nemen mögen vnd sollen* (n.p., 1522), A2v: "eyn yeder tragt den alten adam bey sich" (cf. *Apologia pro M. Bartolomeo praeposito qui uxorem in sacerdotio duxit*). See also Buckwalter, *Priesterehe*, 79–81, 94–98, 133–34.

20. Simon Reuter, *Ein Christliche frage*, A2v: "von eebrecherey hürerey vnd den Sodomitischen sundenn (welche alle auß gezwungener keuscheit zühalten kummen)."

21. Hans Sachs, "Historia: Paphnutius erhelt die pfaffen-ehe" (1562), in *Werke*, 15:501. In Catholicism, marriage is prohibited "against divine and natural law" (*Wider gott und natürlich recht*, 502).

22. Johannes Bugenhagen, *Von dem ehelichen stande der Bischoffe vnd Diaken / an Herrn Wolffgang Reyssenbusch / der Rechte Doctor vnd / Preceptor zu Lichtemberg Sant Anthonius ordens*, trans. Stephan Rodt (Wittenberg: J. Klug, 1525), A3v: "auss den banden des Antichristischen iochs erlöset / mit dem lieben Loth auss dem lande der Sodomer sich reyssen mügen."

23. See Susan Karant-Nunn, *The Reformation of Ritual: An Interpretation of Early Modern Germany* (London: Routledge, 1997).

24. Roderick Phillips, *Putting Asunder: A History of Divorce in Western Society* (Cambridge: Cambridge University Press, 1988), 44, quoting Heinrich Bullinger, *Fiftie Godlie and Learned Sermons, diuided into fiue Decades, conteyning the Chiefe and principall pointes of Christian Religion* (1577).

25. Joel Harrington, *Reordering Marriage and Society in Reformation Germany* (Cambridge: Cambridge University Press, 1995), 274; with reference to Steven Ozment, *The Age of Reform, 1250–1550: An Intellectual and Religious History of Late Medieval and Reformation Europe* (New Haven, Conn.: Yale University Press, 1980), 383. See also Buckwalter, *Priesterehe*, 71.

26. "Die Basler Reformationsordnung vom 1. April 1529," in *Aktensammlung zur Geschichte der Basler Reformation in den Jahren 1519–1534*, vol. 3 (1937), 396–98; "Reformationsmandat für das Gebiet von Bern vom 7. Februar 1528," in *Aktensammlung zur Geschichte der Berner Reformation 1521–1532*, vol. 1 (1932), 629–34; Ernst Gerhard Rüsch, ed., "Die Schaffhauser Reformationsordnung von 1529," *Schaffhauser Beiträge zur Geschichte* 56 (1979): 17–23; "Das Zürcher Mandat 'Christenlich ansehung des gemeinen kilchgangs etc.' vom 26. März 1530," in *Aktensammlung zur Geschichte der Zürcher Reformation in den Jahren 1519–1533* (1879): 702–11. See also Susanna Burghartz, *Zeiten der Reinheit: Orte der Unzucht: Ehe und Sexualität in Basel während der frühen Neuzeit* (Paderborn: Schöningh, 1999).

27. To be sure, the older categories of sexual sins did not disappear altogether. As Hull notes, some of them, like adultery, even gained in prominence (*Sexuality, State, and*

Civil Society, 22). Others lived on in *summa*-like manuals, compilations in which Protestant scholars followed Catholic models.

28. See Erika Kartschoke et al., eds. *Repertorium deutschsprachiger Ehelehren der Frühen Neuzeit*, vol. 1, part 1: *Handschriften und Drucke der Staatsbibliothek zu Berlin / Preußischer Kulturbesitz (Haus 2)* (Berlin: Akademie, 1996).

29. Albrecht von Eyb, *Ob einem manne sey zunemen ein eelichs weyb oder nicht*, ed. Helmut Weinacht (Darmstadt: Wissenschaftliche Buchgesellschaft, 1982).

30. Kartschoke, *Repertorium*, 195–99, 162–64. In a recent article, Rüdiger Schnell was able to trace the origins of this text back to Jacobus de Voragine's (c. 1226–98) *Sermones dominicales*. See his "Konstanz und Metamorphosen eines Textes: Eine überlieferungs- und geschlechtergeschichtliche Studie zur volkssprachlichen Rezeption von Jacobus' de Voragine Ehepredigten," *Frühmittelalterliche Studien* 33 (1999): 319–95.

31. *Von dem Eelichen stadt* ([Augsburg: J. Schönsberger, c. 1513]): "ain leer . . . wie sich ain eeman halten / vnd sein Eefrawen vnderweisen vnnd ziehen soll Auch widerumb die fraw gegen irm mann."

32. Thomas Stör, *Der Ehelich standt*, A3r. See also "Darumb ist besser die vnlustige Ee / den dye vnlustige keuscheyt" (B1r).

33. Ibid., A3v: "Kein Eebrecher / bůb / noch zodomiter / werden das Reych Gottes besitzen." See also 1 Cor 6:9–10. Also quoted in Reuter, *Ein Christliche frage*, A2r.

34. See Paul Rebhun, *Haußfried*, G6r.

35. Johann Baumgarten (Pomerarius), *Eine Predigt Vom EheStande / vber das Euangelium von der Hochzeit zu Cana in Galilea* (n.p., 1568), E1r/v: "die aber solches thun / sind die Ketzer vnd Ehefeind vnd Eheschender. Also do sind die Saturniter / Eustachianer / Martianer / Martioniter / Manicheer / Encraticer / Hipponacter / Tatianer / Malakoiter / Asmokoiter / Sodomiter / Florentiner / Widerteuffer / Papisten / Priapisten / Welsche Hochzeit leute / Mönche / Nonnen / etc." Similarly, E3r/v.

36. Michael Caelius, *Ein Sermon / Auff der Heimfart der Durchlauchten Hochgebornen Fürstin / Frawen Dorothea / Geborne Hertzogin in Pomern etc. Greffin zu Manesfelt / geprediget. Wider drey nichtige Einreden etlicher Ehelosen Papisten / zuwider dem Standt der heiligen Ehe* (Eisleben: U. Kaubisch, 1555).

37. Ibid., B4r/v: "denn wie kan er [God] auch zuletzt zu sehen vnd leiden / das man seine Göttliche ordenung den heiligen Ehestand nicht alleine verachtet / sondern mit Ehebruch / Hurerey / vnd andern schanden vnd lastern / die nicht zu nennen sein / vnd wol stumme Sůnden genennet werden / schendet / vnd vnehret / darumb so mögen sich alle Ehebrecher vnd hurer / Sodoma / vnd Gomorra / wol fur sehen / vnd Busse thun / denn die Ehe sol vnd mus doch endlich fur Gott / vnd allen Creaturen mit Ehren bestehen"; D2r.

38. See chapters 6 and 7 for evidence.

39. Davies, "Continuity and Change in Literary Advice on Marriage," 62. Both Mark D. Jordan (*Invention of Sodomy*, 151) and Elizabeth Keiser (*Courtly Desire*, 55) apply the term *vague* or *vagueness* with regard to the treatment of sodomy in medieval theology.

40. Martin Luther, "Katechismuspredigten" (1528), in *WA*, vol. 30.1 (1910), 1–122; "Deudsch Catechismus (Der Große Katechismus)" (1529), in *WA*, vol. 30.1, 123–238; "Der Kleine Katechismus" (1529), in *WA*, vol. 30.2 (1909), 239–425; Andreas Althammer, *Catechismus* (Marburg: n.p., 1529); Andreas Osiander d.Ä., "Katechismuspredigten," in *Gesamtausgabe*, vol. 5 (1983), 233–38; David Chytraeus, *Catechesis in Academia Rostochiana* (Rostock: L. Dietz, 1554); Johannes Monheim, *Katechismus 1560* (Cologne: Rheinland,

1987); Chytraeus, *Der Fürnembsten Heubtstuck Christlicher Lehr Nützliche vnd kurtze erklerung* (Rostock: J. Lucius, 1572), 63v; Johannes Gigas, *Catechismus* (Frankfurt a.d.Oder: J. Eichhorn, 1579); Polykarp Leyser, *Christianismus* (Dresden: n.p., 1599). The following works contain brief allusions, Cyriacus Spangenberg, *Catechismus* (Schmalkalden: Michael Schmuck, 1566), E8v, F3r; Simon Musaeus, *Catechismus mit kurtzen Fragen vnnd Antworten von den aller notwendigsten vnd wichtigsten Artickeln Christlicher Lehre* (Frankfurt am Main: Nikolaus Basse, 1580), M8r/v; Johannes Mathesius, *Catechismus* (Leipzig: J. Beyer, 1586), 154, 176–77.

41. Georg Witzel, *Catechismus Ecclesiae: Lere vnd Handelunge des heiligen Christenthums* (Leipzig: M. Lotter, 1535), Q4r/v, R1r; Johann Dietenberger, *Catechismus: Euangelische berichtinge vnde Christlike vnderwysynge* (Cologne: Peter Quentel, 1539), 16r; Friedrich Nausea, *Sermones adventales* (Cologne: Peter Quentel, 1536), 129r; Johannes Gropper, *Institutio Catholica, elementa Christianae pietatis succincta breuitate complectens* (Cologne: I. Gennepaeus, 1550), 81, 499; Gropper, *Capita institutionis ad pietatem ex Sacris scripturis et Orthodoxa Catholicae Ecclesiae doctrina et traditione excerpta* (Antwerp: I. Latius, 1555), 69r; Michael Helding, *Catechismus, Das ist Christliche Vnderweisung* (Mainz: Franz Behem, 1557), 125r; Petrus Canisius, *Catechismus, siue summa doctrinae Chistianae, in usum Christianae pueritiae* (Cologne: M. Cholinus, 1560), 196; Canisius, *Catholischer Catechismus oder Summarien Christlicher Lehr* (Cologne: M. Cholinus, 1563), S1v, S2v, S3r; Canisius, *Der klain Catechismus sampt kurtzen gebetlein für die ainfeltigen* (n.p., 1563); Canisius, *Institutiones Christianae pietatis seu paruus catechismus Catholicorum* (Dillingen: S. Mayer, 1572), 23v; Pedro de Soto, *Methodus confessionis seu verius doctrinae pietatisque Christianae praecipuorum capitum epitome* (Dillingen: S. Mayer, 1576), 30v, 71r. Most of these texts treat sodomy in the context of the sixth commandment, some also in the context of the "crying sins" (*peccata clamantia*). There is no mention of sodomy in Pedro de Soto, *Institutionis Christianae libri tres* (Augsburg: V. Othmar, 1548), 22r; *Brevis institutio ad pietatem Christianam secundum Doctrinam Catholicam* (Mainz: Ivo Schoeffer, 1552); Pedro de Soto, *Compendium doctrinae Catholicae* (n.p., 1554); *Confessio Catholicae fidei Christiana* (Mainz: Franciscus Behem, 1557); Stanislaus Hosius, *Confession, das ist: Ein Christliche Bekantnuß des Catholischen Glaubens* (Ingolstadt: A. Weissenhorn, 1560).

42. Martin Luther, "Eine kurze Unterweisung, wie man beichten soll" (1519), in *WA*, vol. 2 (1884), 63. For bibliographical references to his catechisms of 1529, see n. 40 above.

43. See chapter 6.

44. Johannes Mathesius, *Ehespiegel Mathesij* (Leipzig: J. Beyer, 1591), 27r: "Mechtige grosse vnordentliche Brunst / Vnzucht / Hurerey / Ehebrecherey / Florentinisch Vnreinigkeiten vnd Römische Hochzeiten / vnnd andere erschreckliche Vnfleterey / dauon wir nicht sagen mögen / sind vom Teuffel vnd von bösen Naturen eingeführet worden."

45. Heinrich Bullinger, *Der Christlich Eestand* (first printed edition 1540; Zurich: Christoph Froschauer, 1579), fol. 2: "Das kompt alles dahaer / das die laster nit mer iren rechten nammen tragend; allerley unreinigkeit."

46. Paracelsus [Theophrast Bombast von Hohenheim], "Von der ehe ordnung und eigenschaft," in *Sämtliche Werke*, 2. Abteilung: *Theologische und religionsphilosophische Schriften*, ed. Kurt Goldammer, vol. 2 (Wiesbaden: Franz Steiner, 1965), 247: "die ehe ist die höchste eher und heiliger stand undtern menschen und ist in gottes gewalt behalten."

47. Anderson, *Imagined Communities*. Compare, for instance, the role of pamphlets in Reformation Germany with the role of newspapers and novels in molding a community. Anderson's concept is akin to Goertz's "symbolic integration" (*Pfaffenhaß und groß Geschrei*, 247).

48. Matheson, *Rhetoric of the Reformation*, 241.

49. See, however, Alfeld, *Wyder den Wittenbergischen*, 26–27, 34–35.

50. For matrimony, see Steven Ozment, *When Fathers Ruled: Family Life in Reformation Europe* (Cambridge, Mass.: Harvard University Press, 1983), 1–49.

51. Roper, *Holy Household*, 252, 257–58, and passim.

52. See, however, B. Schuster on prostitution: *Die unendlichen Frauen;* and *Die freien Frauen: Dirnen und Frauenhäuser im 15. und 16. Jahrhundert* (Frankfurt am Main: Campus, 1995).

53. Thomas Max Safley, *Let No Man Put Asunder: The Control of Marriage in the German Southwest, 1550–1600* (Kirksville: Northeast Missouri State University Press, 1984), 195.

54. Harrington, *Reordering Marriage*, 271.

55. Kartschoke, ed., *Repertorium*, vii. See also Walter Behrendt, "Übersetzungen und Bearbeitungen des Pseudo-Bernhardus-Briefs 'De cura rei familiaris' im 16. Jahrhundert (Joachim Himmel, Johannes Spangenberg, Adam Walasser)," *Leuven Contributions in Linguistics and Philology* 83 (1994): 351–52.

56. Kartschoke, ed., *Repertorium*, nos. 6, 8, 13, 14, 19, 39. About 20 of the 104 texts in the *Repertorium* came out before 1517; no information on confessional identity is available for about fifteen authors or texts. For the scope of the treatises included, see the preface.

57. Aegidius Albertinus based his *Weiblicher Lustgarten* (1605) on Juan de la Cerda's *Vida politica de todos los estados de mugeres* (1599); Christoph Bruno adapted Juan Luis Vives's *De institutione foeminae Christianae* (1524) and *De officio mariti* (1529) for a German audience (1544); the anonymous *Hauszucht und Regiment*, printed in Dillingen in 1569, emulated Ps-Bernhard's *Epistola de cura rei familiaris* and Petrus Canisius (1521–97).

58. See, for instance, the case of journeymen who were not allowed to marry in many cities and also actively resisted fellow journeymen who were married: Merry E. Wiesner, "Guilds, Male Bonding, and Women's Work in Early Modern Germany," in *Gender, Church, and State*, 170–71.

59. See Klaus-Joachim Lorenzen-Schmidt, "Zur Stellung der Frauen in der frühneu-zeitlichen Städtegesellschaft Schleswigs und Holsteins," *Archiv für Kulturgeschichte* 61 (1979): 323–25. For the fifteenth century, see Erich Maschke, "Die Unterschichten der mittelalterlichen Städte Deutschlands," in *Gesellschaftliche Unterschichten in den südwestdeutschen Städten*, ed. E. Maschke and Jürgen Sydow (Stuttgart: Kohlhammer, 1967), 27.

60. See Maryanne Kowaleski, "Singlewomen in Medieval and Early Modern Europe: The Demographic Perspective," in *Singlewomen in the European Past, 1250–1800*, ed. Judith Bennett and Amy Froide (Philadelphia: University of Pennsylvania Press, 1999), 38–81, 325–44; Merry E. Wiesner, "Having Her Own Smoke: Employment and Independence for Singlewomen in Germany, 1400–1750," in *Singlewomen*, 193–94, 196–99. On the median age of marriage, see Winfried Schulze, *Deutsche Geschichte im 16. Jahrhundert* (Frankfurt am Main: Suhrkamp, 1987), 28.

Conclusion

1. Martin Luther, "Warnung an seine lieben Deutschen" (1531), in *WA*, vol. 30.3 (1910), 303: "solche unbusfertige, unverschampte Puseronen."

Bibliography

Primary Sources

Manuscript Sources

Staatsarchiv Basel-Stadt (StABS)
Criminalia 31 F 1
Criminalia 4 12 (1647)
Missiven B 11
Ratsbücher A 3 (*Leistungsbuch* 2)
Straf- und Polizeiakten C 15

Staatsarchiv Luzern (StALU)
A1 F9 SCH 826
Archiv 1, Personalien, AKT 113/90; 113/132; 113/161; 113/213; 113/334; 113/373
 113/579; 113/904; 113/928 113/937; 113/956; 113/962 113/964; 113/978; 113/1033;
 113/1103; 113/1151; 113/1180; 113/1253; 113/1341; 113/1412; 113/1806; 113/1844;
 113/1863; 113/1901; 113/1952; 113/1963; 113/2055; 113/2076; 113/2093; 113/2115;
 113/2159; 113/2241; 113/2251; 113/2266; 113/2270; 113/2283
COD 1256/1 (*Regierungsverordnungen*)
COD 4435, 4445, 4500, 4530 (*Turmbücher*)
RP 1ff. (*Ratsprotokolle*)

Staatsarchiv Schaffhausen (StASCH)
Justiz, D 1 (*Vergichtbuch*)

Staatsarchiv Solothurn (StASO)
Bürgerarchiv, "Wyss Buech," E I 61
Copiae 1524–1525, AB 2.9
Denkwürdige Sachen (DS) 33
Missiven 1515–1519, AB 1.6
Ratsmanual 1523–1525, A 1.12
Ratsmanual 1523–1526, A 1.14
Ratsmanual, vol. 66 (1566)
Vergichtbuch (*Ratsmanual rot* 19) 1478–1552

Vergichtbuch und Thurn Roedel 1553–1579, 1583–1587
Vergichtbuch und Thurn Roedel 1600–1613

Staatsarchiv Zürich (StAZ)
A 27.3, 27.8, 27.9, 27.10, 27.13, 27.14, 27.15, 27.16, 27.26, 27.35, 27.37a, 27.39,
27.43, 27.44, 27.45 (*Kundschaften und Nachgänge*)
B VI 209, 245, 253, 255, 257, 259, 262 (*Rats- und Richtbücher*)
B VII 21.2
A 10 (*Bestialität und Sodomiterei* 1561–1765)
Ratsbuch B VII 21.2
E II 336; 356a

Stadtarchiv Augsburg
Strafamt, Urgichten, Nr. 7: Wolfgang Keck, Bernhart Wagner (November 16, 1529);
Nr. 9: Jacob Miller (April 3–May 7, 1532); Bernhart Wagner (April 4–June 8,
1532); Christoff Schmidt (May 1–8, 1532); Philipp Zeller (May 8–June 11, 1532);
Michel Will (December 1, 1533–March 19, 1534)

Stadtarchiv Freiburg im Breisgau
C1 Criminalia C9 (1547)

Stadtarchiv Konstanz
B I.11, B I.14, L 843
Schultheiß Coll A I 8/1

Stadtarchiv München
Zimelie 17
Ratsbuch III 1362–1384
KR (Kammerrechnung) 1378

Stadtarchiv St. Gallen (StArchiv St. Gallen)
Malefiz-Buch nr. 192

Stadtarchiv Speyer
1A 704/II

Stadtarchiv Strassburg
AA 261, nr. 29

Archives de l'ancien Evêché de Bâle, Porrentruy
A 85 (*Officialitas Basiliensis*)

Erzbischöfliches Archiv Freiburg
Liber conceptorum, B (1441–46), Sign. Ha 315

Manuscripts
Basel, Universitätsbibliothek (UB), F VIII 15
Berthold von Regensburg, *Sermones*, Fribourg/CH, Couvent des Cordeliers, cod. 117,
vol. 2
Kalocsa, Föszékesegyházi Könyvtár (Hungary), Ms 629
Vienna, Austrian National Library (ÖNB), Series nova 3616

Printed Sources

Agrippa, Henricus Cornelius. *Declamation on the Nobility and Preeminence of the Female Sex.* Edited by Albert Rabil, Jr. Chicago: University of Chicago Press, 1996.

Albrecht von Eyb. *Ob einem manne sey zunemen ein eelichs weyb oder nicht.* Edited by Helmut Weinacht. Darmstadt: Wissenschaftliche Buchgesellschaft, 1982.

Alfeld, Augustin von. *Wyder den Wittenbergischen Abgot Martin Luther (1524).* Edited by Käthe Büschgens. *Erklärung des Salve Regina (1527).* Edited by Leonhard Lemmens. Münster: Aschendorff, 1926.

Althammer, Andreas. *Catechismus / Das ist Vnderricht zum Christlichen glauben / wie man die Jugent leren vnd ziehen sol / ynn frag vnd antwort gestelt.* Marburg: n.p., 1529.

"Annales Basileenses." Edited by Philipp Jaffé. In *Annales aevi suevici,* edited by Georg Heinrich Pertz. Monumenta Germaniae Historica: Scriptores 17, 193–202. Hannover: Hahnsche Buchhandlung, 1861.

"Annales Sancti Disibodi." Edited by Georg Waitz. In *Annales aevi suevici,* edited by Georg Heinrich Pertz. Monumenta Germaniae Historica: Scriptores 17, 4–30. Hannover: Hahnsche Buchhandlung, 1861.

Anshelm, Valerius. *Die Berner Chronik des Valerius Anshelm.* Edited by Historischer Verein des Kantons Bern. Bern: K. J. Wyss, 1884/1901.

Anthony of Florence [Antoninus]. *Summa.* Basel: Amerbach/Petri/Froben, [1511].

Astesanus, *Summa de casibus conscientiae.* [Strasbourg: Johann Mentel, 1489].

Basilea Latina. Edited by Alfred Hartmann. Basel: Lehrmittelverlag des Erziehungs-Departementes, 1931.

Basler Chroniken. 7 vols. Edited by Historische und Antiquarische Gesellschaft zu Basel. Leipzig: S. Hirzel, 1872–1915.

"Die Basler Reformationsordnung vom 1. April 1529." *Aktensammlung zur Geschichte der Basler Reformation in den Jahren 1519–1534,* 3 (1937): 396–98.

Baumgarten, Johann [Pomerarius]. *Eine Predigt Vom EheStande / vber das Euangelium von der Hochzeit zu Cana in Galilea.* N.p., 1568.

Bebel, Heinrich. *Heinrich Bebels Facetien Drei Bücher.* Edited by Gustav Bebermeyer. Leipzig: W. Hiersemann, 1931.

Beccuti, Francesco Coppetta, and Giovanni Guidiccioni. *Rime.* Edited by E. Chiorboli. Bari: Laterza, 1912.

Beclagung Tütscher Nation. Schnersheim a. Kochersberg, 1526 [Schlettstadt: Nikolaus Küffer, 1521] [*Lamentationes Germanicae nationis,* German].

Beheim, Michel. *Die Gedichte des Michel Beheim.* 2 vols. Edited by Hans Gille and Ingeborg Spriewald. Berlin: Akademie, 1968–70.

Berg, Klaus, and Monika Kasper, eds. *"Das bůch der tugenden": Ein Compendium des 14. Jahrhunderts über Moral und Recht nach der "Summa theologiae" II-II des Thomas von Aquin und anderen Werken der Scholastik und Kanonistik.* 2 vols. Tübingen: Niemeyer, 1984.

Bericht: Welches die rechte wahre vnnd allgemain Kirchen Gottes sey / ausser welcher niemand die Seligkait erlangen kan. Wien: n.p., 1560.

Bernhardi, Bartholomäus. *Das die Priester Ee weyber nemen mögen vnd sollen.* N.p., 1522.

Berthold. *Die "Rechtssumme" Bruder Bertholds: Eine deutsche abecedarische Bearbeitung der "Summa Confessorum" des Johannes von Freiburg: Synoptische Edition der Fassungen B, A und C.* 7 vols. Edited by Georg Steer, Wolfgang Klimanek, Daniela Kuhlmann, Freimut Löser, and Karl-Heiner Südekum. Tübingen: Niemeyer, 1987–91.

Berthold von Regensburg. *Predigten.* Edited by Franz Pfeiffer. Berlin: de Gruyter, 1965.

[Boccaccio, Giovanni]. *Cento Nouella Johannis Bocatij: Das ist Hundert Newer Historien* [*Decamerone*]. Strasbourg: Paul Messerschmidt, 1561.

Bodenstein, Andreas (named Karlstadt). *Super coelibatu, monachatu et viduitate axiomata.* Wittenberg: Nikolaus Schirlentz, 1521.

—————. *Von gelubden vnterrichtung.* Wittenberg: [Nickel Schirlentz], 1521.

Bodin, Jean. *De la demonomanie des sorciers.* Paris: Jacques du Puys, 1580.

Bossi, Egidio. *Tractatus varii, qui omnem fere criminalem materiam excellenti doctrina complectuntur.* Lyon: Haeredes Iacobi Iunti, 1562.

Brandenburgische balßgerichtsordnung. Nuremberg: n.p., 1516.

Brevis institutio ad pietatem Christianam secundum Doctrinam Catholicam. Mainz: Ivo Schoeffer, 1552.

Bucer, Martin. *Eyn schoner dialogus vnd gesprech zwischen áim Pfarrer vnd eym Schultheß / betreffendt alle vbel des Stands der geystlichen: Vnd bóß handlung der weltlichen.* [Wittenberg: Johann Rhau-Grünenberg, 1521].

[Bucer, Martin]. *Gesprech biechlin neüw Karsthans.* [Strasbourg: Matthias Schürer, 1521].

Bugenhagen, Johannes. *Von dem ehelichen stande der Bischoffe vnd Diaken / an Herrn Wolfgang Reyssenbusch / der Rechte Doctor vnd / Preceptor zu Lichtemberg Sant Anthonius ordens.* Translated by Stephan Rodt. Wittenberg: Joseph Klug, 1525.

Büheler, Sebald, Jr. *La chronique strasbourgeoise de Sébald Büheler.* Edited by Léon Dacheux. *Bulletin de la société pour la conservation des monuments historiques d'alsace,* n.s. 13 (1888): 23–149.

Bujanda, J. M., ed. *Index de Rome 1557, 1559, 1564: Les premiers index romains et l'index du Concile de Trente.* Sherbrooke: Centre d'études de la Renaissance, 1990.

Bujanda, J. M., René Davignon, and Ela Stanek, eds. *Index de Venise, 1549, et Milan, 1554.* Sherbrooke: Centre d'études de la Renaissance, 1987.

Bullinger, Heinrich. *Der Christlich Eestand.* Zurich: Christoph Froschauer, 1579.

Burger, Helene, ed. *Nürnberger Totengeläutbücher.* 2 vols. Neustadt a.d.Aisch: Kommissionsverlag, 1961/67.

Caelius, Michael. *Ein Sermon / Auff der Heimfart der Durchlauchten Hochgebornen Fürstin / Frawen Dorothea / Geborne Hertzogin in Pomern etc. Greffin zu Mansfelt / geprediget: Wider drey nichtige Einreden etlicher Ehelosen Papisten / zuwider dem Standt der heiligen Ehe.* Eisleben: Urban Kaubisch, 1555.

Cammermeister, Hartung. *Die Chronik Hartung Cammermeisters.* Edited by Robert Reiche. Halle: Otto Hendel, 1896.

Canisius, Petrus. *Catechismus, sive summa doctrinae Chistianae, in usum Christianae pueritiae.* Cologne: Maternus Cholinus, 1560.

—————. *Catholischer Catechismus oder Summarien Christlicher Lehr.* Cologne: Maternus Cholinus, 1563.

—————. *Der klain Catechismus sampt kurtzen gebetlein für die ainfeltigen.* N.p., 1563.

—————. *Institutiones Christianae pietatis seu parvus catechismus Catholicorum.* Dillingen: Sebald Mayer, 1572.

Carpzov, Benedikt. *Practica imperialis saxonicae rerum criminalium.* Edited by Johann Samuel Friedrich Böhmer. Frankfurt am Main: Franciscus Varentrapp, 1758.

Celtis, Conrad. *Selections from Conrad Celtis.* Edited by Leonard Forster. Cambridge: Cambridge University Press, 1948.

Cephalus [?], Sigismund. *Warer Grundt vnnd beweisung / das die vnrecht handlen / die jren*

Predigern verbieten / das Antichristisch Bapstumb mit seinen greweln zustraffen. Magdeburg: Christian Rödinger, 1551.

Ain Christenliches lustigs gesprech / das besser . . . seye auß den Klöstern zůkommen / vnd Eelich zůwerden / dann darinnen zůbeleyben. N.p., 1524.

Chroniken der deutschen städte vom 14. bis in's 16. jahrhundert. Edited by Bayerische Akademie der Wissenschaften. Leipzig: S. Hirzel, 1862–.

Chytraeus, David. *Catechesis in Academia Rostochiana.* Rostock: Ludwig Dietz, 1554.

———. *Der Fürnembsten Heubtstuck Christlicher Lehr Nützliche vnd kurtze erklerung.* Rostock: Jacob Lucius, 1572.

Civilius [Mathias Flaccius Illyricus?]. *Ein freidige vermanung zu klarem vnd öffentlichem bekentnis Jhesu Christi.* N.p., 1550.

Clarmund, Adolf. *Vitae clarissimorum in re literaria virorum,* part 9. Wittenberg: Christian Gottlieb Ludwig, 1710.

Code historique et diplomatique de la ville de Strasbourg. Strasbourg: Silbermann, 1845.

Confessio Catholicae fidei Christiana: vel potius explicatio quaedam confessionis a patribus factae in synodo provinciali. Mainz: Franciscus Behem, 1557.

Corpus iuris civilis. Edited by Christoph Heinrich Freiesleben. Neukölln: E. Thurneysen, 1775.

Coryat, Thomas. *Coryat's Crudities.* 2 vols. Glasgow: J. MacLehose, 1905.

Coste, Jean, ed. *Boniface VIII en procès: Articles d'accusation et dépositions des témoins (1303–1311).* Rome: "L'erma" di Bretschneider, 1995.

Cronberg, Hartmuth von. *Drey Christliche schrift.* Wittenberg: Melchior Lotter, [1522].

———. [title page not preserved], call number: Herzog August Bibliothek, Wolfenbüttel: 435.9 Theol. (44).

Crusius, Christophorus. *Tractatvs de indiciis delictorum specialibus.* Frankfurt am Main: Wolfgang Hoffmann, 1635.

Damian, Peter [Petrus Damian]. *Die Briefe des Petrus Damiani.* 4 vols. Edited by Kurt Reindel. Munich: Monumenta Germaniae Historica, 1983–93.

———. *Letters.* Edited by Owen J. Blum. Washington, D.C.: Catholic University of America Press, 1989–.

Della Casa, Giovanni. *Giovanni della Casa's Poem Book "Ioannis Casae Carminum Liber."* Edited by John B. Van Sickle. Tempe, Ariz.: Arizona Center for Medieval and Renaissance Studies, 1999.

———. *Opere di Monsignor Giovanni della Casa.* 3 vols. Venice: Angiolo Pasinelli, 1752.

———. *Prose.* Edited by Arnaldo di Benedetto. Turin: Unione tipografico-editrice torinese, 1991.

———. *Rime, et prose di M. Giovanni della Casa.* Venice: Marc'Antonio Bonibelli, 1616.

———. *Le terze rime.* Usecht: J. Broedelet, 1726.

———. *Le terze rime piacevoli.* Benevent: n.p., 1727.

Denis the Carthusian. *Opera omnia.* 43 vols. Monstrolii and Tournai: Cartusiae S. M. de Pratis, 1896–1913.

De Soto, Pedro. *Compendium doctrinae Catholicae in usum plebis Christianae recte instituendae.* N.p., 1554.

———. *Institutionis Christianae libri tres.* Augsburg: Valentin Othmar, 1548.

———. *Methodus confessionis seu verius doctrinae pietatisque Christianae praecipuorum capitum epitome.* Dillingen: Sebald Mayer, 1576.

Dialogus vere elegans et lepidus, apud inferos habitus, inter Papas, Leonem et Clementem, atque Cardinalem Spinolam. N.p., 1538 (see also the German translation, Ein kleglich gesprech).

Diehl, Adolf, ed. Dionysius Dreytweins Esslingische Chronik (1548–1564). Tübingen: H. Laupp, 1901.

Dierauer, Johannes, ed. Chronik der Stadt Zürich. Basel: A. Geering, 1900.

Dietenberger, Johann. Catechismus: Euangelische berichtinge vnde Christlike vnderwysynge. Cologne: Peter Quentel, 1539.

Eberlin von Günzburg, Johann. Ausgewählte Schriften, vols. 1–3. Edited by Ludwig Enders. Halle a.d. Saale: Max Niemeyer, 1896–1902.

————. Eyn freundtlichs zuschreyben an alle stendt teutscher nation. N.p., 1524.

————. Ein klägliche klag an den christlichen Römischen Keyser. N.p., [1521].

————. Wie gfarlich sey: So ein Priester kein Eeweyb hat. N.p., 1522.

Edlibach, Gerold (bis 1498). "Gerold Edlibach's Chronik." Edited by Joh. Mart. Usterj. In Mitteilungen der antiquarischen Gesellschaft in Zürich. Vol. 4. Zurich, n.p., 1847.

Ellenbog, Nikolaus. Briefwechsel. Edited by Andreas Bigelmair and Friedrich Zoepfl. Münster: Aschendorff, 1938.

Engelbrecht, Anton. "Abconterfeyung Martin Butzers" (1546). Edited by Werner Bellardi. Münster: Aschendorff, 1974.

Epistell des heyligen Bischoffs Hulderici czu Augspurg wyder die Constitution unnd ansatzung. von der keuscheit und Enthaldung der priesterschaft offenlich den geyst der Apostolischen lere. außsprechende. N.p., [1521?].

Epistolae obscurorum virorum aliaque aevi decimi sexti monimenta rarissima. Edited by Ernst Münch. Leipzig: J. C. Hinrichssche Buchhandlung, 1827.

Erasmus von Rotterdam. Ausgewählte Schriften. 8 vols. Edited by Werner Welzig. Darmstadt: Wissenschaftliche Buchgesellschaft, 1967–80.

————. Opera omnia. Amsterdam: North-Holland Pub., 1969–.

————. The Praise of Folly and Other Writings. Edited by Robert M. Adams. New York: Norton, 1989.

[Fabricius, Lactantius?]. Ware Abcontereytung vnnd vergleichung des Bapstumbs / Mit andern grössesten Ketzereien. N.p., n.d. [after 1546].

Fischart, Johann. Aller Practick Großmutter. Strasbourg: Bernhard Jobin, 1572.

————. Vom Außgelasnen Wütigen Teüffelsheer Allerhand Zauberern / Hexen vnnd Hexenmeistern / Vnholden / Teufelsbeschwerern / Warsagern / Schwartzkünstlern / Vergifftern / Augenverblendern / etc. Strasbourg: Bernhard Jobin, 1591 [Jean Bodin, De la demonomanie, German].

Flacius Illyricus, Matthias, ed. Epistola S. Hvlrici Episcopi. Magdeburg: n.p., 1550.

————. Des h. Hulrichs etwa vor sechshundert jaren Bischoffs zu Augspurg schrifft wider das ehelos leben der Priester jtzt sehr nützlich zulesen. Augsburg: n.p., 1553.

Folz, Hans. Die Reimpaarsprüche. Edited by Hanns Fischer. Munich: Beck, 1961.

Francisci, Erasmus. Neu=polirter Geschicht= Kunst= und Sitten=Spiegel ausländischer Völcker. Nuremberg: Johann Andreas Endter, n.d.

Freder, Johann. Ein Dialogus dem Ehestand zu ehren geschrieben. Wittenberg: Nickel Schirlentz, 1545.

Eyn freüntlichs gesprech zwischen eynem Parfusser münch / auß der Prouintz Osterreich / der Obseruantz / vnd einem Löffelmacher / mit namen / Hans Stösser / gar lustig zúlesen. N.p., n.d.

Frey, Jakob. Jakob Freys Gartengesellschaft (1556). Edited by Johannes Bolte. Tübingen: Bibliothek des Litterarischen Vereins, 1896.

Frischlin, Nikodemus. Facetiae selectiores. Strasbourg: Bernhard Jobin, 1600.

Gagliardi, Ernst, ed. *Dokumente zur Geschichte des Bürgermeisters Hans Waldmann.* 2 vols. Basel: Adolf Geering, 1911–13.

Gast, Hiob. *Ein Trostpredige vnd Christenliche trewe vermanung.* Nuremberg: Leonhard Milchtaler, 1540.

Geffcken, Johannes. *Der Bildercatechismus des funfzehnten Jahrhunderts und die catechetischen Hauptstücke in dieser Zeit bis auf Luther.* Vol. 1, *Die zehn Gebote.* Leipzig: T. O. Weigel, 1855.

Geiler von Kaisersberg, Johann. *Die brösamlin doct. Keiserspergs vffgelesen.* Translated by Johannes Pauli. Strasbourg: Johannes Grüninger, 1517.

———. *Der dreieckecht Spiegel.* Strasbourg: M. Schürer, n.d.

———. *Ain gaistliche bedeütung des Häßlins / wie man das in dem pfeffer bereyten sol.* [Strasbourg: Johann Knoblauch, 1511].

———. *Les plus anciens écrits.* Edited by L. Dacheux. Colmar: M. Hoffmann, 1882.

———. *Sermones funebres.* Lyon: Johannes Klein, 1504.

———. *Die siben hauptsünd die da bedeüt seind bey den gaistlichen schwertern / mitt denen der böß veind der teüfel / die seelen der menschen schlecht / verwundt vnd ertödtet.* [Strasbourg: Johann Knoblauch, 1511].

———. "Von der beycht." In *Les plus anciens écrits,* edited by L. Dacheux. Colmar: M. Hoffmann, 1882.

Genequand, Jean-Etienne. "Quelques 'Petites Annales bourguignonnes' à Genève." *Publications du Centre d'Etudes burgundo-médianes* 14 (1972): 51.

Gerson, Jean. *Oeuvres complètes.* 10 vols. Paris: Desclée, 1960–73.

Geschichte des Kantons Zürich. Zurich: Werd, 1995–96.

Gesner, Conrad. *Bibliotheca.* Edited by Georg Simler. Zurich: Christoph Froschauer, 1574.

Gigas, Johannes. *Catechismus.* Frankfurt a.d.Oder: Johann Eichhorn, 1579.

Gropper, Johannes. *Capita institutionis ad pietatem ex Sacris scripturis et Orthodoxa Catholicae Ecclesiae doctrina et traditione excerpta.* Antwerp: I. Latius, 1555.

———. *Institutio Catholica, elementa Christianae pietatis succincta breuitate complectens.* Cologne: Iaspar Gennepaeus, 1550.

Der grosse Seelentrost: Ein niederdeutsches Erbauungsbuch des vierzehnten Jahrhunderts. Edited by Margarete Schmitt. Cologne: Böhlau, 1959.

Grünbeck, Joseph. *Spiegel der naturlichen himlischen vnd prophetischen sehungen aller trubsalen.* Leipzig: Wolfgang Stöckel, 1522.

Guilelmus Alvernus. *Opera omnia.* Vol. 2. Paris: Ludovicus Billaine, 1674.

Gundling, Nikolaus H. *Observationes selectae ad rem litterariam spectantes.* 2 vols. 2d ed. Halle: Renger, 1737.

Hartmann, Alfred, and Beat Rudolf Jenny, eds. *Die Amerbachkorrespondenz.* Basel: Verlag der Universitätsbibliothek, 1942–83.

Heinrich von Friemar. *Preceptorium.* Cologne: n.p., 1505.

Helding, Michael. *Catechismus, Das ist Christliche Vnderweisung.* Mainz: Franz Behem, 1557.

Hemmerli, Felix. "De Matrimonio." In *Septimum volumen tractatuum doctorum iuris.* Lyon: Dionysius de Harsy, 1535.

Herolt, Johannes. *Sermones discipuli.* Mainz: n.p., 1612.

Herp, Henricus. *Speculum Aureum de preceptis diuine legis.* Basel: Johannes Froben, 1496.

Hieronymus. *Opera.* Turnhout: Brepols, 1959–.

Höfer, Michael. *Wes man sich in disen gefehrlichen zeyten halten / vnd wie man dem zorn Gottes /*

so vber die Welt entzúndet ist / *zuuorkommen soll*. Nuremberg: Johann vom Berg/Ulrich Neuber, 1546.

Hosius, Stanislaus. *Confession* / *das ist: Ein Christliche Bekantnuß des Catholischen Glaubens.* Ingolstadt: Alexander Weissenhorn, 1560.

Hutten, Ulrich von. *Clag und vormanung*. [Strasbourg: Johann Schott], n.d.

————. *Drey ding findt man tzu Rhom*. [Leipzig: Martin Landsberg, 1519].

————. *Eyn lustiger vnd nuczlicher Dialogus* [Vadiscus]. Strasbourg: Balthasar Beck, 1544.

————. *Des teutschen Ritters Ulrich von Hutten auserlesene Werke*. Edited by Ernst Münch. Leipzig: Georg Reimer, 1822.

Iulius: Dialogus viri cuiuspiam eruditissimi, festiuus sane ac elegans. N.p., n.d.

Jacques de Vitry. *Historia orientalis*. Douai: Balthasarus Bellerus, 1597.

Kaufmann, Arthur, ed. *Die Peinliche Gerichtsordnung Kaiser Karls V. von 1532 (Carolina)*. Stuttgart: Reclam, 1996.

Keller, Adelbert von, ed. *Decameron von Heinrich Steinhöwel*. Stuttgart: Litterarischer Verein, 1860.

Kirchhof, Hans Wilhelm. *Wendunmuth*. 5 vols. Edited by Hermann Österley. Stuttgart: H. Laupp, 1869.

Ein kleglich gesprech Babsts Leonis / *vnd Babsts Clementen* / *mit jrem Kemmerer* / *Cardinaln Spinola* / *in der Helle gehalten* / *den jetzigen Kirchenstand belangend. Kurtzlich in Jtalien außgangen*. N.p., 1538 (see also the Latin version, *Dialogus vere elegans*).

Knapp, Hermann, ed. *Das Rechtsbuch Ruprechts von Freising (1328)*. Leipzig: R. Voigtländer, 1916.

Knebel, Johannes. "Diarium." In *Basler Chroniken*, edited by Wilhelm Vischer and Heinrich Boes. Vol. 2. Leipzig: S. Hirzel, 1880.

Kolde, Dietrich. *Der Christenspiegel des Dietrich Kolde von Münster*. Edited by Clemens Drees. Werl: Dietrich-Coelde-Verlag, 1954.

Koller, Heinrich, ed. *Reformation Kaiser Sigismunds*. Stuttgart: A. Hiersemann, 1964.

Langenberg, Rudolf. *Quellen und Forschungen zur Geschichte der deutschen Mystik*. Bonn: P. Hanstein, 1902.

[Las Casas, Bartolomé de]. *Warhafftiger vnd gründlicher Bericht* / *Der Hispanier grewlich: vnd abschewlichen Tryannrey von jhnen in den West Jndien* / *die newe Welt genant* / *begangen*. Oppenheim: Theodor de Bry, 1613.

Las Casas, Bartolomé de. *Werkauswahl*. Edited by Mariano Delgado. Translated by Ulrich Kunzmann. Paderborn: Ferdinand Schöningh, 1994–.

Leonardus de Utino. *Quadragesimale de legibus seu anime fidelis*. Lyon: n.p., 1494.

Leyser, Polykarp. *Christianismus, Das ist: Acht Bußpredigten* / *nach Ordnung des Christlichen Catechismi herrn Doctoris Martini Lutheri*. Dresden: n.p., 1599.

Libelli de lite imperatorum et pontificum saeculis XI. et XII. conscripti. Monumenta Germaniae Historica. Hannover: Hahnsche Buchhandlung, 1891–97.

Linck, Wenzeslaus. *Ein schöne Christliche Sermon von dem außgang der kinder Gottes auß des Antichrists gefengknüß*. N.p., 1524.

[Luther, Martin]. *Adversus papatum Romae a Sathana fundatum*. N.p., 1545.

Luther, Martin. *Briefwechsel: Kritische Gesamtausgabe*. Weimar: Böhlau, 1930–85.

————. *Contra papatum Romanum, a diabolo inventum, D. Doct. Mar. Luth. E germa. latine redditum, per Iustum Ionam*. Translated by Justus Jonas. N.p., 1545.

————. *Offenbarung des Endtchrists*. Wittenberg: n.p., 1524.

————. *Werke: Kritische Gesamtausgabe.* Weimar: Böhlau, 1883–. (Cited in the notes as WA.)

————. *Works.* 55 vols. Edited by Jaroslav Jan Pelikan, Helmut T. Lehmann, and Milton C. Oswald. St. Louis, Mo.: Concordia, 1955–86.

Luther, Martin, ed. *Epistola divi Hulderichi Augustensis Episcopi, adversus constitutionem de Cleri Coelibatu, plane referens Apostolicon Spiritum.* Wittenberg: [Melchior Lotter d.J.], 1520.

Major, Georg. *Ewiger Göttlicher / Allmechtiger Maiestat Declaration.* N.p., n.d.

Marcus von Weida. *Spigell des ehlichen ordens.* Edited by Anthony van der Lee. Assen: Van Gorcum, 1972.

Marquard von Lindau, O.F.M. *Das Buch der zehn Gebote (Venedig 1483): Textausgabe mit Einleitung und Glossar.* Edited by Jacobus Willem van Maren. Amsterdam: Rodopi, 1984.

Marschalck, Haug (named Zoller). *Von dem weyt erschollen Namen Luther.* Strasbourg [Erfurt: Johann Loersfeld], 1523.

Martin von Amberg. *Der Gewissensspiegel.* Edited by Stanley Newman Werbow. Berlin: Erich Schmidt, 1958.

Mathesius, Johannes. *Catechismus.* Leipzig: J. Beyer, 1586.

————. *Ehespiegel Mathesij.* Leipzig: Johann Beyer, 1591.

Meffret. *Sermones Meffret. alius Ortulus regine de tempore pars Estiualis.* N.p., n.d.

Melanchthon, Philipp. *Melanchthons Briefwechsel: Kritische und kommentierte Gesamtausgabe.* Edited by Richard Wetzel. 10 vols. and vols. T1–T3. Stuttgart-Bad Cannstatt: Frommann Holzboog, 1977–.

————. *Eine Schrifft Philip. Melanth. newlich latinisch gestellet / Widder den vnreinen Bapsts Celibat / vnd verbot der Priesterehe.* Translated by Justus Jonas. Wittenberg: Joseph Klug, 1541.

Ménage, Gilles. *Anti-Baillet ou critique du livre de Mr. Baillet, intitulé "Jugement des savans."* La Haye: Louis & Henry van Dole, 1690.

Meyer, Christian, ed. *Das Stadtbuch von Augsburg, insbesondere das Stadtrecht vom Jahre 1276, nach der Originalhandschrift zum ersten Male herausgegeben und erläuter.* Augsburg: F. Butsch, 1872.

Monheim, Johannes. *Katechismus 1560.* Cologne: Rheinland-Verlag, 1987.

Mörlin, Joachim. *Von dem Beruff der Prediger.* Eisleben: Urban Gaubisch, 1555.

Mundt, Lothar, ed. *Lemnius und Luther: Studien und Texte zur Nachwirkung ihres Konflikts (1538/39).* Bern: Peter Lang, 1983.

Musaeus, Simon. *Catechismus / Mit kurtzen Fragen vnnd Antworten / von den aller notwendigsten vnd wichtigsten Artickeln Christlicher Lehre.* Frankfurt am Main: Nikolaus Basse, 1580.

Nashe, Thomas. *Works.* 5 vols. Edited by Ronald B. McKerrow. London: Bullen, 1904–10.

Nausea, Friedrich. *Sermones adventales.* Cologne: Peter Quentel, 1536.

Newe zeytung auß Rom: Vom newen Babst Paulo / dem Vierdten dises namens / in disem M.D.LV. Jare erwelet. N.p., 1555.

Nider, Johannes. *Praeceptorium divinae legis.* N.p., n.d.

Oberndorff, Kunz von [Urbanus Rhegius?]. *Dialogus ader eyn ghespreche / wieder Doctor Ecken Büchlein.* [Braunschweig: Hans Dorn, 1521].

Osiander d.Ä., Andreas. *Gesamtausgabe.* 10 vols. Edited by Gerhard Müller and Gottfried Seebaß. Gütersloh: Gütersloher Verlagshaus, 1975–97.

———. *Verantwortung des Nürmbergischen Catechismi / Wider den vngelerten zenckischen Sophisten / Hansen Mayr zu Jngelstat.* Nuremberg: Leonhard Milchtaler, 1539.

Pagnotti, F. "Nicollò da Calvi e la sua *Vita d'Innocenzo IV,* con una breve introduzione sulla istoriografia pontificia nei secoli XIII e XIV." *Archivio Storico della R. Società Romana di Storia Patria* 21 (1898): 5–120.

Der Papisten handtbüchlein fleissig zu mercken / vnd heymlich zu lesen / Damit es die Leyen / denen der Bapst die heylige Schrifft zu lesen verbotten hat / nicht erfaren. N.p., 1546.

Paracelsus [Theophrast Bombast von Hohenheim]. *Sämtliche Werke.* 1. Abteilung. Edited by Karl Sudhoff and Wilhelm Matthießen. Munich: O. W. Barth and Berlin: R. Oldenbourg, 1922–33. Reprint, Hildesheim: Olms, 1996.

———. *Sämtliche Werke.* 2. Abteilung, *Theologische und religionsphilosophische Schriften.* Edited by Kurt Goldammer. Wiesbaden: Franz Steiner, 1955–.

Pasquillus: New Zeytung Vom Teuffel. N.p., 1546.

Pauli, Johannes. *Schimpf und Ernst.* 2 vols. Edited by Johannes Bolte. Berlin: H. Stubenrauch, 1924.

P. C. D. [?]. *Antwort. Auff den Sendbrieff / so H. S. . . . geschriben hatt.* N.p., n.d. [c. 1546].

Peraldus, Guilelmus. *Summa de vitiis et virtutibus.* N.p., n.d.

———. *Summae virtutum ac vitiorum.* 2 vols. Lyon: Guilelmus Rovillius, 1585.

Pfeiffer-Belli, Wolfgang, ed. *Thomas Murner im Schweizer Glaubenskampf.* Münster: Aschendorff, 1939.

Philipp of Novara. *The Wars of Frederick II against the Ibelins in Syria and Cyprus.* Edited by John L. La Monte. New York: Columbia University Press, 1936.

Raimundus de Pennaforte. *Summa de paenitentia.* Edited by Xaverius Ochoa and Aloisius Diez. Rome: Commentarium pro religiosis, 1976.

Ratschlag eins ausschus etlicher Cardinel / Bapst Paulo des namens dem dritten / auff seinen befelh geschrieben vnd vberantwortet: Mit einer vorrede D. Mart. Luth. Wittenberg: Hans Luft, 1538.

Rauscher, Hieronymus. *Ein nützliches gesprech eines Christlichen Fursten mit seynen Reten.* [Magdeburg: Christian Rödinger], n.d.

Rebhun, Paul. *Haußfried: Was für Ursachen den Christlichen eheleuten zubedencken.* Nuremberg: D. Gerlatz, 1569.

"Reformationsmandat für das Gebiet von Bern vom 7. Februar 1528." *Aktensammlung zur Geschichte der Berner Reformation 1521–1532* 1 (1932): 629–34.

Reuter, Simon. *Ein Christliche frage Simonis Reuters vonn Schlaytz / an alle Bischoffe / vnnd anndere geystliche auch zum teil weltliche regenten / Warumb sy doch: an priestern: vnnd andern geistlich geferbten leuten / den elichen standt nicht mügenn leyden.* N.p., 1523.

Reynmann, Leonhard. *Practica vber die grossen vnd manigfeltigen Coniunction der Planeten.* Nuremberg: Hieronymus Hölzel, 1523.

Rockinger, L., ed. "Briefsteller und formelbücher des eilften bis vierzehnten jahrhunderts." *Quellen zur bayerischen und deutschen Geschichte* 9 (1863).

Römer, Johann. *Das ist der hochthuren Babel id est Confusio Pape.* [Strasbourg: Matthias Schürer Erben, 1521].

Roth, Simon. *Ein Teutscher Dictionarius.* Augsburg: Michael Mayer, 1571.

Ruppert, Philipp, ed. *Die Chroniken der Stadt Konstanz.* Konstanz: R. Ruppert, 1891.

Rüsch, Ernst Gerhard, ed. "Die Schaffhauser Reformationsordnung von 1529." *Schaffhauser Beiträge zur Geschichte* 56 (1979): 17–23.

Rütiner, Johannes. *Diarium 1529–1539.* 5 vols. Edited by Ernst Gerhard Rüsch. St. Gallen: Vadiana, 1996.

Sachs, Hans. *Werke.* Edited by Adelbert von Keller et al. Hildesheim: Olms, 1964.

Sammlung schweizerischer Rechtsquellen. Edited by Schweizerischer Juristenverein. Aarau: Sauerländer, 1898–.

Schade, Oskar, ed. *Satiren und Pasquille aus der Reformationszeit.* 2d ed. 3 vols. Hannover: C. Rümpler, 1858–63.

Schelhorn, Johann Georg. *Apologia pro Petro Paulo Vergerio Episcopo Ivstinopolitano adversus Ioannem Casam Archiepiscopum Beneventanvm accedvnt qvaedam monvmenta inedita.* Ulm: Lieberkühn, 1760.

Schilling, Diebold. *Die Berner Chronik des Diebold Schilling 1468–1484.* 2 vols. Edited by Gustav Tobler. Bern: K. J. Wyss, 1897–1901.

———. *Diebold Schilling's des Lucerners Schweizer-Chronik: Abgedruckt nach der Originalhandschrift auf der Bürgerbibliothek der Stadt Lucern.* Lucerne: F. J. Schiffmann, 1862.

———. *Luzerner Bilderchronik.* Edited by Robert Durrer and Paul Hilber. Geneva: Sadag, 1932.

———. *Die Schweizer Bilderchronik des Luzerners Diebold Schilling 1513.* Edited by Alfred A. Schmid, Gottfried Boesch, Pascal Ladner, Carl Pfaff, Peter Rück, and Eduard Studer. Lucerne: Faksimile-Verlag, 1981.

Schmeink, Hermann Klein, ed. *Iohanens Fisher, Sacri sacerdotii defensio contra Lutherum (1525).* Münster: Aschendorff, 1925.

Schrot, Martin. *Apocalipsis: Ain frewden geschray über das gefallen Bapstumb so yetz diser zeit durch Gottes wort vnd schwerdt überwunden ist.* N.p., n.d.

Sebastus, Alphonsus Aemilius [pseud.]. *Pasquillus: Der vertriben von Rhom / so yetzund diser zeyt in Teütschland im ellend / vmb zeücht.* N.p., n.d.

Seel, Otto, ed. *Der Physiologus.* Zurich: Artemis, 1960.

Sinistrari, Ludovico Maria. *Peccatum Mutum: The Secret Sin,* ed. Montague Summers. Paris, n.d.

Sleidan, Johannes. *De statu religionis et reipublicae Carolo Quinto Caesare commentarii.* 3 vols. Edited by Johann Gottlob Boehm. Frankfurt am Main: Varentrapp/Wenner, 1785–86.

Spangenberg, Cyriacus. *Catechismus: Die Fünff Heuptstück der Christlichen Lere / Sampt der Haußtafel / vnd dem Morgen vnd Abendt Gebet / Benedicite vnd Gratias / etc.* Schmalkalden: Michael Schmuck, 1566.

Speculum exemplorum omnibus christicolis salubriter inspiciendum: vt exemplis discant disciplinam. Hagenau: Heinrich Gran, 1512.

Steinhausen, Georg, ed. *Deutsche Privatbriefe des Mittelalters.* Vol. 1, Berlin: R. Gaertners Verlagsbuchhandlung, 1899. Vol. 2, Berlin: Weidmannsche Buchhandlung, 1907.

Stör, Thomas. *Der Ehelich standt vonn got mit gebendeyung auffgeseczt.* N.p., 1524.

Strauss, Gerald, ed. *Manifestations of Discontent in Germany on the Eve of the Reformation: A Collection of Selected Documents.* Bloomington: Indiana University Press, 1971.

Tanner, Norman P., S.J., ed. *Decrees of the Ecumenical Councils.* Vol. 1: *Nicaea I to Lateran V.* Washington, D.C.: Georgetown University Press, 1990.

Tenngler, Ulrich. *Laienspiegel: Von rechtmässigen ordnungen inn Burgerlichenn vnd Peinlichen Regimenten.* Strasbourg: Wendel Rihel, 1550.

―――. *Laÿen Spiegel: Von rechtmässigen ordnungen in Burgerlichen vnd peinlichen regimenten.* Augsburg: H. Ottmar, 1509.

―――. *Der neü Layenspiegel Von rechtmässigen ordnungen in Burgerlichen vnd peinlichen Regimenten.* Augsburg: Hans Ottmar, 1511.

Thomas Aquinas. *Summa theologiae.* Edited by Pietro Caramello. Turin: Marietti, 1986.

Torrentinus, Hermann. *Bucolica: P. Virgilij Maronis cum verborum contextu in poetices tyrunculorum sublevamen.* [Cologne: Quentel, 1503].

Tschamser, Malachias. *Annales oder Jahrs-Geschichten der Baarfüseren.* Edited by A. Merklen. Colmar: n.p., 1864.

Ulric, Saint, Bishop of Augsburg. *See* Flacius Illyricus, Matthias; Luther, Martin

van den Broek, M. A., ed. *Der Spiegel des Sünders: Ein katechetischer Traktat des fünfzehnten Jahrhunderts: Textausgabe und Beobachtungen zum Sprachgebrauch.* Amsterdam: Rodopi, 1976.

Vergerio, Pietro Paolo. *Il catalogo de libri, li qvali nvovamente nel mese di maggio nell'anno presente M.D.XLVIIII. sono stati condannati, & scomunicati per heretici, Da M. Giouan. della Casa legato di Vinetia.* [Zurich?: Poschiavo?]: 1549.

―――. *A gl'inqvisitori che sono per l'Italia: Del catalogo di libri eretici, stampato in Roma nell'Anno presente.* [Tübingen]: 1549.

―――. *Postremus catalogus haereticoum Romae conflatus, 1559.* Pforzheim: Corvinus, 1560.

Vintler, Hans. *Die Pluemen der Tugent des Hans Vintler.* Edited by Ignaz V. Zingerle. Innsbruck: Wagner, 1874.

Virdung, Hans. *Practica von dem Entcrist vnd dem jüngsten tag auch was geschehen sal vor dem Ende der welt.* [Speyer: Jakob Schmidt, 1523].

Volz, Hans, ed. *Drei Schriften gegen Luthers Schmalkaldische Artikel von Cochläus, Witzel und Hoffmeister.* Münster: Aschendorff, 1932.

Vom Ende der Welt / Vnd zukunfft des Endtchrists. Frankfurt am Main: Hermann Gülfferich, n.d.

Von dem Eelichen stadt. [Augsburg: Johann Schönsberger, c. 1513].

Von dem gewalt vnd haupt der kirchen / ein gesprech. N.p., n.d.

Vrsprung vnd Vrsach diser Auffrur / Teutscher Nation. N.p., n.d.

Waga, Friedrich, ed. *Die Welsch-Gattung.* Breslau: M. & H. Marcus, 1910.

Wann, Paul. *Sermones de septem vitijs criminalibus eorumque remediis.* Hagenau: Heinrich Gran, 1514.

―――. *Sermones dominicales per anni circulum.* Hagenau: Heinrich Gran, 1512.

Watt, Joachim von [Vadian]. *Vadianische Briefsammlung.* 7 vols. Edited by Emil Arbenz and Hermann Wartmann. St. Gallen: Huber, 1890–1913.

Wickram, Jörg. *Sämtliche Werke.* Berlin: de Gruyter, 1967–.

Wilhelm, Balthasar. *Practica oder Prenostication auff tzükunfftig tzeythe / auss der heyligen schrifft getzogenn.* N.p., [1524].

William of Peyraud. *See* Peraldus, Guilelmus

Wimpfeling, Jakob. *Adolescentia.* Edited by Otto Herding. Munich: W. Fink, 1965.

―――. *Briefwechsel.* 2 vols. Edited by Otto Herding and Dieter Mertens. Munich: W. Fink, 1990.

Wimpina, Conrad, Johann Mensing, Wolfgang Redorffer, and Rupert Elgersima. *Gegen die bekanntnus Martini Luthers auff den ytzigen angestellten Reychstag zu Augspurg.* [Leipzig: Valentin Schumann, 1530].

Witzel, Georg. *Catechismus Ecclesiae: Lere vnd Handelunge des heiligen Christenthums.* Leipzig: Melchior Lotter, 1535.

————. *Von der Christlichen Kyrchen: wider Jodocum Koch / der sich nennet / Justum Jonam.* Leipzig: Nickel Schmidt, 1540.

Wolff, Johannes. "Beichtbüchlein" (1478). In *Drei Beichtbüchlein nach den zehn Geboten aus der Frühzeit der Buchdruckerkunst,* edited by Franz Falk. Münster: Aschendorff, 1907.

Zedler, Johann Heinrich. *Grosses vollständiges Universal-Lexicon.* 64 vols. Reprint, Graz: Akademische Druck- und Verlagsanstalt, 1962.

Zimmermann, Anton. *Vom vbeln der Eyde / so ynn offenlichen gerichten geschehen.* [Erfurt: Johann Loersfeld], 1523.

"Das Zürcher Mandat 'Christenlich ansehung des gemeinen kilchgangs etc.' vom 26. März 1530." In *Aktensammlung zur Geschichte der Zürcher Reformation in den Jahren 1519–1533,* edited by Emil Egli, 702–11. Zurich: n.p., 1879. Reprint, Nieuwkoop: de Graaf, 1973.

Zwinger, Theodor. *Theatri Humani Vitae.* Basel: Henricpetri, 1604.

Secondary Literature

Abray, Lorna Jane. *The People's Reformation: Magistrates, Clergy, and Commons in Strasbourg, 1500–1598.* Ithaca, N.Y.: Cornell University Press, 1985.

Albert, Thomas D. *Der gemeine Mann vor dem geistlichen Richter: Kirchliche Rechtsprechung in den Diözesen Basel, Chur und Konstanz vor der Reformation.* Stuttgart: Lucius & Lucius, 1998.

Anderson, Benedict. *Imagined Communities: Reflections on the Origin and Spread of Nationalism.* Rev. ed. London: Verso, 1991.

Andreadis, Harriette. *Sappho in Early Modern England: Female Same-Sex Literary Erotics 1550–1714.* Chicago: University of Chicago Press, 2001.

Anzelewski, Fedja. *Dürer: Werk und Wirkung.* Erlangen: Karl Müller, 1988.

Arnold, Klemens. "St. Ursus in Solothurn." In *Die Weltlichen Kollegiatstifte der deutsch- und französischsprachigen Schweiz,* edited by Guy P. Marchal. Abteilung 2, Teil 2 of *Helvetia Sacra.* Bern: Francke, 1977.

Arnold, Werner, et al., eds. *Die Erforschung der Buch- und Bibliotheksgeschichte in Deutschland.* Wiesbaden: Harrassowitz, 1987.

Babcock, Barbara A. Introduction to *The Reversible World: Symbolic Inversion in Art and Society.* Edited by Barbara A. Babcock. Ithaca, N.Y.: Cornell University Press, 1978.

Bagchi, David N. N. *Luther's Earliest Opponents: Catholic Controversialists, 1518–1525.* Minneapolis, Minn.: Fortress Press 1991.

Bakhtin, Mikhail. *Rabelais and His World.* Translated by Hélène Iswolsky. Bloomington: Indiana University Press, 1984.

Baldwin, John W. "Five Discourses on Desire: Sexuality and Gender in Northern France around 1200." *Speculum* 66 (1991): 797–819.

————. *The Language of Sex: Five Voices from Northern France around 1200.* Chicago: University of Chicago Press, 1994.

Baptist-Hlawatsch, Gabriele. *Das katechetische Werk Ulrichs von Pottenstein: Sprachliche und rezeptionsgeschichtliche Untersuchungen.* Tübingen: Niemeyer, 1980.

Baptist-Hlawatsch, Gabriele, and Ulrike Bodemann. "Ulrich von Pottenstein." In *Die deutsche Literatur des Mittelalters: Verfasserlexikon*, 2d ed., edited by Stammler, Langosch, and Wachinger. Vol. 10, 10–17. Berlin: de Gruyter, 1996.

Barber, Malcolm. *The Trial of the Templars*. Cambridge: Cambridge University Press, 1978.

Barkan, Leonard. *Transuming Passion: Ganymede and the Erotics of Humanism*. Stanford, Calif.: Stanford University Press, 1991.

Baron, Frank. *Faustus: Geschichte, Sage, Dichtung*. Munich: Winkler, 1982.

Barstow, Anne Llewellyn. *Married Priests and the Reforming Papacy: The Eleventh-Century Debates*. Lewiston, N.Y.: Mellen, 1982.

Battaglia, Salvatore, ed. *Grande dizionario della lingua italiana*. Turin: Unione tipografico-editrice torinese, 1961–.

Baumann, Karin. *Aberglaube für Laien: Zur Programmatik und Überlieferung spätmittelalterlicher Superstitionenkritik*. Würzburg: Königshausen & Neumann, 1989.

Bayle, Pierre. *Dictionnaire historique et critique*. 5th ed. of 1740. Geneva: Slatkine, 1995.

————. *Historisches und Critisches Wörterbuch: Nach der neuesten Auflage von 1740 ins Deutsche übersetzt*. 4 vols. Edited by Johann Christoph Gottsched. Hildesheim: Olms, 1974–78.

Behrendt, Walter. "Übersetzungen und Bearbeitungen des Pseudo-Bernhardus Briefs 'De cura rei familiaris' im 16. Jahrhundert (Joachim Humel, Johannes Spangenberg, Adam Walasser)." *Leuvense Bijdragen: Leuven Contributions in Linguistics and Philology* 83 (1994): 343–62.

Bein, Thomas. "Orpheus als Sodomit: Beobachtungen zu einer mhd. Sangspruchstrophe mit (literar)historischen Exkursen zur Homosexualität im hohen Mittelalter." *Zeitschrift für deutsche Philologie* 109 (1990): 33–55.

Bennett, Judith M. "'Lesbian-Like' and the Social History of Lesbianisms." *Journal of the History of Sexuality* 9 (2000): 1–24.

Bennett, Judith M., and Amy M. Froide, eds. *Singlewomen in the European Past, 1250–1800*. Philadelphia: University of Pennsylvania Press, 1999.

Bihrer, Andreas, Sven Limbeck, and Paul Gerhard Schmidt, eds. *Exil, Fremdheit und Ausgrenzung in Mittelalter und früher Neuzeit*. Würzburg: Ergon, 2000.

Bleys, Rudi C. *The Geography of Perversion: Male-to-Male Sexual Behaviour Outside the West and the Ethnographic Imagination, 1250–1918*. London: Cassell, 1996.

Blickle, Peter. "Antiklerikalismus um den Vierwaldstättersee 1300–1500." In *Anticlericalism in Late Medieval and Early Modern Europe*, edited by Peter A. Dykema and Heiko A. Oberman. Leiden: E. J. Brill, 1993.

Bloch, R. Howard. "Modest Maids and Modified Nouns: Obscenity in the Fabliaux." In *Obscenity, Social Control, and Artistic Creation in the European Middle Ages*, edited by Jan M. Ziolkowski, 293–307. Leiden: Brill, 1998.

Bodmer, Jean-Pierre. "Werner Steiners Pilgerführer." *Zwingliana* 12, no. 1 (1964): 69–73.

————. "Werner Steiner und die Schlacht bei Marignano" *Zwingliana* 12, no. 4 (1965, no. 2): 241–47.

Boes, Maria R. "The Treatment of Juvenile Delinquents in Early Modern Germany: A Case Study." *Continuity and Change* 11 (1996): 43–60.

Boner, Georg. "Das Predigerkloster in Basel von der Gründung bis zur Klosterreform 1233–1429." *Zeitschrift für Basler Altertumskunde* 33 (1934): 195–303; 34 (1935): 107–259.

Boockmann, Hartmut, Ludger Grenzmann, Bernd Moeller, and Martin Staehelin, eds.

Recht und Verfassung im Übergang vom Mittelalter zur Neuzeit. Göttingen: Vandenhoeck & Ruprecht, 1998.

Boone, Marc. "State Power and Illicit Sexuality: The Persecution of Sodomy in Late Medieval Bruges." *Journal of Medieval History* 22 (1996): 135–53.

Boswell, John. *Christianity, Social Tolerance, and Homosexuality: Gay People in Western Europe from the Beginning of the Christian Era to the Fourteenth Century.* Chicago: University of Chicago Press, 1980.

———. "Dante and the Sodomites." *Dante Studies* 112 (1994): 33–51.

Boureau, Alain. *The Myth of Pope Joan.* Chicago: University of Chicago Press, 2001.

Boyle, Leonard E., "The *Summa Confessorum* of John of Freiburg and the Popularization of the Moral Teaching of St. Thomas and of Some of His Contemporaries." In *St. Thomas Aquinas 1274–1974: Commemorative Studies,* edited by Etienne Gilson, 245–68. Toronto: Pontifical Institute, 1974.

Brady, Thomas A., Jr. "'You Hate Us Priests': Anticlericalism, Communalism, and the Control of Women at Strasbourg in the Age of the Reformation." In *Anticlericalism in Late Medieval and Early Modern Europe,* edited by Peter A. Dykema and Heiko A. Oberman, 167–207. Leiden: E. J. Brill, 1993.

Brall, Helmut. "Reflections of Homosexuality in Medieval Poetry and Chronicles." In *Queering the Canon: Defying Sights in German Literature and Culture,* edited by Christoph Lorey and John Plews, 89–105. Columbia, S.C.: Camden House, 1998.

Brändly, Willy. "Die Zuger Humanisten." *Innerschweizerisches Jahrbuch für Heimatkunde* 8–10 (1946): 206–20.

———. "Jodocus Müller (Molitor)." *Zwingliana* 7, no. 5 (1941): 319–30.

———. "Peter Kolin von Zug." *Zwingliana* 9, no. 3 (1950, no. 1): 150–76.

Bray, Alan. "Homosexuality and the Signs of Male Friendship in Elizabethan England." In *Queering the Renaissance,* edited by Jonathan Goldberg. Durham, N.C.: Duke University Press, 1994. First published in *History Workshop Journal* 29 (1990): 1–19.

———. *Homosexuality in Renaissance England.* London: Gay Men's Press, 1982.

———. "To Be a Man in Early Modern Society: The Curious Case of Michael Wigglesworth." *History Workshop Journal* 41 (Spring 1996): 155–65.

Breitenberg, Mark. *Anxious Masculinity in Early Modern England.* New York: Cambridge University Press, 1996.

Briggs, Robin. *Witches and Neighbors: The Social and Cultural Context of European Witchcraft.* New York: Penguin, 1996.

Brooten, Bernadette J. *Love between Women: Early Christian Responses to Female Homoeroticism.* Chicago: University of Chicago Press, 1996.

Brown, Judith C. *Immodest Acts: The Life of a Lesbian Nun in Renaissance Italy.* New York: Oxford University Press, 1986.

———. "Lesbian Sexuality in Medieval and Early Modern Europe." In *Hidden from History,* edited by Martin B. Duberman, Martha Vicinus, and George Chauncey, Jr. New York: NAL Books, 1989.

Brückner, Wolfgang. "Exempelsammlungen." In *Enzyklopädie des Märchens.* Vol. 4. Berlin: de Gruyter, 1984.

Brundage, James A. *Law, Sex, and Christian Society in Medieval Europe.* Chicago: University of Chicago Press, 1987.

———. "Politics of Sodomy: Rex vs. Pons Hugh de Ampurias (1311)." In *Sex in the Middle Ages,* edited by Joyce E. Salisbury, 239–46. New York: Garland, 1991.

Brunnenmeister, Emil. *Die Quellen der Bambergensis: Ein Beitrag zur Geschichte des Strafrechts.* Leipzig: Engelmann, 1879.

Buckwalter, Stephen E. *Die Priesterehe in Flugschriften der frühen Reformation.* Gütersloh: Gütersloher Verlagshaus, 1996.

Buff, Adolf. "Verbrechen und Verbrecher in Augsburg in der zweiten Hälfte des 14. Jahrhunderts." *Zeitschrift des Historischen Vereins für Schwaben und Neuburg* 4 (1877/78): 160–231.

Bullough, Vern L., and James A. Brundage, eds. *Handbook of Medieval Sexuality.* New York: Garland, 1996.

Burckhardt, Jacob. *Die Kultur der Renaissance in Italien.* Edited by Horst Günther. Frankfurt am Main: Deutscher Klassikerverlag, 1989. Translated by S. G. C. Middlemore under the title *The Civilization of the Renaissance in Italy* (London: Penguin, 1990).

Burghartz, Susanna. *Leib, Ehre und Gut: Delinquenz in Zürich Ende des 14. Jahrhunderts.* Zurich: Chronos, 1990.

———. *Zeiten der Reinheit: Orte der Unzucht: Ehe und Sexualität in Basel während der frühen Neuzeit.* Paderborn: Schöningh, 1999.

Burke, Peter. "The Art of Insult in Early Modern Italy." *Culture and History* 2 (1987): 68–79.

———. *The Historical Anthropology of Early Modern Italy.* Cambridge: Cambridge University Press, 1987.

Busch, Alexandra, and Dirck Linck, eds. *Frauenliebe—Männerliebe: Eine lesbisch-schwule Literaturgeschichte in Essays.* Stuttgart: Metzler, 1997.

Buschbell, Gottfried. *Reformation und Inquisition in Italien um die Mitte des 16. Jahrhunderts.* Paderborn: Ferdinand Schöningh, 1910.

Butler, Judith. *Bodies That Matter: On the Discursive Limits of "Sex."* New York: Routledge, 1993.

———. *Excitable Speech: A Politics of the Performative.* New York: Routledge, 1997.

Cady, Joseph. "'Masculine Love,' Renaissance Writing, and the 'New Invention' of Homosexuality." In *Homosexuality in Renaissance and Enlightenment England,* edited by Claude J. Summers. New York: Haworth Press, 1992.

Cano, Melchior. *Opera.* Vol. 2. Rome: n.p., 1890.

Canosa, Romano. *Storia di una grande paura: La sodomia a Firenze e a Venezia nel Quattrocento.* Milano: Feltrinelli, 1991.

Casid, Jill H. "Queer(y)ing Georgic: Utility, Pleasure, and Marie-Antoinette's Ornamented Farm." *Eighteenth-Century Studies* 30 (1997): 304–18.

Charland, Thomas-Marie, O.P. *Artes praedicandi: Contribution à l'histoire de la rhétorique au moyen âge.* Paris: J. Vrin, 1936.

Chartier, Roger. "L'histoire culturelle entre 'Linguistic Turn' et retour au sujet." In *Wege zu einer neuen Kulturgeschichtsschreibung,* edited by Hartmut Lehmann, 29–58. Göttingen: Wallstein, 1995.

———. *On the Edge of the Cliff: History, Language, and Practices.* Translated by Lydia G. Cochrane. Baltimore: Johns Hopkins University Press, 1996.

Chiffoleau, Jacques. "'Contra naturam': Pour une approche casuistique et procédurale de la nature médiévale." *Micrologus* 4 (1996): 265–312.

———. "Dire l'indicible: La catégorie du 'nefandum' du XIIe au XVe siècle." *Annales esc.* 45 (1990): 289–324.

Chrisman, Miriam Usher. *Conflicting Visions of Reform: German Lay Propaganda Pamphlets, 1519–1530.* Atlantic Highlands, N.J.: Humanities Press, 1996.

———. "From Polemic to Propaganda: The Development of Mass Persuasion in the Late Sixteenth Century." *Archiv für Reformationsgeschichte* 73 (1982): 175–95.

Church, Frederic C. *The Italian Reformers 1534–1564.* New York: Columbia University Press, 1932.

Cohen, William A. *Sex Scandal: The Private Part of Victorian Fiction.* Durham, N.C.: Duke University Press, 1996.

Colberg, Katharina. "Felix Hemmerli." In *Die deutsche Literatur des Mittelalters: Verfasserlexikon,* 2d ed., edited by Stammler, Langosch, and Wachinger. Vol. 3, cols. 989–1001. Berlin: de Gruyter, 1981.

Cole, Richard G. "Reformation Pamphlet and Communication Processes." In *Flugschriften als Massenmedium der Reformationszeit,* edited by Hans-Joachim Köhler. Stuttgart: Klett-Cotta, 1981.

Crompton, Louis. "The Myth of Lesbian Impunity: Capital Laws from 1270 to 1791." In *The Gay Past,* edited by Salvatore J. Licata and Robert P. Petersen. New York: Harrington Park Press, 1985.

dall'Orto, Giovanni. " 'Socratic Love' as a Disguise for Same-Sex Love in the Italian Renaissance." In *The Pursuit of Sodomy: Male Homosexuality in Renaissance and Enlightenment Europe,* edited by Kent Gerard and Gert Hekma, 33–65. London: Harrington Park Press, 1989.

Davies, Kathleen M. "Continuity and Change in Literary Advice on Marriage." In *Marriage and Society: Studies in the Social History of Marriage,* edited by R. B. Outhwaite, 58–80. New York: Europa Publications, 1982.

Davis, Natalie Zemon. *Society and Culture in Early Modern France.* Stanford, Calif.: Stanford University Press, 1975.

De Certeau, Michel. *The Writing of History.* Translated by Tom Conley. New York: Columbia University Press, 1988.

Degler-Spengler, Brigitte. "Die Beginen in Basel." *Basler Zeitschrift für Geschichte und Altertumskunde* 69 (1970): 5–83; 70 (1970): 29–118.

Dekker, Rudolf M., and Lotte C. van de Pol. *The Tradition of Female Transvestism in Early Modern Europe.* London: Macmillan, 1989.

Deleuze, Gilles. "Ecrivain non: un nouveau cartographe," *Critique* 343 (1975): 1207–27.

———. *Foucault.* London: Athlone, 1988.

Delumeau, Jean, ed. *Injures et blasphèmes.* Paris: Editions Imago, 1989.

Dictionnaire de la langue française du seizième siècle. Edited by Edmond Huguet. Paris: Didier, 1961.

Dictionnaire de la langue française et de tous les dialectes du IXe au XVe siècle. Edited by Frédéric Godefroy. Paris: F. Vieweg, 1880–1902. Reprint, New York: Kraus Reprint, 1961.

Diener, Ernst. *Das Haus Landenberg im Mittelalter: Mit besonderer Berücksichtigung des 14. Jahrhunderts.* Zurich: Friedrich Schulthess, 1898.

Dietrich, Christian. *Die Stadt Zürich und ihre Landgemeinden während der Bauernunruhen von 1489 bis 1525.* Frankfurt am Main: Peter Lang, 1985.

Dinshaw, Carolyn. "Chaucer's Queer Touches/A Queer Touches Chaucer." *Exemplaria* 7 (1995): 75–92.

———. *Getting Medieval: Sexualities and Communities, Pre- and Postmodern.* Durham, N.C.: Duke University Press, 1999.

Dipple, Geoffrey. *Antifraternalism and Anticlericalism in the German Reformation: Johann Eberlin von Günzburg and the Campaign against the Friars.* Brookfield, Vt.: Ashgate, 1996.

Donoghue, Emma. "Imagined More than Women: Lesbians as Hermaphrodites, 1671–1766." *Women's History Review* 2 (1993): 199–216.

Duberman, Martin Bauml, Martha Vicinus, and George Chauncey, Jr., eds. *Hidden from History: Reclaiming the Gay and Lesbian Past.* New York: NAL Books, 1989.

Du Boulay, Francis Robin H. *Germany in the Later Middle Ages.* London: Athlone Press, 1987.

Du Cange, Charles Du Fresne. *Glossarium mediae et infimae latinitatis.* Paris: Didot, 1840–50.

Duggan, Lisa. "The Discipline Problem: Queer History Meets Lesbian and Gay History." *GLQ* 2 (1995): 179–91.

Dülmen, Richard van, ed. *Kultur und Alltag in der Frühen Neuzeit.* 3 vols. Munich: Beck, 1990–94.

————. *Theatre of Horror: Crime and Punishment in Early Modern Germany.* Translated by Elisabeth Neu. Cambridge: Polity Press, 1990.

Dykema, Peter A., and Heiko A. Oberman, eds. *Anticlericalism in Late Medieval and Early Modern Europe.* Leiden: E. J. Brill, 1993.

Dynes, Wayne R., ed. *Encyclopedia of Homosexuality.* 2 vols. New York: Garland, 1990.

Edwards, Mark U., Jr. *Luther's Last Battles: Politics and Polemics, 1531–46.* Ithaca, N.Y.: Cornell University Press, 1983.

Egger, Franz. *Beiträge zur Geschichte des Predigerordens: Die Reform des Basler Konvents 1429 und die Stellung des Ordens am Basler Konzil 1431–1448.* Bern: Peter Lang, 1991.

Eickels, Klaus van. *Vom inszenierten Konsens zum systematisierten Konflikt: Die englisch-französischen Beziehungen und ihre Wahrnehmung an der Wende vom Hoch- zum Spätmittelalter.* Stuttgart: Thorbecke, 2002.

Eisenhardt, Ulrich. *Die kaiserliche Aufsicht über Buchdruck, Buchhandel und Presse im Heiligen Römischen Reich Deutscher Nation, 1496–1806.* Karlsruhe: C. F. Müller, 1970.

Elliott, Dyan. *Fallen Bodies: Pollution, Sexuality, and Demonology in the Middle Ages.* Philadelphia: University of Pennsylvania Press, 1998.

Eriksson, Brigitte, ed. "A Lesbian Execution in Germany, 1721: The Trial Records." In *The Gay Past: A Collection of Historical Essays,* edited by Salvatore J. Licata and Robert P. Petersen, 27–40. New York: Harrington Park Press, 1985.

Esch, Arnold. "Mit Schweizer Söldnern auf dem Marsch nach Italien: Das Erlebnis der Mailänderkriege 1510–1515 nach bernischen Akten." *Mitteilungen und Forschungen aus italienischen Archiven und Bibliotheken* 70 (1990): 348–440.

Farnell, Lewis Richard. *The Cults of the Greek States.* Vol. 5. Oxford: Clarendon, 1909.

Feller, Richard, and Edgar Bonjour. *Geschichtsschreibung der Schweiz vom Spätmittelalter zur Neuzeit.* 2d ed. Basel: B. Schwabe, 1979.

Forey, Alan J. *The Military Orders: From the Twelfth to the Early Fourteenth Centuries.* London: Macmillan, 1992.

Foucault, Michel. *The History of Sexuality.* Vol. 1, *An Introduction.* New York: Vintage, 1980.

————. "Nietzsche, Genealogy, History." In *The Foucault Reader.* Edited by Rabinow, Paul. New York: Pantheon, 1984.

Fradenburg, Louise O., and Carla Freccero. "The Pleasures of History." *GLQ* 1 (1995): 371–84.

Frank, Isnard W. "Das lateinische theologische Schrifttum im österreichischen Spätmittelalter." In *Die österreichische Literatur: Ihr Profil von den Anfängen im Mittelalter bis ins 18. Jahrhundert (1050–1750)*, edited by Herbert Zeman, 261–93. Graz: Akademische Druck- und Verlagsanstalt, 1986.

Frank, Michael. "Ehre und Gewalt im Dorf der Frühen Neuzeit: Das Beispiel Heiden (Grafschaft Lippe) im 17. und 18. Jahrhundert." In *Verletzte Ehre: Ehrkonflikte in Gesellschaften des Mittelalters und der Frühen Neuzeit*, edited by Klaus Schreiner and Gerd Schwerhoff. Cologne: Böhlau, 1995.

Frantzen, Allen J. *Before the Closet: Same-Sex Love from "Beowulf" to "Angels in America."* Chicago: University of Chicago Press, 1998.

———. "Between the Lines: Queer Theory, the History of Homosexuality, and Anglo-Saxon Penitentials." *Journal of Medieval and Early Modern Studies* 26 (1996): 255–96.

———. "The Disclosure of Sodomy in *Cleanness*." *PMLA* 111 (1996): 451–64.

Frauenknecht, Erwin. *Die Verteidigung der Priesterehe in der Reformzeit.* Hannover: Hahnsche Buchhandlung, 1997.

Freddi, Silvan. *Das Kollegiatstift St. Ursus in Solothurn: Von den Anfängen bis 1520: Ursprung—Innere Organisation—Verhältnis zur Stadt.* Lizentiatsarbeit, University of Zurich, 1995.

Fretz, Diethelm. "Steineri fata." *Zwingliana* 4, no. 12 (1926, no. 2): 377–84.

Fudge, Thomas A. *The Magnificent Ride: The First Reformation in Hussite Bohemia.* Aldershot: Ashgate, 1998.

Füser, Thomas. "Der Leib ist das Grab der Seele: Der institutionelle Umgang mit sexueller Devianz in Cluniazensischen Klöstern des 13. und frühen 14. Jahrhunderts." In *De ordine vitae: Funktionen und Formen von Schriftlichkeit im mittelalterlichen Ordenswesen*, edited by Gert Melville. Munich: Lit, 1996.

Gade, Kari Ellen. "Homosexuality and Rape of Males in Old Norse Law and Literature." *Scandinavian Studies* 58 (1986): 124–41.

Gagliardi, Ernst. *Hans Waldmann und die Eidgenossenschaft des 15. Jahrhunderts.* Basel: Verlag der Basler Buch- und Antiquariatshandlung, 1912.

———. "Mailänder und Franzosen in der Schweiz 1495–1499: Eidgenössische Zustände im Zeitalter des Schwabenkriegs." *Jahrbuch für schweizerische Geschichte* 39 (1914): 1*–283*.

Gärtner, Kurt, and Gerhard Hanrieder, eds. *Findebuch zum mittelhochdeutschen Wortschatz.* Stuttgart: S. Hirzel, 1992.

Giesecke, Michael. *Der Buchdruck in der frühen Neuzeit: Eine historische Fallstudie über die Durchsetzung neuer Informations- und Kommunikationstechnologien.* Frankfurt am Main: Suhrkamp, 1991.

Gilmour-Bryson, Anne. "Sodomy and the Knights Templar." *Journal of the History of Sexuality* 7 (1996): 151–83.

Gilomen, Hans-Jörg. "Innere Verhältnisse der Stadt Zürich, 1300–1500." In *Geschichte des Kantons Zürich*, vol. 1. Zurich: Werd, 1995.

Ginzburg, Carlo. *History, Rhetoric, and Proof: The Menahem Stern Jerusalem Lectures.* Hanover, N.H.: University Press of New England, 1999.

Gluckman, Max. "Gossip and Scandal." *Current Anthropology* 4 (1963): 307–16.

Goertz, Hans-Jürgen. "Kleruskritik, Kirchenzucht und Sozialdisziplinierung in den täuferischen Bewegungen der Frühen Neuzeit." In *Kirchenzucht und*

Sozialdisziplinierung im frühneuzeitlichen Europa, edited by Heinz Schilling, 183–98. Berlin: Duncker & Humblot, 1994.

—————. *Pfaffenhaß und groß Geschrei: Die reformatorischen Bewegungen in Deutschland 1517–1529*. Munich: C. H. Beck, 1987.

Goldberg, Jonathan. *Sodometries: Renaissance Texts, Modern Sexualities*. Stanford, Calif.: Stanford University Press, 1992.

Goldberg, Jonathan, ed. *Queering the Renaissance*. Durham, N.C.: Duke University Press, 1994.

Göllner, Carl. *Tvrcica: Die europäische Türkendrucke des 16. Jahrhunderts*. Vol. 1, *1501–1550*. Berlin: Akademie 1961. Vol. 2, *1551–1600*. Baden-Baden: Heitz, 1968. Vol. 3, *Die Türkenfrage in der öffentlichen Meinung Europas im 16. Jahrhundert*. Baden-Baden: Valentin Koerner, 1978.

Goodich, Michael. "Sodomy in Ecclesiastical Law and Theory." *Journal of Homosexuality* 1 (1976): 427–34.

—————. "Sodomy in Medieval Secular Law." *Journal of Homosexuality* 1 (1976): 295–302.

—————. *The Unmentionable Vice: Homosexuality in the Later Medieval Period*. Santa Barbara, Calif.: Dorset Press, 1979.

Gössi, Anton. "Das Werden des modernen Staates: Luzern von 1550–1650." In *Renaissancemalerei in Luzern 1560–1650: Ausstellung im Schloss Wyher, Ettiswil*, edited by Anton Gössi. Lucerne: Lehrmittelverlag Luzern, 1986.

Gossman, Lionel. *Basel in the Age of Burckhardt: A Study in Unseasonable Ideas*. Chicago: University of Chicago Press, 2000.

Gottlieb, Gunther, et al., eds. *Geschichte der Stadt Augsburg von der Römerzeit bis zur Gegenwart*. 2d ed. Stuttgart: Konrad Theiss, 1985.

Gowing, Laura. *Domestic Dangers: Women, Words, and Sex in Early Modern London*. New York: Oxford University Press, 1996.

—————. "Language of Insult in Early Modern London." *History Workshop Journal* 35 (1993): 1–21.

Grafton, Anthony T. *Defenders of the Text: The Traditions of Scholarship in an Age of Science, 1450–1800*. Cambridge, Mass.: Harvard University Press, 1991.

Greenberg, David F. *The Construction of Homosexuality*. Chicago: University of Chicago Press, 1988.

Grendler, Paul F. *The Roman Inquisition and the Venetian Press*. Princeton, N.J.: Princeton University Press, 1977.

Grimm, Jacob, and Wilhelm Grimm, eds. *Deutsches Wörterbuch*. Leipzig: S. Hirzel, 1854–.

Grüter, Sebastian. *Geschichte des Kantons Luzern im 16. und 17. Jahrhundert*. Luzern: Räber, 1945.

Gyger, Patrick J. *L'épée et la corde: Criminalité et justice à Fribourg (1475–1505)*. Lausanne: Section d'histoire médiévale Faculté des Lettres, 1998.

Haefliger, Hans. *Solothurn in der Reformation*. Solothurn: Gassmann, 1945.

Hagemann, Rudolf. *Aus dem Rechtsleben im alten Basel*. Basel: Basler Zeitung, 1989.

—————. *Basler Rechtsleben im Mittelalter*. 2 vols. Basel: Helbing & Lichtenhahn, 1981–87.

Haggerty, George E. *Men in Love: Masculinity and Sexuality in the Eighteenth Century*. New York: Columbia University Press, 1999.

Hain, Ludwig. *Repertorium bibliographicum, in quo libri omnes ab arte typographica inventa usque ad annum MD. typis expressis ordine alphabetico vel simpliciter enumerantur.* 4 vols. Stuttgart & Tübingen: J. G. Cotta, 1826–38.

Halperin, David M. "Forgetting Foucault: Acts, Identities, and the History of Sexuality." *Representations* 63 (1998): 93–120.

—————. "How to Do the History of Male Homosexuality." *GLQ* 6 (2000): 87–124.

Harrington, Joel F. *Reordering Marriage and Society in Reformation Germany.* Cambridge: Cambridge University Press, 1995.

Hartweg, Frédéric. "Die Rolle des Buchdrucks für die frühneuhochdeutsche Sprachgeschichte." In *Sprachgeschichte: Ein Handbuch zur Geschichte der deutschen Sprache und ihrer Erforschung.* Vol. 2. Edited by Werner Besch, Oskar Reichmann, and Stefan Sonderegger. Berlin: de Gruyter, 1985.

Hauser, A. *Pietro Paolo Vergerios protestantische Zeit.* Ph.D. diss., University of Tübingen, 1980.

Heimpel, Hermann. "Reformatio Sigismundi, Priesterehe und Bernhard von Chartres." *Deutsches Archiv für Geschichte des Mittelalters* 17 (1961): 526–37.

Herdt, Gilbert, ed. *Third Sex, Third Gender: Beyond Sexual Dimorphism in Culture and History.* New York: Zone Books, 1994.

Hergemöller, Bernd-Ulrich. "Dietrich Koldes *Verclaringhe* und *Een prophetye gepreect by broeder Dierick van Munster*: Zur Arbeitsweise und Rezeptionsgeschichte des Christenspiegels." In *Vestigia Monasteriensia: Westfalen—Rheinland—Niederlande,* edited by Ellen Widder, Mark Mersiowsky, and Peter Johanek, 73–99. Bielefeld: Verlag für Regionalgeschichte, 1995.

—————. *Einführung in die Historiographie der Homosexualitäten.* Tübingen: Edition diskord, 1999.

—————. "Homosexuelle als spätmittelalterliche Randgruppe." *Forum Homosexualität und Literatur* 2 (1987): 53–91.

—————. *Krötenkuß und schwarzer Kater: Ketzerei, Götzendienst und Unzucht in der inquisitorischen Phantasie des 13. Jahrhunderts.* Warendorf: Fahlbusch, 1996.

—————. "Ludwig der Bayer, Friedrich der Schöne, Friedrich von Tirol—Verwirrungen und Verwechslungen." *Capri: Zeitschrift für schwule Geschichte* 1 (1991): 31–41.

—————. *Männer, "die mit Männer handeln," in der Augsburger Reformationszeit.* Munich: Forum Homosexualität und Geschichte, 2000.

—————. "Sodomiter—Erscheinungsformen und Kausalfaktoren des spätmittelalterlichen Kampfes gegen Homosexuelle." In *Randgruppen der spätmittelalterlichen Gesellschaft: Ein Hand- und Studienbuch,* edited by Bernd-Ulrich Hergemöller, 361–403. 2d ed. Warendorf: Fahlbusch, 1994.

—————. "Sodomiterverfolgung im christlichen Mittelalter: Diskussionsstand und Forschungsperspektiven." *Zeitschrift für Sexualforschung* 2 (1989): 317–36.

—————. *Sodom und Gomorrha: Zur Alltagswirklichkeit und Verfolgung Homosexueller im Mittelalter.* Hamburg: MännerschwarmSkript Verlag, 1998.

—————. "Die 'unsprechliche stumme Sünde' in Kölner Akten des ausgehenden Mittelalters." *Geschichte in Köln* 22 (1987): 5–43.

—————. "Das Verhör des 'Sodomiticus' Franz von Alsten (1536/37): Ein Kriminalfall aus dem nachtäuferischen Münster." *Westfälische Zeitschrift* 140 (1990): 31–47.

————. "Die 'widernatürliche Sünde' in der theologischen Pest- und Leprametaphorik des 13. Jahrhunderts." *Forum Homosexualität und Literatur* 21 (1994): 5–19.

Herrup, Cynthia. *A House in Gross Disorder: Sex, Law, and the 2nd Earl of Castlehaven.* New York: Oxford University Press, 1999.

Hexter, Ralph J. *Ovid and Medieval Schooling: Studies in Medieval School Commentaries on Ovid's "Ars Amatoria," "Epistulae ex Ponto," and "Epistulae Heroidum."* Munich: Arbeo-Gesellschaft, 1986.

Hirsch, Rudolf. "Pre-Reformation Censorship of Printed Books." *Library Chronicle* 21 (1955): 100–105.

Hohmann, Thomas. "'Die recht gelerten maister': Bemerkungen zur Übersetzungsliteratur der Wiener Schule des Spätmittelalters." In *Die österreichische Literatur: Ihr Profil von den Anfängen im Mittelalter bis ins 18. Jahrhundert (1050–1750),* edited by Herbert Zeman, 349–66. Graz: Akademische Druck- und Verlagsanstalt, 1986.

Holenstein, Pia. *Der Ehediskurs der Renaissance in Fischarts "Geschichtklitterung": Kritische Lektüre des fünften Kapitels.* Bern: Peter Lang, 1991.

Horodowich, Elizabeth A. *Blasphemy, Insults, and Gossip in Renaissance Venice.* Ph.D. diss., University of Michigan, 2000.

Hubert, Friedrich. *Vergerios publizistische Thätigkeit nebst einer bibliographischen Übersicht.* Göttingen: Vandenhoeck & Ruprecht, 1893.

Hull, Isabel V. *Sexuality, State, and Civil Society in Germany, 1700–1815.* Ithaca, N.Y.: Cornell University Press, 1996.

Hunt, Lynn. *The Family Romance of the French Revolution.* Berkeley: University of California Press, 1992.

Hunt, Lynn, ed. *The Invention of Pornography: Obscenity and the Origins of Modernity, 1500–1800.* New York: Zone Books, 1993.

Hupp, Otto. *Scheltbriefe und Schandbilder—ein Rechtsbehelf aus dem 15. und 16. Jahrhundert.* Munich: G. J. Manz, 1930.

Hurteau, Pierre. "Catholic Moral Discourse on Male Sodomy and Masturbation in the Seventeenth and Eighteenth Centuries." *Journal of the History of Sexuality* 4 (1993): 1–26.

Iggers, Georg G., and Konrad von Moltke, eds. *The Theory and Practice of History: Leopold von Ranke.* New York: Irvington Press, 1983.

IJsewijn, Jozef. "I rapporti tra Erasmo, l'umanesimo italiano, Roma e Giulio II." In *Erasmo, Venezia e la cultura padana nel '500.* Edited by Achille Olivieri, 117–29. Rovigo: Minelliana, 1995.

Jaeger, C. Stephen. *Ennobling Love: In Search of a Lost Sensibility.* Philadelphia: University of Pennsylvania Press, 1999.

Jenkins, Keith. "A Postmodern Reply to Perez Zagorin." *History and Theory* 39 (2000): 181–200.

Jenny, Beat Rudolf. *Graf Froben Christoph von Zimmern: Geschichtsschreiber—Erzähler—Landesherr: Ein Beitrag zur Geschichte des Humanismus in Schwaben.* Lindau: Jan Thorbecke, 1959.

Jerouschek, Günter. "Die Herausbildung des peinlichen Inquisitionsprozesses im Spätmittelalter und in der frühen Neuzeit." *Zeitschrift für die gesamte Strafrechtswissenschaft* 104 (1992): 328–60.

Johansson, Warren. "Sixteenth-Century Legislation." In *Encyclopedia of Homosexuality*, edited by Wayne R. Dynes. Vol. 2, 1198–1200. New York: Garland, 1990.

Jones, William Jervis, ed. *Sprachhelden und Sprachverderber: Dokumente zur Erforschung des Fremdwortpurismus im Deutschen (1478–1750)*. Berlin: de Gruyter, 1995.

Jordan, Mark D. *The Invention of Sodomy in Christian Theology*. Chicago: University of Chicago Press, 1997.

Jussen, Bernhard, and Craig Koslofsky, eds. *Kulturelle Reformation: Sinnformationen im Umbruch 1400–1600*. Göttingen: Vandenhoeck & Ruprecht, 1999.

Kamensky, Jane. *Governing the Tongue: The Politics of Speech in Early New England*. New York: Oxford University Press, 1997.

Karant-Nunn, Susan. *The Reformation of Ritual: An Interpretation of Early Modern Germany*. London: Routledge, 1997.

Kartschoke, Erika, et al., eds. *Repertorium deutschsprachiger Ehelehren der Frühen Neuzeit*. Vol. 1, part 1: *Handschriften und Drucke der Staatsbibliothek zu Berlin / Preußischer Kulturbesitz (Haus 2)*. Berlin: Akademie, 1996.

Keiser, Elizabeth B. *Courtly Desire and Medieval Homophobia: The Legitimation of Sexual Pleasure in "Cleanness" and Its Contexts*. New Haven, Conn.: Yale University Press, 1997.

Kleinschmidt, Erich. "Die Colmarer Dominikaner-Geschichtsschreibung im 13. und 14. Jahrhundert: Neue Handschriftenfunde und Forschungen zur Überlieferungsgeschichte." *Deutsches Archiv für Erforschung des Mittelalters* 28 (1972): 371–496.

Knonau, Gerold Meyer von. *Der Canton Zürich, historisch-geographisch-statistisch geschildert von den ältesten Zeiten bis auf die Gegenwart*. 2 vols. St. Gallen: Huber, 1844–46.

Knox, Dilwyn. "*Disciplina*: The Monastic and Clerical Origins of European Civility." In *Renaissance Society and Culture: Essays in Honor of Eugene F. Rice, Jr.*, edited by John Monfasani and Ronald G. Musto, 107–35. New York: Italica Press, 1991.

Koebner, Richard. "Die Eheauffasung des ausgehenden Mittelalters." *Archiv für Kulturgeschichte* 9 (1911/12): 136–98, 279–318.

Köhler, Hans-Joachim. *Bibliographie der Flugschriften des 16. Jahrhunderts*. 2 vols. Tübingen: Bibliotheca Academica, 1991.

—————. "Erste Schritte zu einem Meinungsprofil der frühen Reformationszeit." In *Martin Luther: Probleme seiner Zeit*, edited by Volker Press and Dieter Stievermann, 244–81. Stuttgart: Klett-Cotta, 1986.

—————. "Die Flugschriften der frühen Neuzeit: Ein Überblick." In *Die Erforschung der Buch- und Bibliotheksgeschichte in Deutschland*, edited by Werner Arnold et al., 307–45. Wiesbaden: Harrassowitz, 1987.

Köhler, Hans-Joachim, ed. *Flugschriften als Massenmedium der Reformationszeit: Beiträge zum Tübinger Symposion 1980*. Stuttgart: Klett-Cotta, 1981.

Könsgen, Ewald, ed. *Arbor Amoena Comis: 25 Jahre Mittellateinisches Seminar in Bonn*. Stuttgart: Franz Steiner, 1990.

Körber, Esther-Beate. *Öffentlichkeiten der Frühen Neuzeit: Teilnehmer, Formen, Institutionen und Entscheidungen öffentlicher Kommunikation im Herzogtum Preußen von 1525 bis 1618*. Berlin: de Gruyter, 1998.

Kornrumpf, Gisela. "Der Tugendhafte Schreiber." In *Die deutsche Literatur des Mittelalters: Verfasserlexikon*, 2d ed., edited by Stammler, Langosch, and Wachinger. Vol. 9, cols. 1138–41. Berlin: de Gruyter, 1995.

Kowaleski, Maryanne. "Singlewomen in Medieval and Early Modern Europe: The Demographic Perspective." In *Singlewomen in the European Past, 1250–1800*, edited by Judith Bennett and Amy Froide, 38–81. Philadelphia: University of Pennsylvania Press, 1999.

Krekić, Bariša. "'Abominandum crimen': Punishment of Homosexuals in Renaissance Dubrovnik." *Viator* 18 (1987): 337–45.

Krings, Stefanie. "Sodomie am Bodensee: Vom gesellschaftlichen Umgang mit sexueller Abartigkeit in spätem Mittelalter und früher Neuzeit auf St. Galler Quellengrundlage." *Schriften des Vereins für Geschichte des Bodensees und seiner Umgebung* 113 (1995): 1–45.

Krohn, Rüdiger. "Erotik und Tabu in Gottfrieds 'Tristan': König Marke." In *Stauferzeit: Geschichte, Literatur, Kunst*, edited by Rüdiger Krohn, Bernd Thum, and Peter Wapnewski. Stuttgart: Klett-Cotta, 1979.

Künast, Hans-Jörg. "Entwicklungslinien des Augsburger Buchdrucks von den Anfängen bis zum Ende des Dreißigjährigen Krieges." In *Augsburger Buchdruck und Verlagswesen: Von den Anfängen bis zur Gegenwart*, edited by Helmut Gier and Johannes Janota. Wiesbaden: Harrassowitz, 1997.

———. *"Getruckt zu Augsburg": Buchdruck und Buchhandel zwischen 1468 und 1555.* Tübingen: Niemeyer, 1996.

Kunzle, David. "World Upside Down: The Iconography of a European Broadsheet Type." In *The Reversible World: Symbolic Inversion in Art and Society*. Edited by Barbara A. Babcock. Ithaca, N.Y.: Cornell University Press, 1978.

Kuster, Harry J., and Raymond J. Cormier. "Old Views and New Trends: Observations on the Problem of Homosexuality in the Middle Ages." *Studi medievali*, 3d ser., 25 (1984): 587–610.

Kuster, Hendrikus Johannes. *Over Homoseksualiteit in Middeleeuws West-Europa: Some Observations on Homosexuality in Medieval Western Europe*. Ph.D. diss., Universiteit Utrecht, 1977.

Labalme, Patricia H. "Sodomy and Venetian Justice in the Renaissance." *Tijdschrift voor Rechtsgeschiedenis: Revue d'histoire du droit: The Legal History Review* 52 (1984): 217–55.

Langbein, John H. *Prosecuting Crime in the Renaissance: England, France, Germany.* Cambridge, Mass.: Harvard University Press, 1974.

Lankewish, Vincent A. "Assault from Behind: Sodomy, Foreign Invasion, and Masculine Identity in the *Roman d'Enéas*." In *Text and Territory: Geographical Imagination in the European Middle Ages*, edited by Sylvia Tomasch and Sealy Giles, 207–44. Philadelphia: University of Pennsylvania Press, 1998.

Laun, Christiane. *Bildkatechese im Spätmittelalter: Allegorische und typologische Auslegungen des Dekalogs*. Ph.D. diss., Munich University, 1979.

Lechot, Pierre Olivier. "Puncto Criminis Sodomiae: Un procès pour bestialité dans l'ancien Evêché de Bâle au XVIIIe siècle." *Schweizerische Zeitschrift für Geschichte* 50 (2000): 123–40.

Lenzen, Rolf. "Sodomitenschelte: Eine Invektive des Serlo von Bayeux?" In *Arbor amoena comis: 25 Jahre Mittellateinisches Seminar in Bonn*, edited by Ewald Könsgen, 189–92. Stuttgart: Franz Steiner, 1990.

Lerch, Christoph. *Die Rechtsgrundlagen für Frevel- und Malefizsachen in Solothurn seit dem Stadtrecht von 1604.* Diplomarbeit, n.d.

Lesnick, Daniel R. "Insults and Threats in Medieval Todi." *Journal of Medieval History* 17 (1991): 71–89.

Levin, Eve. *Sex and Society in the World of the Orthodox Slavs, 900–1700.* Ithaca, N.Y.: Cornell University Press, 1989.

Lexer, Matthias. *Mittelhochdeutsches Handwörterbuch.* 3 vols. Reprint, Leipzig: S. Hirzel, 1992.

———. *Mittelhochdeutsches Taschenwörterbuch.* 37th ed. Stuttgart: A. Hiersemann, 1986.

Ley, Klaus. *Giovanni della Casa (1503–1556) in der Kritik.* Heidelberg: Winter, 1984.

Licata, Salvatore J., and Robert P. Petersen, eds. *The Gay Past: A Collection of Historical Essays.* New York: Harrington Park Press, 1985.

Liebenwirth, R. "Ertränken." In *Handwörterbuch zur deutschen Rechtsgeschichte,* edited by Stammler and Kaufmann, 4th installment, cols. 1009–10. Berlin: Erich Schmidt, 1967.

Liliequist, Jonas. "State Policy, Popular Discourse, and the Silence on Homosexual Acts in Early Modern Sweden." *Journal of Homosexuality* 35 (1998): 15–52.

Limbeck, Sven. "Mittelalter." In *Frauenliebe—Männerliebe: Eine lesbisch-schwule Literaturgeschichte in Essays,* edited by Alexandra Busch and Dirck Linck, 290–95. Stuttgart: Metzler, 1997.

———. "Plautus in der Knabenschule: Zur Eleminierung homosexueller Inhalte in deutschen Plautusübersetzungen der frühen Neuzeit." In *Erinnern und Wiederentdecken,* edited by Dirck Linck, Wolfgang Popp, and Annette Runte. Berlin: Verlag rosa Winkel, 1999.

———. "'Sacrista'—'Hypocrita'—'Sodomita': Komödiantische Konstruktion sexueller Identität in Mercurino Ranzos 'De falso hypocrita.'" In *Exil, Fremdheit und Ausgrenzung in Mittelalter und früher Neuzeit,* edited by Andreas Bihrer, Sven Limbeck, and Paul Gerhard Schmidt, 91–112. Würzburg: Ergon, 2000.

Linck, Dirck, Wolfgang Popp, and Annette Runte, eds. *Erinnern und Wiederentdecken: Tabuisierung und Enttabuisierung der männlichen und weiblichen Homosexualität in Wissenschaft und Kritik.* Berlin: Verlag rosa Winkel, 1999.

Lindemann, Mary. "Die Jungfer Heinrich: Transvestitin, Bigamistin, Lesbierin, Diebin, Mörderin." In *Von Huren und Rabenmüttern: Weibliche Kriminalität in der Frühen Neuzeit,* edited by Otto Ulbricht, 259–79. Cologne: Böhlau, 1995.

Livia, Anna, and Kira Hall, "'It's a Girl!' Bringing Performativity Back to Linguistics." In *Queerly Phrased: Language, Gender, and Sexuality,* edited by Anna Livia and Kira Hall. New York: Oxford University Press, 1997.

Lochrie, Karma. *Covert Operations: The Medieval Uses of Secrecy.* Philadelphia: University of Pennsylvania Press, 1998.

Lochrie, Karma, Peggy McCracken, and James A. Schultz, eds. *Constructing Medieval Sexuality.* Minneapolis: University of Minnesota Press, 1997.

Loetz, Francisca. *Mit Gott handeln: Von den Zürcher Gotteslästern der Frühen Neuzeit zu einer Kulturgeschichte des Religiösen.* Göttingen: Vandenhoeck, 2002.

Lorenzen-Schmidt, Klaus-Joachim. "Zur Stellung der Frauen in der frühneuzeitlichen Städtegesellschaft Schleswigs und Holsteins." *Archiv für Kulturgeschichte* 61 (1979): 317–39.

Mages, Emma. "Die Rücknahme der Pfandschaft Tännesberg 1466: Das Verfahren gegen Konrad von Murbach wegen der 'ungenannten Sünde.'" *Zeitschrift für bayerische Landesgeschichte* 62 (1999): 201–12.

Maier, Christoph. *Regiment und Rechtschaffenheit: Regelungen des öffentlichen "Benehmens" in Basel, 1415–1460.* Lizentiatsarbeit, University of Basel, 1985.

Marius, Richard. *Martin Luther: The Christian between God and Death.* Cambridge, Mass.: Harvard University Press, 1999.

Martin, Hervé. *Le métier de prédicateur en France septentrionale à la fin du moyen âge (1350–1520).* Paris: Cerf, 1988.

Maschke, Erich. "Die Unterschichten der mittelalterlichen Städte Deutschlands." In *Gesellschaftliche Unterschichten in den südwestdeutschen Städten,* edited by Erich Maschke and Jürgen Sydow. Stuttgart: Kohlhammer, 1967.

Matheson, Peter. *The Rhetoric of the Reformation.* Edinburgh: Clark, 1998.

May, Georg. *Die geistliche Gerichtsbarkeit des Erzbischofs von Mainz im Thüringen des späten Mittelalters: Das Generalgericht zu Erfurt.* Leipzig: St. Benno, 1956.

McFarlane, Cameron. *The Sodomite in Fiction and Satire, 1660–1750.* New York: Columbia University Press, 1997.

Messmer, Kurt, and Peter Hoppe. *Luzerner Patriziat: Sozial- und wirtschaftsgeschichtliche Studien zur Entstehung und Entwicklung im 16. und 17. Jahrhundert.* Lucerne: Rex-Verlag, 1976.

Meulengracht Sørensen, Preben. *The Unmanly Man: Concepts of Sexual Defamation in Early Northern Society.* Translated by Joan Turville-Petre. Odense: Odense University Press, 1983.

Meuthen, Erich. *Das 15. Jahrhundert.* Munich: Oldenbourg, 1980.

Meyer, Christian. *Das Stadtbuch von Augsburg, insbesondere das Stadtrecht vom Jahre 1276, nach der Originalhandschrift zum ersten Male herausgegeben und erläutert.* Augsburg: F. Butsch, 1872.

Meyer, Kurt. *Solothurnische Verfassungszustände zur Zeit des Patriziats.* Olten: Dietschi, 1921.

Meyer, Wilhelm. *Der Chronist Werner Steiner 1492–1542: Ein Beitrag zur Reformationsgeschichte von Zug.* Stans: Ad. & P. von Matt, 1910.

Michaud-Quantin, Pierre. *Sommes de casuistique et manuels de confession au moyen âge (XII–XVI siècles).* Louvain: Nauwelaerts, 1962.

Michelsen, Jakob. "Von Kaufleuten, Waisenknaben und Frauen in Männerkleidern: Sodomie im Hamburg des 18. Jahrhunderts." *Zeitschrift für Sexualforschung* 9 (1996): 205–37.

Miller, D. A. *The Novel and the Police.* Berkeley: University of California Press, 1988.

Mitteis, Heinrich. *Deutsche Rechtsgeschichte: Ein Studienbuch.* Edited by Heinz Lieberich. 19th ed. Munich: Beck, 1992.

Monter, E. William. "Sodomy and Heresy in Early Modern Switzerland." In *The Gay Past,* edited by Salvatore J. Licata and Robert P. Petersen, 41–55. New York: Harrington Park Press, 1985. First appeared as "La Sodomie à l'époque moderne en Suisse romande," *Annales esc.* 29 (1974): 1023–33.

Moogk, Peter N. "'Thieving Buggers' and 'Stupid Sluts': Insults and Popular Culture in New France." *William and Mary Quarterly,* 3d ser., 36 (1979): 524–47.

Moore, Robert Ian. *The Formation of a Persecuting Society: Power and Deviance in Western Europe, 950–1250.* Oxford: Basil Blackwell, 1987.

Mormando, Franco. *The Preacher's Demons: Bernardino of Siena and the Social Underworld of Early Renaissance Italy.* Chicago: University of Chicago Press, 1999.

Mourin, Louis. *Jean Gerson: Prédicateur français.* Bruges: De Tempel, 1952.

Müller, Arnd. "Die Zensurpolitik der Reichsstadt Nürnberg." *Mitteilungen des Vereins für Geschichte der Stadt Nürnberg* 49 (1949): 66–169.

Müller, Roland. "Der schweizerische Bauernkrieg von 1653." In *Bauern und Patrizier: Stadt und Land im Ancien Régime,* edited by Silvio Bucher. Lucerne: Lehrmittelverlag Luzern, 1986.

Murray, Jacqueline. "Twice Marginal and Twice Invisible: Lesbians in the Middle Ages." In *Handbook of Medieval Sexuality,* edited by Vern L. Bullough and James A. Brundage. New York: Garland, 1996.

Niccoli, Ottavia. *Prophecy and People in Renaissance Italy.* Translated by Lydia G. Cochrane. Princeton, N.J.: Princeton University Press, 1990.

Noordam, Dirk Jaap. *Riskante relaties: Vijf eeuwen homoseksualiteit in Nederland, 1233–1733.* Hilversum: Verloren, 1995.

Norton, Mary Beth. "Gender and Defamation in Seventeenth-Century Maryland." *William and Mary Quarterly,* 3d ser., 44, no. 1 (January 1987): 3–39.

Oberman, Heiko A. *The Dawn of the Reformation: Essays in Late Medieval and Reformation Thought.* Edinburgh: Clark, 1986.

————. "Hus und Luther: Der Antichrist und die zweite reformatorische Entdeckung." In *Jan Hus: Zwischen Zeiten, Völkern, Konfessionen,* edited by Ferdinand Seibt, 319–46. Munich: Oldenbourg, 1997.

Oehmig, Stefan. "Bettler und Dirnen, Sodomiter und Juden: Über Randgruppen und Minderheiten in Erfurt im Spätmittelalter und in der frühen Neuzeit." *Mitteilungen des Vereins für die Geschichte und Altertumskunde von Erfurt* 56, n.s. 3 (1995): 69–102.

Oexle, Otto Gerhard, ed. *Memoria als Kultur.* Göttingen: Vandenhoeck & Ruprecht, 1995.

Olivieri, Achille, ed. *Erasmo, Venezia e la cultura padana nel '500: Atti del XIX Convegno Internazionale di Studi Storici.* Rovigo: Minelliana, 1995.

Orgel, Stephen. *Impersonations: The Performance of Gender in Shakespeare's England.* Cambridge: Cambridge University Press, 1996.

Ortalli, Gherardo. " . . . pingatur in Palatino . . .": *La pittura infamante nei secoli XIII–XVI.* Rome: Jouvance, 1979.

Ozment, Steven E. *The Age of Reform, 1250–1550: An Intellectual and Religious History of Late Medieval and Reformation Europe.* New Haven, Conn.: Yale University Press, 1980.

————. *The Reformation in the Cities: The Appeal of Protestantism to Sixteenth-Century Germany and Switzerland.* New Haven, Conn.: Yale University Press, 1975.

————. "The Social History of the Reformation." In *Flugschriften als Massenmedium der Reformationszeit,* edited by Hans-Joachim Köhler. Stuttgart: Klett-Cotta, 1981.

————. *When Fathers Ruled: Family Life in Reformation Europe.* Cambridge, Mass.: Harvard University Press, 1983.

Park, Katharine. "The Rediscovery of the Clitoris: French Medicine and the Tribade, 1570–1620." In *The Body in Parts: Fantasies of Corporeality,* edited by David Hillman and Carla Mazzio, 184–87. London: Routledge, 1997.

Paul, Hermann. *Deutsche Grammatik.* 5 vols. 4th ed. Halle a.d.S.: Max Niemeyer, 1956–59.

Pavan, Elisabeth. "Police des moeurs, société et politique à Venise à la fin du Moyen Age." *Revue historique* 104 (1980): 241–88.

Payer, Pierre J. *Sex and the Penitentials: The Development of a Sexual Code, 550–1150.* Toronto: University of Toronto Press, 1984.

Perry, Mary Elizabeth. *Crime and Society in Early Modern Seville.* Hanover, N.H.: University Press of New England, 1980.

Peyer, Hans Conrad. *Verfassungsgeschichte der alten Schweiz.* Zurich: Schulthess Polygraphischer Verlag, 1978.

Pfyffer, Kasimir. *Der Kanton Luzern, historisch-geographisch-statistisch geschildert.* St. Gallen: Huber, 1858.

Phillips, Roderick. *Putting Asunder: A History of Divorce in Western Society.* Cambridge: Cambridge University Press, 1988.

Plummer, Marjorie Elizabeth. *Reforming the Family: Marriage, Gender, and the Lutheran Household in Early Modern Germany, 1500–1620.* Ph.D. diss., University of Virginia, 1996.

Poirier, Guy. *L'homosexualité dans l'imaginaire de la Renaissance.* Paris: Champion, 1996.

Price, David. "When Women Would Rule: Reversal of Gender Hierarchy in Sixteenth-Century German Drama." *Daphnis* 20 (1991): 147–66.

Puff, Helmut. "Acts 'Against Nature' in the Law Courts of Early Modern Germany and Switzerland." In *The Moral Authority of Nature,* edited by Lorraine Daston and Fernando Vidal. Chicago: University of Chicago Press, forthcoming.

———. "'Allen menschlichen nuczlichen': Publikum, Gebrauchsfunktion und Aussagen zur Ehe bei Ulrich von Pottenstein." In *Text und Geschlecht: Mann und Frau in Eheschriften der frühen Neuzeit,* edited by Rüdiger Schnell, 176–96. Frankfurt am Main: Suhrkamp, 1997.

———. "Female Sodomy: The Trial of Katherina Hetzeldorfer (1477)." *Journal of Medieval and Early Modern Studies* 30 (2000): 41–61.

———. "Localizing Sodomy: The 'Priest and Sodomite' in Pre-Reformation Germany and Switzerland." *Journal of the History of Sexuality* 8 (1997): 165–95.

———. "Überlegungen zu einer Rhetorik der 'unsprechlichen Sünde': Ein Basler Verhörprotokoll aus dem Jahr 1416." *Österreichische Zeitschrift für Geschichtswissenschaften* 9 (1998): 342–57.

Puff, Helmut, and Wolfram Schneider-Lastin. "Quellen zur Homosexualität im Mittelalter: Ein Basler Projekt." *Forum Homosexualität und Literatur* 13 (1991): 119–24.

Ranke, Leopold von. *Geschichten der romanischen und germanischen Völker von 1494 bis 1514.* 3d ed. Leipzig: Duncker & Humblot, 1885. Translated by Philip A. Ashworth under the title *History of the Latin and Teutonic Nations from 1494 to 1514* (London: George Bell, 1887).

Rauh, Hans Dieter. *Das Bild des Antichrist im Mittelalter: Von Tyconius zum deutschen Symbolismus.* Münster: Aschendorff, 1973.

Reinle, Christine. "Konflikte und Konfliktstrategien eines elsässischen Adligen." In *"Raubritter" oder "Rechtschaffene vom Adel"? Aspekte von Politik, Friede und Recht im späten Mittelalter,* edited by Kurt Andermann, 89–113. Sigmaringen: Thorbecke, 1997.

———. "Zur Rechtspraxis gegenüber Homosexuellen: Eine Fallstudie aus dem Regensburg des 15. Jahrhunderts." *Zeitschrift für Geschichtswissenschaft* 44 (1996): 307–26.

Richards, Jeffrey. *Sex, Dissidence and Damnation: Minority Groups in the Middle Ages.* London: Routledge, 1990.

Richter, Mario. *Giovanni della Casa in Francia nel secolo XVI.* Roma: Edizioni di storia e letterature, 1966.

Ritscher, Alfred. *Literatur und Politik im Umkreis der ersten Habsburger: Dichtung, Historiographie und Briefe am Oberrhein.* Frankfurt am Main: Peter Lang, 1992.

Robert, Paul, ed. *Le Grand Robert de la langue Française.* 9 vols. Paris: Le Robert, 1985.

Robinson, Ian S. *Authority and Resistance in the Investiture Contest: The Polemical Literature of the Late Eleventh Century.* New York: Manchester University Press, 1978.

Rocke, Michael. *Forbidden Friendships: Homosexuality and Male Culture in Renaissance Florence.* New York: Oxford University Press, 1996.

Rodt, Emanuel von. *Die Feldzüge Karls des Kühnen, Herzogs von Burgund, und seiner Erben.* 2 vols. Schaffhausen: Hurter, 1843–44.

Roecken, Sully, and Carolina Brauckmann, eds. *Margaretha Jedefrau.* Freiburg i.Br.: Kore, 1989.

Roper, Lyndal. *The Holy Household: Religion, Morals, and Order in Reformation Augsburg.* Oxford: Oxford University Press, 1989.

———. *Oedipus and the Devil: Witchcraft, Sexuality, and Religion in Early Modern Europe.* London: Routledge, 1994.

Rordorf-Gwalter, Sal. "Die Geschwister Rosilla und Rudolf Rordorf und ihre Beziehungen zu Zürcher Reformatoren." *Zwingliana* 3, no. 6 (1915): 180–93.

Roth, Detlef. "'An uxor ducenda': Zur Geschichte eines Topos von der Antike bis zur Frühen Neuzeit." In *Geschlechterbeziehungen und Textfunktionen: Studien zu Eheschriften der Frühen Neuzeit,* edited by Rüdiger Schnell, 171–232. Tübingen: Niemeyer, 1998.

Rouse, Richard H., and Mary A. Rouse. *Preachers, Florilegia, and Sermons: Studies on the "Manipulus florum" of Thomas of Ireland.* Toronto: Pontifical Institute, 1979.

Rousseau, G. S. "The Pursuit of Homosexuality in the Eighteenth Century: 'Utterly Confused Category' and/or Rich Repository." In *'Tis Nature's Fault: Unauthorized Sexuality during the Enlightenment.* edited by Robert P. Maccubin, 137–68. Cambridge: Cambridge University Press, 1987.

Rowland, Ingrid D. "Revenge of the Regensburg Humanists, 1493." *Sixteenth Century Journal* 25 (1994): 307–22.

Rozzo, Ugo, ed., *Pier Paolo Vergerio il Giovane, un polemista attraverso l'Europa del Cinquecento.* Udine: Forum, 2000.

Rublack, Ulinka. "Anschläge auf die Ehre: Schmähschriften und -zeichen in der städtischen Kultur des Ancien Régime." In *Verletzte Ehre: Ehrkonflikte in Gesellschaften des Mittelalters und der Frühen Neuzeit,* edited by Klaus Schreiner and Gerd Schwerhoff, 391–411. Cologne: Böhlau, 1995.

Rücker, Brigitte. *Die Bearbeitung von Ovids "Metamorphosen" durch Albrecht von Halberstadt und Jörg Wickram und ihre Kommentierung durch Gerhard Lorichius.* Göppingen: Kümmerle, 1997.

Ruggiero, Guido. *The Boundaries of Eros: Sex, Crime, and Sexuality in Renaissance Venice.* New York: Oxford University Press, 1985.

Russell, Paul A. *Lay Theology in the Reformation: Popular Pamphleteers in Southwest Germany, 1521–1525.* Cambridge: Cambridge University Press, 1986.

Sabean, David Warren. *Power in the Blood: Popular Culture and Village Discourse in Early Modern Germany.* Cambridge: Cambridge University Press, 1984.

———. "Soziale Distanzierungen: Ritualisierte Gestik in deutscher bürokratischer Prosa der Frühen Neuzeit." *Historische Anthropologie* 4 (1996): 216–33.

Safley, Thomas Max. *Let No Man Put Asunder: The Control of Marriage in the German Southwest: A Comparative Study, 1550–1600.* Kirksville: Northeast Missouri State University Press, 1984.

Samuel, Raphael. "Reading the Signs." *History Workshop Journal* 32 (1992): 88–109; 33 (1993): 220–51.

Santosuosso, Antonio. *The Bibliography of Giovanni della Casa: Books, Readers, and Critics 1537–1975.* Florence: L. S. Olschki, 1979.

Schilling, Heinz, ed. *Kirchenzucht und Sozialdisziplinierung im frühneuzeitlichen Europa.* Berlin: Duncker & Humblot, 1994.

Schilling, Michael. *Bildpublizistik der frühen Neuzeit: Aufgaben und Leistungen des illustrierten Flugblatts in Deutschland bis um 1700.* Tübingen: Niemeyer, 1990.

Schimmelpfennig, Bernhard. "Religiöses Leben im späten Mittelalter." In *Geschichte der Stadt Augsburg,* edited by Gunther Gottlieb. Stuttgart: Konrad Theiss, 1985.

Schleiner, Winfried. "Burton's Use of *praeteritio* in Discussing Same-Sex Relationships." In *Renaissance Discourses of Desire,* edited by Claude J. Summers and Ted-Larry Pebworth. Columbia: University of Missouri Press, 1993.

———. "Linguistic 'Xeno-Homophobia' in Sixteenth-Century France: A Page from Early Modern Gay Philology." Forthcoming.

———. "'That Matter Which Ought Not to Be Heard Of': Homophobic Slurs in Renaissance Cultural Politics." *Journal of Homosexuality* 26 (1994): 41–75.

Schmeller, J. Andreas. *Bayerisches Wörterbuch.* Stuttgart: Cotta, 1827–37.

Schmidinger, Andreas. *Das Entlebuch zur Zeit der Glaubensspaltung und der katholischen Reform.* Schüpfheim: n.p., 1972.

Schmidt, Charles. *Histoire littéraire de l'Alsace à la fin du XVe et au commencement du XVIe siècle.* 2 vols. Paris, 1879. Reprint, Hildesheim: Olms, 1966.

Schmidt, Günter. *Libelli famosi: Zur Bedeutung der Schmähschriften, Scheltbriefe, Schandgemälde und Pasquille in der deutschen Rechtsgeschichte.* Ph.D. diss., University of Cologne, 1970.

Schmidt, Heinrich-Richard. "Pazifizierung des Dorfes: Struktur und Wandel von Nachbarschaftskonflikten vor Berner Sittengerichten 1570–1800." In *Kirchenzucht und Sozialdisziplinierung im frühneuzeitlichen Europa,* edited by Heinz Schilling, 91–128. Berlin: Duncker & Humblot, 1994.

Schmugge, Ludwig. "Stadt und Kirche im Spätmittelalter am Beispiel der Schweiz: Ein Überblick." In *Variorum Munera Florum: Festschrift für Hans F. Haefele zum 60. Geburtstag,* edited by Adolf Reinle, Ludwig Schmugge, and Peter Stotz. Sigmaringen: Thorbecke, 1985.

Schneider-Lastin, Wolfram, and Helmut Puff. "'Vnd solt man alle die so das tuend verbrennen, es bliben nit funffzig mannen jn Basel': Homosexualität in der deutschen Schweiz im Spätmittelalter." In *Lust, Angst und Provokation: Homosexualität in der Gesellschaft,* edited by Helmut Puff, 79–103. Göttingen: Vandenhoeck & Ruprecht, 1993.

Schnell, Rüdiger. "Konstanz und Metamorphosen eines Textes: Eine überlieferungs- und geschlechtergeschichtliche Studie zur volkssprachlichen Rezeption von Jacobus' de Voragine Ehepredigten." *Frühmittelalterliche Studien* 33 (1999): 319–95.

Schnell, Rüdiger, ed. *Geschlechterbeziehungen und Textfunktionen: Studien zu Eheschriften der Frühen Neuzeit.* Tübingen: Niemeyer, 1998.

—————. *Text und Geschlecht: Mann und Frau in Eheschriften der Frühen Neuzeit.* Frankfurt am Main: Suhrkamp, 1997.

Scholz Williams, Gerhild. *Defining Dominion: The Discourses of Magic and Witchcraft in Early Modern France and Germany.* Ann Arbor: University of Michigan Press, 1995.

Schreiner, Klaus, and Gerd Schwerhoff, eds. *Verletzte Ehre: Ehrkonflikte in Gesellschaften des Mittelalters und der Frühen Neuzeit.* Cologne: Böhlau, 1995.

Schulze, Winfried. *Deutsche Geschichte im 16. Jahrhundert.* Frankfurt am Main: Suhrkamp, 1987.

Schuster, Beate. *Die freien Frauen: Dirnen und Frauenhäuser im 15. und 16. Jahrhundert.* Frankfurt am Main: Campus, 1995.

—————. *Die unendlichen Frauen: Prostitution und städtische Ordnung in Konstanz im 15./16. Jahrhundert.* Konstanz: Universitätsverlag Konstanz, 1996.

Schuster, Peter. *Der gelobte Frieden: Täter, Opfer und Herrschaft im spätmittelalterlichen Konstanz.* Konstanz: Universitätsverlag Konstanz, 1995.

Schutte, Anne Jacobson. *Pier Paolo Vergerio: The Making of an Italian Reformer.* Geneva: Droz, 1977.

Schütte, Bernd. "'Multi de illo multa referunt': Zum Lebenswandel Heinrichs IV." In *Arbor Amoena Comis: 25 Jahre Mittellateinisches Seminar in Bonn,* edited by Ewald Könsgen, 143–50. Stuttgart: Franz Steiner, 1990.

Schwennicke, Detlev, ed. *Europäische Stammtafeln: Stammtafeln zur Geschichte der europäischen Staaten.* N.s. 16: *Bayern und Franken.* Berlin: J. A. Stargardt, 1995.

Schwerhoff, Gerd. *Köln im Kreuzverhör: Kriminalität, Herrschaft und Gesellschaft in einer frühneuzeitlichen Stadt.* Bonn: Bouvier, 1991.

Schwitalla, Johannes. *Deutsche Flugschriften 1460–1525: Textsortengeschichtliche Studien.* Tübingen: Niemeyer, 1983.

—————. *Flugschrift.* Tübingen: Niemeyer, 1999.

Scott, James C. *Domination and the Arts of Resistance: Hidden Transcripts.* New Haven, Conn.: Yale University Press, 1990.

Scribner, Robert W. "Antiklerikalismus in Deutschland um 1500." In *Europa 1500: Integrationsprozesse im Widerstreit,* edited by Ferdinand Seibt and W. Eberhard, 368–82. Stuttgart: Klett-Cotta, 1987.

—————. "Flugblatt und Analphabetentum: Wie kam der gemeine Mann zu reformatorischen Ideen?" In *Flugschriften als Massenmedium der Reformationszeit,* edited by Hans-Joachim Köhler, 65–76. Stuttgart: Klett-Cotta, 1981.

—————. *For the Sake of Simple Folk: Popular Propaganda for the German Reformation.* Oxford: Clarendon Press, 1981.

—————. "Luther's Anti-Roman Polemics and Popular Belief." *Luther-Jahrbuch* 57 (1990): 93–113.

—————. *Popular Culture and Popular Movements in Reformation Germany.* London: Hambledon Press, 1987.

Sedgwick, Eve Kosofsky. *Between Men: English Literature and Male Homosocial Desire.* New York: Columbia University Press, 1985.

—————. *Epistemology of the Closet.* Berkeley: University of California Press, 1990.

Segesser, Anton Philipp von. *Rechtsgeschichte der Stadt und Republik Lucern.* 4 vols. Lucerne: n.p., 1851–58.

Sharpe, J. A. *Defamation and Sexual Slander in Early Modern England: The Church Courts at York.* York: Bothwick Institute of Historical Research, [1980].

Sieber-Lehmann, Claudius. Introduction to *In Helvetios—Wider die Kuhschweizer: Fremd-und Feindbilder von den Schweizern.* Edited by Claudius Sieber-Lehmann and Thomas Wilhelmi. Bern: Paul Haupt, 1998.

————. *Spätmittelalterlicher Nationalismus: Die Burgunderkriege am Oberrhein und in der Eidgenossenschaft.* Göttingen: Vandenhoeck & Ruprecht, 1995.

Siegmund, Stefanie. *From Tuscan Households to Florentine Ghetto: The Construction of a Jewish Community, 1560–1610.* Ph.D. diss., American Theological Seminary, 1995.

Sigrist, Hans. "Benedikt Hugi der Jüngere, Niklaus Conrad, zwei Lebensbilder." *Jahrbuch für solothurnische Geschichte* 22 (1949): 36–79.

Silver, Larry. "Germanic Patriotism in the Age of Dürer." In *Dürer and His Culture,* edited by Dagmar Eichenberger and Charles Zika, 38–68. Cambridge: Cambridge University Press, 1998.

Simon-Muscheid, Katharina. "Frauen in Männerrollen." In *Arbeit—Liebe—Streit: Texte zur Geschichte des Geschlechterverhältnisses und des Alltags, 15 bis 18. Jahrhundert.* Edited by Dorothee Rippmann, Katharina Simon-Muscheid, and Christian Simon, 102–21. Liestal: Verlag des Kantons Basel-Landschaft, 1996.

Slenczka, Ruth. *Lehrhafte Bildtafeln in spätmittelalterlichen Kirchen.* Cologne: Böhlau, 1998.

Sozzi, Lionello. "La polémique anti-italienne en France au XVIe siècle." *Atti della Accademia della Scienze di Torino: Classe di Scienze Morali, Storiche e Filologiche* 206 (1972): 99–190.

Spiegel, Gabrielle M. *The Past as Text: The Theory and Practice of Medieval Historiography.* Baltimore: Johns Hopkins University Press, 1997.

Spierenburg, Pieter. *The Broken Spell: A Cultural and Anthropological History of Preindustrial Europe.* New Brunswick, N.J.: Rutgers, 1991.

Spreitzer, Brigitte. *Die stumme Sünde: Homosexualität im Mittelalter mit einem Textanhang.* Göppingen: Kümmerle, 1988.

Stadlin, Franz Karl. *Der Topographie des Kantons Zug erster Theil.* Lucerne: n.p., 1824.

Stadtwald, Kurt. *Roman Popes and German Patriots: Antipapalism in the Politics of the German Humanist Movement from Gregor Heimburg to Martin Luther.* Geneva: Droz, 1996.

Staedtke, Joachim. "Heinrich Bullingers Bemühungen um eine Reformation im Kanton Zug." *Zwingliana* 10, no. 1 (1954): 24–47.

Stallybrass, Peter, and Allon White. *The Politics and Poetics of Transgression.* Ithaca, N.Y.: Cornell University Press, 1986.

Stammler, Adalbert, and Ekkehard Kaufmann, eds. *Handwörterbuch zur deutschen Rechtsgeschichte.* Berlin: Erich Schmidt, 1964–.

Stammler, H. Wolfgang, Karl Langosch, and Burghart Wachinger, eds. *Die deutsche Literatur des Mittelalters: Verfasserlexikon.* 2d ed. Berlin: de Gruyter, 1977–.

Stammler, Wolfgang. *Kleine Schriften zur Literaturgeschichte des Mittelalters.* Berlin: Erich Schmidt, 1953.

Staub, Friedrich, and Ludwig Tobler, eds. *Schweizerisches Idiotikon: Wörterbuch der schweizerdeutschen Sprache.* Frauenfeld: Huber, 1881–.

Steiner, Alois. "Luzern als Vorort der katholischen Eidgenossenschaft vom 16. bis zum 18. Jahrhundert." In *Bauern und Patrizier: Stadt und Land im Ancien Régime,* edited by Silvio Bucher, 96–103. Lucerne: Lehrmittelverlag Luzern, 1986.

Stepto, Michele, and Gabriel Stepto, eds. *Lieutenant Nun: Memoir of a Basque Transvestite in the New World: Catalina de Erauso.* Boston: Beacon, 1996.

Stewart, Alan. *Close Readers: Humanism and Sodomy in Early Modern England.* Princeton, N.J.: Princeton University Press, 1997.

Stolt, Birgit. *Wortkampf: Frühneuhochdeutsche Beispiele zur rhetorischen Praxis.* Frankfurt am Main: Athenäum, 1974.

Störmer-Caysa, Uta. *Gewissen und Buch: Über den Weg eines Begriffes in die deutsche Literatur des Mittelalters.* Berlin: de Gruyter, 1998.

Strauss, Gerald. *Law, Resistance, and the State: The Opposition to Roman Law in Reformation Germany.* Princeton, N.J.: Princeton University Press, 1986.

Ström, Folke. *nið, ergi and Old Norse Moral Attitudes.* The Dorothea Coke Memorial Lecture in Northern Studies. London: published for University College by the Viking Society for Northern Research, 1974.

Stucki, Heinzpeter. "Das 16. Jahrhundert." In *Geschichte des Kantons Zürich,* vol. 2. Zürich: Werd, 1996.

Studer, Julius. *Die Edeln von Landenberg: Geschichte eines Adelsgeschlechts der Ostschweiz.* Zurich: Schulthess, 1904.

Summers, Claude J. "English Literature: Renaissance." In *The Gay and Lesbian Literary Heritage: A Reader's Companion to the Writers and Their Works: From Antiquity to the Present,* edited by Claude J. Summers. New York: Henry Holt, 1995.

————. *Homosexuality in Renaissance and Enlightenment England: Literary Representations in Historical Context.* Binghamton, N.Y.: Haworth Press, 1992.

Suntrup, Rudolf, Burghart Wachinger, and Nicola Zotz. "'Zehn Gebote' (Deutsche Erklärungen)." In *Die deutsche Literatur des Mittelalters: Verfasserlexikon,* 2d ed., edited by Stammler, Langosch, and Wachinger. Vol. 10, cols. 1484–1503. Berlin: de Gruyter, 1981.

Teasley, David. "The Charge of Sodomy as a Political Weapon in Early Modern France: The Case of Henry III in Catholic League Polemic, 1585–1589." *Maryland Historian* 18 (1987): 17–30.

Tentler, Thomas N. *Sin and Confession on the Eve of the Reformation.* Princeton, N.J.: Princeton University Press, 1977.

Tervooren, Helmut, and Thomas Bein. "Ein neues Fragment zum Minnesang und zur Sangspruchdichtung: Reinmar von Zweter, Neidhart, Kelin, Rumzlant und Unbekanntes." *Zeitschrift für deutsche Philologie* 107 (1988): 1–26.

Thieme, Hans. *Ideengeschichte und Rechtsgeschichte: Gesammelte Schriften.* Cologne: Böhlau, 1986.

Tobler, Alfred, and Erhard Lommatzsch, eds. *Altfranzösisches Wörterbuch.* Wiesbaden: Franz Steiner, 1925–.

Traub, Valerie. "The (In)Significance of 'Lesbian' Desire in Early Modern England." In *Queering the Renaissance,* edited by Jonathan Goldberg, 66–70. Durham, N.C.: Duke University Press, 1994.

————. *The Renaissance of Lesbianism in Early Modern England.* Cambridge: Cambridge University Press, 2002.

Trexler, Richard. "Correre la Terra: Collective Insults in the Late Middle Ages." *Mélanges de l'Ecole française de Rome: Moyen Age: Temps Modernes* 96 (1984): 845–902.

————. *Sex and Conquest: Gendered Violence, Political Order, and the European Conquest of the Americas*. Ithaca, N.Y.: Cornell University Press, 1995.

Trumbach, Randolph. "The Birth of the Queen: Sodomy and the Emergence of Gender Equality in Modern Culture, 1660–1750." In *Hidden from History*, edited by Martin B. Duberman, Martha Vicinus, and George Chauncey, Jr., 129–40. New York: NAL Books, 1989.

————. "Erotic Fantasy and Male Libertinism in Enlightenment England." In *The Invention of Pornography*, edited by Lynn Hunt, 253–82. New York: Zone Books, 1993.

————. "London's Sapphists: From Three Sexes to Four Genders in the Making of Modern Culture." In *Third Sex, Third Gender: Beyond Sexual Dimorphism in Culture and History*, edited by Gilbert Herdt. New York: Zone Books, 1994.

————. *Sex and the Gender Revolution*. Vol. 1, *Heterosexuality and the Third Gender in Enlightenment London*. Chicago: University of Chicago Press, 1998.

Usteri, Emil. *Marignano: Die Schicksalsjahre 1515/1516 im Blickfeld der historischen Quellen*. Zurich: Kommissionsverlag Berichthaus, 1974.

Van der Meer, Theo. "Sodom's Seed in The Netherlands: The Emergence of Homosexuality in the Early Modern Period." *Journal of Homosexuality* 34 (1997): 1–16.

————. *Sodoms zaad in Nederland: Het ontstaan van homoseksualiteit in de vroegmoderne tijd*. Nijmegen: SUN, 1995.

————. "Tribades on Trial: Female Same-Sex Offenders in Late Eighteenth-Century Amsterdam." *Journal of the History of Sexuality* 1 (1991): 424–45.

Verzeichnis der im deutschen Sprachbereich erschienenen Drucke des 16. Jahrhunderts (VD-16). Stuttgart: A. Hiersemann, 1983–2000.

Vocabolario della lingua italiana. 4 vols. Rome: Istituto della Enciclopedia italiana, 1986–94.

Walter, Tilmann. *Unkeuschheit und Werk der Liebe: Diskurse über Sexualität am Beginn der Neuzeit in Deutschland*. Berlin: de Gruyter, 1998.

Walther, Hans. *Das Streitgedicht in der lateinischen Literatur des Mittelalters*. Munich: Beck, 1920.

Walz, Rainer. "Schimpfende Weiber: Frauen in lippischen Beleidigungsprozessen des 17. Jahrhunderts." In *Weiber, Menschen, Frauenzimmer: Frauen in der ländlichen Gesellschaft 1500–1800*, edited by Heide Wunder and Christina Vanja. Göttingen: Vandenhoeck & Ruprecht, 1996.

Wechsler, Elisabeth. *Ehre und Politik: Ein Beitrag zur Erfassung politischer Verhaltensweisen in der Eidgenossenschaft (1440–1500) unter historisch-anthropologischen Aspekten*. Zurich: Chronos, 1991.

Weeks, Jeffrey. *Coming Out: Homosexual Politics in Britain, from the Nineteenth Century to the Present*. London: Quartet, 1977.

Weibel, Thomas. "Der zürcherische Stadtstaat." In *Geschichte des Kantons Zürich*, vol. 2. Zurich: Werd, 1996.

Weidenhiller, P. Egino. *Untersuchungen zur deutschsprachigen katechetischen Literatur des späten Mittelalters: Nach den Handschriften der Bayerischen Staatsbibliothek*. Munich: Beck, 1965.

Weimann, Robert. *Authority and Representation in Early Modern Discourse*. Baltimore: Johns Hopkins University Press, 1996.

Wellmann, Hans. *Deutsche Wortbildung: Typen und Tendenzen in der Gegenwartssprache: Zweiter Hauptteil: Das Substantiv*. Düsseldorf: Schwann, 1975.

Wendehorst, Alfred. *Das Bistum Würzburg*. Germania Sacra, n.s. 26. Part 2, *Die Bischöfe von 1254 bis 1455*. Berlin: de Gruyter, 1969.

————. *Das Bistum Würzburg*. Part 4, *Das Stift Neumünster in Würzburg*. Germania Sacra, n.s. 26. Berlin: de Gruyter, 1989.

Wettstein, Erich. *Die Geschichte der Todesstrafe im Kanton Zürich*. Winterthur: H. Schellenberg, 1958.

Whitman, James Q. *The Legacy of Roman Law in the German Romantic Era: Historical Vision and Legal Change*. Princeton, N.J.: Princeton University Press, 1990.

Wickham, Chris. "Gossip and Resistance among the Medieval Peasantry." *Past and Present* 160 (August 1998): 3–24.

Wiesner, Merry E. *Gender, Church, and State in Early Modern Germany*. London: Longman, 1998.

————. "Having Her Own Smoke: Employment and Independence for Singlewomen in Germany, 1400–1750." In *Singlewomen in the European Past, 1250–1800*, edited by Judith Bennett and Amy Froide, 192–216. Philadelphia: University of Pennsylvania Press, 1999.

Witte, Heinrich. *Der letzte Puller von Hohenburg: Ein Beitrag zur politischen und Sittengeschichte des Elsasses und der Schweiz im 15. Jahrhundert sowie zur Genealogie des Geschlechts der Püller*. Beiträge zur Landes- und Volkskunde von Elsass-Lothringen. Vierter Band (Heft 16–20). Strasbourg: J. H. E. Heitz, 1893.

Zagorin, Perez. "History, the Referent, and Narrative: Reflections on Postmodernism Now." *History and Theory* 38 (1999): 1–24.

————. "Rejoinder to a Postmodernist." *History and Theory* 39 (2000): 201–9.

Zanger, Alfred. "Wirtschaft und Sozialstruktur." In *Geschichte des Kantons Zürich*. Zurich: Werd, 1995–96.

Zorach, Rebecca E. "The Matter of Italy: Sodomy and the Scandal of Style in Sixteenth-Century France." *Journal of Medieval and Early Modern Studies* 26 (1996): 581–609.

Index

adultery, 27, 37, 58, 63, 133, 148, 168, 170, 173–75, 192n. 8, 263n. 27
age: of offender, 75, 87; of sexual partners, 29. *See also* persecution of sodomites; same-sex sexual behavior
age differences between partners, 29, 43, 91, 97–98, 118, 128, 130, 148, 197n. 29. *See also* pederasty
Agricola, Johann, 134–35
Agrippa of Nettesheim, Henricus Cornelius, 60
Albert, Thomas, 37
Albert the Great, 22
Alberus, Erasmus, 148
Albrecht of Halberstadt, 73
Albrecht von Eyb, 125, 172, 219n. 147
alcoholism, 127
Alexis, 218n. 129
Alfeld, Augustin von, 155
Amerbach, Bonifacius, 231n. 166
Americas, 128–29
Anabaptists, 178, 225n. 103
anal sex, 29, 94–95, 99, 159, 160
ancient literature, 58–60, 70–72. *See also* *specific authors*
Anderson, Benedict, 141, 176
Andreadis, Harriette, 6
Anthony of Florence, Archbishop, 206n. 1, 207n. 6
Antichrist, 137, 145, 149, 165, 249n. 23
anticlericalism, 127, 139
antimonasticism, 127, 173
anus licking, 133, 134

apocalypse, sodomy as sign of, 154–55
apprentices, 81, 82, 84–86, 94
Aquinas, Thomas, 17, 22, 54, 58
archives, 22
artisans, 24, 79, 174
Astesanus d'Asti, 40
audience, 58, 65–67, 237n. 77
Augsburg, 18, 40, 57, 63, 78–80, 176
authorship, concepts of, 162, 165
avarice, 127, 131

Bagchi, David, 155
banishment, 23, 28, 33, 36, 38, 40, 88, 90, 91, 112, 115
Basel, 17, 27, 30, 33, 37–39, 44, 101–2; council of, 28, 38, 171
baths, 23, 79, 98
Baumgarten, Johann, 173
Beccuti, Francesco (il Coppetta), 258n. 120
Beeke, Hermann von der. *See* Torrentinus, Hermann
Beguines, 38
Behaim, Michel, 208n. 17
Benedictines, 41
Bennett, Judith, 10
Bern, 46, 75, 117–18, 122
Berthold, Brother, 53, 113, 215n. 94
Berthold of Regensburg, 54, 56, 57, 68
bestiality, 8, 26, 29, 90, 91, 133–34, 146, 170, 222n. 42, 223n. 47, 228n. 131, 237n. 77
Bible, 49, 54, 72. *See also* Decalogue; Sodom and Gomorrah
bigamy, 133

Constance, 24, 32, 88, 237n. 77; bishop of, 41, 88
Constitutio Criminalis Bambergensis, 30
Constitutio Criminalis Carolina, 29–30, 102
"conversations" (genre of pamphlet literature), 146
Coryat, Thomas, 158
courts: ecclesiastical vs. secular, 35–36; spreading sodomy, 132; urban, 37, 41, 42, 48. *See also* execution(s); judges
Cronberg, Hartmuth von, 154
cross-dressing, 32–34
"crying sins" (*peccata clamantia*), 56, 59, 214n. 85
Curia, 142
Curio, Celio Secundo, 163
customary law, 28, 30
cynaedus, 126, 129, 137, 142, 153, 159

Damian, Peter, 21, 110
Decalogue, 8, 27, 59, 64, 67, 174
decapitation, 29, 82, 90, 148
defamation, sodomy, 48, 88, 107–9, 122–24, 206n. 77; history of, 110–12; literary, 132–35; political protest and, 116–18; and the rhetoric of inversion, 135–38; *sodomiticus redivivus*, 119–22. *See also* Della Casa; *fama*; humanists; libel; slander
Della Casa, Giovanni, 158–66, 258n. 120, 260–61n. 148
Delsberg (Delémont), 101–3
demons, 55–56, 82
Denis the Carthusian, 55, 61, 67
De obitu Julii. See Julius exclusus
Derrida, Jacques, 10
desire, 107–8. *See also* lust
destruction. *See* Sodom and Gomorrah
detraction, 18, 38, 47, 108, 111–14
devil(s), 56, 57, 65, 82, 147, 175
dialogues, 146
dichotomies in sexual discourse, 95–96, 174–75. *See also* purity; "unchastity"
didactic literature. *See* literature, didactic
diffamatio, 112
difference, category of, 10
difference, sexual, 115–16
dildos, 32, 34
Dinshaw, Carolyn, 107, 115
discipline, notion of, 20, 23

disclosure, 136
disease, metaphors of, 67, 130, 132, 134–35
disgust, rhetoric of, 56, 64–65, 93–96, 102, 126, 129, 147, 149, 152, 197n. 22
divorce, 110
Dominicans, 17, 36–38, 67, 239n. 11
"don't ask, don't tell" policy, 66, 68
drowning, 32, 33
drunkenness, 80–82, 87, 88; and alcoholism, 127
Dülmen, Richard van, 168
Dürer, Albrecht, 125

Eberlin von Günzburg, Johann, 150, 169, 170
ecclesiastical courts, 35–36
ecclesiastical elites. *See* elites, ecclesiastical
ecclesiastical jurisdiction, 40, 41, 80, 115, 120, 171
Edwards, Mark U., Jr., 143
effeminacy, 33, 78, 142–43, 145, 149
ejaculation, 23, 28, 41
elites, 45–48, 59, 99, 100, 119, 121, 152, 226n. 105; ecclesiastical, 110, 111, 145, 147–49; political, 103
Elliott, Dyan, 110
Engelbrecht, Anton, 156
Entlebuch, 116
enumeration, 138
"epicurism," Italian, 135
Epistolae obscurorum virorum, 71, 128
Erasmus, 70–72, 152, 254n. 72
Erfurt, 36
Esch, Arnold, 117
evil spirits. *See* demons; devil(s)
execution(s) for sodomy, 5, 28–29, 91, 94, 101, 119; by breaking on the wheel, 18, 90; of Burgundian mercenaries, 43–48; by burning at the stake, 18, 23, 24, 29, 40, 41, 46, 77, 82, 89, 90, 237n. 72; and the Church, 36–37, 40, 41; in Constance, 24; customary law and, 28; by decapitation, 29, 82, 90, 148; by drowning, 32, 33; earliest documented, 17, 32; general methods of, 90, 94; in Lucerne, 90–91; Regensburg trial, 26; in Solothurn, 25; in Zurich, 25, 90, 91
exile. *See* banishment
experience, category of, 146–47

humanists, 71, 72, 75; defaming and
defamed, 124–27, 130–31, 158, 164
humor, 57, 164, 169, 179
Hus, Jan, 137–38
Hutten, Ulrich von, 125, 145, 146

idolatry, 170, 255n. 88
incest, 63, 73, 110, 137
indexes, Catholic (of prohibited books),
160–62, 164–65
inn(s), 77–79, 84, 112, 113
intercourse, 29; frequency, 28; intercrural,
29. *See also* penetration
interrogations, 24, 32–33, 88
inversio, 124, 167
inversion, rhetoric of, 135–38, 165
"Italian weddings," 133, 137
Italy, 25–26, 81; association with sodomy,
117–18, 125–28, 139, 155; images of, 126,
132, 251n. 35

Jerome, 54
Jewish persons and religion, 128, 197n. 22
Jonas, Justus, 153, 155
Jordan, Mark, 7, 9, 54, 130
judges, 17–20, 24, 26–29, 35, 37, 42, 48, 81,
82, 115, 180
Julius exclusus, 151–53
Julius II, Pope, 148
Julius III, Pope, 148, 151
jurisdiction, 20–21; ecclesiastical, 40, 41,
115, 120, 171; secular, 17, 40, 48, 120, 171

Kaisersberg. *See* Geiler von Kaiserberg,
Johann
Karlstadt, Andreas, 146, 170
Keiser, Elizabeth, 67
ketzerie. *See* heresy
Knebel, Johann, 44
Köhler, Hans-Joachim, 140
Kyburg, 93, 231n. 170

laborers, 25, 33–34, 37, 81, 82, 84, 92, 97
laity: clergy as teachers of, 52–58; dissemination of Christian dogma to, 52–53,
58–59, 65
language, 10, 75–76; of documents, 60–61.
See also terminology
Las Casas, Bartolomé de, 129

Laterin Council, Fifth, 138
Laterin Council, Third, 35, 38
Latin literature, 60, 61, 68, 72–73, 153
latrine, 24
law: customary, 28, 30; handbooks of, 53,
112, 215n. 94
law code(s), 18, 49; Justinian's, 26, 28;
vernacular, 18, 112. *See also* law
law enforcement, changing patterns of
communication in, 102–3
legal cooperation, 89
legal language, 26–27, 92–103, 226n. 112
legislation, legal framework of, 27–30. See
also *Constitutio Criminalis Bambergensis*;
Constitutio Criminalis Carolina
Lemnius, Simon, 156, 257n. 106
Leo X, Pope, 148, 152, 153
lesbianism, 14; and cross-dressing, 32–34;
and male homosexuality, 5–6, 181; and
nuns, 150–1. *See also* women offenders
lèse-majesté, 7
libel, 46–47, 130–31. *See also* defamation;
fama; polemics; slander
Lichtenberger, Johann, 154
Linck, Wenzeslaus, 154
literary expression, 165; modes of, 165
literature: didactic, 18, 62, 72, 107, 124, 130,
138, 172, 174; religious, 58–67, 173–75.
See also poetry
Lombardy, 43–44, 117
Lorichius, Gerhard, 71–73
Louis of Bavaria, King, 111
love, 39, 71
Lucerne, 30, 41, 42, 75, 78, 84, 86–88,
90–91, 96, 101, 112, 118; council of, 87
lust, 70, 137. *See also* desire; *luxuria*
Luther, Martin, 133, 162, 170, 249n. 23–24;
criticisms of, 155, 156; on Germany, 131,
133, 135; on marriage, 137; on popes
and papacy, 137–38, 142–43, 145–46;
publications and polemics, 128, 131,
135–37, 139, 142–44, 150, 151, 154;
Against the Roman Papacy, 142, 156, 157;
on Rome and Italy, 126–27, 135
luxuria (lust), 54, 63, 64

macarelli, 132–33, 244n. 58
maendlaer, 196n. 7
magic, 82

Scribner, Robert W., 141
Sedgwick, Eve Kosofsky, 14, 107
seduction, 69, 80–81
selfhood, notions of, 5, 80–83, 98–99
semiotics, 108
sermons, 50, 52, 54, 57, 67–70, 174
sexology, 3
sexual advances, negative responses to,
    83–85. See also seduction
sexual culture, 92
sexual identity, labeling, 162–63
sexual roles, 32–34, 91, 149
shame, rhetoric of, 54–56, 91–93, 147, 209n.
    29, 251n. 41
sharing beds, 77–87, 89, 97. See also sleep
shouting. See outcry
Sieber-Lehmann, Claudius, 44
silence, enforced on sodomy, 100–101, 103,
    138. See also "mute sin"; "unspeakable," the
simony, 21, 110, 111, 145, 205n. 72
single women and men, 178
sin(s): hierarchy of, 63, 73, 139, 145, 147–49;
    against nature, 8, 35, 55, 57, 59–63, 67,
    68, 72, 73, 131, 139, 170, 206n. 1, 208n.
    18, 209 nn. 29, 32, 209–10 n. 36, 215n.
    95. See also "unnatural" acts
slander, 47; execution for, 237n. 77;
    gendered nature of, 116, 142; regulation
    of, 109, 121–22; slanderous media, 113
    (see also pamphlets); spoken vs. written,
    113, 114. See also defamation; fama; libel
sleep, 23, 81–83, 88
Sleidan, Johannes, 159
social and sexual strata, 91, 98, 123, 147–49
Sodom and Gomorrah, 18, 26, 55, 56, 65,
    153–55, 157, 174
sodomia, 23, 50, 53, 55, 56, 63, 64, 67, 80,
    109, 110, 175, 181, 206n. 1; defined, 110
sodomiphobia, 123, 141, 176. See also
    homophobia
sodomy: definitions and meanings, 7–10,
    29; as divisive concept, 180; rhetorics of,
    180–81; stability as a term, 7–9; use of
    term, 229n. 140
Solothurn, 25, 79, 119
Speculum exemplorum, 50–51
Speyer, 32, 33
Spiegel, Gabrielle, 10
spirits. See demons

Stadtwald, Kurt, 126, 143
state formation, and sexual discipline in late
    Middle Ages, 19–23
Steiner, Werner, 97–100, 229nn. 141–45
St. Gallen, 25, 75, 101
Stör, Thomas, 150, 173
Strasbourg, 46, 69–70, 82; Strasbourg
    council, 23–24
Stricker, 55, 196n. 7, 209n. 34
Summa de casibus/Summa Astesana, 40
Sweden, 230n. 154
Swiss Confederacy, 19, 41, 46–48, 89, 90,
    116, 160

tagsatzung, 116
teachers, 1, 39, 43, 49, 52–54, 65, 70, 71, 74,
    79, 92, 150, 178
teacher-student relations, 130
teaching: by clergy, 52–58; the unspeakable
    sin of the Romans, 70–74; in a vernacular
    summa, 58–62
Ten Commandments. See Decalogue
Tenngler, Ulrich, 28
terminology, 26–27, 42, 92–93, 206n. 1;
    Puff's, 12–13; vilifying, 138. See also
    defamation, literary
Torrentinus, Hermann, 71
torture, 43, 45, 46, 96, 116
translation, 72–73, 129, 132–35, 151–53,
    178, 219n. 147, 250n. 31, 254–55n. 82
treason, 7, 18, 44, 47, 116, 117
Trent, Council of, 164
tribade, 34
Trithemius, Johannes, 243n. 44
Trumbach, Randolph, 4–5, 145
Turkey, 128, 131, 137, 149
Turks, 142, 146
tyranny, 44, 137–38, 146, 152

Ulrich, Bishop of Augsburg (Huldericus),
    170, 251n. 42, 262–63n. 18
Ulrich of Pottenstein, 27, 58–60, 62, 63,
    211n. 61
"unchastity," 26, 29, 53, 55, 59, 64, 67, 101,
    102, 173
"unchristian acts," 18, 24, 27, 87, 94–96, 101
University of Vienna, 59
"unnatural" acts, 26, 92, 95–96
unspeakability, 62, 64; notions of, 66, 68